Universal Design in Higher Education

Universal Design in Higher Education

From Principles to Practice

Edited by

Sheryl E. Burgstahler and Rebecca C. Cory

HARVARD EDUCATION PRESS

Cambridge, Massachusetts

Library of Congress Control Number 2007941439

Paperback ISBN 978-1-891792-90-8
Library Edition ISBN 978-1-891792-91-5

Published by Harvard Education Press,
an imprint of the Harvard Education Publishing Group

Harvard Education Press
8 Story Street
Cambridge, MA 02138

Cover Design: Nancy Goulet/studio;wink

The typefaces used in this book are ITC Stone Serif for text and ITC Stone Sans for display.

Contents

Foreword   ix

Acknowledgments   xi

PART 1 INTRODUCTION   1

1 Universal Design in Higher Education   3
    Sheryl E. Burgstahler

PART 2 UNIVERSAL DESIGN OF INSTRUCTION IN HIGHER EDUCATION   21

2 Universal Design of Instruction: From Principles to Practice   23
    Sheryl E. Burgstahler

3 Universal Design for Learning in Postsecondary Education:
Reflections on Principles and Their Application   45
    David H. Rose
    Wendy S. Harbour
    Catherine Sam Johnston
    Samantha G. Daley
    Linda Abarbanell

4 The Faculty Perspective: Implementation of Universal Design
in a First-Year Classroom   61
    Jeanne L. Higbee

5 Universal Design of Assessment   73
    Martha L. Thurlow
    Christopher J. Johnstone
    Leanne R. Ketterlin-Geller

6 Universal Design of Instruction: Reflections of Students   83
    Imke Durre
    Michael Richardson
    Carson Smith
    Jessie Amelia Shulman
    Sarah Steele

7   The Benefits of Universal Design for Students with
    Psychiatric Disabilities   97
        Al Souma
        Deb Casey

8   The Contribution of Universal Design to Learning
    and Teaching Excellence   105
        Adele Darr
        Richard Jones

9   Universal Course Design: A Model for Professional Development   109
        Kirsten Behling
        Debra Hart

10 Small Victories: Faculty Development and Universal Design   127
        Susan Yager

11 A Case Study Approach to Promote Practical Application
    of Universal Design for Instruction   135
        Sally S. Scott
        Joan M. McGuire

12 Engaging Higher Education Faculty in Universal Design:
    Addressing Needs of Students with Invisible Disabilities   145
        Andrea M. Spencer
        Olga Romero

13 Incorporating Universal Design into Administration Courses:
    A Case Study   157
        Karen A. Myers

PART 3 UNIVERSAL DESIGN OF STUDENT SERVICES, PHYSICAL SPACES,
AND TECHNOLOGICAL ENVIRONMENTS IN HIGHER EDUCATION   165

14 Universal Design of Student Services: From Principles to Practice 167
        Sheryl E. Burgstahler

15 Applications of Universal Design to Student Services:
    Experiences in the Field   177
        Alice Anderson
        Rebecca C. Cory
        Pam Griffin
        Patricia J. Richter
        Scott Ferguson
        Eric Patterson
        Lacey Reed

16   Universal Design of Physical Spaces: From Principles to Practice   187
        Sheryl E. Burgstahler

17   Applications of Universal Design to Higher Education Facilities   199
        Elisabeth Goldstein

18   Universal Design of Technological Environments:
     From Principles to Practice   213
        Sheryl E. Burgstahler

19   Problems and Solutions for Making Multimedia Web-Based
     Lectures Accessible: A Case Study   225
        Alice Anderson
        Mike Litzkow

20   Universal Design of Computing Labs   235
        Terry Thompson

**PART 4   INSTITUTIONALIZATION OF UNIVERSAL DESIGN
IN HIGHER EDUCATION**   **245**

21   Indicators of Institutional Change   247
        Sheryl E. Burgstahler
        Rebecca C. Cory

22   A Change Process for Creating a Universally Designed Campus   255
        Cathy Jenner

23   Implementing Universal Design: Collaborations Across Campus   267
        Donald E. Finn
        Elizabeth Evans Getzel
        Susan B. Asselin
        Virginia Reilly

24   Promoters and Inhibitors of Universal Design in Higher Education   279
        Sheryl E. Burgstahler

     Appendix: Project Teams and Resources   285

     About the Authors   295

     Index   303

Foreword

Mark A. Emmert, Ph.D.
President, University of Washington

The University of Washington has an enduring commitment to diversity in all aspects of our educational mission. Our understanding of diversity, however, has evolved over time. Early efforts toward achieving an inclusive campus included the appointment of a vice president for minority affairs to ensure increased opportunities for students of color. Four decades later, our chief diversity officer has a title—Vice President for Minority Affairs and Vice Provost for Diversity—that reflects a significant expansion of our definition of diversity to encompass race, gender, class, ethnicity, sexuality, religion, age, socioeconomic status, nationality, and disability. Today, the value we place on human differences in the university community is prominent in the university's six core values: integrity, innovation, excellence, collaboration, respect, and diversity.

We believe that meeting the challenges of our time requires the energy and perspectives of all populations. We recruit the best, most diverse and innovative faculty and staff from around the world and support a vibrant intellectual community. Scholars and practitioners from traditionally underrepresented groups bring perspectives and insights that contribute in unique ways to the university's capacity to address pressing societal issues, enrich course curricula, and engage diverse external communities. Preparing all our students for global citizenship requires new understanding of diversity, access, equity, and inclusiveness, as well as new styles of leadership.

We strive to focus on the strengths of individuals—on what they can do rather than on what they cannot. There are many concrete expressions of our understanding of disability as one aspect of diversity. For example, since 1992, we have hosted the Disabilities, Opportunities, Internetworking, and Technology (DO-IT) Center, directed by Dr. Sheryl Burgstahler, the lead author of this book, to undertake activities nationwide that increase the success of individuals with disabilities in higher education and careers. With federal, state, corporate, and private funding, DO-IT's activities have grown to include the creation of the Center for Universal Design in Education. In addition, we have created a tri-campus Disability Studies minor and in 2007 cosponsored the annual meeting of the Society for Disability Studies. We actively recruit faculty and students with disabilities, and our growing cadre of scholars at the university are making tremendous contributions to our knowledge about disability and disability studies.

We see the practice of universal design, the topic of this book, as a promising approach that reflects the value we place on diversity. Instead of creating courses, services, information technology, and physical spaces for the "typical" student and then making modifications for students for whom they are inaccessible, this approach proactively addresses the needs of people with the broadest range of characteristics during the design process. This approach leads to educational products and environments that are welcoming, accessible, and inclusive and that address all aspects of diversity, including disability.

In this book, forty-one scholars, practitioners, and students, representing twenty-six postsecondary institutions and other organizations, share perspectives and a wide range of applications of universal design in higher education. For campuses with a long history of embracing diversity, the content reinforces the rationale and structure for supporting a diverse educational community and provides suggestions for strengthening existing programs and exploring new approaches. Campuses that do not yet have a strong commitment to diversity can benefit from models and case studies on how to be responsive to vastly changing social, political, and legal contexts in higher education. Campuses can embrace universal design as part of their commitment to transformative change, which builds diversity into the institution's mission, core values, planning processes, resource allocation, and accountability measures.

Acknowledgments

This book is a product of the Disabilities, Opportunities, Internetworking, and Technology (DO-IT) Center at the University of Washington. It could not have been published without generous funding from DO-IT's primary sponsors: the National Science Foundation, U.S. Department of Education, and the state of Washington. DO-IT has worked to increase the successful participation of individuals with disabilities in higher education and employment since 1992.

The inspiration and content for this book emerged from three projects funded by the Office of Postsecondary Education (OPE) of the U.S. Department of Education (grant numbers P333A990042, P333A020044, P333A050064). In each project, DO-IT staff worked with collaborating institutions from more than twenty states in creating professional development materials and programs to help postsecondary faculty and administrators fully include students with disabilities in their courses and services. The Center for Universal Design in Education (http://www.washington.edu/doit/CUDE) was created to disseminate guidelines and resources for the application of universal design to instruction, services, physical spaces, and technology.

DO-IT's OPE-funded projects have been complemented by projects funded by the National Science Foundation as part of AccessSTEM—the Alliance for Access to Science, Technology, Engineering, and Mathematics (Cooperative Agreement number HRD-0227995)—and AccessComputing—the Alliance for Access to Computing Careers (grant number CNS-0540615). AccessSTEM and AccessComputing staff developed content related to science, technology, engineering, and mathematics for Web sites and for this book.

Together, these projects have led to the development of a comprehensive collection of Web sites with content tailored to the needs and interests of specific audiences. Each includes a searchable knowledge base of questions and answers, case studies, and promising practices. The five Web sites most relevant to the content of this book are as follows.

- *The Faculty Room,* for instructors and academic administrators
- *The Student Services Conference Room,* for student service administrators and staff
- *The Board Room,* for college and university administrators
- *The Student Lounge,* for students with disabilities
- *The Center for Universal Design in Education,* with guidelines for creating inclusive courses, services, physical spaces, and technological environments

Questions, findings, and conclusions or recommendations expressed in this book are those of the authors and do not necessarily reflect the views of the funding sources. The Principles of Universal Design were conceived and developed by the Center for Universal Design at North Carolina State University. Use or application of the Principles in any form is separate and distinct from the Principles and does not constitute or imply acceptance or endorsement by the Center for Universal Design of the use or application.

I would like to acknowledge the efforts of project team members to make their campuses more inclusive. They are listed in the appendix along with project descriptions and resources. I am grateful to the forty-one authors and peer reviewers of book chapters for generously sharing their diverse experiences and perspectives on the application of universal design in higher education. DO-IT staff members also contributed to the creation of this work. I would especially like to thank coeditor Rebecca Cory, publications manager Linda Tofle, and publications coordinator Rebekah Peterson. Without the contributions of all these individuals, this book would not have been possible.

Sheryl Burgstahler, Ph.D.
Founder and Director, DO-IT and Accessible Technology
University of Washington Technology Services,
College of Engineering, College of Education

PART 1

Introduction

In Part One, Sheryl Burgstahler provides an overview of the history, principles, and applications of universal design (UD). She highlights approaches to implementing UD in higher education and explains the book's organization.

Universal Design in Higher Education

Instruction	Services	Information Technology	Physical Spaces
Class climate	Planning, policies, and evaluation	Procurement/ development policies	Planning, policies, and evaluation
Interaction	Physical environments/ products	Physical environments/ products	Appearance
Physical environments/ products	Staff	Information	Entrances/ routes of travel
Delivery methods	Information resources/ technology	Input/control	Fixtures/ furniture
Information resources/ technology	Events	Output	Information resources/ technology
Feedback		Manipulations	Safety
Assessment		Safety	Accommodation
Accommodation		Compatibility with assistive technology	

Source: S. Burgstahler (2007). *Applications of Universal Design in Education*. Seattle: University of Washington. http://www.washington.edu/doit/Brochures/Academics/app_ud_edu.html

1

Universal Design in Higher Education

Sheryl E. Burgstahler

Universal design (UD) has a rich history in applications to commercial products and architecture and is now being applied to instruction and student services. UD holds promise for making educational products and environments more inclusive of all students, faculty, staff, and visitors. This chapter is an overview of topics covered in this book, including the definition and principles of UD, the process of UD, and applications of UD in higher education (UDHE). The chapter ends with an outline of the content of the book and a guide for locating answers to specific questions addressed within.

What if there was a paradigm for higher education that would simultaneously address issues of equality, accessibility, social integration, and community? What if it could create more inclusive classrooms? What if it provided guidance for physical spaces, student services, and technology? Universal design (UD) in higher education can do all this and more. While you can never finish implementing UDHE, it is easy to get started and then to continue taking incremental steps. Applying UDHE is a journey and, like any other journey, requires planning, diligence, and flexibility. This chapter gives an overview of the world of UDHE, and the remaining chapters provide road maps for the journey itself.

The design of any product or environment, including education, involves myriad factors, among them purpose, aesthetics, safety, industry standards, usability, and cost. Traditional design often focuses on the average user, and accessible or "barrier-free" design focuses on people with disabilities. In contrast, UD promotes an expanded goal to make products and environments welcoming and useful to groups that are diverse in many dimensions, including gender, race and ethnicity, age, socioeconomic status, ability, disability, and learning style. Originally applied in the fields of architecture and consumer product design, UD has more recently emerged as a paradigm to address diversity in the design of a broad range of educational products and environments, including Web sites, educational software, instruction, student services, and physical spaces.

DIVERSITY IN HIGHER EDUCATION

Diversity has become a fact of life in higher education. Once the domain of the young, able-bodied, Caucasian male, the postsecondary student body of today has been estimated as one-fourth racial and ethnic minorities, more than half women, with a rising average age (Higher Education Research Institute, 2006). In addition, 6% or more of students have disabilities (Horn & Nevill, 2006; Lewis & Farris, 1999; National Center for Education Statistics, 2000). Of the students who report having disabilities, the largest and fastest-growing group is students who have "invisible disabilities," such as those that affect learning and the ability to attend. Veterans of recent wars are adding to the growing pool of college students with disabilities. Many other aspects of diversity are reflected in the student body, as represented in Figure 1.1.

A rich body of research and practice in the areas of civil rights, social justice, and multicultural education sheds light on postsecondary diversity issues with respect to socioeconomic, racial and ethnic, and gender status (e.g., Hackman & Rauscher, 2004; Nieto, 1996; Pliner & Johnson, 2004). In addition, research suggests that the most effective teaching methods differ by age group (e.g., Knowles, 1980). The discussion below elucidates a few of the challenges faced by students with diverse physical, sensory, learning, attention, and communication characteristics and shares examples of ways to ameliorate those challenges.

FIGURE 1.1   Student Characteristics

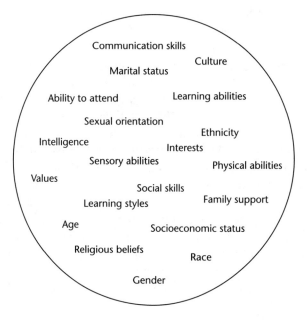

- *Physical differences.* Some facilities are not designed for students who are large; providing a few larger chairs in a classroom can make these students more comfortable. Spaces that are not wheelchair accessible cannot be used by some students and instructors. Standard keyboards and mice are not accessible to some people; to operate computers or lab equipment they need access to expanded or minikeyboards, speech input technology, and other assistive technologies.
- *Visual differences.* Web content that requires the ability to distinguish one color from another presents a barrier to access for people who are color-blind. A standard computer screen is inaccessible to individuals who are blind; they need computer systems that are able to convert screen text to braille or speech. Since this technology can only read text, students who are blind can make sense of the content within graphic images only if alternative text descriptions are provided. Individuals who have limited vision and use software to enlarge screen images can view only a small portion of content at one time. For these users, cluttered Web pages and inconsistent page layouts make navigation difficult. Printed materials, videos, televised presentations, and other materials with visual content also erect access barriers unless large print formats, tactile materials, audio versions, or electronic text is provided.
- *Hearing differences.* Unless the audio content of videos and other multimedia is captioned or transcribed, it is inaccessible to students who are deaf. Although some communication methods, such as e-mail, are fully accessible to individuals with hearing impairments, they may be unable to participate in on-site, telephone, or videoconferencing discussions unless sound amplification, sign language interpreters, real-time captions, or other accommodations are provided.
- *Learning differences.* Course content delivered in a single mode, such as lecture, creates a barrier to access for students with a wide variety of learning styles, strengths, and preferences (e.g., Claxton & Ralston, 1978; Dunn & Griggs, 2000; Gardner, 1983; Rose, Meyer, & Hitchcock, 2005). Just as Web sites that change formats from one page to the next or crowd too much content on the screen are inaccessible to users who use screen-magnifying software, they also present barriers for students with specific learning disabilities that affect the ability to read, write, or process information. When time provided to complete a test is inadequate, students with learning disabilities that affect processing speed are placed at a disadvantage unless they are allowed extra time to compensate. Some students with learning disabilities that affect their ability to interpret written text require audio-tape books or speech output software on computers.
- *Attention differences.* Students exhibit a wide range in their ability to attend. Some students may find it difficult to pay attention to a lecture, lab, or other activity without a printed outline or other organizational tool.
- *Communication differences.* Communication differences can relate to hearing ability, brain injuries, autism spectrum disorders, native language, culture, age, or other factors. E-mail and other modes of communication that do not require the ability to hear or speak are fully accessible to individuals with speech and hearing impairments and may also be desirable for students in courses where the spo-

ken language is not their native language. However, fast-paced, on-site, or online discussions; teleconferences; or audio conferences may limit the participation of these individuals.

Understanding how institutions of higher education can use the UD paradigm to address diversity issues is enhanced by awareness of the history of UD, which is presented in the next section.

HISTORY, MEANING, AND PRINCIPLES OF UNIVERSAL DESIGN

UD of products and environments has a history that predates the use of the term *universal design*. Marc Harrison (1928–1996), who became a professor of industrial engineering at the Rhode Island School of Design, was a pioneer in what later became known as UD. Harrison sustained a traumatic brain injury as a child. His experiences through years of rehabilitation gave him insight and inspiration in his academic and professional work. He challenged the design philosophy at the time, which focused on design for individuals of average size and ability, by promoting the idea that products and environments should be designed for people of all abilities. For example, his design of a food processor—with large and easily pressed buttons; large grasp handles; and bold, high-contrast labels—demonstrated that making a product more usable by consumers with visual and mobility impairments made it more usable by everyone (Hagley Museum and Library, n.d.).

Ronald Mace, an internationally recognized architect, product designer, and educator, coined the term *universal design* in the 1970s. Like Harrison, Mace challenged the conventional practice of designing products for the average user and promoted a design approach that led to a more accessible and usable world. At the Center for Universal Design (CUD) at North Carolina State University, he defined UD as "the design of products and environments to be usable by all people, to the greatest extent possible, without the need for adaptation or specialized design" (The Center for Universal Design, 1997a, p. 1). UD features in a product or environment are integrated into the design so that they foster social integration and do not stand out. An example of UD is a sidewalk that has curb cuts to make it usable by people who are walking, using wheelchairs, pushing baby strollers, and rolling delivery carts. The curb cut exemplifies "design for all."

Meaning of Universal Design

Some researchers and practitioners have tailored the general definition of UD to specific applications. For example, Universal Smart Home Design has been described as "the process of designing products and housing environments that can be used to the greatest extent possible for people of all ages, abilities and physical disabilities" (Schwab, 2004). With a focus on information technology, UD is defined in the Assistive Technology Act of 1998 as follows:

> a concept or philosophy for designing and delivering products and services that are usable by people with the widest possible range of functional capabilities, which include products and services that are directly usable (without requiring assistive

technologies) and products and services that are made usable with assistive technologies.

The common thread in all definitions of UD is that a diverse group of potential users can fully benefit from a product or environment in an inclusive setting (National Council on Disability, 2004). With UD, the consumer is not expected to adjust to the limitations of an inflexible product or environment; rather, the application adjusts to the needs and preferences of any user.

The *universal* in UD represents an ideal with respect to the audience for a specific product or environment. No application will be fully usable by every human being; in many cases this is not even desirable. For example, designing an electric saw that can be easily operated by everyone, including a 5-year-old child, is neither necessary nor desirable. UD does, however, require inclusive practices that address access and use issues related to diverse characteristics of members of the population for whom the application is intended. Considerations include level of ability to move, see, hear, read, learn, and process information; stature; age; race; ethnicity; culture; socioeconomic status; learning style and preference; dexterity; native language; intelligence; and gender. Considering that most characteristics (e.g., the ability to see) are measured on a continuum, the traditional view of a person "having a disability" or "not having a disability" is simplistic. Everyone has different abilities that are likely to change over the course of a lifetime. The need for a specific ability depends on the design of a product or environment with which an individual wishes to interact and the specific task at hand. An uncaptioned video requires the ability to hear; a captioned one does not.

The *design* in UD reinforces the characteristic that UD is a proactive process rather than a reactive one. Universally designed products and environments have built-in features that anticipate the needs of a diverse group of users. For example, the director of a registration office is applying UD when she anticipates that a student who is blind may at some time need to register for a class, and she takes steps now to ensure that the online registration system will be accessible to someone who is blind and using text-to-speech technology.

Principles of Universal Design

At the CUD, a group of product developers, architects, environmental designers, and engineers established a set of seven principles of UD to consider in the design of any product or environment and then developed guidelines for each principle (The Center for Universal Design, 1997b):

1. *Equitable use.* The design is useful and marketable to people with diverse abilities. Guidelines for this principle are as follows:
   - Provide the same means of use for all users: identical whenever possible; equivalent when not.
   - Avoid segregating or stigmatizing any users.
   - Provisions for privacy, security, and safety should be equally available to all users.
   - Make the design appealing to all users.

2. *Flexibility in use.* The design accommodates a wide range of individual preferences and abilities. Guidelines for this principle are as follows:
   - Provide choice in methods of use.
   - Accommodate right- or left-handed access and use.
   - Facilitate the user's accuracy and precision.
   - Provide adaptability to the user's pace.

3. *Simple and intuitive use.* Use of the design is easy to understand, regardless of the user's experience, knowledge, language skills, or current concentration level. Guidelines for this principle are as follows:
   - Eliminate unnecessary complexity.
   - Be consistent with user expectations and intuition.
   - Accommodate a wide range of literacy and language skills.
   - Arrange information to be consistent with its importance.
   - Provide effective prompting and feedback during and after task completion.

4. *Perceptible information.* The design communicates necessary information effectively to the user, regardless of ambient conditions or the user's sensory abilities. Guidelines for this principle are as follows:
   - Use different modes (pictorial, verbal, tactile) for redundant presentation of essential information.
   - Provide adequate contrast between essential information and its surroundings.
   - Maximize "legibility" of essential information.
   - Differentiate elements in ways that can be described (i.e., make it easy to give instructions or directions).
   - Provide compatibility with a variety of techniques or devices used by people with sensory limitations.

5. *Tolerance for error.* The design minimizes hazards and the adverse consequences of accidental or unintended actions. Guidelines for this principle are as follows:
   - Arrange elements to minimize hazards and errors: most used elements, most accessible; hazardous elements eliminated, isolated, or shielded.
   - Provide warnings of hazards and errors.
   - Provide fail-safe features.
   - Discourage unconscious action in tasks that require vigilance.

6. *Low physical effort.* The design can be used efficiently, comfortably, and with a minimum of fatigue. Guidelines for this principle are as follows:
   - Allow user to maintain a neutral body position.
   - Use reasonable operating forces.
   - Minimize repetitive actions.
   - Minimize sustained physical effort.

7. *Size and space for approach and use.* Appropriate size and space is provided for approach, reach, manipulation, and use regardless of the user's body size, posture, or mobility. Guidelines for this principle are as follows:

- Provide a clear line of sight to important elements for any seated or standing user.
- Make reach to all components comfortable for any seated or standing user.
- Accommodate variations in hand and grip size.
- Provide adequate space for the use of assistive devices or personal assistance.

Some researchers and practitioners have used CUD's seven principles of UD as a foundation on which to develop unique guidelines, performance indicators, or checklists to help practitioners begin to implement UD in specific situations. For example, Vanderheiden and Vanderheiden (1992) developed guidelines for information technology. Similarly, Hogan (2003) developed an Inclusive Employment Checklist and an Inclusive Marketing Checklist for companies to use when applying UD to issues regarding employees and products, respectively. Ensign (1993) developed a UD checklist for playgrounds. Disabilities, Opportunities, Internetworking, and Technology (DO-IT), which now hosts the Center for Universal Design in Education, developed and field-tested checklists for UD of computer labs (Burgstahler, 2007b), instruction (Burgstahler, 2007c), student services (Burgstahler, 2007d), and specific student service units (DO-IT, n.d.). Although the CUD principles of UD are intentionally general in order to make them applicable to all products and environments, some practitioners have reworded (e.g., Mason & Orkwis, 2005) or expanded them (McGuire, Scott, & Shaw, 2003) for specific applications.

ACCESSIBLE DESIGN, USABLE DESIGN, UNIVERSAL DESIGN, AND ACCOMMODATIONS

Products that are universally designed are both accessible and usable for a broad audience and, therefore, minimize the need for accommodations. However, the concept of UD is broader than the concepts of *accessible design*, *usable design*, and *accommodations*. This section discusses the relationship between these related terms.

Accessible Design

The term *accessible* is commonly associated with the physical environment (Iwarsson & Stahl, 2003). Veterans who suffered injuries in World War II, other people with disabilities, and their advocates led a barrier-free movement that drove changes in public policies, laws, and design standards. Further inspired by the civil rights movement of the 1960s, disability rights leaders made a positive impact on the accessibility of education, public places, transportation, and information technology (U.S. Department of Justice, 2005). For example, the Architectural Barriers Act of 1968 requires that all buildings designed, constructed, altered, or leased with federal funds meet minimum accessibility requirements to remove physical barriers to individuals with disabilities. Section 504 of the Rehabilitation Act of 1973 prohibits discrimination on the basis of disability in covered public programs and services. However, accessible design came to the forefront of public awareness in the United States with the passage of the Americans with Disabilities Act of 1990 (ADA). As a result of this legislation, the U.S. Architectural and Transportation Barriers Compliance Board (Access Board) created standards for the construction and renovation of facilities. People often equate accessible design to compliance with these standards and even label accessible environments as "ADA-compliant" (Iwarsson & Stahl, 2003).

Although the focus of the ADA is on disability, it is often observed that making a product or environment accessible to individuals who have disabilities benefits others, as illustrated in the following examples.

- Constraints imposed by a noisy environment that prohibit the effective use of audio features are similar to those faced by people with hearing impairments; captions ensure access by a broad audience.
- Some people for whom English is a second language experience reading difficulties similar to those of people with some types of learning disabilities; software that provides vocabulary support (e.g., easy access to definitions) benefits both groups.
- Workers who need to operate a computer when their hands are performing other tasks face access challenges similar to those who use a hands-free input method because of physical limitations; speech control benefits many people.

Usable Design

Usability has been defined as "the extent to which a product can be used by specified users to achieve specified goals with effectiveness, efficiency and satisfaction in a specified context of use" (International Organization for Standardization, 1998). Usability engineers are concerned with subjective views on how well a design enables performance and contributes to well being (Iwarsson & Stahl, 2003). Usability takes into account how easily specific users can learn how to operate a product, achieve their goals, and remember how to perform tasks when they return to the product at a later time. Some usability professionals today do not routinely include people with disabilities in usability tests (Bergman & Johnson, 1995; Burgstahler, Jirikowic, Kolko, & Eliot, 2004). Others, however, consider accessibility "a necessary precondition for usability" (Iwarsson & Stahl, 2003, p. 62). In this view, a design cannot be highly rated for usability if it is not accessible to people with disabilities.

Accommodations

The ADA (Americans with Disabilities Act of 1990) considers a person with a disability to be any individual who is found to

> (1) have a physical or mental impairment that substantially limits one or more major life activities of such individual [including walking, seeing, hearing, speaking, breathing, learning, and working], (2) have a record of such an impairment, or (3) be regarded as having such an impairment.

Disabilities covered by legislation include, but are not limited to, those that are related to hearing, learning, mental health, speech, mobility, and sight. According to these laws, no otherwise qualified individual with a disability shall, solely by reason of that disability, be excluded from, denied the benefits of, or subjected to discrimination under programs of a covered entity, including an institution of higher education.

In the Americans with Disabilities Act of 1990 *qualified*, with respect to postsecondary education, means

> an individual with a disability who, with or without reasonable modifications to rules, policies, or practices, the removal of architectural, communication, or transportation barriers, or the provision of auxiliary aids and services, meets the essential eligibility requirements for the receipt of services or the participation in programs or activities provided by a public entity.

The term *accommodation* means offering an adjustment or modification to make a product or environment accessible to an individual with a disability. Accommodation is grounded in the medical model of disability. In this model, a professional typically identifies an individual's functional limitations or "deficits" and prescribes adjustments that allow this person to participate to some degree in the "normal" environment (Gill, 1987; Hahn, 1988; Jones, 1996; Swain & Lawrence, 1994). Examples of accommodations include printed materials in alternate formats (e.g., braille), extra time on an exam, a sign language interpreter, assistive technology, and a class moved to a wheelchair-accessible location. In higher education, the student must disclose and document a disability to a specified individual or office at the institution and request accommodations. The institutional representative determines what is a reasonable accommodation and shares this information with a faculty or staff member, directly or through the student. Some accommodations (e.g., producing materials in braille) are handled directly by the campus disability service unit.

Access Approaches Compared

Whereas accommodation is a *reactive* approach to provide access to an *individual*, accessible, usable, and UD processes are *proactive* approaches to ensure access for *groups* of potential participants. UD integrates both accessible and usable design features and seeks to make it possible for everyone to participate in an inclusive setting where no one is singled out. In contrast, designs that are technically accessible to people with disabilities may not be very usable. For example, a very complicated table presented on a Web site could be marked up in such a way that a person who is blind could access the content with text-to-speech technology, but because of the table's complexity, this mode of presentation might be too confusing for this individual to use. Designs that are technically accessible also may not be very inclusive. For example, a ramp to provide wheelchair access to a main entrance with stairs is technically accessible. However, this approach is not as inclusive as a sloping ramp to a main entrance without stairs, in which case everyone approaches and enters the building together.

UD is consistent with an understanding of disability not simply as a deficit within the individual but as a social construct much like those regarding gender, racial, and ethnic status. UD promoters argue that disadvantages associated with disabilities are primarily imposed by the inaccessible design of products and environments (Gill, 1987; Hahn, 1988; Jones, 1996; Swain & Lawrence, 1994). Many campus buildings used to have steps with no convenient way for a wheelchair user to enter or advance to another floor. Later, campuses retrofitted buildings with ramps and elevators to give individuals using wheelchairs access to facilities. People began to realize that the "problem" of facility access lay not in the wheelchair user but rather in the design of a building. Now institutions routinely design buildings to be wheelchair accessible. Some researchers and practitioners, including authors of chapters in this book, consider the practice of infusing UD into all aspects of higher education a next step toward destigmatizing disability while making all members of the campus community feel welcome. The result is inclusive educational programs that benefit from the unique perspectives of all participants.

Changing attitudes about diversity and, specifically, disability are embodied in how the postsecondary community discusses access problems. For example, a professor might say, "My podcasts are not accessible to Dylan because *he* is deaf." A newly "UD-enlightened" professor might say, "Dylan cannot access my podcasts because I neglected to provide transcriptions." A fully UD-enlightened professor could say, "Dylan can access my podcasts because I provide transcriptions to benefit students who are deaf and to those whose native language is not mine, who wish to search through the content for specific topics, and who want to reformat the content into their own study materials." UD-enlightened individuals recognize that many accessibility barriers reside in a product or environment and take proactive steps to avoid them. Rather than viewing disability as an individual's problem, they see inclusion as a responsibility of the institution.

THE PROCESS OF UNIVERSAL DESIGN

The term *design* can be used as a verb or as a noun. Similarly, UD is a process as well as a goal. As Story, Mueller, and Mace (1998, p. 2) have written:

> It is possible to design a product or an environment to suit a broad range of users, including children, older adults, people with disabilities, people of atypical size or shape, people who are ill or injured, and people inconvenienced by circumstance. [Yet] it is unlikely that any product or environment could ever be used by everyone under all conditions. Because of this, it may be more appropriate to consider universal design a process, rather than an achievement.

Vanderheiden and his colleagues at the University of Wisconsin's Trace Center (Vanderheiden & Tobias, n.d., p. 1) have used the following definition of UD as a process for designing consumer products:

> Universal design is the process of creating products (devices, environments, systems, and processes) which are usable by people with the widest possible range of abilities, operating within the widest possible range of situations (environments, conditions, and circumstances), as is commercially practical. Universal design has two major components:
>
> 1. Designing products so that they are flexible enough that they can be directly used (without requiring any assistive technologies or modifications) by people with the widest range of abilities and circumstances as is commercially practical, given current materials, technologies, and knowledge; and

2. Designing products so that they are compatible with the assistive technologies that might be used by those who cannot efficiently access and use the products directly.

In applying UD to consumer electronics, the Electronic Industries Alliance suggested that companies (1) know the user; (2) make the product adjustable; (3) provide alternatives and redundancies; (4) make functions conspicuous; (5) provide adequate feedback; (6) make the design forgiving; (7) strive first for accessibility, then for compatibility (with assistive technology); and (8) evaluate the product (Electronic Industries Alliance, 1996).

UD as a process requires a macro view of an application, as well as a micro view of subparts of the application. A review of the literature regarding how UD has been applied in a wide variety of settings suggests the following process for applying UDHE (Burgstahler, 2007f, pp. 1–2). These steps are also summarized in Figure 1.2.

1. *Identify the application.* Specify the product or environment to which you wish to apply universal design.
2. *Define the universe.* Describe the overall population (e.g., users of service), and then describe the diverse characteristics of potential members of the population for which the application is designed (e.g., students, faculty, and staff with diverse characteristics with respect to gender; age; size; ethnicity and race; native language; learning style; and abilities to see, hear, manipulate objects, read, and communicate).
3. *Involve consumers.* Consider and involve people with diverse characteristics (as identified in Step 2) in all phases of the development, implementation, and evaluation of the application. Also gain perspectives through diversity programs, such as the campus disability services office.

FIGURE 1.2   A Process of Universal Design

Identify the application

Define the universe

Involve consumers

Adopt guidelines/standards

Apply guidelines/standards

Plan for accommodations

Train and support

Evaluate

4. *Adopt guidelines or standards.* Create or select existing universal design guidelines or standards. Integrate them with other best practices within the field of the specific application.

5. *Apply guidelines or standards.* Apply universal design in concert with best practices within the field, as identified in Step 4, to the overall design of the application, all subcomponents of the application, and all ongoing operations (e.g., procurement processes, staff training) to maximize the benefit of the application to individuals with the wide variety of characteristics identified in Step 2.

6. *Plan for accommodations.* Develop processes to address accommodation requests (e.g., purchase of assistive technology, arrangement for sign language interpreters) from individuals for whom the design of the application does not automatically provide access.

7. *Train and support.* Tailor and deliver ongoing training and support to stakeholders (e.g., instructors, computer support staff, procurement officers, volunteers). Share institutional goals with respect to diversity and inclusion and practices for ensuring welcoming, accessible, and inclusive experiences for everyone.

8. *Evaluate.* Include universal design measures in periodic evaluations of the application; evaluate the application with a diverse group of users; and make modifications based on feedback. Provide ways to collect input from users (e.g., through online and printed instruments and communications with staff).

APPLICATIONS OF UNIVERSAL DESIGN IN HIGHER EDUCATION

With roots in commercial product design and architecture, UD principles have been applied to many educational products, (e.g., Web sites, curricula, scientific equipment) and environments, (e.g., classrooms, student union buildings, libraries, online courses) (The Center for Universal Design in Education, n.d.). Practicing UDHE instead of providing accommodations alone holds promise for making institutions more inclusive of students who disclose disabilities and request accommodations and those with disabilities who do not disclose, an estimated 60% of the population of students with disabilities (Wagner, Newman, Cameto, Garza, & Levine, 2005). Other beneficiaries of UDHE are students with various learning styles, whose native language is not English, who are older than the average student, and who are members of racial and ethnic minority groups.

Although the basic definition and principles of UD can be applied to any situation, strategies for applying UD are unique to a specific application. Table 1.1 lists the seven principles of UD developed by the Center for Universal Design, each matched with examples of its application to products and environments in higher education (Burgstahler, 2007e).

To be more useful to individuals with specific roles in the institution, UD strategies can be organized according to where they are applied, such as instruction, services, information technology, and physical spaces (Burgstahler, 2007a, p. 2). Figure 1.3 provides examples of UDHE practices in these four areas.

UD is a promising approach for integrating all we know about gender, race and ethnicity, age, disability, and other diversity issues into an implementation model

TABLE 1.1   Examples of Universal Design Principles Applied to Higher Education Practices

UD Principle	Example of UDHE Practice
1. *Equitable use.* The design is useful and marketable to people with diverse abilities.	*Career services.* Job postings in formats accessible to people with a broad range of abilities, disabilities, ages, and racial/ethnic backgrounds.
2. *Flexibility in use.* The design accommodates a wide range of individual preferences and abilities.	*Campus museum.* A design that allows a visitor to choose to read or listen to the description of the contents of display cases.
3. *Simple and intuitive.* Use of the design is easy to understand, regardless of the user's experience, knowledge, language skills, or current concentration level.	*Assessment.* Testing in a predictable, straightforward manner.
4. *Perceptible information.* The design communicates necessary information effectively to the user, regardless of ambient conditions or the user's sensory abilities.	*Dormitory.* An emergency alarm system with visual, aural, and kinesthetic characteristics.
5. *Tolerance for error.* The design minimizes hazards and the adverse consequences of accidental or unintended actions.	*Instructional software.* A program that provides guidance when the student makes an inappropriate selection.
6. *Low physical effort.* The design can be used efficiently, comfortably, and with a minimum of fatigue.	*Curriculum.* Software with on-screen control buttons that are large enough for students with limited fine motor skills to select easily.
7. *Size and space for approach and use.* Appropriate size and space is provided for approach, reach, manipulation, and use, regardless of the user's body size, posture, or mobility (The Center for Universal Design, 1997).	*Science lab.* An adjustable table and flexible work area that is usable by students who are right- or left-handed and have a wide range of physical characteristics and abilities (Burgstahler, 2007e).

that highly values diversity and equity and can be routinely applied to all aspects of higher education. UD

- is a goal;
- is a proactive process that can be implemented in incremental steps;
- is accessible, usable, and inclusive;
- does not lower quality or standards.

Applying UDHE may reorient the roles of faculty, student service administrators, and disability services. In an accommodation model, the student is responsible for presenting documentation to disability service staff who determine reasonable accommodations and, as appropriate, tell faculty and staff to implement them. In the UDHE model, there is more shared responsibility as faculty and staff take on greater responsibilities to create welcoming, accessible, and inclusive environments; disability service personnel act in a consulting role regarding these efforts in addition to their traditional role of specifying accommodations for individuals. Effective results with both models, however, requires active engagement of the student as well. Table 1.2 articulates the potential roles of students with disabilities, disability services staff, faculty, and student service administrators when UDHE is embraced.

FIGURE 1.3 Examples of Universal Design in Higher Education

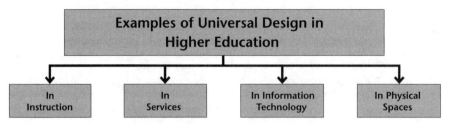

In Instruction	In Services	In Information Technology	In Physical Spaces
• A statement on a syllabus that invites students to meet with the instructor to discuss learning needs. • Multiple delivery methods that motivate and engage all learners. • Flexible curriculum that is accessible to all learners. • Examples that appeal to students with a variety of characteristics with respect to race, ethnicity, gender, age, and interest. • Regular, accessible, and effective interactions between students and the instructor. • Allowing students to turn in parts of a large project for feedback before the final project is due. • Class outlines and notes that are on an accessible Web site. • Assessing student learning using multiple methods. • Faculty awareness of process and resources for disability-related accommodations.	• Part of a service counter that is at a height accessible from a seated position. • Staff that are aware of resources and procedures for providing disability-related accommodations. • Pictures in publications and on Web sites that include people with diverse characteristics with respect to race, age, gender, and disability. • A statement in publications that states how to request special assistance, such as a disability-related accommodation. • A student service Web site that adheres to accessibility standards of the U.S. federal government (see http://www.section508.gov/). • Printed materials that are easy to reach from a variety of heights and without furniture blocking access. • Printed publications that are available in alternate formats (e.g., electronic, large print, braille).	• Captioned videos. • Alternative text for graphic images on Web pages so that individuals who are blind and using text-to-speech technology can access the content. • Procurement policies and procedures that promote the purchase of accessible products. • Standards for the universal design of Web sites. • Comfortable access to computers for both left- and right-handed students. • Software and Web sites that are compatible with assistive technology. • Computers that are on adjustable-height tables.	• Clear directional signs that have large, high-contrast print. • Restrooms, classrooms, and other facilities that are physically accessible to individuals who use wheelchairs or have other mobility challenges. • Furniture and fixtures in classrooms that are adjustable in height and allow arrangements for different learning activities and student groupings. • Emergency instructions that are clear and visible and address the needs of individuals with sensory and mobility impairments. • Nonslip walking surfaces.

TABLE 1.2 Stakeholder Roles on a Universally Designed Campus

Stakeholder	Role
Student with disability	Apply self-determination skills, including self-advocacy to address access issues.
Disability services staff	Consult on universal design. Authorize and arrange reasonable accommodations.
Faculty or student service administrator	Apply universal design. Provide reasonable accommodations.

CONCLUSION

In an era of rapidly changing demographics, it is impossible (and not particularly useful) to describe the "typical" student; it is easier and more useful to describe diversity within the student body. However, bringing diverse groups into an institution that does not adequately address diversity issues limits the ability of specific groups to thrive and limits the institution's ability to achieve its academic goals. UDHE shows promise as a framework for addressing diversity by creating educational products and environments that are welcoming, inclusive, and usable for everyone.

THE AUTHORS AND CONTENT OF THIS BOOK

The content of this book emerged from decades of experience of educators, administrators, and researchers who share a common goal of making higher education more welcoming, accessible, usable, and inclusive for everyone. The authors share a passion for creating educational environments that value all learners, and they recognize the promise of UD to do that. The authors present a variety of perspectives, experiences, and outcomes with respect to the application of UDHE to:

- instruction (including curriculum and assessment);
- physical spaces;
- technological environments;
- student services.

Many of the authors have disabilities, but no one knows for sure exactly how many because the process for developing the publication was universally designed and, thus, accommodations were not needed. To limit the size of this volume, specific benefits of UD to students with disabilities are emphasized; we also acknowledge the value of UD to other student populations, as well as faculty, staff, and visitors.

UD strategies are employed in presenting the content of this book. It is available in alternate formats for people with disabilities. The chapters are organized into four parts that guide its readers:

- Part One: Introduction
- Part Two: Universal Design of Instruction in Higher Education
- Part Three: Universal Design of Student Services, Physical Spaces, and Technological Environments in Higher Education
- Part Four: Institutionalization of Universal Design in Higher Education

Each part begins with a summary of the section's focus and a recurring diagram of UDHE examples that highlights the section topic. Each chapter begins with an abstract summarizing its content. There are overview chapters for each of the four major UDHE application areas covered in the book: instruction, student services, physical spaces, and technological environments. These chapters are easy to identify by the inclusion of "From Research to Practice" in their titles. Each overview chapter ends with a description of the subsequent chapters that relate to the topic. Chapters are ordered so that the content builds on previous chapters, but they are self-contained and can be read out of the order presented. The book includes a traditional table of contents and index. In addition, Table 1.3 helps readers locate answers to specific questions.

TABLE 1.3   Questions Answered in This Book

If This Is Your Question	Find Your Answer in Chapter(s):
What are the history and applications of UDHE?	1, 2, 14,16, 18
How can I take the definition and principles of UD and apply them to instruction?	2, 3, 11
How does UD relate to teaching and learning theories, philosophies, and models?	2, 3, 4, 6, 11
How can I apply UD to assessments?	2, 5
How can I apply UD to an online distance learning course? To an entire program?	2, 18, 19
What are examples of UD applied to specific courses?	3, 4, 13
How do students with disabilities perceive the value of UD for their learning?	6
How does UD benefit students with psychiatric, learning, and other "invisible" disabilities?	7, 12
How can I provide faculty development on UD?	8, 9, 10, 11, 12, 23
How can I apply UD to a student service unit?	14, 15
How is a universally designed physical space different than one that is simply "ADA-compliant"?	16, 17
How can I design Web content to be accessible and usable by all students?	18, 19, 20
How can I promote a campuswide adoption of UD?	21, 22, 23, 24

REFERENCES

Americans with Disabilities Act of 1990. 42 U.S.C.A. § 12101 *et seq.*

Architectural Barriers Act of 1968. 42 U.S.C. § 4151 *et seq.*

Assistive Technology Act of 1998 Pub.L. No. 105-394 Stat 2432.

Bergman, E., & Johnson, E. (1995). Towards accessible human-computer interaction. In J. Nielsen (Ed.), *Advances in human-computer interaction* (Vol. 5). Norwood, NJ: Ablex.

Burgstahler, S. (2007a). *Applications of universal design in education.* Seattle: University of Washington. Retrieved November 1, 2007, from http://www.washington.edu/doit/Brochures/Academics/app_ud_edu.html

Burgstahler, S. (2007b). *Equal access: Universal design of computer labs.* Seattle: University of Washington. Retrieved November 1, 2007, from http://www.washington.edu/doit/Video/equal.html

Burgstahler, S. (2007c). *Equal access: Universal design of instruction.* Seattle: University of Washington. Retrieved November 1, 2007, from http://www.washington.edu/doit/Brochures/Academics/equal_access_ud.html

Burgstahler, S. (2007d). *Equal access: Universal design of student services.* Seattle: University of Washington. Retrieved November 1, 2007, from http://www.washington.edu/doit/Brochures/Academics/equal_access_ss.html

Burgstahler, S. (2007e). *Universal design in education: Principles and applications.* Seattle: University of Washington. Retrieved November 1, 2007, from http://www.washington.edu/doit/Brochures/Academics/ud_edu.html

Burgstahler, S. (2007f). *Universal design: Process, principles, and applications.* Seattle: University of Washington. Retrieved November 1, 2007, from http://www.washington.edu/doit/Brochures/Programs/ud.html

Burgstahler, S., Jirikowic, T., Kolko, B., & Eliot, M. (2004). Software accessibility, usability testing and individuals with disabilities. *Information Technology and Disabilities, 10*(2). Retrieved November 1, 2007, from http://www.rit.edu/%7Eeasi/itd/itdv10n2/burghsta.htm

The Center for Universal Design. (1997a). *About UD*. Raleigh: North Carolina State University. Retrieved November 1, 2007, from http://www.design.ncsu.edu/cud/about_ud/about_ud.htm

The Center for Universal Design. (1997b). *The principles of universal design, version 2.0*. Raleigh: North Caroline State University. Retrieved November 1, 2007, from http://www.design.ncsu.edu/cud/about_ud/udprincipleshtml

The Center for Universal Design in Education. (n.d.). Seattle: University of Washington. Retrieved November 1, 2007, from http://www.washington.edu/doit/CUDE

Claxton, C. S., & Ralston, Y. (1978). *Learning styles: Their impact on teaching and administration*. Washington, DC: American Association for Higher Education.

DO-IT (Disabilities, Opportunities, Internetworking, and Technology). (n.d.). *Resources for student services staff*. Seattle: University of Washington. Retrieved November 1, 2007, from http://www.washington.edu/doit/Conf/staff_resources.html

Dunn, R., & Griggs, S. A. (2000). *Practical approaches to using learning styles in higher education*. Westport, CT: Greenwood.

Electronic Industries Alliance. (1996). *Resource guide for accessible design of consumer electronics: Linking product design to the needs of people with functional limitations*. Arlington, VA: Author.

Ensign, A. (Ed.). (1993). *Universal playground design*. Lansing, MI: PAM Assistance Centre.

Gardner, H. (1983). *Frames of mind*. New York: Basic Books.

Gill, C. J. (1987). A new social perspective on disability and its implications for rehabilitation. In F. S. Cromwell (Ed.), *Sociocultural implications in treatment planning in occupational therapy* (pp. 49–55). New York: Haworth Press.

Hackman, H., & Rauscher, L. (2004). A pathway to access for all: Exploring the connections between universal instructional design and social justice education. *Equity & Excellence in Education, 37*, 114–123.

Hagley Museum and Library. (n.d.). *The Marc Harrison collection*. Wilmington, DE: Author. Retrieved November 1, 2007, from http://www.hagley.org/A2193D.HTM

Hahn, H. (1988). The politics of physical differences: Disability and discrimination. *Journal of Social Issues, 44*(1), 39–47.

Higher Education Research Institute. (2006). *The American freshman, forty-year trends: 1966–2006*. Los Angeles: University of California–Los Angeles Graduate School of Education & Information Studies.

Hogan, G. (2003). *The inclusive corporation*. Athens, OH: Swallow Press/Ohio University Press.

Horn, L., & Nevill, S. (2006). *Profile of undergraduates in U.S. postsecondary education institutions: 2003–04* (NCES 2006-184). Washington, DC: National Center for Education Statistics, U.S. Department of Education.

International Organization for Standardization. (1998). *Guidance on usability*. (ISO 9241-11).

Iwarsson, S., & Stahl, A. (2003). Accessibility, usability and universal design—positioning and definition of concepts describing person-environment relationships. *Disability and Rehabilitation, 25*(2), 57–66.

Jones, S. R. (1996). Toward inclusive theory: Disability as social construction. *NASPA Journal, 33*, 347–354.

Knowles, M. S. (1980). *The modern practice of adult education*. Englewood Cliffs, NJ: Cambridge Adult Education.

Lewis, L., & Farris, E. (1999). An institutional perspective on students with disabilities in postsecondary education. *Education Statistics Quarterly, 1*(3). Retrieved November 20, 2007 from http://nces.ed.gov/programs/quarterly/vol_1/1_3/4-esq13-b.asp

Mason, C., & Orkwis., R. (2005). Instructional theories supporting universal design for learning—Teaching to individual learners. In Council for Exceptional Children (Ed.), *Universal design for learning: A guide for teachers and education professionals*. Upper Saddle River, NJ: Pearson Prentice Hall.

McGuire, J. M., Scott, S. S., & Shaw, S. F. (2003). Universal design for instruction: The paradigm, its principles, and products for enhancing instructional access. *Journal of Postsecondary Education and Disability, 17*(1), 11–21.

National Center for Education Statistics. (2000). *Services and accommodations for students with disabilities.* Retrieved November 20, 2007 from http://nces.ed.gov/programs/coe/2003/section5/tables/se34_1.asp

National Council on Disability. (2004). *Design for inclusion: Creating a new marketplace.* Washington, DC: Author. Retrieved November 1, 2007, from http://www.ncd.gov/newsroom/publications/2004/online_newmarketplace.htm#afbad

Nieto, S. (1996). *Affirming diversity: The sociopolitical context of multicultural education* (2nd ed.). White Plains, NY: Longman.

Pliner, S., & Johnson, J. (2004). Historical, theoretical, and foundational principles of universal instructional design in higher education. *Equity & Excellence in Education, 37*, 105–113.

Rose, D. H., Meyer, A., & Hitchcock, C. (Eds.). (2005). *The universally designed classroom: Accessible curriculum and digital technologies.* Cambridge, MA: Harvard Education Publishing Group.

Schwab, C. (2004). A stroll through the universally designed smart home for the 21st century. *The Exceptional Parent, 34*(7), 24–28.

Section 504 of the Rehabilitation Act of 1973, as amended. 29 U.S.C. § 794.

Section 508 of the Rehabilitation Act of 1973, as amended. 29 U.S.C. § 794(d).

Story, M. F., Mueller, J. L., & Mace, R. L. (1998). *The universal design file: Designing for people of all ages and abilities.* Retrieved November 1, 2007, from http://www.udeducation.org/resources/readings/mueller_mace.asp

Swain, J., & Lawrence, P. (1994). Learning about disability: Changing attitudes or challenging understanding? In S. French (Ed.), *On equal terms: Working with disabled people* (pp. 87–102). Oxford: Butterworth Heinemann.

United States Department of Justice. (2005). *A guide to disability rights laws.* Washington, DC: U.S. Department of Justice, Civil Rights Division. Retrieved November 1, 2007, from www.ada.gov/cguide.pdf

Vanderheiden, G., & Tobias, J. (n.d.). *Universal design of consumer products: Current industry practice and perceptions.* Madison: University of Wisconsin Trace Research and Development Center. Retrieved November 1, 2007, from http://trace.wisc.edu/docs/ud_consumer_products_hfes2000/index.htm

Vanderheiden, G. C., & Vanderheiden, K. R. (1992). *Guidelines for the design of consumer products to increase their accessibility to people with disabilities or who are aging* (Working Draft 1.7). Madison: University of Wisconsin Trace Research and Development Center. Retrieved November 1, 2007, from http://trace.wisc.edu/docs/consumer_product_guidelines/toc.htm

Wagner, M., Newman, L., Cameto, R., Garza, N., & Levine, P. (2005). *After high school: A first look at the postschool experiences of youth with disabilities. A report from the National Longitudinal Transition Study2 (NLTS2).* Menlo Park, CA: SRI International.

This chapter is based on work supported by the U.S. Department of Education Office of Postsecondary Education (grant numbers P333A990042, P333A020044, and P333A050064) and the National Science Foundation (Cooperative Agreement number HRD-0227995). Any opinions, findings, and conclusions or recommendations are those of the author and do not necessarily reflect the policy or views of the federal government, and you should not assume its endorsement.

PART 2

Universal Design of Instruction in Higher Education

In Part Two, the authors explore applications of universal design (UD) to instruction. They share issues, perspectives, and strategies for applying UD to teaching methods, curriculum, and assessment. The section begins with a chapter by Sheryl Burgstahler that provides an overview of history, principles, and applications of universal design of instruction.

Universal Design in Higher Education

Instruction	Services	Information Technology	Physical Spaces
Class climate	Planning, policies, and evaluation	Procurement/ development policies	Planning, policies, and evaluation
Interaction	Physical environments/ products	Physical environments/ products	Appearance
Physical environments/ products	Staff	Information	Entrances/ routes of travel
Delivery methods	Information resources/ technology	Input/control	Fixtures/ furniture
Information resources/ technology	Events	Output	Information resources/ technology
Feedback		Manipulations	Safety
Assessment		Safety	Accommodation
Accommodation		Compatibility with assistive technology	

Source: S. Burgstahler (2007). Applications of Universal Design in Education. Seattle: University of Washington. http://www.washington.edu/doit/Brochures/Academics/app_ud_edu.html

2

Universal Design of Instruction
From Principles to Practice

Sheryl E. Burgstahler

Articles about the application of universal design (UD) to instruction in higher education have appeared in the literature over the past decade. This chapter provides an overview of various approaches to applying UD to teaching methods, curricula, and assessments in on-site and online learning environments. Educators may find these insights useful as the characteristics of the students in their courses become increasingly diverse.

What might be the first response of a professor when a student who is blind enrolls in her art history class? Would she look forward to the unique perspective this student brings to her field and classroom? Would she be eager to learn how a person with a visual impairment might experience art? An important first step in creating a welcoming and inclusive classroom environment for all students is to truly value diversity in its many forms, in this case, to see differences in visual abilities as simply a normal part of the human experience.

Universal design (UD) offers a proactive approach to making courses inclusive of all potential students, including those with disabilities. The application of UD to instruction—UD principles applied to curricula, teaching methods, and assessments—holds promise as faculty try to effectively teach a student body that is increasingly diverse. Consistent with other applications of UD discussed in chapter 1, universally designed instruction is welcoming, accessible, and inclusive for all students qualified (e.g., they meet the prerequisites) to take a course without giving unfair advantage to anyone.

From the perspective of an instructor, the *universe* referred to in the UD paradigm includes anyone who is qualified to enroll in a specific course. With respect to disabilities, relevant legislation in the United States specifically defines an "otherwise qualified" student with a disability as one who meets the academic and technical standards requisite for enrollment in the course (Americans with Disabilities Act, 1990; Section 504 of the Rehabilitation Act of 1973; U.S. Department of Justice, 2005). As discussed in chapter 1, for those who submit appropriate documentation, the institution is expected to provide reasonable accommodations that allow the student to access instructional content. In contrast to the legalistic and reactive approach in providing accommodations for an individual, UD is proactive and has as its goal the full inclusion of *all* students—regardless of gender, race, place of origin, first language, learning style, culture, background knowledge, disability, or other characteristics.

UD of instruction (UDI)—also known as UD for instruction, universally designed instruction, universal instructional design, and universal course design—ensures that all students have meaningful access to course curricula, instructional activities, and assessments in an integrated setting (Bar, Galluzzo, & Sinfit, 1999; Campbell, 2004; Mino, 2004). With built-in alternatives, UDI allows students with diverse abilities and backgrounds to learn and demonstrate knowledge through multiple channels, including reading, listening, viewing, manipulating, experimenting, discussing, responding to questions, each of which are available in formats accessible to all students. UDI avoids erecting physical barriers for students with mobility impairments, sensory barriers for students with visual and hearing impairments, language barriers for students whose first language is not English, learning barriers for students with cognitive challenges, social barriers for students with social challenges, and cultural barriers for students with a broad range of backgrounds.

Applying UDI reduces, but does not eliminate, the need for accommodations for students with disabilities. For example, providing a sign language interpreter in every class, just in case someone might need one, is unreasonable; this service is best provided as an accommodation for a specific student in a specific course. However, designing course Web resources in an accessible format means that no accommodations or product redevelopment will be necessary if a blind student enrolls in the class. Planning ahead through UD may save time in the long run.

This chapter provides an overview of a process for UDI; principles of UDI; and strategies for applying UDI to teaching methods, curricula, and assessments in on-site and online learning environments in higher education.

A PROCESS FOR UNIVERSAL DESIGN OF INSTRUCTION

To implement UDI, an instructor can choose a range of teaching strategies for a course and then apply UD to each strategy, course curriculum, and assessment of student learning. Adapting the general process for applying UD as presented in chapter 1 of this book, the instructor can take the following steps, which are also summarized in Figure 2.1 (Burgstahler, 2007b).

1. *Identify the course.* Describe the course, its learning objectives, and its overall content.
2. *Define the universe.* Describe the overall population of students eligible to enroll in the course and then consider their potential diverse characteristics (e.g., with respect to gender; age; ethnicity and race; native language; learning style; and abilities to see, hear, manipulate objects, read and communicate).
3. *Involve students.* Consider perspectives of students with diverse characteristics, as identified in Step 2, in the development of the course. If they are not avail-

FIGURE 2.1   A Process of Universal Design for Instruction

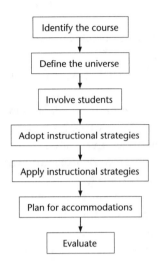

able directly from students, gain student perspectives through diversity programs such as the campus disability services office.

4. *Adopt instructional strategies.* Adopt overall learning and teaching philosophies and methods (e.g., Chickering & Gamson, 1987; Svinicki, 1999). Integrate these practices with UD guidelines or strategies for learning or instruction (e.g., Bowe, 2000; Burgstahler, 2007b; Rose, Meyer, & Hitchcock, 2005; Scott, McGuire, & Shaw, 2003).

5. *Apply instructional strategies.* Apply UD strategies in concert with good instructional practices (both identified in Step 4) to the overall choice of course teaching methods, curricula, and assessments. Then apply UD to all lectures, classroom discussions, group work, handouts, Web-based content, labs, fieldwork, assessment instruments, and other academic activities and materials to maximize the learning of students with the wide variety of characteristics identified in Step 2.

6. *Plan for accommodations.* Learn campus procedures for addressing accommodation requests (e.g., arranging for sign language interpreters) from specific students for whom the course design does not automatically provide full access.

7. *Evaluate.* Monitor the effectiveness of instruction through observation and feedback from students with the diverse set of characteristics identified in Step 2, assess learning, and modify the course as appropriate.

PRINCIPLES OF UNIVERSAL DESIGN APPLIED TO INSTRUCTION

Three approaches to adopting UD principles for learning and instruction have been discussed in the literature: (1) apply the seven principles of UD to instructional products and environments, (2) modify the seven principles, and (3) create a new set of principles tailored to instructional settings. The rationale for subscribing to a given approach and an example of how the approach leads to strategies for applying UD to teaching and learning are described in the following three sections.

Approach 1: Apply the Seven Basic Principles of Universal Design to Universal Design of Instruction

The Center for Universal Design (CUD) at North Carolina State University defines UD as "the design of products and environments to be usable by all people, to the greatest extent possible, without the need for adaptation or specialized design" (The Center for Universal Design, 1997). At CUD, a group of architects, product designers, engineers, and environmental design researchers established seven principles of UD to provide guidance in the design of products and environments (The Center for Universal Design, 1997). As described in chapter 1, researchers and practitioners have applied these principles to specific products and environments, including information technology (e.g., telephones, Web sites, educational software, video presentations), physical spaces (e.g., classrooms, labs), and services (e.g. registration, career services). Consistent with this approach, some educators have applied the CUD definition and seven principles to instruction and, from that foundation, developed specific guidelines or strategies for UDI. To demonstrate this approach, each of the seven principles of UD is listed in Table 2.1, along with one example of its application to postsecondary instruction.

Frank Bowe takes this approach in his book *Universal Design in Education* (2000). Bowe developed guidelines for the application of each principle in an educational setting and highlighted a few key instructional strategies as a "Tip Sheet for Universally Designed Teaching" (Bowe, 2000, pp. 5–6) with the following eight subcategories:

1. Become aware of your own culture's teachings and how those affect you as an educator.
2. Provide students with options for demonstrating knowledge and skills.
3. Offer instruction, and accept student work, at a distance.
4. Alert students to availability of digitized texts (e-books).
5. Offer students information in redundant media.
6. Provide the support students need to improve accuracy and speed.
7. Translate important materials to other languages as needed by your students.
8. Choose physically accessible locations for your classes.

At the Center for Universal Design in Education (CUDE), hosted by the Disabilities, Opportunities, Internetworking, and Technology (DO-IT) Center at the University of Washington–Seattle (DO-IT, n.d.), staff and collaborators also concluded that the CUD definition and principles of UD for products and environments can be applied specifically to instructional products and environments. However, after providing professional development to faculty, they concluded that the terminology used in the CUD principles of UD are somewhat foreign to educators (DO-IT, n.d., 2006, 2007a; Burgstahler, 2007a,c). Postsecondary instructors requested practical strategies for the application of UDI to specific instructional products (e.g., textbooks, Web sites) and environments (e.g., classrooms, computer labs, online learning). Checklists developed through these efforts reveal how the seven principles of

TABLE 2.1 Applications of the Seven Principles of Universal Design to Instruction

UD Principle	Example of How UD Might Be Applied to Instruction
Equitable use. The design is useful and marketable to people with diverse abilities.	A professor's Web site is designed so that it is accessible to everyone, including students who are blind and use text-to-speech software.
Flexibility in use. The design accommodates a wide range of individual preferences and abilities.	A museum, visited as a field trip for a course, allows each student to choose to read or listen to a description of the contents of display cases.
Simple and intuitive. Use of the design is easy to understand regardless of the user's experience, knowledge, language skills, or current concentration level.	Control buttons on science equipment are labeled with text and symbols that are simple and intuitive to understand.
Perceptible information. The design communicates necessary information effectively to the user regardless of ambient conditions or the user's sensory abilities.	A video presentation projected in a course includes captions.
Tolerance for error. The design minimizes hazards and the adverse consequences of accidental or unintended actions.	Educational software provides guidance and/or background information when the student makes an inappropriate response.
Low physical effort. The design can be used efficiently and comfortably and with a minimum of fatigue.	Doors to a lecture hall open automatically for people with a wide variety of physical characteristics.
Size and space for approach and use. Appropriate size and space is provided for approach, reach, manipulation, and use regardless of the user's body size, posture, or mobility (The Center for Universal Design, 1997).	A flexible science lab work area has adequate workspace for students who are left- and right-handed and for those who need to work from a standing or seated position (Burgstahler, 2007e, p. 2).

UD can be applied to the overall design of instruction as well as to specific areas, such as class climate, physical environment and products, delivery methods, information resources and technology, interaction, feedback, assessment, and accommodations (Burgstahler, 2007b,d). UD can also apply to specific teaching techniques, such as lectures, large- and small-group discussions, video presentations, online instruction, case studies, and role-playing. Accommodation is built into this UDI model by requiring that instructors have a plan for accommodating students with disabilities who are not fully served by their instructional design.

Approach 2: Add Unique Instructional Principles to the Seven Principles of Universal Design

A second approach to adopting principles for UD to instruction is to modify existing principles and add more principles to address instructional issues that practitioners feel are not adequately covered in the seven principles developed by CUD. For example, at the University of Connecticut, a review of the literature on UD, effective instruction, and teaching students with learning disabilities motivated researchers to add two UD principles to CUD's list of seven, to create a total of nine principles for instruction (McGuire, Scott, & Shaw, 2003). Per McGuire, Scott, & Shaw (2003, p. 13), the two extra principles and their definitions are:

8. *A community of learners:* The instructional environment promotes interaction and communication among students and between students and faculty.

9. *Instructional climate:* Instruction is designed to be welcoming and inclusive. High expectations are espoused for all students.

There are two key differences between this model and the one described in the previous section. First, in the approach used by Bowe and DO-IT, CUD's seven principles of UD for products and environments are considered adequate for applications to instructional products and environments. Principles 8 and 9 of the second approach are considered covered by other CUD principles—in part, by Principle 1 (Equitable use: The design is useful and marketable to people with diverse abilities) and associated guidelines that ensure the same means of use for all participants; avoid segregating or stigmatizing anyone; make the design appealing to all users; and ensure privacy, security, and safety for everyone (The Center for Universal Design, 1997). Second, the University of Connecticut combines UD with principles of good practice for students with disabilities and, specifically, for those with learning disabilities, thereby creating a combined list of principles of good *and* universally designed instruction. In contrast, the approach of Bowe and DO-IT does not consolidate UD principles with any particular teaching or learning philosophies or instructional practices; rather, it considers UD as a characteristic that can be applied in any general philosophy or approach to instruction or any specific instructional practice, such as lectures, large- and small-group discussions, video presentations, and distance learning.

Approach 3: Create a New Set of Principles Tailored to Instructional Settings

Since the late 1980s, the Center for Applied Special Technology (CAST) has led efforts in the application of UD to educational software, especially for children. CAST concluded that "The *idea* of UD transfers readily from the built environment to the learning environment, but the *principles* and *techniques* do not" (Rose, Harbour, Johnston, Daley, & Abarbanell, 2006, p. 1). Applying the results of brain and learning research and the capabilities of information technology, CAST defined UD for learning (UDL) as "a research-based set of principles that together form a practical framework for using technology to maximize learning opportunities for every student" (Rose & Meyer, 2002, p. 5). UDL supports the goal of *differentiated instruction* to effectively teach students with different backgrounds, levels of readiness, primary languages, preferences, interests, and abilities in the same class. UDL provides "rich supports for learning, and reduces barriers to the curriculum, while maintaining high achievement standards for all" (CAST, n.d., p. 1). A key premise of UDL is that a curriculum should include alternatives to make it accessible and applicable to students with different backgrounds, learning styles, abilities, and disabilities and minimizes the need for assistive technology.

UDL is structured around three sets of learning networks—recognition learning, strategic learning, and affective learning (Rose, Meyer, & Hitchcock, 2005)—and three guiding principles for applying UDL to curriculum and assessment (Rose, Meyer, & Hitchcock, 2005; Orkwis & McLane, 1998). The three principles of UDL are

1. multiple means of representation;
2. multiple means of expression;
3. multiple means of engagement.

In short, according to Hitchcock, Meyer, Rose & Jackson (2002, p. 8), in a UDL curriculum:

- *Goals* provide an appropriate challenge for all students.
- *Materials* have a flexible format, supporting transformation between media and multiple representations of content to support all students' learning.
- *Methods* are flexible and diverse enough to provide appropriate learning experiences, challenges, and support for all students.
- *Assessment* is sufficiently flexible to provide accurate, ongoing information that helps teachers adjust instruction and maximize learning.

When UD is applied to the development of instructional materials and assessments, students and teachers do not need to adapt themselves to the limits of the material because the materials are flexible enough to address their specific needs and preferences. With UDL materials, students with disabilities have access to content at the same time as their peers. Flexible components are built into digital materials to benefit students with learning disabilities; with attention issues; with behavioral problems; or with physical or sensory disabilities. They also benefit those who are learning a new language; who have attention deficits; or who have other characteristics that make taking notes, reading, understanding auditory information, paying attention, handwriting, or spelling difficult.

UNIVERSAL DESIGN AND TEACHING/LEARNING PHILOSOPHIES

Although the three sets of principles for applying UD to instruction are not identical, there is considerable agreement on the part of researchers and practitioners, including the authors of this book, on specific strategies that represent the application of UD to curricula, teaching strategies, and assessments. UD does not require that educators abandon their adopted teaching and learning philosophies, theories, and models, such as differentiated instruction, behaviorism, constructivism, learner-centered instruction, and sociocultural models of teaching and learning (Svinicki, 1999). Instead, UD requires that instructors rethink the mix of strategies they use and ensure that the overall mix, as well as the implementation of each strategy, is inclusive and accessible for everyone. Table 2.2 provides examples of how UD might be applied to specific strategies common to a sampling of teaching and learning philosophies.

The wide variety of learning styles, strengths, and preferences of students in a typical course presents challenges regardless of the instructional approach (Claxton & Ralston, 1978; Kolb, 1981; Wooldridge, 1995). Learning style has been described as a combined reaction to the environment, emotions, sociological factors, and physiolog-

TABLE 2.2   Universal Design Applied to Strategies of Sample Teaching/Learning Philosophies

Strategy Employed by a Specific Teaching/Learning Philosophy	Example of How UD Might Be Applied to the Strategy
The *differentiated instruction* strategy of initial and ongoing assessment of student readiness and growth (Hall, Strangman, & Meyer, 2003; Tomlinson, 2001).	Use multiple and accessible assessments (e.g., oral presentations, demonstrations, portfolios, and projects) that take into account the diverse characteristics of potential students, including disabilities.
Computer-assisted self-paced instruction based on *behaviorist theory* (Svinicki, 1999).	Ensure that content is culturally relevant to a broad audience, that captions or transcriptions are provided for auditory output, and that text descriptions are provided for the content of graphic images.
The *constructivist* approach for the instructor to serve as a resource to help students access and utilize information resources and share information with peers (Fosnot, 1996; Hodson & Hodson, 1998; Osborne, 1996).	Make sure resources and communication options are accessible to all learners, including those for whom English is a second language; those with low-level reading skills; and those who have physical, learning, or sensory disabilities.
The *learning-centered instruction* focus on the student as learner and the instructor as the facilitator of learning (Barr & Tagg, 1995; Harrison, 2006; Kame'enui, Carnine, Dixon, Simmons, & Coyne, 2002).	Ensure that learning is defined in such a way that it does not discriminate against any students and is assessed in multiple ways.
The *sociocultural approach* to teaching and learning based on the notions that learning is situated in contexts, each student has a unique cultural perspective, and communication in the learning process is very important (O'Loughlin, 1992).	Ensure that the views of *all* students are heard, considered, and valued in the classroom.

ical factors (Dunn & Griggs, 2000). Learning preferences include those that are auditory, visual, tactile, and kinesthetic (Wooldridge, 1995). Another theoretical framework for learning styles focuses on how people experience learning according to their dominant style as a converger, diverger, assimilator, or accommodator (Claxton & Ralston, 1978; Svinicki & Dixon, 1987). The theory of multiple intelligences—linguistic, logical-mathematical, spatial, bodily-kinesthetic, musical, interpersonal, intrapersonal, and naturalistic (Gardner, 1983)—describes how people perceive the world and sheds light on aspects of diversity in the classroom. Although the linguistic and logical-mathematical intelligences are most frequently addressed in traditional curricula, educators who apply UD consider a more balanced offering of curricula and teaching approaches that address all types of learning differences and include multiple modes of delivery, multiple ways for students to interact with each other and the course content, and multiple ways for students to demonstrate what they have learned. The following summary by Svinicki (1999, p. 19) further supports the UD strategy to engage in multiple modes of instruction.

It is appropriate to acknowledge that there are individual variables among students that can influence the effectiveness of instruction. However, more research is needed

TABLE 2.3   Universal Design of Instruction Applied to Principles of Good Practice

Principle of Good Practice in Undergraduate Education:	Example of How UD Might Be Applied to the Principle
Encourages contact between students and faculty.	Include a statement on class syllabus inviting students to meet with instructor to discuss disability-related and other learning needs.
Develops reciprocity and cooperation among students.	Assign group work for which learners must support each other and that places a high value on different skills and roles. Encourage multiple ways for students to interact with each other (e.g., in-class questions and discussion, group work, Internet-based communications).
Encourages active learning.	Provide multiple ways for students to participate, ensuring that all students, including those with disabilities, can actively participate in class activities.
Gives prompt feedback.	Regularly assess student progress using multiple, accessible methods and tools and adjust instruction accordingly.
Emphasizes time on task.	Ensure that all students have adequate time to complete tasks, including students with disabilities.
Communicates high expectations.	Keep expectations high, including those for students with disabilities, and provide accommodations to level the playing field rather than give unfair advantage.
Respects diverse talents and ways of learning (Chickering & Gamson, 1997).	Adopt practices that reflect high values with respect to both diversity *and* inclusiveness.

to verify which of the proposed differences is most strongly grounded in empirical data and has the best record of relating to learning. Until those data have been gathered and properly analyzed, our best instructional strategy to cope with individual differences is to provide an array of learning alternatives and let the learner choose among them rather than trying to force one on everyone or even on a single individual.

The popular principles of good practice in undergraduate education were distilled by Chickering & Gamson (1987) from research on teaching and learning in postsecondary education. Table 2.3 shows how UD can enhance the implementation of each of these principles. Similarly, educators who embrace specific academic supports for postsecondary students can apply UD to these approaches. For example, instructors can apply UD to freshman learning communities (Hotchkiss, Moore, & Pitts, 2006; Minkler, 2002; Soldner, Lee, & Duby, 1999)—environments in which freshmen engage in courses and extracurricular activities as a cohort—by ensuring that all aspects of these communities are welcoming, accessible to, and inclusive of a broad audience. As one step toward universally designed learning communities, coordinators of such communities can ensure that participating instructors employ UDI in their courses. They can also make sure that publications and Web sites for their communities are welcoming and accessible to a broad audience through pictures of participants with diverse characteristics, accessible formats, and content that tells how to obtain accommodations and other assistance.

As demonstrated in these examples, UD does not replace, but rather complements, principles of good teaching and related practices in the same way that applying UD to an entrance complements overall building construction standards, aesthetics, and functionality. Just as applying UD to a poorly conceived product makes the features of a poor product accessible to everyone, applying UD to poorly designed or implemented instructional strategies simply results in making poor instruction accessible to all students. Thus, one could argue that all universally designed instruction is not necessarily good instruction, but that all good instruction is universally designed.

But which teaching qualities provide the greatest benefit to students with a variety of abilities? In an informal online discussion conducted by the author of this chapter, high school and college students with disabilities were asked, "What are the qualities of a good teacher?" Their responses can be summarized as follows: A good teacher

- is well prepared;
- is a good role model;
- makes expectations clear;
- is approachable;
- gets to know students;
- respects students and maintains privacy;
- does not make assumptions about a student's capabilities;
- encourages students;
- is patient;
- challenges students;
- helps students apply knowledge;
- is open to new ideas;
- is enthusiastic;
- facilitates the exchange of ideas between students and between teacher and students;
- adjusts to the unique needs of students.

No one in the discussion specifically mentioned disability, but some of the qualities mentioned reflect the inclusive nature of a universally designed course. Simply stated, good teaching for students with disabilities is good teaching for all students. This should be welcome news to professors who thought they needed to adopt entirely new teaching approaches in order to fully include students with diverse characteristics in their courses.

STRATEGIES FOR APPLYING UNIVERSAL DESIGN TO INSTRUCTION

Good teachers have long used teaching methods that reach a diverse student body. For example, in an exploratory study, postsecondary faculty reported that flexible instructional strategies and the ability to monitor and quickly adjust methods benefit students with a range of disabilities, as do the general strategies of cooperative learning, contextual learning, computer-assisted instruction, constructive learning, scaffolding, online instruction and assessment, the provision of organizing tools for students, multimodal instruction, peer editing, criterion-based learning, extended time for exams and projects, and testing in the same manner as teaching (Silver, Bourke, & Strehorn, 1998). Making instruction appropriate for a diverse audience has been recognized as fostering the academic and social growth of all students (Gurin, Dey, Hurtado, & Gurin, 2002).

DO-IT has developed a list of guidelines and examples for faculty to use to begin applying UD to their instruction (Burgstahler, 2007b). The initial list was created after a review of research papers, published articles, and comprehensive Web sites that identified specific instructional strategies considered to be applications of UDI (Bowe, 2000; Bruch, 2003; Burgstahler & Doe, 2006; Burgstahler, Corrigan, & McCarter, 2005; Hitchcock & Stahl, 2003; Johnson & Fox, 2003; Mason & Orkwis, 2005; McAlexander, 2003; McGuire, Scott, & Shaw, 2003; Mino, 2004; Orkwis, 2003; Orkwis & McLane, 1998; Pedelty, 2003; Rose, Harbour, Johnston, Daley, & Abarbanell, 2006; Rose & Meyer, 2002; Silver, Bourke, & Strehorn, 1998).

DO-IT's list of UDI examples was initially built from various sources by combining similar items and discarding items considered too specific to a content area or to the needs of a specific student (i.e., an *accommodation* rather than a UD feature). Further revisions were based on the formative feedback of faculty and administrators from postsecondary institutions as part of three three-year projects funded by the U.S. Department of Education Office of Postsecondary Education (DO-IT, 2006, 2007a, 2007b). Always a working document, the most current list of UDI strategies is maintained in the regularly updated publication *Equal Access: Universal Design of Instruction* (Burgstahler, 2007b) on the CUDE Web site (DO-IT, n.d.). Educators are encouraged to suggest improvements and to take the electronic copy of the checklist and tailor it to specific courses.

A single document cannot capture all potential applications of UDI. However, DO-IT's evolving checklist provides a place to start. Table 2.4 includes a partial list of UDI practices organized around specific aspects of instruction. It should be noted that an example may overlap several guidelines but is listed only once to emphasize one aspect of its importance and to reduce redundancies.

As an example of how the UDI checklist might be used, suppose a professor decides that lecture followed by large-group discussion is the best way to deliver a specific lesson. In applying UDI, the instructor might choose to:

- Welcome all students by name, interacting with them as they enter the classroom.
- Arrange seating to encourage participation, giving each student a clear line of sight to the instructor and visual aids and allowing room for wheelchairs, personal assistants, and assistive technology.
- Give students scaffolding tools (e.g., provide outlines, class notes, summary, graphic organizer, copy of projected materials with room for taking notes) and provide alternative formats (e.g., large print, braille), if they have been requested by students with disabilities.

TABLE 2.4   DO-IT Universal Design of Instruction Guidelines and Examples

UDI Guideline	Example of UDI Practice
Class climate. Adopt practices that reflect high values with respect to *both* diversity and inclusiveness.	*Avoid stereotyping.* Offer instruction and support based on student performance and requests, not simply on assumptions that members of certain groups (e.g., students with certain types of disabilities or from a specific racial/ethnic group) will automatically do well or poorly or require certain types of assistance.
Interaction. Encourage regular and effective interactions between students and the instructor and ensure that communication methods are accessible to all participants.	*Promote effective communication.* Employ interactive teaching techniques. Face the class, speak clearly, use a microphone if your voice does not project adequately for all students, and make eye contact with students. Consider requiring a meeting with each student. Supplement in-person contact with online communication. Use straightforward language; avoid unnecessary jargon and complexity; and use student names in electronic, written, and in-person communications.
Physical environments/ products. Ensure that facilities, activities, materials, and equipment are physically accessible to and usable by all students, and that all potential student characteristics are addressed in safety considerations	*Arrange instructional spaces to maximize inclusion and comfort.* Arrange seating to encourage participation, giving each student a clear line of sight to the instructor and visual aids and allowing room for wheelchairs, personal assistants, sign language interpreters, captionists, and assistive technology. Minimize distractions for students with a range of attention abilities (e.g., put small groups in quiet work areas). Work within constraints to make the environment as inclusive as possible. Encourage administrators to apply UD principles in facility design and renovation.
Delivery methods. Use multiple, accessible instructional methods that are accessible to all learners.	*Provide cognitive supports.* Summarize major points, give background/ contextual information, deliver effective prompting, provide scaffolding tools (e.g., outlines, class notes, summaries, study guides, and copies of projected materials with room for notes), and other cognitive supports. Deliver these materials in printed form and in a text-based electronic format. Provide opportunities for gaining further background information, vocabulary, and different levels of practice with variable levels of support. Encourage and support students to develop their own scaffolding materials.
Information resources/technology. Ensure that course materials, notes, and other information resources are engaging, flexible, and accessible for all students.	*Select materials early.* Choose printed materials and prepare a syllabus early to allow students the option of beginning to read materials and work on assignments before the course begins. Allow adequate time to arrange for alternate formats, such as books in audio format or in braille (which, for textbooks, can take longer than a month).
Feedback. Provide specific feedback on a regular basis.	*Provide regular feedback and corrective opportunities.* Allow students to turn in parts of large projects for feedback before the final project is due. Give students resubmission options to correct errors in assignments and exams. Arrange for peer feedback when appropriate.
Assessment. Regularly assess student progress using multiple, accessible methods and tools, and adjust instruction accordingly.	*Set clear expectations.* Keep academic standards consistent for all students, including those who require accommodations. Provide a syllabus with clear statements of course expectations, assignment descriptions, deadlines, and expectations, as well as assessment methods and dates. Include a straightforward grading rubric.
Accommodation. Plan for accommodations for students whose needs are not met by the instructional design.	*Know how to arrange for accommodations.* Know campus protocols for getting materials in alternate formats, rescheduling classroom locations, and arranging for other accommodations for students with disabilities. Make sure that assistive technology can be made available in a computer or science lab in a timely manner. Ensure that the course experience is equivalent for students with accommodations and those without (Burgstahler, 2007b, pp. 2–5).

- Face the class; speak clearly; use a microphone, if appropriate; and make eye contact with all students.
- Use large, bold fonts on uncluttered overhead displays and speak aloud all content presented with visual aids.
- Present content in a logical, straightforward manner and in an order that reflects levels of importance. Avoid unnecessary jargon and complexity; define new terms and acronyms. Summarize major points. Give background or contextual information.
- Provide multiple examples of specific concepts to make them relevant to individuals with diverse characteristics with respect to age, ability, gender, ethnicity, race, socioeconomic status, interests, and so on.
- In discussions, encourage the sharing of multiple perspectives. Demonstrate and demand mutual respect. Seek out a student's point of view and respond patiently.
- Avoid segregating or stigmatizing any student by drawing undue attention to a difference (e.g., a disability).
- Repeat a question a student asks to ensure that all have heard it.
- Put class notes and assignments on a Web site in a text-based format.

If these strategies simply sound like good teaching practices, they should. UD is one characteristic of a well-taught course.

Besides curricula and assessments for specific courses, UD principles have also been applied to large-scale assessments, such as statewide tests required for high school graduation and college entrance examinations (Dolan & Hall, 2001; Thompson, Johnstone, & Thurlow, 2002). Like other applications of UD, the result is testing instruments and practices that accurately assess the skills of a diverse group of test takers.

UNIVERSAL DESIGN OF DISTANCE LEARNING

Information technology is well suited to delivering the multiple options required to implement UDI. However, many educational Web sites and distance learning courses unintentionally erect barriers for individuals with disabilities (Burgstahler, 2002, 2006, 2007a; National Council on Disability, 2004; Schmetzke, 2001). To create an accessible environment, UD can be applied to specific course features. For example, to ensure that a Web site for a course is accessible and usable by all students, accessible design methods can be employed (e.g., providing text alternatives to the content in graphic images). In addition, the instructor should ensure that communication methods used in the course (e.g., blogs, bulletin boards) are accessible to potential students with all types of disabilities.

UD can also be built into specific assignments for students. For example, if working in small groups is selected as a general teaching strategy for an assignment in an online course, instead of individual groups being told they need to use a specific communication tool (e.g., phone conferencing, electronic mail, bulletin board, online chat), students could be told that the first order of business for their group is to select a communication method through which everyone can actively participate in group "meetings." For example, a group member who is deaf is unlikely to recommend a phone conference, as are members who live in different time zones or have different daily schedules; a group is unlikely to use online chat if someone in the group is uncomfortable with the fast pace of chat communications (perhaps because the language of the course is not their first language, they are slow typists, or they cannot compose their thoughts quickly). Members of a specific group should not be required to disclose their disabilities or any other characteristics that contribute to their communication preference; they just need to reach consensus on the communication tool they will use. When this strategy was applied in a distance learning course taught by the author of this chapter, one group reported that they used electronic mail, primarily as a result of scheduling conflicts but also because one student disclosed that she was unable to use the telephone effectively for a phone conference. If not for her voluntary disclosure that she was deaf, no one would have known that she had a disability, since class assignments were universally designed and captions were provided on all video presentations.

Accessible and universal design can also be applied to a distance learning program as a whole as well as to individual courses. Efforts by educators on sixteen campuses (DO-IT, 2007b) to guide distance learning administrators in making their overall programs accessible to all students led to the list of characteristics of an accessible distance learning program documented in Table 2.5.

ACCEPTANCE AND PROMOTION OF UNIVERSAL DESIGN TO INSTRUCTION

At a meeting in 1997, a group of researchers and developers recommended steps for implementing UD in curricula (Orkwis & McLane, 1998, p. 13):

> Publishers should prepare, and teachers should select, instructional materials that are supportive and inclusive of students who have wide disparities in their abilities to see, hear, speak, read, etc. . . . To achieve that end, we recommend that all developers of instructional materials adopt the concept of universal design and implement it in their products. Further, we recommend that teacher-training programs prepare teachers for teaching in environments where the goals, methods, and materials are universally designed.

Meeting participants hoped that publishers would collaborate with educators to make the flexibility of UD standard for all curricula. They recommended the following first steps for curriculum developers (Orkwis & McLane, 1998, pp. 14–15):

1. Provide all text in digital format.
2. Provide captions for all audio.
3. Provide educationally relevant descriptions for images and graphical layouts.
4. Provide captions and educationally relevant descriptions for video.
5. Provide cognitive supports for content and activities:
   - Summarize big ideas.
   - Provide scaffolding for learning and generalization.

- Build fluency through practice.
- Provide assessments for background knowledge.
- Include explicit strategies to make clear the goals and methods of instruction.

The U.S. Secretary of Education in 1998, Richard Riley, expressed optimism that universally designed curricula would soon become readily available (Orkwis & McLane, 1998, p. 15):

> As developers of computer hardware and software recognize the benefit that can be derived from all individuals (those with and without disabilities) being able to use the same computer equipment and software applications, the concept of universal design, in the development of new products, becomes more accepted, and built-in access should become more readily available.

TABLE 2.5   Characteristics of Distance Learning Programs That Are Accessible to All Students

For Students and Potential Students

1. The distance learning home page is accessible to individuals with disabilities (e.g., it adheres to Section 508, World Wide Web Consortium, or institutional accessible-design guidelines/standards).

2. A statement about the distance learning program's commitment to accessible design for all potential students, including those with disabilities, is included prominently in appropriate publications and Web sites, along with contact information for reporting inaccessible design features.

3. A statement about how distance learning students with disabilities can request accommodations is included in appropriate publications and Web pages.

4. A statement about how people can obtain alternate formats of printed materials is included in publications.

5. The online and other course materials of distance learning courses are accessible to individuals with disabilities.

For Distance Learning Designers

6. Publications and Web pages for distance learning course designers include:
     a. a statement of the program's commitment to accessibility;
     b. guidelines/standards regarding accessibility;
     c. resources.

7. Accessibility issues are covered in regular course designer training.

For Distance Learning Instructors

8. Publications and Web pages for distance learning instructors include:
     a. a statement of the distance learning program's commitment to accessibility;
     b. guidelines/standards regarding accessibility;
     c. resources.

9. Accessibility issues are covered in training sessions for instructors.

For Program Evaluators

10. A system is in place to monitor the accessibility of courses and, based on this evaluation, the program takes actions to improve the accessibility of specific courses and to update information and training given to potential students, actual students, course designers, and instructors (Burgstahler, 2006, p. 86).

Although research is not plentiful, some published studies support the efficacy of universally designed curricula (e.g., Gordon, 2002; O'Neill & Dalton, 2002; Pisha & Coyne, 2001). Although pedagogical, legal, and ethical arguments have been made for developing educational materials that are accessible to students with diverse characteristics, few available curriculum products at any educational level fully embrace UD (Rose, Harbour, Johnston, Daley, & Abarbanell, 2006). For example, when 25 award-winning companies who produce instructional software were surveyed, only 2 of the 19 who responded to the survey reported that they were aware of software accessibility issues. Sixty-five percent (65%) of the remaining 17 companies were not aware of accessibility issues; 100% were not currently addressing accessibility issues in their product development; and 88% had no plans to do so in the future (Golden, 2002).

Because so little universally designed software exists, educators at all levels continue to rely on cumbersome approaches of curriculum modification and media conversion to accommodate students for whom the design is inaccessible. This problem might be solved, at least in part, with increased awareness of software developers, teachers, and people with disabilities regarding accessibility barriers imposed by current products and potential solutions that lead to increased demand for universally designed materials.

Progress in addressing the needs of students with disabilities to access curricula has been enhanced by the U.S. Department of Education's endorsement of a common National Instructional Materials Accessibility Standard (NIMAS) (Rose, Meyer, & Hitchcock, 2005). NIMAS provides a foundation for the development of a variety of alternate-format versions of printed materials. However, until NIMAS is widely implemented, educators will continue to struggle with acquiring textbooks and other printed materials in alternate format for students with print-related disabilities.

With respect to the design of distance learning courses, most publications about distance learning do not address UD or access issues for people with disabilities (Burgstahler, 2007a). Not surprisingly, many distance learning courses are not accessible to all students with disabilities. In one survey on distance learning programs offered by postsecondary institutions, only 18% of the respondents indicated that they followed established Web site accessibility guidelines to a major extent; 28% followed guidelines to a moderate extent; 18% followed guidelines to a minor extent; 3% did not follow guidelines at all; and 33% did not know if their Web sites adhered to accessibility guidelines (Waits & Lewis, 2003). The results of three studies (Burgstahler, 2007a) suggest the need for accessibility training for distance learning personnel that includes content related to access challenges for people with disabilities, legislative requirements, UD guidelines, design techniques, and resources.

There is evidence that UD is being taught to faculty nationwide (e.g., Burgstahler, 2007c; Burgstahler & Doe, 2006; Getzel, Briel, & McManus, 2003; Harrison, 2006; Kame'enui, Carnine, Dixon, Simmons, & Coyne, 2002; Ouellett, 2004; Shaw & Scott, 2003). Much of the training has been conducted by institutions of higher education and funded by more than 60 three-year grants from the Office of Postsecondary Education (OPE) of the U.S. Department of Education (n.d.). Much of this training has included UD as a strategy to help faculty serve students with disabilities more effectively in their courses (Getzel, Briel, & McManus, 2003; Office of Postsecondary Education, n.d.).

Three OPE-funded projects have been hosted at the University of Washington (DO-IT, 2006, 2007a, 2007b). Each project was a collaboration between institutions of higher education from twenty states. Their combined efforts resulted in the creation and ongoing maintenance of five Web sites with content tailored to the interests of faculty, student service personnel, administrators, students, and nationwide leaders in higher education. These Web sites include publications, video presentations, and searchable knowledge bases of questions and answers, case studies, and promising practices that are regularly updated. For example, *The Faculty Room* includes practical content on UDI and accommodations for postsecondary faculty. All materials are universally designed to ensure accessibility to anyone with interests in applications of UD to higher education. To consult any of these Web sites, select *"AccessCollege"* from the DO-IT home page at http://www.washington.edu/doit. There you will find links to

- *The Faculty Room* for instructors and academic administrators;
- *The Student Services Conference Room* for student service administrators and staff;
- *The Board Room* for college and university administrators;
- *The Student Lounge* for students with disabilities;
- *The CUDE* for those interested in applying UD to educational products and environments.

The Association of Higher Education and Disability (AHEAD), the professional organization for disability service providers nationwide, also endorses UD. In 2001, it launched its Universal Design Initiative in support of AHEAD's mission to "dynamically address current and emerging issues with respect to disability, education, and accessibility to achieve universal access" (AHEAD, n.d., p. 1). This initiative was established to promote the concepts of UD in higher education, explore strategies that can be used by AHEAD members to promote UD concepts in their institutions, identify strategies to ensure access to the curriculum for diverse populations, promote new conceptualizations of disability, and provide resources and training in these emerging philosophies to AHEAD members.

CONCLUSION

Although it is a relatively new concept, UD's applications to on-site and online teaching methods, curricula, and assessments are beginning to appear in the literature. The authors of the remaining chapters in Part Two further explore the application of UD to teaching and learning. In chapter 3, David Rose, Wendy Harbour, Catherine Sam Johnston, Samantha Daley, and Linda Abarbanell share how they have universally designed a course at Harvard University. Similarly, in the next chapter, Jeanne Higbee shares how she has applied UD to a college course at the University of Minnesota. In chapter 5, Martha Thurlow, Christopher Johnstone, and Leanne Ketterlin-Geller tell how UD principles can be applied to assessments in higher education, building guidelines from applications of UD to large-scale testing instruments in precollege education. In chapter 6, past and present students with disabilities—Imke Durre, Sarah Steele, Michael Richardson, Carson Smith, and Jessie Amelia Shulman—share their perspectives on UDI.

Al Souma and Deb Casey discuss the benefits of UD for students with psychiatric disabilities in chapter 7. Adele Darr and Richard Jones in chapter 8 report experiences in incorporating UDI concepts into faculty training at Arizona State University. In chapter 9, Kirsten Behling and Debra Hart share details regarding a universal course design project at the University of Massachusetts that developed a model for professional development. In chapter 10, Susan Yager shares experiences in campuswide efforts to implement UDI at Iowa State University. Sally Scott and Joan McGuire in chapter 11 propose the use of a case study approach to promote applications of UD by higher education faculty. Then, Andrea Spencer and Olga Romero share their experiences promoting UD to faculty at Bank Street College of Education. Finally, Karen Myers shares her experience with incorporating UD in administration courses.

REFERENCES

Americans with Disabilities Act of 1990. 42 U.S.C.A. § 12101 *et seq.*

Association on Higher Education and Disability (AHEAD). (n.d.). AHEAD's universal design initiative. Huntersville, NC: Author. Retrieved November 1, 2007, from http://www.ahead.org/resources/ud_intro.php

Bar, L., Galluzzo, J., & Sinfit, S. D. (1999). The accessible school: Universal design for educational settings. Berkeley, CA: MIG Communications.

Barr, R. B., & Tagg, J. (1995). From teaching to learning—a new paradigm for undergraduate education. Change, 27(6), 12–25.

Bowe, F. G. (2000). Universal design in education: Teaching nontraditional students. Westport, CT: Bergin and Garvey.

Bruch, P. L. (2003). Interpreting and implementing universal instructional design in basic writing. In J. L. Higbee (Ed.), Curriculum transformation and disability: Implementing universal design in higher education (pp. 93–103). Minneapolis: University of Minnesota, Center for Research on Developmental Education and Urban Literacy.

Burgstahler, S. (2002). Distance learning: Universal design, universal access. AACE Journal, 10(1), 32–61. Retrieved November 1, 2007, from http://www.editlib.org/index.cfm?fuseaction=Reader.ViewAbstract&paper_id=17776

Burgstahler, S. (2006). The development of accessibility indicators for distance learning programs. Association for Learning Technology Journal, 14(1), 79–102.

Burgstahler, S. (2007a). Accessibility training for distance learning personnel. Access Technologists Higher Education Network (ATHEN) E-Journal, 2. Retrieved November 1, 2007, from http://athenpro.org/node/56

Burgstahler, S. (2007b). Equal access: Universal design of instruction. Seattle: University of Washington. Retrieved November 1, 2007, from http://www.washington.edu/doit/Brochures/Academics/equal_access_udi.html

Burgstahler, S. (2007c). Lessons learned in The Faculty Room. Journal on Excellence in College Teaching, 18(3).

Burgstahler, S. (2007d). Universal design in education: Principles and applications. Seattle: University of Washington. Retrieved November 1, 2007, from http://www.washington.edu/doit/Brochures/Academics/ud_edu.html

Burgstahler, S. (2007e). Universal design of instruction: Definition, principles, guidelines, and examples. Seattle: University of Washington. Retrieved November 1, 2007, from http://www.washington.edu/doit/Brochures/Academics/instruction.html

Burgstahler, S., Corrigan, B., & McCarter, J. (2005). Steps toward making distance learning accessible to students and instructors with disabilities. Journal of Information Technology and Disabilities, 11(1). Retrieved November 1, 2007, from http://www.rit.edu/~easi/itd/itdv11n1/brgstler.htm

Burgstahler, S., & Doe, T. (2006). Improving postsecondary outcomes for students with disabilities: Designing professional development for faculty. Journal of Postsecondary Education and Disability, 18(2), 135–147.

Campbell, D. (2004). Assistive technology and universal instructional design: A postsecondary perspective. Equity and Excellence in Education, 37(2), 167–173.

Center for Applied Special Technology (CAST). (n.d.). What is universal design for learning? Retrieved November 1, 2007, from http://www.cast.org/research/udl/

The Center for Universal Design. (1997). The principles of universal design, version 2.0. Raleigh: North Carolina State University. Retrieved November 1, 2007, from http://www.design.ncsu.edu/cud/about_ud/udprincipleshtmlformat.html

Chickering, A. W., & Gamson, Z. F. (1987). Seven principles for good practice in undergraduate education. Washington, DC: American Association for Higher Education. (ERIC Document Reproduction Service No. ED282491).

Claxton, C. S., & Ralston, Y. (1978). Learning styles: Their impact on teaching and administration. Washington, DC: American Association for Higher Education.

DO-IT (Disabilities, Opportunities, Internetworking, and Technology). (n.d.). The Center for Universal Design in Education. Seattle: University of Washington. Retrieved November 1, 2007, from http://www.washington.edu/doit/CUDE/

DO-IT. (2006). DO-IT Prof: A project to help postsecondary educators work successfully with students who have disabilities. Seattle: University of Washington. Retrieved November 1, 2007, from http://www.washington.edu/doit/Brochures/Academics/prof.html

DO-IT. (2007a). AccessCollege: Systemic change for postsecondary institutions. Seattle: University of Washington. Retrieved November 1, 2007, from http://www.washington.edu/doit/Brochures/Academics/access_college.html

DO-IT. (2007b). DO-IT Admin: A project to help postsecondary campus services administrators work successfully with students who have disabilities. Seattle: University of Washington. Retrieved November 1, 2007, from http://www.washington.edu/doit/Brochures/Academics/admin.html

Dolan, R. P., & Hall, T. E. (2001). Universal design for learning: Implications for large-scale assessment. IDA Perspectives, 27(4), 22–25.

Dunn, R., & Griggs, S.A. (2000). Practical approaches to using learning styles in higher education. Westport, CT: Greenwood.

Fosnot, C. T. (1996). Constructivism: Theory, perspectives, and practice. New York: Teachers College Press.

Gardner, H. (1983). Frames of mind: The theory of multiple intelligences. New York: Basic Books.

Getzel, E. E., Briel, L. W., & McManus, S. (2003). Strategies for implementing professional development activities on college campuses: Findings from the OPE-funded project sites (1999–2002). Journal of Postsecondary Education and Disability, 17(1), 59–78.

Golden, D. C. (2002). Instructional software accessibility: A status report. Journal of Special Education Technology, 17(1), 57–60. Retrieved November 1, 2007, from http://www.ataporg.org/instructionalreport.asp

Gordon, D. T. (2002, January/February). Curriculum access in the digital age. Harvard Education Letter. Retrieved November 1, 2007, from http://edletter.org/past/issues/2002-jf/digitalage.shtml

Gurin, P., Dey, E. L., Hurtado, S., & Gurin, G. (2002). Diversity and higher education: Theory and impact on educational outcomes. Harvard Educational Review, 72(3), 330–366.

Hall, T., Strangman, N., & Meyer, A. (2003). Differentiated instruction and implications for UDL implementation. Wakefield, MA: National Center for Accessing the General Curriculum. Retrieved November 1, 2007, from http://www.cast.org/publications/ncac/ncac_diffinstructudl.html

Harrison, E. G. (2006). Working with faculty toward universally designed instruction: The process of dynamic course design. Journal of Postsecondary Education and Disability, 19(2), 152–162.

Hitchcock, C., Meyer, A., Rose, D., & Jackson, R. (2002). Providing new access to the general curriculum: Universal design for learning. Teaching Exceptional Children, 35(2), 8–17.

Hitchcock, C., & Stahl, S. (2003). Assistive technology, universal design, universal design for learning: Improved learning opportunities. Journal of Special Education Technology, 18(4). Retrieved November 1, 2007, from http://jset.unlv.edu/18.4/hitchcock/first.html

Hodson, D., & Hodson. J. (1998). From constructivism to social constructivism. A Vygotskian perspective on teaching and learning science. School Science Review, 79(289), 33–41.

Hotchkiss, J., Moore, R. E., & Pitts, M. M. (2006). Freshman learning communities, college performance, and retention. Education Economics, 14(2), 197–210.

Johnson, D. M., & Fox, J. A. (2003). Creating curb cuts in the classroom: Adapting universal design principles to education. In J. Higbee (Ed.), Curriculum transformation and disability: Implementing universal design in higher education (pp. 7–22). Minneapolis: University of Minnesota, Center for Research on Developmental Education and Urban Literacy.

Kame'enui, E. J., Carnine, D. W., Dixon, R. C., Simmons, D. C., & Coyne, M. D. (2002). Effective teaching strategies that accommodate diverse learners (2nd ed.). Upper Saddle River, NJ: Pearson Prentice Hall.

Kolb, D. (1981). Learning styles and disciplinary differences. In A. W. Chickering (Ed.), The modern American college. San Francisco: Jossey-Bass.

Mason, C., & Orkwis., R. (2005). Instructional theories supporting universal design for learning—Teaching to individual learners. In Council for Exceptional Children (Ed.), Universal design for learning: A guide for teachers and education professionals. Upper Saddle River, NJ: Pearson/Merrill Prentice Hall.

McAlexander, P. J. (2003). Using principles of universal design in college composition courses. In J. Higbee (Ed.), Curriculum transformation and disability: Implementing universal design in higher education (pp. 105–114). Minneapolis: University of Minnesota, Center for Research on Developmental Education and Urban Literacy.

McGuire, J. M., Scott, S. S., & Shaw, S. F. (2003). Universal design for instruction: The paradigm, its principles, and products for enhancing instructional access. Journal of Postsecondary Education and Disability, 17(1), 11–21.

Minkler, J. E. (2002). ERIC review: Learning communities at the community college. Community College Review, 30(3), 46–63. Retrieved November 1, 2007, from http://crw.sagepub.com/cgi/content/abstract/30/3/46

Mino, J. (2004). Planning for inclusion: Using universal instructional design to create a learner-centered community college classroom. Equity & Excellence in Education, 37(2), 154–160.

National Council on Disability. (2004). Design for inclusion: Creating a new marketplace. Washington, DC: Author. Retrieved November 1, 2007, from http://www.ncd.gov/newsroom/publications/2004/online_newmarketplace.htm

Office of Postsecondary Education. (n.d.). Demonstration projects to ensure students with disabilities receive a quality higher education. Washington, DC: U.S. Department of Education. Retrieved November 1, 2007, from http://www.ed.gov/programs/disabilities/index.html

O'Loughlin, M. (1992). Rethinking science education: Beyond Piagetian constructivism toward a sociocultural model of teaching and learning. Journal of Research in Science Teaching, 29(8), 791–820.

O'Neill, L. M., & Dalton, B. (2002). Thinking readers: Supporting beginning reading in children with cognitive disabilities through technology. Exceptional Parent, 32(6), 40–43.

Orkwis, R. (2003). Universally designed instruction. Arlington, VA: ERIC Clearinghouse on Disabilities and Gifted Education. (ERIC Document Reproduction Service No. ED475386).

Orkwis, R., & McLane, K. (1998). A curriculum every student can use: Design principles for student access. ERIC/OSEP Topical Brief. Reston, VA: ERIC/OSEP Special Project. (ERIC Document Reproduction Service No. ED423654). Retrieved November 1, 2007, from http://eric.ed.gov/ERICDocs/data/ericdocs2sql/content_storage_01/0000019b/80/16/e9/bd.pdf

Osborne, J. (1996). Beyond constructivism. Science Education, 80(1), 53–82.

Ouellett, M. L. (2004). Faculty development and universal instructional design. Equity and Excellence in Education, 37, 135–144.

Pedelty, M. (2003). Making a statement. In J. Higbee (Ed.), Curriculum transformation and disability: Implementing universal design in higher education (pp. 71–78). Minneapolis: University of Minnesota, Center for Research on Developmental Education and Urban Literacy.

Pisha, B., & Coyne, P. (2001) Smart from the start: The promise of universal design for learning. Remedial and Special Education, 22(4), 197–203.

Rose, D. H., Harbour, W. S., Johnston, C. S., Daley, S. G., & Abarbanell, L. (2006). Universal design for learning in postsecondary education: Reflections and principles and their applications. Journal of Postsecondary Education and Disability, 19(2), 135–151.

Rose, D. H., & Meyer, A. (2002). Teaching every student in the digital age: Universal design for learning. Alexandria, VA: Association for Supervision and Curriculum Development.

Rose, D. H., Meyer, A., & Hitchcock, C. (Eds.). (2005). The universally designed classroom: Accessible curriculum and digital technologies. Cambridge, MA: Harvard Education Press.

Schmetzke, A. (2001). Online distance education: "Anytime, anywhere" but not for everyone. Information Technology and Disabilities, 7(2). Retrieved November 1, 2007, from http://www.rit.edu/~easi/itd/itdv07n2/axel.htm.

Scott, S., McGuire, J., & Shaw, S. (2003). Universal design for instruction: A new paradigm for adult instruction in postsecondary education. Remedial and Special Education, 24(6), 369–379.

Section 504 of the Rehabilitation Act of 1973, as amended. 29 U.S.C. § 794.

Shaw, S. F., & Scott, S. S. (2003). New directions in faculty development. Journal of Postsecondary Education and Disability, 17(1). 3–9.

Silver, P., Bourke, A., & Strehorn, K. C. (1998). Universal instructional design in higher education: An approach for inclusion. Equity & Excellence in Education, 31(2), 47–51.

Soldner, L., Lee, Y., & Duby, P. (1999). Welcome to the block: Developing freshman learning communities that work. Journal of College Student Retention, 1(2), 115–129.

Svinicki, M. D. (1999). New directions in learning and motivation. New Directions for Teaching and Learning, 80, 5–27.

Svinicki, M. D., & Dixon, N. M. (1987). The Kolb model modified for classroom activities. College Teaching, 35, 141–146.

Thompson, S. J., Johnstone, C. J., & Thurlow, M. L. (2002). Universal design applied to large-scale assessments (NCEO Synthesis Report 44). Minneapolis: University of Minnesota, National Center on Educational Outcomes.

Tomlinson, C. A. (2001). How to differentiate instruction in mixed-ability classrooms (2nd ed.). Alexandria, VA: Association for Supervision and Curriculum Development.

United States Department of Justice. (2005). A guide to disability rights laws. Washington, DC: U.S. Department of Justice Civil Rights Division. Retrieved November 1, 2007, from www.ada.gov/cguide.pdf

Waits, T., & Lewis, L. (2003). Distance education at degree-granting postsecondary institutions: 2000–2001. U.S. Department of Education, National Center for Education Statistics. NCES 2003-017. Retrieved November 1, 2007, from http://nces.ed.gov/pubsearch/pubsinfo.asp?pubid=2003017

Wooldridge, B. (1995). Increasing the effectiveness of university/college instruction: The results of learning style research into course design and delivery. In R. R. Simms and S. J. Sims (Eds.), The importance of learning styles (pp. 49–68). Westport, CT: Greenwood Press.

This chapter is based on work supported by the U.S. Department of Education Office of Postsecondary Education (grant numbers P333A990042, P333A020044, and P333A050064) and the National Science Foundation (Cooperative Agreement number HRD-0227995). Any opinions, findings, and conclusions or recommendations are those of the author and do not necessarily reflect the policy or views of the federal government, and you should not assume its endorsement.

3

Universal Design for Learning in Postsecondary Education
Reflections on Principles and Their Application

David H. Rose
Wendy S. Harbour
Catherine Sam Johnston
Samantha G. Daley
Linda Abarbanell

Written by the teaching staff of the course T-560: Meeting the Challenge of Individual Differences, at the Harvard Graduate School of Education, this chapter reflects on potential applications of universal design for learning (UDL) in university courses, illustrating major points with examples. The authors emphasize the ongoing developmental nature of the course and UDL principles as tools or guidelines for postsecondary faculty, rather than a set of definitive rules. UDL is proposed as a way to address diversity and disabilities in higher education classrooms by shifting the burden of being flexible and responsive from the student to the curriculum.

Although the concept of universal design is now familiar to many educators, its application in education lags far behind its application in the built environment. In this chapter, we illustrate the principles of what we call universal design for learning (UDL) in a university course. This chapter is essentially an excerpt from an article that appeared in the *Journal of Postsecondary Education and Disability*. The longer article includes a discussion of the roots of UDL in cognitive neuroscience.

This chapter is an excerpt from an article originally published as D. H. Rose et al. (2006). Universal design for learning in postsecondary education: Reflections on principles and their application. *Journal of Postsecondary Education and Disability, 19*(2): 135–151.

Universal design focuses on the elimination of barriers through initial designs that consider the needs of diverse people rather than the overcoming of barriers later through individual adaptation. Because the intended users are whole communities, universally designed environments are engineered for flexibility and designed to anticipate the need for alternatives, options, and adaptations to meet the challenge of diversity. UDL is one part of the overall movement toward universal design. The term emphasizes the special purpose of learning environments: They are created not only to transmit information or to shelter but also to support and foster the changes in knowledge and skills that we call learning. Although providing access to information or to materials is often essential to learning, it is not sufficient. UDL requires that we design not only accessible information but also an accessible pedagogy through

- multiple means of representation;
- multiple means of expression;
- multiple means of engagement.

THE APPLICATIONS OF UNIVERSAL DESIGN FOR LEARNING IN A UNIVERSITY COURSE

In this section we describe our semester-long course called T-560: Meeting the Challenge of Individual Differences, offered at the Harvard Graduate School of Education. In the 2004–05 academic year, ninety-three graduate students were registered (mostly master's students, but also doctoral students), an enrollment that is quite large for Harvard's Graduate School of Education. The students who take the course are diverse in background and interests, and a significant number have cross-registered from other colleges (e.g., law, public health) or other universities (e.g., the Massachusetts Institute of Technology). In general, however, the majority of students come from three areas within the Graduate School of Education: human development (especially those interested in mind, brain, and education), technology in education, and teaching and curriculum development. Many students interested in disabilities and special education also take the course, although there are no particular degree programs or concentrations in those subjects at Harvard University.

From the outset, we acknowledge that T-560 is not a perfect demonstration of UDL. Many aspects of the course would fail to meet any standard for UDL. Like UDL itself, the course is a work in progress, not a destination. We offer our observations merely as travelers on a journey, and we look forward to your suggestions as fellow travelers. Furthermore, we encourage readers not to take our observations as rules or steps to follow. UDL emerges differently in different contexts. The ideas here are merely a set of starter tools, not a complete vision, and we expect to learn a great deal as we travel ahead and incorporate additional advice, research, and experiences.

Goals of T-560

Like many postsecondary courses, T-560 originally began with goals that were largely ambiguous. Set in the context of a university, the implicit goal was to teach information and ideas, specifically about applying neuroscience to education. Its methods were completely traditional, including lectures and readings that were selected to transfer facts and ideas from the instructor and authors to eager (and sometimes not so eager) students.

Over time, that course content migrated somewhat, as did its instructional methods, and finally its goals. The current course description reads as follows:

> In the era of No Child Left Behind and IDEA [Individuals with Disabilities Education Act], the challenge of individual differences faces every teacher, administrator, and curriculum designer. The media and materials of the general education curriculum, once designed primarily for a narrow and illusive group of "regular" students, must now ensure results for students with a much wider range of abilities and disabilities. This course will explore recent advances that are critical to meeting this challenge. The first half of the course will address recent research in the neuroscience of learning—providing a new framework for understanding the range of individual differences that must be addressed. The second half will address recent advances in the design of educational media and technologies—advances that meet the challenge of individual differences through universal design.

With this basic information about the outline of the course, it is instructive to consider its goals from a UDL perspective, including consideration of three aspects of the goals following the three primary principles of UDL.

First, there is the obvious goal: teaching information. The course is clearly intended to teach information on a variety of topics: neuroscience, learning in the brain, individual differences in the way our brains learn, the limits and strengths of various educational media for teaching, as well as the ways in which they can be individualized. This goal has remained fairly consistent over the last decade. The first principle of UDL reminds us that information must be presented in multiple ways in order for that goal to be achieved for a wide range of students.

But the UDL framework requires a broader understanding of goals and objectives. The framework reminds us that it is not enough for students merely to acquire information; they must also have some way to express what they have learned and some way to apply that information as knowledge. Only in its expression is knowledge made useful. Thus, the goals for the course must have an expressive component. It is important that students not only have information but also know how to apply the information in appropriate settings, including the kinds of work they will likely perform during their lives ahead. The second principle reminds us that there must be multiple means for expressing their knowledge and multiple means for learning the skills that will underlie that expression.

The third UDL principle reminds us also that there is an affective component to reaching any goal. While the explicit goals of a course tend to focus on the first two principles—the knowledge students will learn and the skills to express that knowledge—the third is just as critical. Students will never use knowledge they don't care about, nor will they practice or apply skills they do not find valuable. Therefore, another goal of the course is affective. We want students to be engaged fully in learning the content, to be eager to apply what they know, to leave the course wanting to learn even more, and to want to apply their knowledge everywhere. Unfortunately, we currently do not evaluate this third goal systematically enough. As members of the teaching staff for T-560, we do conduct regular weekly check-in discussions with each other before and after classes to talk about our individual observations, engagements, or motivations with that week's material, as well as any feedback or concerns from students. We informally assess student engagement through observation during classes and discussions, as well as through formal written course evaluations mandated by the Harvard Graduate School of Education. Yet ongoing evaluation of engagement and motivation remains a challenge.

Applying Universal Design for Learning Principles to Course Lectures

Typical courses in universities are dominated by two types of media: lectures and textbooks. It is legitimate to ask whether such a prominent position is warranted: Are lectures and textbooks effective media for instruction? Not surprisingly the answer is, it depends. While lectures and textbooks play an important role in instruction everywhere, both of them are ineffective for some students in all content areas and for all students in some content areas.

While that caution is worth stating at the outset, we are not going to try to slay that dragon here. At this time, and for the immediate future, it is a given that universities will use lectures and textbooks as the predominant means of mass instruction. And so lectures and books are very central to T-560, too. For that reason, we will begin our discussion of the course materials with them, highlighting how they are modified and used within the context of UDL. But it is important to clarify that lectures and books are presented within a somewhat different overall context in our course. The lectures and readings, as well as other media and activities, are embedded in a course Web site that forms the primary *container* or *backbone* of the course. Elements of this site will be described throughout this section, and the site itself is discussed in more detail later.

First, it is important to reflect on the strengths of lectures. Why are they important in postsecondary education? What is important to capture or save in any form of alternative representation? The strengths of a lecture derive from the enormous expressivity of the human voice. It is not the content or language itself—neither the semantics nor syntax—that is uniquely powerful; in fact, those aspects of a lecture are often conveyed more accessibly in a printed version of the lecture. What sets lectures apart is the enormous expressive capacity of spoken language, including its ability to stress what is significant and important, to clarify tone and intent, to situate and contextualize meaning, and to provide an emotional background. The feeble use of graphic equivalents to indicate significance (e.g., exclamation points and italics) cannot match the ability of spoken language to convey affect, such as irony or scorn, or to emphasize for clarity. This is why when a printed speech is read aloud, the power of language usually evaporates for any audience, unless the speaker is a gifted reader or actor. Speech coaches usually discourage public speakers from reading speeches because the natural expressivity of spoken speech is difficult to mimic when text has been provided in written form. It is not only the sounds of speech that lend meaning, clarity, and emphasis; many speeches and lectures are embedded in a full multimodal display. Good lecturers use facial expression, gesture, and body motion to further convey meaning and affect. Moreover, lecturers frequently combine voice with additional media, such as PowerPoint slides. Altogether, this is a rich multimedia experience that overpowers the expressive strength of written text.

For these reasons, and to meet expectations of students and the university, lectures play an important role in T-560. Nevertheless, their limitations as an instructional medium are obvious. For some students (especially those who are deaf) lectures are completely inaccessible in their raw form. For many others the words are accessible because they can be heard and their meanings recognized, but they raise barriers of different kinds, stemming principally from high demands on linguistic and cognitive abilities, including memory, attention, and the amount of background knowledge they assume. In T-560, we use multiple strategies in our efforts to overcome the limitations and differential demands that lectures present.

First, in deference to the first principle of UDL, we give alternative representations of the lectures. Several types of alternatives are provided, differing in the kinds of problems they seek to address, the ease of implementation, and the kinds of technologies they require (from no-tech to high-tech). For example, the lecture's content is made available in alternate sensory modalities. The university provides sign language interpreters whenever there is a deaf student or teaching assistant in the class, as there has been for the last three years. Good interpreters capture not only the semantics of what they hear but also, through body movements, facial expressions, and gestures, the affect and stress. In addition, the lecturer attempts (not always consistently) to describe the visuals. At this time, this is the only real adaptation of the lecture we provide for students who are visually impaired or blind.

Second, we videotape each lecture in its entirety and post that video on the course Web site, where it can be accessed at any time. This permanent recording of the lecture is an alternative representation, which has several uses. For many students, it is convenient to access the recording of the lecture at any time of day or night, and a good backup if they are late or absent from class. For other students, the information in online lectures is much more accessible than the live version. Students for whom English is a second language or who have a wide variety of language-based disabilities, for example, find that the linguistic demands of understanding a live lecture are steep. For some of them, the flexibility of the video version is superior because it can be reviewed at any time to fill in gaps, stopped and started to hear difficult segments repeated, and even replayed in its entirety. Finally, for other students, the length and passivity of lectures and their demand for sustained attention and concentration are significant barriers that render lectures ineffective. Lectures are inherently evanescent and impermanent. The linear, one-time-only stream of a lecture is highly demanding on concentration and executive abilities. Lapses are inevitable and create difficult-to-repair gaps in a lecture's structure and meaning. For some students, therefore, the online video presentation is especially helpful because it allows them to articulate the larger whole of the lecture into manageable chunks or to replay segments that have been missed during lapses in concentration or attention. In truth, however, the videos of lectures are not used that much by the typical student in T-560. They are a fallback that is essential for some students but are far too time consuming, low in quality, and passive for most. It is interesting and important to note, for example, that in spite of all lectures being available on the course Web site in digital video (and thus very convenient for viewing anytime and anywhere), students overwhelmingly come to class anyway.

Third, and perhaps most interestingly, we collect student notes from the lecture and display them for everyone in T-560. This may seem both time consuming and redundant, especially in light of the online video availability, but we have found this simple technique to be enormously beneficial and a wonderful example of the unexpected benefits of universal design. While it is possible to have volunteer or paid note-takers as an accommodation for students with disabilities, we have found these unsatisfactory in many instructive ways. In brief, "professional" note-takers are typically first-time students in the course, and their own skills at making sense of things are highly variable. Since their background knowledge, interests, and learning preferences often differ considerably from the disabled student for whom they are taking notes, their notes are often poorly directed, sampled, or leveled. Instead, we have hit on a very simple alternative. Each week, several students (in our case, five or six per lecture) are responsible for taking notes on the lecture, including whatever discussion happens. Within several days, they are required to send their notes to a teaching assistant, who posts them on the course Web site. The notes are then available to everyone, regardless of their disability or lack thereof. Though the notes are not graded, they are required as part of a student's participation grade.

There are several unexpected benefits of this note-taking process. First, the notes are more universally designed than the lecture itself; that is to say, different students capture and express very different content from the lecture, and they represent it in very different ways. In addition, despite being ungraded, students are highly engaged with the notes, responding to student notes in online discussions on the course Web site and using them as examples during class lecture. The variance in T-560 notes is astonishing. Some students post notes that are almost perfect linear outlines of the lecture. Some of these are very short and succinct with bullet outlines only, while others are much longer, more expressive, and expansive. Others are different in kind. For example, some students do not outline the talk at all and are much more anecdotal than taxonomic, capturing more of the stories of the lecture than its structure. That is only the beginning of the variation. Some students take very graphic notes instead of ones that rely primarily on text. Their notes range from doodles that accompany text, to heavy use of illustration and visual highlighting that clarify and connect parts of the text, to notes that are literally superimposed on the PowerPoint slides of the lecture, to full-scale visual representations of the main ideas and concepts in the lecture that have almost no words, just labels. The latter are often a big hit with other students who find them immediately a strong complement to the outline view. A second benefit derives from the public posting of these notes. Students, seemingly already engaged with the notes, recognize that their notes are about to become public to their peers. As a result, they often enhance the notes in various ways: by bringing in additional information, commentary, or questions; adding images or drawings; adding multimedia (like video or sound); or preparing the notes in a particularly cogent and clear way. We have never requested this kind of enhancement. Instead, there is a natural contagion of enthusiasm among the note-takers, who view notes from the previous lecture as a way of preparing to take their own. In fact, they learn to take better notes by informally mentoring each other.

Last, the point of universal design quickly becomes clear to every student, as the kinds of notes they take and what they learn from a given lecture often differ greatly from those of their classmates. Even though the lecture ostensibly conveys the exact same content for all ninety-three students, its reception is highly variable. Students perceive, understand, and prioritize different things within the same lecture. This is often especially interesting (and a big relief) to students who have been told they cannot take notes because of a disability (e.g., having a learning disability or brain injury, being deaf or hard of hearing). Though they may initially dread this aspect of the course requirement because of preexisting beliefs about what constitutes good or acceptable notes, they often quickly realize that their notes will be as good as their classmates' notes. Last year, one student told a T-560 teaching assistant that she felt more like a true member of the class, learned a lot about herself, and gained new insights into her learning disability and what it meant for her learning, simply because of the T-560 note-taking system.

Thus far we have talked about three different representations of the lecture: an alternative sensory presentation, like American sign language; a reviewable alternative in the form of Web-based videos; and multiple notes shared among students. There are actually many other ways to provide alternative means of support within a lecture. Following is one more example.

Cognitively, a lecture places many demands on students. For example, a lecture's structure is generally much more implicit than its textual counterpart. Missing are the explicit reviewable divisions into visible chunks like sentences, paragraphs, and chapters; the structural support provided by explicit and multiple levels of headers; and the use of white space and page layout to emphasize structure. Good lecturers use a variety of techniques to make their structure more explicit and memorable and to reduce the cognitive load in other ways (e.g., by using a great deal more repetition than editors of the written text would tolerate, by explicitly stating the structure of the talk early and often, and by summarizing the argument so far).

In T-560, as in other courses, we seek to provide cognitive and structural supports during the lecture. PowerPoint slides, for example, are a nearly constant accompaniment to the lecture. We use such slides in two primary ways. First, the slides are used to clarify and make explicit the structure of the talk. Most teachers of public speaking rightly criticize the wild overuse of slides in "bullet-point" mode, where speakers essentially read their slides to the audience, often to the detriment of content and meaning (Tufte, 2003). Even though we are sometimes guilty of that as well, PowerPoint slides are most frequently used in T-560 to introduce a new topic or to summarize a previous section. That is, they provide the structure but not the substance of the presentation.

During the main part of lecture presentations, the slides are primarily graphic or visual: They are an alternate representation of the content and a complement to it rather than a restatement of what has been said verbally. In particular, we attempt to use slides that capture the power of graphic images over text, including the ability to clarify and emphasize relationships between facts, concepts, ideas, principles, and processes. The primary power of images is exemplified well in a graph. A quick glance at a graph provides a rich and explicit exposition of the relationships between several variables or sets of things. Providing that same exposition through words is extremely labor intensive and often too opaque. Other images, such as a photograph or video, have the same privileged capacity to convey relationships of interest. For example, an elephant's size relative to a zebra's is much easier to convey in an image than in words. In addition, we try to provide a structural context within slides, such as a header at the top of a graphic slide. The header is a reminder, an element of structure that reminds the student that we are looking at examples of, say, good Web site design or the limits of sound. In a more subtle way than bullet points, we hope to provide structural supports that help students follow and make meaning of the presentation.

These and other means are used to make lectures more accessible to a wide variety of students. In our impression, most students like these alternatives, whether or not they have any disabilities that may require their use. In that way, they exemplify good universal design when taken as a whole.

Discussion Groups and Universal Design for Learning

Discussions are often seen as a supplement to lectures or a complement to assigned texts. For some students, especially students with learning disabilities, the format of small-group discussions is more accessible than lectures or books. The highly interactive nature of small groups, when facilitated correctly, overcomes the passivity of lectures and books; makes material more relevant and engaging for many; and provides the potential for complex, active, group-based construction of knowledge rather than simple delivery of information. For those reasons and many others, it is beneficial to provide discussion groups as components in any course, both as a complement to and an alternative to the other media. Yet small group discussions are also a limited medium for some students. With this in mind, we also apply UDL principles to discussion groups using the following approaches.

First, students may choose among different discussion groups offered during the week. In addition, all discussion groups are optional: Students may choose any, all, or none, although it is one of several ways to fulfill participation requirements (taking notes is another). In practice, some students come to many sessions, some to only a few, and some to none. The sessions differ in several cognitively meaningful respects; however, we have noticed that some students base their choices on the entirely social aspects of who is in the group or who is leading it.

There are *review* sessions, where students have an opportunity to ask questions about the material for the week, participate in guided review discussions of the week's content, discuss implications or highlights of the material, express concerns, and so forth. These are ideal for students who find the content of readings or lectures either too challenging or too abstract. It is also a good place for students to inquire about gaps in background knowledge they may be missing (e.g., some students who are not K–12 teachers may want to know more about lesson plans when we talk about designing curricula).

An alternative is sessions that are called *advanced*. In the advanced sessions, the teaching staff assume students have already read and understood the material for the week and, therefore, discuss something that extends or challenges that material, more deeply connecting it to other knowledge or ideas. In these sessions an additional relevant reading is assigned that is provocative, new, stimulating, controversial, or even contrary to material otherwise presented in the course. Students must read the extra reading before coming to class. Typically about 10–15% of students show up for these kinds of sessions in a given week, although about 25% of students participate in them over the course of the semester. These are ideal sessions for students who find the lectures or readings too elementary or concrete.

Another way in which the discussions differ is in the medium used for participation. Each week students may choose to join either a face-to-face group or an entirely online discussion group (offered as a component of the course Web site). Students differ significantly in terms of the kinds of discussions they consistently prefer. Some students join only face-to-face groups, never participating online. Others choose just the opposite, and some come randomly or attend both types.

We have not done research to understand the basis of the students' choices. Some things seem obvious, though. Students with dyslexia tend to come to face-to-face sessions rather than write online. Students who are constitutionally or culturally shy seem to prefer the online discussions. What is clear is that the medium very significantly biases student participation. Without the opportunity to participate in discussions online, many students are underrepresented in their ability to show what they know, or they experience barriers to engaging in meaningful dialogues about the course material.

By providing options and multiple means for those discussions, we have found higher rates and quality of engagement in these aspects of the course. In our review of the 2004–05 year, we came to the conclusion that all our sessions, both live and online, would be enhanced by providing specific topics or activities that made them more coherent. As a result, we will try to use the discussion sections to emphasize an alternative way of engaging in the course content by using case studies.

Textbooks and Universal Design for Learning

Books and other texts are not a promising foundation for UDL because they are inherently inflexible. The product of mass production, books are designed with a uniform display and identical content for every student. In addition, most books are delivered to colleges and universities in print, a technology that is particularly difficult to modify and thus to meet the needs of many students with disabilities. As a result, books as they are presently delivered create barriers rather than opportunities for many students. Nevertheless, they are popular in universities (and we like them for their virtues, not their liabilities), so in T-560 we use books. For the most part, we use books in typical ways: three or four books assigned and suggested for purchase, with others on a recommended list. Two are textbooks, and the others are trade books or topical readings on education, media, and neuroscience.

When the reading list is distributed, students notice one thing immediately—the two textbooks seem to cover the exact same topic of introductory cognitive neuroscience. Moreover, the syllabus recommends that students purchase and read only one of them. But which one? That choice is left to each student. This is the first place in the course that students typically begin to confront alternatives (while developing an understanding of UDL firsthand). Some are charmed by the choice of alternatives and others become alarmed. For some, the fact that either book will suffice does not square with the ways they have been taught to use textbooks. Whereas there is likely considerable overlap between the books, every student knows that there will be topics, ideas, names, facts, experiments, or methods in one that are not in the other at all. One of the books is even much thicker than the other, so how can one even think about buying the thinner one—maybe critical information is left out?

Students soon note, and we also point out, that the books are really different not only in the content they present but also in the *way* they present the content. One book by Banich (2004) has a great deal more words and is much thicker. It is a highly literate, very well-written and -researched book that is authoritative and scholarly, with occasional illustrations. The main thrust is clearly in the text. The other book, by Carter (1998), is highly visual, loaded with drawings and diagrams. It is thinner than Banich, with fewer words but many more diagrams, illustrations, color, graphics, and maps. Having noticed the differences, students are encouraged to buy the one that seems best for them. Typically, Carter's book sells a bit more. Students are encouraged to borrow each other's books, compare them, and get the best of both, and some clearly do that. A few buy both books. Regardless, this first choice sets the right stage for the course. It is not that either book is perfect, has the "truth" of cognitive neuroscience, or has the right way to present information for all students. Instead, students are confronted right from the start with the fact that they might not all like their information presented in the same way. It's a start.

Later there are other choices about books. One of the books, *Teaching Every Student in the Digital Age: Universal Design for Learning* (Rose & Meyer, 2002), is available at the bookstore and library as usual. With the permission of the publisher, however, the entire book is also available on the Web absolutely free at http://www.cast.org. Nonetheless, most students choose to purchase it in print. For most students, reading a whole book online is not a positive experience. The print version is more convenient, more readable in the long run, and more familiar. Most of the students in this class are adult graduate students, immigrants to the land of digital books instead of natives. However, some students are very pleased to read the book entirely online. These students, including those with dyslexia or those who are blind, for example, do not find that the print version is more convenient, more readable, or more comfortable. For them, it is much better to read the book online using a talking browser. Other students, like those with attention deficit disorder/attention deficit-hyperactivity disorder (ADD/ADHD) or those who are computer-savvy, prefer the online book because they enjoy exploring the format, especially embedded links, which foster connections to relevant material that may not be as easy to access through a print version.

Not all the course books are available in this alternative fashion yet. As a result, students who have dyslexia typically approach the disability services office to scan the printed books into digital versions that they can use. This is an unfortunate, time-consuming, and expensive workaround to overcome the limitations of print, but that will soon change.

In 2004, the U.S. Department of Education endorsed, both houses of Congress passed, and President Bush approved a revision of IDEA that included a new policy: the National Instructional Materials Accessibility Standard (NIMAS). NIMAS stipulates that publishers must provide a digital source file of their printed textbooks to a national repository at the time print versions are distributed. Furthermore, states must distribute accessible versions of those source files to their students in a timely fashion. NIMAS is valuable because it is specifies the format (an XML base with DAISY tags) in which those textbooks must be provided. This makes it vastly faster and easier to generate many types of accessible and digital versions, and the format is consistent for all publishers and for all states and districts.

Officially, NIMAS only applies to preschool, elementary, and secondary education. However, the popularity of NIMAS among states and publishers alike has led many colleges and state systems, as well as publishers, to consider adopting the NIMAS standard for postsecondary use as well. However, these ideas have yet to be implemented in any formal or systemic way. Soon, we believe that there will be readily available textbooks in both print and digitally accessible versions.

Multimedia, the Course Web Site, and Universal Design for Learning

Text and textbooks are a limited presentation medium. In the T-560 course, we try to include a richer set of media as alternatives. The use of video for lectures is an example, but the simplest expansion of media comes from using the Web as the basic skeleton for the course.

The course Web site is central to the course in many ways. It serves as a frame that holds the syllabus, the assignments, the discussion groups, the projects, the class notes, the class videos, the PowerPoint slides for the lectures, and much more. For each week, there are also links to many Web sites, which are presented as additional representations of the topic for the week, or as scaffolds and supports for student learning.

Although in general there are many low-quality materials on the Web, some Web sites are extremely informative and relevant to our class. An advantage of Web sites is the rich set of media from which they are constructed. As an example, one of the course lectures draws heavily on understanding optical illusions. While there are typical examples of illusions in both textbooks, there are several extraordinary Web sites devoted entirely to understanding illusions. These Web sites have extensive collections with accompanying explanations. Moreover, the range of illusions is far more extensive and dramatic than those available in print. For example, illusions of movement or sound cannot be captured in text. During the lecture, which is always done with a live connection to the Web, some of the more dramatic illusions are exhibited and discussed.

In the course Web site, the multimedia syllabus conveys not only the text readings for the week but also the Web sites and other media, all available for easy access through simple clicks of a mouse. These alternatives are mildly engaging for some students, but for others this chance to explore course ideas in a broader and richer context is very important. In fact, for some who were born in a different generation from their professors, this use of contemporary media seems essential for relevance and comprehensive understanding.

Assessment Methods for the Course

It is not enough, of course, to use the framework of UDL only when considering how to present and teach methods, information, or skills. It is also essential to consider UDL as a framework to guide the design of another critical element of instruction: assessment. In considering assessment, we will focus on the second principle of UDL: providing multiple means of action and expression. The other principles are clearly part of assessment, but for brevity we will focus on the obvious fact that assessment draws heavily on the ways students are required to demonstrate and express what they know. From a UDL perspective, it is essential to provide multiple means for that expression.

There are many assessment techniques, the choice of which should be aligned with and constrained by the goals of the course. In our course, we want to develop students who not only can recognize UDL in practice but also can express that knowledge in action. Whether they are designing a curriculum or workshop, choosing from among a number of available curricular options, or preparing to teach a single unit or lecture, we need to know whether they can effectively apply what they have learned. Is it usable knowledge? Administering multiple-choice tests or essay questions is not likely to be an adequate measure of those abilities, nor is writing a traditional paper about how they might apply what they have learned. As a result, we require that students complete two projects on which they are graded.

Midway through the course, students prepare and submit a midterm project that requires them to review the research literature on one type of learner (of any age level, including adults) and to create a Web site. Students are encouraged to choose an atypical learner as their focus. While *atypical* is usually associated with a disability of some kind (e.g., dyslexia, autism, ADD/ADHD, Turner's syndrome, Williams syndrome.), past projects have focused on other types of atypical learners, including those for whom English is a second language and those with gender dysphoria. Students research current neuropsychological literature to identify what is known about the underlying neurology of that type of learner and to articulate their resulting strengths and weaknesses for that learner in a specific subject or educational setting (e.g., dyslexic students in a fifth-grade science lab).

Traditionally, the results of such student research are presented via a 10-page paper. However, the second principle of the UDL framework encourages greater flexibility in the means students can use to express what they have learned. As a result, students in T-560 can use not only text but also images, sound, video, the Web, and so forth. To stimulate their expressive palette somewhat, we artificially limit the word count to approximately 1,500 words. We do that because most students, left to their own devices, tend to limit themselves to text because it is most familiar to them as an academic medium; with a low word limit, they must rely on alternative means to convey complex reviews of neuropsychological research and their conclusions. For some students an expansion of possibilities is a bit threatening, for others the broader palette is very appealing.

When finished, all students must submit their projects in the form of a Web site that then becomes part of an online learning network where all students' Web sites are linked to each other. This manner of submitting work is very challenging for some students, and many have never before created anything on the Web. Nonetheless, we have chosen to use the Web rather than paper as the vehicle for presentation for several reasons.

First, the Web provides a rich and flexible foundation for using multiple media. Students can use a rich variety of other media besides text. Second, the Web provides a way for students to learn from each others' work. Whereas papers have a limited audience of the professor or teaching assistant, all members of the class can access projects on the Web site. Not only is this more motivating for students, it is also more instructive. Each year we see tremendous learning that derives from this ability to view each other's work. In fact, we now emphasize this type of collaborative learning by encouraging students to link their projects to those of other students. Particularly in the final projects, in which students design a lesson or curriculum that considers the profile of the learner in their first projects (and reflects the principles of UDL), students take great advantage of other students' work as part of background research for their own projects. But even more apparent is the explosive effect of particularly strong projects, especially ones that take good advantage of multiple media. The contagion of best practices is easily apparent because high-quality student projects serve as terrific, highly relevant models to emulate and learn from.

How are these public and nontraditional projects graded? Each year students ask anxiously if we will grade on presentation or layout, as opposed to content. Most hope that we will not, primarily because they realize that some students in the class have highly developed skills as Web or media designers. (Some students in the class are majoring in media design.) Thus, some students may be at a considerable advantage in their presentation skills, and this realization usually sparks an important dialogue in class. Inevitably some students, usually students with dyslexia or who have English as a second language, raise the opposite point of view, hoping that presentation will indeed count. For them, the increased palette has leveled the playing field for the first time in their academic careers, and they are delighted to finally have an outlet that more accurately reflects their abilities.

Eventually they learn that presentation does count. Certainly we are forgiving for beginners, but we stress that even beginners can make good choices about the kinds of media that are optimal for expressing different kinds of knowledge. And we provide, in a UDL way, many different ways for students to get support in making their presentations effective; that is, multiple ways to support expression.

Three types of support are customary. First, we give plenty of models. For the first project, models from the previous year's class are typically used. For the second project, there are plenty of models from the first projects of their peers. Second, we provide multiple scaffolds. We offer labs or sections where students can come to learn the basics of both Web design and the use of databases to find relevant literature. In the 2005–06 year, for the first time, we encouraged the students with advanced Web design skills to offer these labs as part of their participation credit, which was a big hit for both instructors and students. All the labs are at different skill levels, so students can learn from any level of prior knowledge. We also encourage students to work collaboratively, and they do, even though they are each responsible for their own Web site. Students who are skilled at media design, even though they may not be knowledgeable in neuroscience or skilled in writing, turn out to be very popular as peer collaborators with educators and researchers who may know how to read a Web page but have never designed one. In a complementary way, students who have excellent backgrounds in education, neuroscience, or research are also popular collaborators for media designers struggling with the class content. The two projects—presenting research and then planning a lesson—draw on the varied strengths of students in the class, giving everyone a chance to have background knowledge and come to the fore.

Affect and Engagement in T-560

From a UDL standpoint, there is a final concern: Does the course succeed affectively, engaging the students? Does it engage different kinds of students? Is that engagement sustained in changes in practice? Overall, there are indications that the course engages a reasonably broad range of students. For one thing, the course is quite popular. This is especially notable because it requires a considerable amount of work in difficult subjects, it is not required for any degree concentration, and there is no special education major at Harvard. What attracts students?

We believe that one of the significant attractions of the class is its attempt to respond to individual differences, providing multiple ways of presenting information, and allowing students to respond. Of particular importance, especially for adult learners, is the ability to make choices (e.g., Cordova & Lepper, 1996).

In the course, as we have noted, students experience choice in almost every arena: choices in the textbooks they choose to read, the kinds of media they prefer to learn from, the timing and level of discussion groups, the media mix they use for their projects, the format for discussions, the amount of support they prefer, and the ways to interact with materials. For some students there are still too few choices, and for some there are too many. But overall, the very fact of choice is a tremendous source of attraction and motivation in the course.

There is a second way that choice is important: in terms of the faculty and teaching assistants. Because there are multiple means of interaction in the course, there are choices for the faculty as well. Throughout the course, we emphasize the different areas in which we members of the teaching staff each have strengths and weaknesses (e.g., content areas, Web design, pedagogical strategies). This *distributed intelligence* eliminates the onerous effects of having to be everything to everyone. It also models for students the value of collaborative teaching and learning. To some extent, the instructors choose the kinds of interactions with which they are most comfortable, and at times they choose situations in which they will be challenged to learn relatively new information or skills with the support of other instructional staff, placing them in the best positions to succeed and to feel engaged.

Last, it is important to emphasize a secondary benefit of universal design. Because there is a richer media mix in the course than in many others, there are opportunities to specialize. It is very clear that, over the previous five years during which the alternative media became more prominent, the lectures have become better. Essentially, just as radio differentiated from television and became more popular in the process, the lectures have been able to differentiate from the other course media. Lectures are used less for information dispensation and more for teaching, modeling, emphasizing, and connecting. They are used more for the kinds of things for which they are optimal.

CONCLUSION AND RECOMMENDATIONS

There are two broad kinds of solutions for addressing the problems of individual students, including those with disabilities. On one hand, the problems can be considered *individual* problems (e.g., the student has a disability that interferes with the ability to access course content, to express knowledge, or to engage optimally in it). Such a view fosters solutions that address weaknesses in the individual. On the other hand, the issues can be considered an *environmental* problem in the design of the learning environment. For example, the typical overreliance on printed text for presenting content and evaluating students clearly, and differentially, raises barriers to achievement for some students and privileges others. Such an environmental view fosters solutions that address the limitations of the learning environment rather than the limitations of the student, while making the student less of a problem and more a part of diversity within the course. The advantage of such universal solutions is that, as with such approaches in built environments, they are very likely to be useful for many individuals: Built once, they are applied many times.

We believe that both approaches are important from a pedagogical standpoint. In their intersection, moreover, we will find solutions that are not only more economical but also more ecological. They reflect the fact that disabilities always reflect mismatches between the environment and the individual. Right now, we believe that universities place too much emphasis on the disabilities in students and not enough on the disabilities in the learning environment. Accommodations and access issues are largely addressed on an individual basis rather than on the level of courses, departments, or universities. Universal design presents other options and perspectives on access that ultimately will benefit all students, disabled and nondisabled.

REFERENCES

Banich, M. (2004). *Cognitive neuroscience and neuropsychology* (4th ed.). Boston: Houghton Mifflin.

Carter, R. (1998). *Mapping the mind.* Berkeley: University of California Press.

Cordova, D. I., & Lepper, M. R. (1996). Intrinsic motivation and the process of learning: Beneficial effects of contextualization, personalization, and choice. *Journal of Educational Psychology, 88*(4), 715–730.

Rose, D. H., & Meyer, A. (2002). *Teaching every student in the digital age: Universal design for learning.* Alexandria, VA: Association for Supervision and Curriculum Development (ASCD). (Also available in digital format at http://www.cast.org).

Tufte, E. R. (2003). *The cognitive style of PowerPoint.* Cheshire, CT: Graphics Press.

4

The Faculty Perspective
Implementation of Universal Design in a First-Year Classroom

Jeanne L. Higbee

The author of this chapter illustrates the implementation of universal instructional design (UID) in a first-year experience course by providing specific examples of essential components, multiple formats for conveying information and assessing learning, and other principles of UID. Benefits and challenges for the faculty member are also addressed.

Universal instructional design (UID) (Bowe, 2000; Higbee, 2003; Silver, Bourke, & Strehorn, 1998) is a means for providing equity in access to higher education for all students by encouraging faculty to rethink their teaching practices to create curricula and courses that include all learners. Although initially many postsecondary educators perceived that the focus of UID was access for students with disabilities, the intent of this theoretical model is to consider all possible students who might be taking a course and then design the course accordingly. All students benefit. In implementation, as in theory, it becomes clear that when this approach to course development is taken, students from other historically underrepresented populations are also likely to experience a more welcoming learning environment. Thus, UID is gradually gaining notice as a tool for social justice and multicultural postsecondary education (Barajas & Higbee, 2003; Hackman & Rauscher, 2004; Higbee & Barajas, 2007; Johnson, 2004; Johnson & Fox, 2003). It is imperative that educators implementing UID consider the broad range and multiple intersections of students' diverse social identities rather than focusing only on disability. It is this notion of inclusion for all that prompted the use of the term *universal*. Within the context of UID, *universal* refers not to "one size fits all"; rather, it prompts universal access to learning for all students, including students with disabilities. The purpose of this chapter is to illustrate the implementation of UID in a first-year experience course, including the benefits for students as well as the rewards and challenges for the faculty member.

UNIVERSAL INSTRUCTIONAL DESIGN AS AN ALTERNATIVE TO INDIVIDUAL ACCOMMODATIONS

Research indicates that faculty members continue to perceive barriers to providing academic accommodations for students with disabilities (Kalivoda, 2003). Particularly at research universities, where faculty are more likely to be rewarded for the quantity of their publications and grant income than the quality of their teaching, barriers included lack of time, resources, and institutional support (Kalivoda, 2003; Smith, 1997). Some faculty members continue to express skepticism about the fairness of providing accommodations for students despite the documentation of their disabilities, especially when considering those that are hidden, such as psychological disabilities, attention deficit/hyperactivity disorder (ADHD), and learning disabilities (Kalivoda, 2003; Williams & Ceci, 1999). Rather than asking faculty to make exceptions for students with disabilities, UID proposes that strategies that might previously have been considered accommodations (e.g., extra time on tests) for students with disabilities are instead made available to all students. As a result, UID enables all students to learn more effectively and to earn grades that reflect their knowledge. Although implementing UID in a course may require additional planning time upfront, often the outcome is a net savings of time for the faculty member because of the decrease in individual requests for accommodations by students with disabilities.

COMPONENTS OF UNIVERSAL INSTRUCTIONAL DESIGN

Components of UID, which are based on the work of Chickering and Gamson (1987), include (a) creating welcoming classrooms; (b) determining the essential components of a course; (c) communicating clear expectations; (d) providing constructive feedback; (e) exploring the use of natural supports for learning, including technology, to enhance opportunities for all learners; (f) designing teaching methods that consider diverse learning styles, abilities, ways of knowing, and previous experience and background knowledge; (g) creating multiple ways for students to demonstrate their knowledge; and (h) promoting interaction among and between faculty and students (Fox & Johnson, 2000; Opitz & Block, 2006). This chapter illustrates the implementation of each of these components in a course offered by the Department of Postsecondary Teaching and Learning (PSTL) at the University of Minnesota–Twin Cities, PSTL 1086: The First-Year Experience. In order to accommodate greater numbers of students, PSTL 1086 meets for 50 minutes per week as a large lecture section facilitated by a tenured faculty member, and for 100 minutes per week in small discussion sections of no more than 20 students facilitated by professional academic advisors. Thus, in describing UID implementation in PSTL 1086, this chapter can provide ideas for large lecture courses as well as more intimate learning settings.

Creating a Welcoming Classroom

Unfortunately, as at many large institutions, the lecture halls in which PSTL 1086 is typically taught do not necessarily convey a sense of a welcoming learning space to students as they enter. To assist in alleviating this barrier to effective teaching and learning, on the first day of lecture, the faculty member and advisors are at the entrances to the lecture hall to welcome students as they come through the door and continue to chat informally with students until it is time for class to start. The class begins with formal introductions of the teaching staff, including calling attention to e-mail addresses and office and home phone numbers provided in the syllabus. Although the faculty member does not go over the syllabus point by point, she does call students' attention to important policies and procedures and "performs" (Pedelty, 2003) or reads aloud the syllabus statement related to accommodations for students with disabilities. The following paragraph from the PSTL 1086 syllabus incorporates all the content of the institution's standard syllabus statement, but it also includes a values statement on the part of the faculty member:

> I believe strongly in providing reasonable accommodations for students with docu-
> mented disabilities on an individualized and flexible basis. The University's Office of
> Disability Services (DS) determines appropriate accommodations through consulta-
> tion with the student. Please contact me and your discussion section leader at the
> beginning of the semester to work out the details of accommodations. If you have a
> documented disability and have not as yet met with staff in DS, I strongly encourage
> you to do so at your earliest convenience. To make an appointment, call . . . .

In the discussion sections this material is repeated, and students are asked to com-
plete a "student information sheet" that includes the question "Is there anything that I should be aware of that might have an impact on your participation in this course (examples: a documented disability, absences for religious observation, or ath-
letic competitions representing the institution)? If so, please describe." Choosing to disclose a disability is a difficult decision for some students (Alexandrin, Schreiber, & Henry, 2008; Henning, 2007; *Uncertain Welcome*, 2002). The student information sheets, which the advisor collects individually as the students leave the room at the end of class, enable students to disclose more privately than by approaching an instructor before or after class, often when surrounded by other students. It also takes some of the responsibility for follow-up off the student and places it on the advisor. Given differences between high school and college in the procedures for securing accommodations, it is important for first-semester freshmen with disabilities to develop self-ad-
vocacy skills (Higbee & Kalivoda, 2003), but it is unlikely that all students will have these skills when they first walk in the door. In fact, I believe that communication skills should be a focus of any first-year experience course like PSTL 1086.

Another important aspect of creating a welcoming learning environment is to assure students that their voices will be heard. Even in the lecture portion of PSTL 1086, there is very little lecture per se. Immediately after the brief review of key com-
ponents of the syllabus on the first day, students are engaged in conversations about their reasons for going to college and the purpose of higher education. The students first work in dyads and triads and then may choose to share their ideas with the class as a whole. Even in a large lecture class, learning individual students' names has become more manageable with the advent of digital photography and the provision of student ID photos by the university via the faculty member's electronic class list. By referring to the ID photos frequently during the initial weeks of class, it is possible for the faculty member to begin linking faces with names in order to call on students

by name. For faculty at institutions where digital ID photos are not provided auto-matically, the ease of taking photos with a digital camera as students enter on the first day of class can also facilitate linking names to faces in the classroom. Especially at larger institutions, letting students know that they are more than a number plays a critical role in making students feel welcomed—a key principle of UID—and encour-aging further interaction.

Determining Essential Components

Considerations in determining essential components include the purpose of the course, intended outcomes, instructional methods for achieving these outcomes, and types of evaluation to be used (Fox & Johnson, 2000). Although the process of learn-ing is important, essential components should focus on learning outcomes. Not all students learn in the same ways; what is important is that they *do learn*. Essential components of a course can vary widely, depending in part on whether the course is a prerequisite for subsequent courses or a requirement in a program governed by specific professional standards, such as those of the allied health professions (Casey, 2007; Sharby & Roush, 2008). For PSTL 1086, which does not have to conform to these types of standards but which requires consistency of content and the grading rubric across sections, the essential components of the course are reflected in the fol-lowing course objectives:

- To explore the purpose of higher education
- To establish individual goals and objectives
- To examine issues of importance to all first-year college students
- To explore how diversity enhances educational and life experiences
- To examine students' responsibility for their own learning
- To introduce the many educational opportunities and resources available at the University of Minnesota
- To begin the career planning process
- To perfect time-management skills
- To develop study strategies to enhance academic success
- To improve critical skills in thinking and problem solving
- To provide a venue for practicing oral and written communication skills
- To assess and reduce sources of stress

The content of both the lectures and the material presented in discussion sections in PSTL 1086, as well as the nature of the course assignments and methods of eval-uation, reflect these essential components. At the end of the semester students are asked to rate on a scale of one to ten the extent to which the course was successful in achieving each of its objectives (Higbee, Lee, Bardill, & Cardinal, 2008).

Communicating Clear Expectations

It is critical that course expectations are communicated in writing, by means of the course syllabus, and then reinforced via various forms of communication between instructors and students. PSTL 1086 uses criterion-referenced grading; final grades are determined through a point system, with a total of 1,000 points available. The grading rubric is presented in the syllabus, but students also receive a "summary of assignments" form that lists each assignment by due date and the maximum number of points the student can earn for that assignment. This form also provides a blank where the student is to record the number of points earned. During the third week of class all students receive an e-mail message explaining how they can calculate their course grade, in the form of a percentage, as of that point in the semester, as well as how to do so in future weeks, by dividing the number of points they have earned by the number possible to date. Examples are provided. This material is also covered briefly in lecture that week. Thus, students are taught how to track their own progress in this and any other course that uses a point system. Students are encouraged to contact the faculty member or the advisor teaching their discussion section if they have any questions. Grading rubrics are also provided for individual assignments, with a greater emphasis on content than on mechanics but with some points for organization, grammar, and so on because development of effective written communication skills is an objective of the course.

Providing Constructive Feedback

Throughout the course, students in PSTL 1086 receive numerous types of feedback from both the faculty member and the advisors teaching the discussion sections. The faculty member responds to each student every week via her comments on the open-ended short-answer and essay-style study guides and "question cards." Upon entering each lecture, students pick up a colored card and respond to a question posted on the screen at the front of the room. Examples of weekly questions include the following:

- What are the top three reasons (in priority order) you are attending college?
- How do you feel about college mathematics? Why? In your opinion, how important is mathematics for college graduation or for your preparation for your career and life after college? Why?
- How do *you personally* benefit from the diversity of the student body at the University of Minnesota?
- What adjective best describes your first semester in college? Why?

The question cards are also used for taking attendance in lectures. Although attendance is technically not required, it is emphasized that research conducted in both PSTL courses and other venues demonstrates that students who attend class earn higher grades (Higbee & Fayon, 2006; Higbee, Schultz, & Goff, 2006; Moore, 2004, 2003; Moore et al., 2003; Thomas & Higbee, 2000). And, although there is no penalty for not attending class, the only opportunity for extra credit in the course is perfect attendance (20 points) or missing only one class meeting (10 points).

After returning the midterm and final exams—which occurs at the next discussion section meetings or, for some sections, on the same day as the test—the faculty member provides an answer key that lists both the correct answer and where in the text or lecture handouts the answer can be found. This is one of those strategies that benefits the faculty member as well as the student; students cannot debate the answers when the source of the material is so clearly spelled out.

The advisors grade students' reflection papers and other writing assignments, commenting on both content and style. For oral presentations and small-group projects, students also receive feedback from their peers. Students also benefit from the process of giving feedback: They learn to think critically and shape comments to be constructive rather than punitive, which is an important life skill.

Feedback on the student's progress in the course is also provided via the University of Minnesota's midsemester report process, which all PSTL faculty and instructional staff members are required to complete for each first-year student enrolled in their classes. Typical information provided in these reports, which are generated electronically and sent to each student via e-mail, includes the student's current grade in the course, the percentage of the course work completed, the student's attendance record, and any individually constructed comments on the student's progress. There is also a checklist that enables the instructor to indicate if the student (a) should be making an appointment to see the faculty member or advisor, (b) needs to attend more regularly, (c) is missing assignments, or (d) should consider dropping the course. Even if students are not tracking their own performance via the course summary of assignments, upon receiving the midsemester report they will have a clear picture of where they stand in the course.

Using Natural Supports

When natural supports for learning are described, the emphasis is frequently on technological supports (Duquaine-Watson, 2008; Fox & Johnson, 2000), which can take the form of course Web pages and other Internet resources such as chat rooms, blogs, and so on. For students with disabilities, these supports may also include a wide variety of assistive technologies, from listening devices to screen readers (Knox, Higbee, Kalivoda, & Totty, 2000; Totty & Kalivoda, n.d.). For PSTL 1086, the faculty member maintains regular communication with all students in the class via e-mail messages sent at least once per week. This practice also encourages the students to be in frequent contact with the faculty member and assists her in becoming better acquainted with the students individually. The faculty member makes a habit of approaching students when they come for lectures and following up on e-mail conversations in person.

For PSTL 1086, the most significant natural support might be the weekly study guides created by the faculty member. The primary purposes of the study guides are to (a) assist the student in learning how to navigate the text and determine what is important, (b) facilitate engagement with the text that goes beyond memorization of facts and figures to application of course content to the student's individual experience, and (c) provide a mechanism for reviewing for the midterm and final exams. Although many textbooks, including the one used in PSTL 1086, provide publisher-generated study guides, by creating her own study guides the faculty member ensures a richer understanding of the course content. Printed copies of the study guides are distributed each week in lecture and are provided electronically via e-mail and on the course Web site. All other faculty-generated instructional materials—from PowerPoint slides (although PowerPoint is used infrequently in this course as a backup for taking notes) to handouts and assessment tools—are also available to students electronically and sent out again as e-mail attachments during the weeks before the midterm and final exams, together with a reminder of what to study. At the end of the semester, students not only complete the university's standard faculty evaluation form, they also rank the helpfulness of the study guides and other natural supports.

Considering Diverse Learning Styles and Abilities

Within PSTL 1086, students complete four assessments related to learning styles, each of which approaches the topic in a different way. Through the combination of large and small class meetings, the faculty member and advisors teaching PSTL 1086 are able to use a wide variety of teaching styles to help overcome the usual diversity in the learning preferences of students, most of whom do not believe that they learn best through reading textbooks and listening passively to lectures (Higbee, Ginter, & Taylor, 1991). In both lecture and discussion, film clips are used frequently to illustrate course topics. In the discussion sections, small-group exercises, such as games and simulations (Ghere, 2003; Hatch, Ghere, & Jirik, 2003), enhance the learning of students who prefer experiential learning and of those who learn best when interacting with others. The final course evaluation asks students whether the course has been successful in addressing individual learning styles and ways of knowing.

Enabling Students to Demonstrate Knowledge in Multiple Ways

Students earn points for a broad range of assignments, including (a) weekly question cards; (b) study guides; (c) a wide variety of self-assessments, including some provided in the course text (Gardner, Jewler, & Barefoot, 2007); (d) attendance at a campus event of the student's choice, approved by the discussion leader; (e) participation in a community service project; (f) reflection papers and other writing assignments; (g) an oral presentation; (h) a small-group multimedia project; and (i) the midterm and final examinations. Not only does this breadth of assignments allow students to demonstrate their knowledge in multiple ways, but it also prepares them for divergent expectations in future courses.

Each of the two exams consists of 50 true-false, multiple choice, and matching items. Most students complete the test within 20 or 25 minutes. However, all students are given the full class period of 50 minutes to complete the test. This is the equivalent of providing all students with extended time. This practice benefits students who read more slowly, those with test anxiety, and students who are not native speakers of English, as well as students with disabilities. However, many students with learning disabilities, ADHD, and other disabilities that often warrant extended time on tests may also benefit from taking exams in less distracting environments and may qualify for an accommodation, like individually administered exams. Since instituting this practice of providing "double time" in PSTL 1086, 100% of the students with disabilities taking the class have chosen to remain in lecture for test days rather than be segregated for separate administration of the exams. In other words, although given the opportunity, they have not chosen to make use of a standard accommodation that, over time, not only segregates them from other students but also is likely to inadvertently breach the confidentiality of students with invisible disabilities. The students with disabilities who could have taken the exams individually have also earned grades that are not significantly lower than those of students without disabilities and, in some cases, have been significantly higher.

Promoting Interaction

As already discussed, both the faculty member and the advisors working with PSTL 1086 try to use a wide array of mechanisms built into the course to encourage inter-action with and among students. In some cases, the weekly question cards provide opportunities for students to pose questions that they might not feel comfortable ask-ing aloud, or that they might not think to ask, such as those on the following prompt used the Friday before the midterm exam:

> What concerns do you have about the midterm exam? What further questions can I answer for you? I will read these cards over the weekend, type up your questions (no names, I promise!), and provide answers to the whole class via e-mail.

When guest speakers on topics like human sexuality, financial planning, or diver-sity present during lecture, students also receive a white card as they enter the room and are prompted to write down any questions they might have for the speaker with-out having to identify themselves. This practice benefits many students, including students with disabilities, students who are not native speakers of English, students who are shy, and students who have questions they consider embarrassing but to which they desperately need answers. Often the speaker does not have time within the lecture period to answer all the questions posed, but these individuals have been thoughtful in providing written responses during the following week; these responses are sent to the entire class via e-mail.

THE FACULTY PERSPECTIVE: BENEFITS AND CHALLENGES OF UNIVERSAL INSTRUCTIONAL DESIGN

Implementing UID benefits the teacher as well as the student. Although some stu-dents with disabilities will still need individual accommodations (e.g., a sign lan-guage interpreter or a text on tape), in planning a course using UID, the faculty mem-ber often reduces the need for individual accommodations, thereby saving time in the long run. Frequently, the faculty member does not have advance notice of the accommodation needs of students with disabilities enrolled in a course prior to the first day of class, when some—but not all—students with disabilities provide a letter from the institution's disabilities services office. At that point there is little time to prepare accommodations like alternative test formats or additional forms of the tests for separate administration. Although students may be encouraged to contact faculty members earlier, some students are hesitant to do so until they can meet with the fac-ulty member in person and gauge the teacher's response to them and their disability (*Uncertain Welcome*, 2002).

One of the challenges of implementing UID is trying to predict the needs of poten-tial students. In 22 years of teaching at large public research universities, the PSTL 1086 faculty member has taught only two students who are blind. During this period, it has become much easier to acquire videos with captioning for students who have hearing impairments and for whom written English is easier to comprehend than spoken English, and to count on the availability of televisions, projectors, monitors, and video players that are equipped for showing captioned films. But it is problematic to request in advance that all videos be described for students who have visual impairments, when no students who are blind may ever enroll in the course, and it may divert resources from the teachers and students who need them most. One solution is to select clips from films that are already available with oral description through the Descriptive Video Service (DVS Home Video, n.d.).

Thus, many of the challenges to implementing UID can be relatively easy to overcome if the faculty member is aware of available resources. Professional development in the areas of universal design and UID can enhance the likelihood that faculty members will perceive the advantages of designing courses that are fully accessible to all students. To the extent possible, it is helpful if faculty receive training from other faculty who are in the same or similar disciplines and can provide concrete examples for implementation in that disciplinary area (e.g., in the chemistry laboratory, in student-teacher placements, in Web pages that illustrate accounting ledger pages). Professional development opportunities are also important for learning center staff members, academic advisors, career counselors, and others who provide services for students.

EVALUATION

As previously noted, the PSTL 1086 instructor augments institutional evaluation processes with her own assessment instruments, which are designed to determine whether the course is meeting its objectives and implementing UID successfully and the extent to which students find class activities, guest speakers, and assignments helpful. Only recently, however, have these data been collected for research purposes. In another, similar first-year course taught by the instructor, the mean rating for implementation of each of the UID principles ranged from 9.6 out of 10 ($n = 31$) for "The required course content was appropriate" (related to essential components) to 9.9 out of 10 ($n = 31$) for three of the eight items: (a) "Dr. _____ created a respectful and welcoming learning environment"; (b) "Dr. _____ provided timely, clear, and accurate feedback"; and (c) "Dr. _____ used multiple teaching strategies (e.g., short lecture, discussion, films, small-group exercises)" (Higbee, Lee, Bardill, & Cardinal, 2008). The faculty member has also achieved high marks for her overall teaching ability on the institution's standard evaluation of teaching.

CONCLUSION

In 1997, Hodge and Preston-Sabin edited a book titled *Accommodations—Or Just Good Teaching?* In many respects, UID could be construed as simply good teaching. But creating universally designed courses and curricula requires intentionality and thorough advance planning. Even the most naturally gifted lecturer is not necessarily a good teacher if other aspects of the course, such as handouts, electronic supports, and exams, do not meet the needs of students. Faculty members who implement UID gain in many ways, not just because they know that they are making their courses more accessible to all students but often in the form of better teaching evaluations and recognition for excellence in teaching as well.

REFERENCES

Alexandrin, J. R., Schreiber, I. L., & Henry, F. (2008). Why not disclose? In J. L. Higbee & E. Goff (Eds.), *Pedagogy and student services for institutional transformation: Implementing universal design in higher education.* Minneapolis: University of Minnesota, Center for Research on Developmental Education and Urban Literacy, Pedagogy and Student Services for Institutional Transformation.

Barajas, H. L., & Higbee, J. L. (2003). Where do we go from here? Universal design as a model for multicultural education. In J. L. Higbee (Ed.), *Curriculum transformation and disability: Implementing universal design in higher education* (pp. 285–290). Minneapolis: University of Minnesota, General College, Center for Research on Developmental Education and Urban Literacy. Retrieved August 21, 2007, from http://www.cehd.umn.edu/CRDEUL/books-ctad.html

Bowe, F. G. (2000). *Universal design in education—Teaching nontraditional students.* Westport, CT: Bergin & Garvey.

Casey, D. A. (2007). Students with psychological disabilities in allied health sciences programs. In J. L. Higbee, D. B. Lundell, & I. M. Duranczyk (Eds.), *Diversity and the postsecondary experience* (pp. 87–102). Minneapolis: University of Minnesota, Center for Research on Developmental Education and Urban Literacy. Retrieved August 21, 2007, from http://www.cehd.umn.edu/CRDEUL/docs/monograph/Diversity.pdf

Chickering, A. W., & Gamson, Z. F. (1987). Seven principles for good practice in undergraduate education. *AAHE Bulletin, 39*(7), 3–7.

Duquaine-Watson, J. M. (2008). Computing technologies, the digital divide, and "universal" instructional methods. In J. L. Higbee & E. Goff (Eds.), *Pedagogy and student services for institutional transformation: Implementing universal design in higher education.* Minneapolis: University of Minnesota, Center for Research on Developmental Education and Urban Literacy, Pedagogy and Student Services for Institutional Transformation.

DVS Home Video. (n.d.). *Descriptive video service catalogue.* Retrieved December 11, 2006, from http://main.wgbh.org/wgbh/pages/mag/resources/dvs-home-video-catalogue.html

Fox, J. A., & Johnson, D. (2000). *Curriculum transformation and disability workshop facilitator's guide.* Minneapolis: University of Minnesota, General College and Disability Services. Retrieved August 21, 2007, from http://www.gen.umn.edu/research/ CTAD/publications.htm

Gardner, J. N., Jewler, A. J., & Barefoot, B. O. (2007). *Your college experience* (7th ed.). Boston, MA: Thomson Wadsworth.

Ghere, D. L. (2003). Best practices and students with disabilities: Experiences in a college history course. In J. L. Higbee (Ed.), *Curriculum transformation and disability: Implementing universal design in higher education* (pp. 149–161). Minneapolis: University of Minnesota, General College, Center for Research on Developmental Education and Urban Literacy. Retrieved August 21, 2007, from http://www.cehd.umn.edu/CRDEUL/books-ctad.html

Hackman, H. W., & Rauscher, L. (2004). A pathway to success for all: Exploring the connections between universal instructional design and social justice education. *Equity & Excellence in Education, 37*(2), 114–123.

Hatch, J. T., Ghere, D. L., & Jirik, K. N. (2003). Empowering students with severe disabilities: A case study. In J. L. Higbee (Ed.), *Curriculum transformation and disability: Implementing universal design in higher education* (pp. 171–183). Minneapolis: University of Minnesota, General College, Center for Research on Developmental Education and Urban Literacy. Retrieved August 21, 2007, from http://www.cehd.umn.edu/CRDEUL/books-ctad.html

Henning, G. (2007). What happens if others find out? *About Campus, 12*(3), 26–29.

Higbee, J. L. (Ed.). (2003). *Curriculum transformation and disability: Implementing universal design in higher education.* Minneapolis: University of Minnesota, General College, Center for Research on Devel-

opmental Education and Urban Literacy. Retrieved August 21, 2007, from http://www.cehd.
umn.edu/CRDEUL/books-ctad.html

Higbee, J. L., & Barajas, H. L. (2007). Building effective places for multicultural learning. *About Campus, 12*(3), 16–22.

Higbee, J. L., & Fayon, A. K. (2006). Attendance policies in developmental education courses: Promoting involvement or undermining students' autonomy? *Research & Teaching in Developmental Education, 22*(2), 71–77.

Higbee, J. L., Ginter, E. J., & Taylor, W. D. (1991). Enhancing academic performance: Seven perceptual styles of learning. *Research & Teaching in Developmental Education, 7*(2), 5–10.

Higbee, J. L., & Kalivoda, K. S. (2003). The first-year experience. In J. L. Higbee (Ed.), *Curriculum transformation and disability: Implementing universal design in higher education* (pp. 203–213). Minneapolis: University of Minnesota, General College, Center for Research on Developmental Education and Urban Literacy. Retrieved August 21, 2007, from http://www.cehd.umn.edu/CRDEUL/books-ctad.html

Higbee, J. L., Lee, P. H., Bardill, J., & Cardinal, H. (2008). Student evaluations of the effectiveness of implementing universal instructional design. In J. L. Higbee & E. Goff (Eds.), *Pedagogy and student services for institutional transformation: Implementing universal design in higher education.* Minneapolis: University of Minnesota, Center for Research on Developmental Education and Urban Literacy, Pedagogy and Student Services for Institutional Transformation.

Higbee, J. L., Schultz, J. L., & Goff, E. (2006). Attendance policies in developmental education courses: The student point of view. *Research & Teaching in Developmental Education, 23*(1), 78–85.

Hodge, B. M., & Preston-Sabin, J. (1997). *Accommodations—Or just good teaching? Strategies for teaching college students with disabilities.* Westport, CT: Praeger.

Johnson, J. R. (2004). Universal instructional design and critical (communication) pedagogy: Strategies for voice, inclusion, and social justice/change. *Equity & Excellence in Education, 37*, 145–153.

Johnson, D. M., & Fox, J. A. (2003). Creating curb cuts in the classroom: Adapting universal design principles to education. In J. L. Higbee (Ed.), *Curriculum transformation and disability: Implementing universal design in higher education* (pp. 7–21). Minneapolis: University of Minnesota, General College, Center for Research on Developmental Education and Urban Literacy. Retrieved August 21, 2007, from http://www.cehd.umn.edu/CRDEUL/books-ctad.html

Kalivoda, K. S. (2003). Creating access through universal instructional design. In J. L. Higbee, D. B. Lundell, & I. M. Duranczyk (Eds.), *Multiculturalism in developmental education* (pp. 25–34). Minneapolis: University of Minnesota, General College, Center for Research on Developmental Education and Urban Literacy. Retrieved August 21, 2007, from http://www.cehd.umn.edu/CRDEUL/pdf/monograph/4-a.pdf

Knox, D. K., Higbee, J. L., Kalivoda, K. S., & Totty, M. C. (2000). Serving the diverse needs of students with disabilities through technology. *Journal of College Reading and Learning, 30*(2), 144–157.

Moore, R. (2003). Students' choices in developmental education: Is it really important to attend class? *Research & Teaching in Developmental Education, 20*(1), 42–52.

Moore, R. (2004). Does improving developmental education students' understanding of the importance of class attendance improve students' class attendance and academic performance? *Research & Teaching in Developmental Education, 20*(2), 24–39.

Moore, R., Jensen, M., Hatch, J., Duranczyk, I., Staats, S., & Koch, L. (2003). Showing up: The importance of class attendance for academic success in introductory science courses. *American Biology Teacher, 65*(5), 325–329.

Opitz, D. L., & Block, L. S. (2006). Universal learning support design: Maximizing learning beyond the classroom. *Learning Assistance Review, 11*(2), 33–45.

Pedelty, M. (2003). Making a statement. In J. L. Higbee (Ed.), *Curriculum transformation and disability: Implementing universal design in higher education* (pp. 71–78). Minneapolis: University of Minnesota, General College, Center for Research on Developmental Education and Urban Literacy. Retrieved August 21, 2007, from http://www.cehd.umn.edu/CRDEUL/books-ctad.html

Sharby, N., & Roush, S. E. (2008). The application of universal instructional design in experiential education. In J. L. Higbee & E. Goff (Eds.), *Pedagogy and student services for institutional transforma-*

tion: Implementing universal design in higher education. Minneapolis: University of Minnesota, Center for Research on Developmental Education and Urban Literacy, Pedagogy and Student Services for Institutional Transformation.

Silver, P., Bourke, A., & Strehorn, K. C. (1998). Universal instructional design in higher education: An approach for inclusion. *Equity & Excellence in Education, 31*(2), 47–51.

Smith, K. L. (1997). Preparing faculty for instructional technology: From education to development to creative independence. *Cause/Effect, 20*(3), 36–44.

Thomas, P. V., & Higbee, J. L. (2000). The relationship between involvement and success in developmental algebra. *Journal of College Reading and Learning, 30*(2), 222–232.

Totty, M. C., & Kalivoda, K. S. (n.d.). *Assistive technology.* Minneapolis: University of Minnesota, Pedagogy and Student Services for Institutional Transformation (PASS IT). Retrieved December 21, 2006, from http://www.cehd.umn.edu/passit/docs/techHandout.doc

Uncertain welcome: Student perspectives on disability and postsecondary education [Video]. (2002). Minneapolis: University of Minnesota, General College and Disability Services. Retrieved December 9, 2006, from http://www.gen.umn.edu/research/CTAD/publications.htm

Williams, W. M., & Ceci, S. J. (1999, August 6). Accommodating learning disabilities can bestow unfair advantages. *Chronicle of Higher Education,* B4–B5.

5

Universal Design
of Assessment

Martha L. Thurlow
Christopher J. Johnstone
Leanne R. Ketterlin-Geller

Universal design is a concept that has been applied to the design of assessments in K–12 education. It originated in architecture but shows promise for educational applications, including postsecondary assessment design. This chapter defines and describes universal design of assessment (UDA), its challenges for application in postsecondary education, and several specific approaches that make its application feasible in postsecondary institutions. This chapter provides steps to take toward designing assessments for classroom use, as well as other tasks and assessments that improve access for all students.

Administration and faculty of higher-education institutions in the United States are challenged to consider the ways in which their institutions are accessible to the increasingly wide variety of students who attend them. Because of major legislation, such as Section 504 of the Rehabilitation Act of 1973 and the Americans with Disabilities Act of 1990, colleges and universities are now required to remove barriers that might deprive qualified persons with disabilities from the opportunity to succeed in postsecondary education. "Accessibility" for a college student with a disability might include anything from physical access to a dormitory to learning and testing accommodations in the classroom.

Because postsecondary students with disabilities are a heterogeneous group, some colleges and universities have adopted a "universal design" approach to meeting the needs of their students. Universal design, originally applied in the field of architecture, is defined as "the design of products and environments to be usable by all people, to the greatest extent possible, without the need for adaptation or specialized design" (Mace, n.d.). In the case of postsecondary education, universal design of environments and learning is especially relevant because only students who disclose their disabilities receive specialized services (Bierwert, 2002). It is likely that there are students who have diagnosed disabilities or other learning and physical challenges who do not receive any formal services in postsecondary education because they have not self-identified. For these students, applying the principles of universal design in assessment might ameliorate this situation.

In this chapter we discuss some of the challenges that higher-education faculty might encounter when designing assessments and then present several approaches to applying the philosophy of universal design when assessing students in postsecondary educational settings. Assessment, broadly defined, is any tool used to evaluate students or to provide data for making adjustments in teaching and learning processes (Roberts & McInnerney, 2006). UDA draws on the philosophy of access to all, but also recognizes that assessments must discriminate between students who have mastered the content and those who have not. Given the purpose of assessments, UDA must maintain the validity of the measures. This means that the needs of a wide range of students are addressed without changing the difficulty of the targeted construct of the assessment.

Because of the tension between open access to assessment content and the underlying function of assessment (to make a valid estimate of student knowledge or skill in a particular area), UDA is understood in different ways. Thompson, Johnstone, & Thurlow (2002) developed *Elements of Universally Designed Assessments* to guide the design of K–12 large-scale assessments. They include seven elements:

1. Inclusive assessment population (e.g., all populations who might take an assessment are considered during assessment development)
2. Precisely defined constructs (i.e., intended material or skills to be tested are transparent)
3. Accessible, nonbiased items (i.e., test items should not be biased against particular populations)
4. Amenability to accommodations (e.g., the test design should allow for the use of accommodations)
5. Simple, clear, and intuitive instructions
6. Comprehensible language
7. Maximum legibility (in both print and graphics)

Dolan, Hall, Banerjee, Chun, & Strangman (2005) and Hall, Strangman, & Meyer (2003) approached UDA from the perspective of technology enhancements to assessment. These researchers viewed UDA as a mechanism for choice and built-in accommodation in assessment. They advocated for multiple means of information retrieval and multiple opportunities for expression (e.g., voice-activated technology to reduce barriers to students who have writing disabilities and screen readers to reduce barriers for students who struggle reading print).

Interpretations of UDA differ but are common in the assumption that accessibility and validity are the hallmarks of high-quality assessments. Such assessment requires that designers discriminate between the actual content they want to test and other nonconstruct information or skills that may act as barriers to students (Ketterlin-Geller, Yovanoff, & Tindal, 2007). Such interpretations echo the American Educational Research Association, American Psychological Association, and National Council on Measurement in Education's *Standards for Educational and Psychological Testing* of 1999. These standards call for improved sensitivity toward students with diverse characteristics while upholding high standards in assessment design and interpretation. UDA research and the 1999 *Test Standards*, however, say little about assessment that is designed by individual teachers for class-specific goals. Therefore, UDA research (which is largely focused on large-scale assessment in K–12 schools) needs to be interpreted carefully within the context of postsecondary education.

CHALLENGES FOR UNIVERSAL DESIGN OF ASSESSMENT IN POSTSECONDARY EDUCATION

Designing assessments is never an easy task, and the design challenges are increased when the student population is diverse. The purpose of assessments administered in individual classes is to evaluate student knowledge in the content area of interest. Assessment results can be used for making a variety of decisions, including determining if the student is making progress in learning assigned materials or has acquired the skills and knowledge in the target content area. The consequences of these decisions range from adjusting instruction to recommending that a student get additional tutoring in a subject area and even to denying matriculation or graduation. Because these decisions often have high stakes, there is increased pressure to develop high-quality assessments that are appropriate for all students.

Even with the increased emphasis on the importance of designing assessments that meet the needs of the range of students in typical college-level courses, faculty receive little support in developing and evaluating their assessment tools. Many faculty members have limited knowledge and experience in designing tests and assignments. Moreover, campuses that offer instructional support through an instructional technology office or center often focus on designing instructional materials or refining classroom-management techniques; little attention is paid to creating assessment tools. Furthermore, few course textbooks have sufficient assessment tools embedded in their materials that address the breadth of course content beyond the material presented in the text. When test banks are provided in textbooks, they are often created by item writers, not the textbook's authors. Furthermore, the technical quality of these tests or assignments is rarely reported; therefore, the validity and reliability of the results are unknown. Thus, faculty members are left with few resources other than their past experience in designing tests and their expertise in the area.

Knowledge of assessment and test-development techniques is critical for designing appropriate assessments. In the context of supporting students with disabilities, test developers need to identify the skills and knowledge that are targeted by the test and those that are not. The targeted skills and knowledge should be those used to make decisions about students. For example, on a botany exam, the targeted skills and knowledge might include cellular respiration and its interrelationship with photosynthesis. Conversely, many skills are unintentionally tested on the assessment that might influence students' ability to demonstrate their skills or knowledge in the targeted content. These skills often are referred to as *access skills* because they are needed to *access* the intended construct. Access skills are especially prevalent in performance assessments that require students to integrate many supplemental skills when demonstrating their knowledge. In the botany example, access skills might include the students' ability to interpret diagrams, express their knowledge in writing, and perform a host of other skills that depend on the structure and format of the actual test. For students with diverse characteristics—including students with disabilities, students whose first language is not English, and students who struggled for a variety of reasons in high school—access skills often limit their ability to demonstrate their content-area knowledge. Access skills can be supported through accommodations for specific students with self-reported disabilities, or the impact of access skills for all students can be minimized by incorporating the principles of universal design.

UDA is an approach that emerged from K–12 education, but many features of UDA are applicable in postsecondary education. For example, the qualities of UDA that Thompson et al. (2002) described can serve to meet the needs of a wide variety of postsecondary students if the assessments are amenable to accommodations; have simple, clear, and intuitive instructions and procedures (see also American Educational Research Association et al., 1999); have maximum readability and comprehensibility (see also Hanson, Hayes, Schriver, LeMahieu, & Brown, 1998); and have maximum legibility (Schriver, 1997). Similarly, the characteristics of UDA that allow for students to use different modalities for the input and output of information described by Dolan et al. (2005) and Hall et al. (2003) can be clearly applied in postsecondary educational settings.

To minimize the effects of deficits in access skills and to provide instructors with a more accurate understanding of student knowledge of material, instructors can ask themselves a series of questions about their assessments and then make adjustments as needed. These questions include the following:

- Are the instructions on this assessment easy for students to understand?
- Is the layout of the assessment easy to navigate?
- Are items formatted consistently throughout the assessment?
- Is the language I am using in the assessment appropriate for the students in my classroom? Will students understand the vocabulary associated with information not directly related to the coursework?
- Is the print large and legible enough for *all* students to read? Are diagrams clear and consistent with text?
- Can the assessment be taken in a variety of formats (e.g., paper, computer-based)?
- Can a potential allowable accommodation for a student be used on this assessment without changing the constructs of what I am testing?

Answering these questions affirmatively results in assessments that apply features of UDA. Such UDA strategies can be easily incorporated into the typical assessment-design work of instructors and the resulting assessments. As Thompson et al. (2002) noted, however, another feature of UDA is that constructs are clearly defined (constructs are the particular content or skill that a test item is intended to measure). Thus, it is important to clearly differentiate target and access skills for any assessment.

Articulating the target and access skills is equally important for understanding how test changes influence the decisions that can be made according to the results. Test changes that support individual students with limited access skills are considered accommodations and should not change the target skills or subsequent decisions about students' ability. However, some test changes might inadvertently change the target skills, thereby invalidating the decisions that result. Without carefully defining the target and access skills, faculty might unintentionally change the meaning of the test scores, thus inflating or deflating student test scores and invalidating interpretations of student knowledge. In assessment terms, the goal is to learn about students' knowledge and skills from construct-relevant variance across test takers (National Accessible Reading Assessment Projects, 2006) while decreasing construct-irrelevant variance (Haladyna & Downing, 2004). It follows that faculty may benefit from additional training in defining the construct of a test and carefully describing what skills and knowledge are and are not intentionally being tested. Only with this information can faculty appropriately apply the principles of UDA.

Even if faculty members are comfortable with test-development techniques, additional challenges are present in postsecondary education when developing tests following the principles of universal design. In K–12 education, new large-scale assessments typically are field-tested and evaluated for technical adequacy. When a teacher uses a test to make decisions about a student, he generally has a high level of confidence in the trustworthiness of the resulting decisions. In postsecondary education, however, opportunities to collect validity evidence or evaluate the reliability of a test prior to administration are often limited. It may be difficult to pilot-test assessments before implementation in postsecondary settings, so faculty are left with little information about the technical qualities of their test results. This is especially important when evaluating the effects of any changes made to the test instrument. Furthermore, if a faculty member was interested in conducting a pilot study to determine if students with disabilities differentially benefited from a test change, the sample size of students with disabilities in postsecondary institutions, which are considerably smaller than in a group of K–12 students, probably would make it impossible to do so.

UNIVERSAL DESIGN OF ASSESSMENT APPROACHES FOR HIGHER EDUCATION

Clearly, there are numerous challenges in applying the elements of universal design to assessments in higher education and other postsecondary settings. However, several specific approaches can make it feasible for UDA to be applied in postsecondary institutions. Following are some steps to start you on your way toward applying universal design elements to your own assessments.

Clearly articulate the decisions you want to make about students' skills and knowledge from the test or assignment. Doing this will help you clarify the construct that you intend to measure. Identify areas in which you are and are not expecting the student to demonstrate proficiency. For example, when assigning a paper to write, are you expecting the student to demonstrate content knowledge about the topic of the paper? Also, you must define the level of specificity (e.g., do you want details from the readings or information from class discussions and lectures?). Are you looking for background knowledge? To what degree is this relevant to the course content and the decisions you have to make? Are you expecting writing skills? For example, is this related to the construct, and do you want to make decisions about their ability to write a thesis statement, use transitions, organize information following standards for writing scientific reports, follow rules of grammar? What level of expertise are you expecting? For example, is it important that these skills be independently mastered or can the student seek help from others?

Think about how students can best demonstrate their skills and knowledge in a way that will help you make decisions. Keep in mind that the role of assessment in postsecondary education is usually to determine the level of skills and knowledge a student has mastered in the content area. You may decide that students can best demonstrate their skills and knowledge through written tests, papers, presentations, demonstrations, observation of students actually performing a task, interviews, and so on. You may want to seek assistance from your instructional support center to help you understand the different types of tasks.

Identify the access skills needed to successfully interpret and respond to assessment items. Identify skills students need to complete the test or assignment that are *not* skills about which you are making decisions. For example, you are assigning an in-class essay about conditions leading to the Vietnam War, and you want to measure students' content knowledge and how they synthesize information from multiple sources; however, you may *not* be interested in the spelling capabilities of students or the speed at which they complete the task. In this example, a professor might agree that students could bring a dictionary or use a computer with spell-checking software to complete the test. Also, time might be extended for students who cannot accurately display their knowledge within the typical time frame. These testing conditions should be determined in advance of the testing session to make sure they do not change the construct of the test. This analysis also helps you clarify which skills really are important to your decision-making and which ones are not. Providing these UDA testing conditions will benefit all students and minimize the need for special accommodations for specific students with disabilities. However, if specific students need additional approved accommodations to support the skills about which you will not be making decisions, provide them. Research on the effects of accommodations has supported this approach, in which students with disabilities receive differential benefit from the use of accommodations they need, confirming that the accommodations are not providing an unfair benefit but instead meeting a need created by the students' disabilities (Sireci, Scarpati, & Li, 2005).

Design a task (test or assignment) that will allow you to make the decisions you want to make.

Explicitly state the expectations for students and which skills you will and will not be evaluating. Make sure the directions are clear; provide straightforward and clear instructions for accomplishing the tasks; provide multiple modalities through which expectations are described (e.g., directions, rubric, listed steps). Understanding the directions should not be the intended construct unless the class is on test-taking skills. Sometimes professors respond that this sounds like spoon-feeding students, but it takes the guesswork out of interpreting the assignment. Having a few people review the directions and provide feedback can help you create clear instructions. You can tell a lot about the clarity of directions for an assignment or a test by asking people to repeat to you what they understand and how they would go about completing the assignment or test.

Design the scoring guide or rubric with the decisions in mind. Tell students what you are trying to measure. If you are not trying to measure grammatical skills, for example, do not include them on the rubric. However, if you are trying to make multiple decisions that go beyond mastery of the content of your course, such as readiness to advance to the next course or general development of advanced skills (e.g., writing, critical thinking), then consider designing rubrics for these skills. Also, you may want to determine if this is something for which students should be formally evaluated or if it should only be informative for students. Consider the possibility that there might be a way for you to record these grades/comments other than through tests or assignments. For instance, some programs have competencies that students must meet to graduate or advance to candidacy (e.g., for doctoral students). If these skills are also assessed across the curriculum, this assessment might be a more appropriate place to note their development of these skills than in your course grade.

MOVING FORWARD: TOWARD ACCESSIBILITY IN ASSESSMENTS FOR ALL STUDENTS

The changing nature of students in postsecondary education environments heightens the importance of accurate information about the meaning of universal design as it applies to assessments and the importance of applying some elements of universal design immediately and additional ones as understanding grows. Discussion of universal design should expand as the diversity of the student body expands. In addition to students who have physical and sensory disabilities, postsecondary institutions now have increasing numbers of students who have learning disabilities, psychological disabilities, autism spectrum disorders, and other disabilities that are not necessarily visible. These students have access needs, too. Understanding the elements of universal design and the approaches outlined in this chapter will help in designing assessments and assignments that improve access for all students.

Besides the push to apply UDA because of the increasing diversity of the student body, other pressures encourage its application. Increasingly, students with disabilities have moved through a K–12 system in which accommodations have been provided frequently. They are accustomed to obtaining the accommodations they need and to participating in assessments designed to allow them to show what they know in diverse ways. In addition, states' large-scale assessment systems have been "encouraged" by federal laws to conform to the principles of universal design (Individuals with Disabilities Education Improvement Act, 2004; No Child Left Behind Act, 2001).

What is lacking—and what is needed for the future—are more training programs that provide those who develop assessments with easier ways to think through the steps and to apply universal design to assessment. Moving from paper and pencil to computer opens up many possibilities, but it also requires more sophistication about ways to improve accessibility to students with disabilities without compromising the content being assessed. Typically, technology can minimize the influence of access skills (e.g., computers can support spelling and print reading), but by its nature, technology presents topics differently from other sources of delivery and therefore needs careful scrutiny to ensure fidelity to the content being tested.

Finally, there is a need for research on the effects of applying universal design elements in classes in higher education and other postsecondary education settings. Research has begun to show effects with small numbers of students (e.g., Johnstone, 2003), and further research is under way. Higher-education settings, with their lack of standardization from institution to institution and instructor to instructor, will require creative approaches to understanding the effects of universal design on course assessments. These creative new methods will help us figure out how to make assessments more accessible and usable without undermining the high standards of postsecondary education.

REFERENCES

American Educational Research Association, American Psychological Association, National Council on Measurement in Education. (1999). *Standards for educational and psychological testing.* Washington, DC: American Educational Research Association.

Americans with Disabilities Act of 1990. 42 U.S.C.A. § 12101 *et seq.*

Bierwert, C. (2002). *Making accommodations for students with disabilities: A guide for faculty and graduate student instructors* (CRLT Occasional Paper No. 17). Ann Arbor: Center for Research on Learning and Teaching, University of Michigan.

Dolan, R. P., Hall, T. E., Banerjee, M., Chun, E., & Strangman, N. (2005). Applying principles of universal design to test delivery: The effect of computer-based read-aloud on test performance of high school students with learning disabilities. *Journal of Technology, Learning, & Assessment, 3*(7).

Haladyna, T. M., & Downing, S. M. (2004). Construct irrelevant variance in high stakes testing. *Educational Measurement: Issues and Practice, 23*(1), 17–27.

Hall, T., Strangman, N., & Meyer, A. (2003). *Differentiated instruction and implications for UDL implementation.* Retrieved June 6, 2006, from http://www.cast.org/publications/ncac/ncac_diffinstruct udl.html

Hanson, M. R., Hayes, J. R., Schriver, K.A, LeMahieu, P. G., & Brown, P. J. (1998). *A plain language approach to the revision of test items.* Paper presented at the annual meeting of the American Educational Research Association, San Diego, CA.

Individuals with Disabilities Education Improvement Act of 2004. 20 U.S.C. § 1400 *et seq.*

Johnstone, C. J. (2003). *Improving validity of large-scale tests: Universal design and student performance* (Technical Report 37). Minneapolis: University of Minnesota, National Center on Educational Outcomes. Retrieved June 24, 2006, from http://www.nceo.info/OnlinePubs/Technical37.htm

Ketterlin-Geller, L. R., Yovanoff, P., & Tindal, G. (2007). Developing a new paradigm for conducting research on accommodations in mathematics testing. *Exceptional Children, 73*(3), 331–347.

Mace, R. (n.d.). *About UD (universal design).* Raleigh: The Center for Universal Design, North Carolina State University. Retrieved October 6, 2007, from http://www.design.ncsu.edu/cud/about_ud/about_ud.htm

National Accessible Reading Assessment Projects. (2006). *Defining reading proficiency for accessible large-scale assessments: Some guiding principles and issues*. Retrieved June 24, 2007, from http://www.narap.info/publications/reports/definingreadingprof.pdf

No Child Left Behind Act of 2001. 20 U.S.C. § 6301 *et seq.*

Rehabilitation Act of 1973. 29 U.S.C. § 794–794a.

Roberts, T., & McInnerney, J. (2006). *Assessment in higher education*. Retrieved August 29, 2007, from http://ahe.cqu.edu.au/introduction.htm

Schriver, K. A. (1997). *Dynamics in document design: Creating text for readers*. New York: Wiley.

Section 504 of the Rehabilitation Acto of 1973, as amended. 29 U.S.C. § 6301

Sireci, S. G., Scarpati, S. E., & Li, S. (2005). Test accommodations for students with disabilities: An analysis of the interaction hypothesis. *Review of Educational Research, 75*(4), 457–490.

Thompson, S. J., Johnstone, C. J., & Thurlow, M. L. (2002). *Universal design applied to large scale assessments* (Synthesis Report 44). Minneapolis: University of Minnesota, National Center on Educational Outcomes. Retrieved June 24, 2006, from http://cehd.umn.edu/NCEO/OnlinePubs/Synthesis44.html

6

Universal Design of Instruction
Reflections of Students

Imke Durre
Michael Richardson
Carson Smith
Jessie Amelia Shulman
Sarah Steele

The coauthors of this chapter, who have a variety of disabilities themselves, share insights from past and present postsecondary experiences regarding the benefits to students of universal design of instruction. Their insights can help professors design their courses to be engaging for all students.

Most literature about the application of universal design to instruction has been written by researchers and practitioners. In contrast, this chapter explores universal design of instruction (UDI) from the student point of view. The coauthors—five successful current and former students who have disabilities with respect to mobility, hearing, vision, learning, and attention—present experiences and insights into the application of UDI. They share their perspectives in the form of responses to a checklist of strategies for the application of UDI. This checklist was originally developed through a literature review and input from participants in the *DO-IT Prof* project, funded by the U.S. Department of Education Office of Postsecondary Education (OPE) and directed through Disabilities, Opportunities, Internetworking, and Technology (DO-IT) at the University of Washington (DO-IT, 2006). It was then updated through an iterative process that was conducted within two more OPE-funded projects, *DO-IT Admin* and *AccessCollege* (DO-IT, 2007a,b). The checklist has been modified based on input from project team members (professionals from postsecondary institutions) who field-tested earlier versions. This working document continues to be updated with feedback from administrators, educators, students, and other stakeholders. The current version of the checklist can be found in the publication *Equal Access: Universal Design of Instruction* on the DO-IT Web site (Burgstahler, 2007).

The content of this chapter is organized into the following sections, which mirror the UDI checklist categories:

- Class climate
- Interaction
- Physical environments and products
- Delivery methods
- Information resources and technology
- Feedback
- Assessment
- Accommodation

Examples of specific strategies are provided under each category in a format similar to the checklist itself. Coauthor perspectives are included as bulleted items under each strategy; a comment that applies to multiple strategies, for the sake of expedience, is included only once. The coauthors hope their feedback will provide guidance not only to DO-IT as they continue to update the checklist but also to instructors who wish to apply universal design in their courses, to educators who provide professional development to faculty, and to service providers who work directly with students and their instructors.

CLASS CLIMATE

Adopt practices that reflect high values with respect to both diversity and inclusiveness.

Welcome everyone. Create a welcoming environment for all students. Encourage the sharing of multiple perspectives. Demonstrate and demand mutual respect.
- When people feel respected, they are more likely to view themselves as valuable members of the student body than when they feel disrespected. The feeling of belonging that is fostered by mutual respect can help retain students in a class or program.

Avoid stereotyping. Offer instruction and support based on student performance and requests, not simply on assumptions that members of certain groups (e.g., students with certain types of disabilities or from a specific racial/ethnic group) will automatically do well or poorly or require certain types of assistance.
- I don't expect professors to have great knowledge about my disability. I see my role as simply articulating the accommodations I need to do my best work.
- My approach has always been to keep the discussion about my disability professional. The objective of the discussion is to arrange appropriate accommodations not to discuss the validity of my disability. The disability services documentation I give the faculty before this discussion helps to keep the meeting on track.

Be approachable and available. Learn students' names. Welcome questions in and outside of class, seek out a student's point of view, and respond patiently. Maintain regular office hours, encourage students to meet with you, and offer alternatives when student schedules conflict with those hours; consider making a student-instructor meeting a course requirement. Be available for online communication as well.

- Being approachable and available to all students allows the student with a disability to feel like an equal part of the class. Rather than being the only student whose name the professor knows, they are simply one of *many* students whose names the professor knows.
- Students are positively motivated when a professor calls on them by name. If they feel known, not anonymous, they feel encouraged to participate in class. This benefits the individual as well as the entire class by invigorating the discussion so real learning can take place.
- Even in large classes, when I visit a professor during office hours and she remembers my name and the history of my previous visits, it has impact.
- Some professors say they have office hours but rarely encourage students to come. Too often students are afraid to look dumb in front of the professor. If the instructor makes more of an overture, more students will come to seek deeper knowledge and build a productive academic relationship with the professor.
- It is also very helpful if the professor has 5 or 10 minutes to spend after class to address individual student questions informally. Some students might not feel comfortable going to office hours but do not have a problem asking a quick question after class. This is particularly convenient for students who use sign language interpreters or captioning services in class because they have ready access to interpretation at that time.

Motivate all students. Use teaching methods and materials that are motivating and relevant to students with diverse characteristics, such as age, gender, and culture.

- In a Differential Equations course I took, the professor actually had a hearing impairment. It was really interesting to watch how he explained this to the students and integrated classroom accommodations to facilitate his teaching. Because of his experience and openness, I felt he was very approachable in terms of requesting accommodations and flexible in his teaching approach.

Address individual needs in an inclusive manner. Both on the syllabus and in class, invite students to meet with you to discuss disability-related accommodations and other learning needs. Avoid segregating or stigmatizing any student by drawing undue attention to a difference (e.g., disability) or sharing private information (e.g., a specific student's need for an accommodation) unless the student brings up the topic in front of others. Remind students of their role in making requests early and contributing to a positive relationship. Communicate effectively with teaching assistants (TAs) about student accommodations.

- Many professors advise on the course syllabus that students with disabilities should make an office appointment if they need to discuss accommodations. This gesture makes students feel more comfortable about approaching the professor.
- Our campus disability service protocol for requesting accommodations asks students to meet and discuss needed accommodations with faculty members. I have always felt this was an important process in terms of self-advocacy, as well as a way to add clarity and set coursework off on the right foot.

- When instructors address individual needs in a confidential manner, this encourages students to come forward with specific needs, thus increasing their chances of reaching their full potential in the class.
- It is important for students to recognize their roles in making requests early and otherwise developing positive relationships with faculty by applying skills in self-advocacy and problem-solving.
- Being flexible is a good skill to have in the self-advocacy tool kit. I usually initiate my accommodation request with the primary course instructor. In the Physics Department I worked with the course program director for exam accommodations. When I took courses in the Psychology and Mathematics departments, I would often take exams in a department conference room. Being flexible is a good skill to have in the self-advocacy tool kit.
- There were occasional instances when I arranged my accommodations with the course faculty, but the TA wasn't informed. This happened in a chemistry course, where I was instructed to return to a TA mailbox an exam I took at Disability Services. When the TA found the exam in her box, I was accused of cheating and not turning in my exam at the end of class. This was frustrating and demeaning. The incident was resolved after I explained to the TA that I had a disability and had arranged accommodations with the professor. I told the TA I was following the professor's instructions and if there was a concern, he should be consulted.

INTERACTION

Encourage regular and effective interactions between students and the instructor and ensure that communication methods are accessible to all participants.

Promote effective communication. Employ interactive teaching techniques. Face the class, speak clearly, use a microphone if your voice does not project adequately for all students, and make eye contact with students. Consider requiring a meeting with each student. Supplement in-person contact with online communication. Use straightforward language, avoid unnecessary jargon and complexity, and use student names in electronic, written, and in-person communications.

- Several of my professors required a student-instructor meeting. Those who did this tended to develop a strong rapport with their students. Personal connections are an important part of learning for many students.
- Effective communication is crucial. Most students default to using e-mail, which is an accessible form of communication for most students, including those with disabilities. Phone and in-person meetings are also used to coordinate work between students.
- Although e-mail is technically accessible to most students, it is important for an instructor to understand that there are students for whom written communication is less efficient than verbal communication. The use of e-mail should not replace the availability of the instructor after class and during office hours.
- For prearranged appointments with my instructor, I am usually able to secure a sign language interpreter. However, there are times when I may want to communi-

cate with the instructor on short notice. It is helpful when the instructor is open to regular communication through e-mail.

Make interactions accessible to all participants. For example, use a telephone conference only if all students can participate, given their abilities to hear, speak, and meet, and their schedule constraints. Also, require that small groups communicate in ways that are accessible to all group members. Be flexible regarding interaction strategies.

- Professors who are approachable and have some knowledge of disability issues can help make a student comfortable by suggesting an alternative communication strategy, if needed.
- E-mail is an accessible method of communication for many students with disabilities. It also provides the best options for students and faculty with conflicting schedules.

Encourage cooperative learning. Assign group work for which learners must support each other and employ different skills and roles. Encourage different ways for students to interact with each other (e.g., in-class discussion, group work, and Internet-based communication). Ensure full participation by insisting that all students participate; facilitate their participation as needed.

- Group work can make it possible for students with disabilities to build on their strengths. For example, a student who has a mobility impairment and cannot perform the physical manipulations required in an assignment can take on a different role, such as reading the instructions or taking notes with a laptop computer equipped with assistive technology.
- To ensure the active participation of everyone, an instructor asked all students in a group, including one who was deaf, to select communication strategies and task assignments so that everyone was able to participate.

PHYSICAL ENVIRONMENTS AND PRODUCTS

Ensure that facilities, activities, materials, and equipment are physically accessible to and usable by all students, and that all potential student characteristics are addressed in safety considerations.

Ensure physical access to facilities. Use classrooms, labs, workspaces, and fieldwork sites that are accessible to individuals with a wide range of physical abilities.

- In an organic chemistry lab, many of the tasks involved fine motor skills and students needed to stand for the duration of 3- to 4-hour lab sessions. The professor could have addressed these issues through UDI.

Arrange instructional spaces to maximize inclusion and comfort. Arrange seating to encourage participation, giving each student a clear line of sight to the instructor and visual aids and allowing room for wheelchairs, personal assistants, sign language interpreters, captionists, and assistive technology. Minimize distractions for students with a range of attention abilities (e.g., put small groups in quiet work areas). Work within constraints to make the environment as inclusive as possible. Encourage administrators to apply UD principles in facility design and renovation.

- A clear line of sight is particularly important when an oral interpreter or sign language interpreter is present.
- Ideally, seats with sufficient room for wheelchairs and assistive technology are scattered around the room, so that each student can choose a seat that is comfortable and maximizes learning.

Ensure that everyone can use equipment and materials. Minimize nonessential physical effort and provide options for operation of equipment, handles, locks, cabinets, and drawers from different heights, with different physical abilities, with one hand, and by right- and left-handed students. Use large print to clearly label controls on lab equipment and other educational aids, using symbols as well as words. Provide straightforward, simple oral and printed directions for operation and use.

- It is helpful when instructors put students who have complementary skills in each group.

Ensure safety. Develop procedures for all students, including those who are blind, deaf, or wheelchair users. Label safety equipment in simple terms, in large print, and in a location viewable from a variety of angles. Consider the impact of specific disabilities on emergency procedures. Provide safety instructions, as well as instructions for specific equipment, in writing prior to class. Repeat printed directions orally.

- When safety instructions are provided in electronic format before class, it gives students who rely on computers for access a chance to familiarize themselves with the instructions ahead of time and refer back to them as needed.
- Quite often, laboratory work includes the use of hazardous materials and substances. For people who are deaf or hard of hearing, it is imperative that oral instructions on safe handling and disposal of materials are also supplemented with instructions in a printed format.

DELIVERY METHODS

Use multiple instructional methods that are accessible to all learners.

Select flexible curriculum. Choose textbooks and other curriculum materials that address the needs of students with diverse abilities, interests, learning styles, preferences, and other characteristics. When possible, use curriculum materials that are well organized, emphasize important points, provide references for gaining background knowledge, include comprehensive indices and glossaries, and have chapter outlines, study questions, and practice exercises. Consider technology-based materials that provide prompting, feedback, opportunities for multiple levels of practice, background information, vocabulary, and other supports based on student responses.

- Using technology is often the best approach to making learning more flexible. Students find it helpful when a course instructor makes good use of a course Web site for the course syllabus, calendar, and other materials.
- It is important that Web-based materials be offered in a format that is accessible, particularly to students who are blind and using text-to-speech technology, which can only access Web content that is in text-based format. For example, often PDF

documents cannot be read by students who are blind and using speech- or braille-output technology. Text-based materials are accessible to these students and also more convenient to those using word-finding features to locate specific passages.

- A search engine course I took had one of the worst course Web pages I have ever used. The Web page consisted of a long, single page that listed course policies, materials, and resources and required excessive scrolling. It was very difficult for any student to use. Materials were easily buried, and there were no chapters or navigational controls. What is interesting is that the informatics program, like many other departments, provides templates for course Web sites, so that students do not need to acclimate themselves and learn how to use a new Web site every quarter. I am not sure why the professor chose not to use the template. These templates also provide an e-mail address that can be used to give anonymous feedback to the course instructor.

Make content relevant. Put learning in context. Incorporate multiple examples and perspectives with respect to specific concepts to make them relevant to individuals with diverse characteristics such as age, ability, gender, ethnicity, race, socioeconomic status, and interests.

- A portion of the informatics course work is borrowed from the library science field. In many of our theory-based courses, we would read a number of seminal papers. These readings were valuable to me because the teachers would go to great lengths to augment them with discussions of historic significance by providing real-world examples.
- The ability of instructors to relate the subject matter to their own experience helps students understand both the material and its importance.
- One of my favorite classes was Computer-Supported Collaborative Work. This class was based on a lot of theory; every article we read cited a real-world case study. It was easy for students to relate what they were learning to something they had experienced in a job or internship.
- The university can benefit students by hiring staff with diverse backgrounds and perspectives so that a college education as a whole can be seen as a mosaic of different and authentic perspectives.

Provide cognitive supports. Summarize major points, give background and contextual information, deliver effective prompting, provide scaffolding tools (e.g., outlines, class notes, summaries, study guides, and copies of projected materials with room for taking notes), and other cognitive supports. Deliver these materials in printed form and in a text-based electronic format. Provide opportunities for gaining further background information, vocabulary, and different levels of practice with variable levels of support. Encourage and support students to develop their own scaffolding materials.

- When they are made available online before a course begins, outlines or notes can be used by students to prepare for the first class session. Providing such materials is particularly helpful in courses without textbooks.
- I find it very helpful when professors make copies of their PowerPoint slides available to students in electronic and paper format. Without them, I was stressed during class and too focused on taking down all the material in my notes that was

covered in the PowerPoint slides. As a result, I didn't participate in class discussions, and I think it may have distracted me from the lecture.

- I learn most effectively from generating and organizing my own outline, notes, and study guides. I learn best and make sense of the material when I read the text, process the information, and then think about it again as I formulate and compose my notes. Although it is time-consuming, I prefer to write my notes by hand because I am a very kinesthetic person and physically writing out notes, instead of typing, helps to reinforce material in my brain. These personalized notes are also very important when I refer back to the material because they are often written to emphasize material that I struggled with.

Provide multiple ways to gain knowledge. Keep in mind that learning styles and levels of familiarity with background material vary among students. Use multiple modes to deliver content; when possible allow students to choose from multiple options for learning; and motivate and engage students. Consider lectures, collaborative learning options, small group discussions, hands-on activities, Internet-based communications, online review materials, educational software, fieldwork, and so forth.

- For those who do not catch the concept the first time, a second mode of presentation can enhance the understanding of that concept.

Deliver instructions clearly and in multiple ways. Provide instructions both orally and in printed form. Ask for questions and have students repeat directions and give feedback.

- There is a certain amount of stress associated with receiving only verbal instructions for a homework assignment or paper. Though I take detailed notes, I can never be sure I have recorded all the instructions correctly. Providing a written document (either paper-based, electronic, or both) and supplementing it with a verbal explanation is most helpful to all students.
- Most students are not familiar enough with the objective of an assignment when it is first introduced to formulate all the questions they may have. It is helpful when professors provide their e-mail addresses, a class list, or a message board for students to ask questions on their own as they arise.

Make each teaching method accessible to all students. Consider a wide range of abilities, disabilities, interests, learning styles, and previous experiences when selecting instructional methods. Provide the same means of participation to all students—identical when possible, equivalent when not. Vary teaching methods.

- Supplementing a lecture with visuals and printed materials, such as a lecture outline, not only benefits a student who is deaf or hard of hearing but also provides a richer experience for all students. This idea is great in theory but more difficult to realize in practice.
- Part of the student's role is learning to adapt to different delivery methods; this will serve them well in the work world.
- Some instructors continue to lecture with their back to the class while writing on the white board. This makes it impossible for me to lip-read and follow what is being written. If an instructor can take the time first to write and then face the

class, not only would it be easier for me but also the eye contact and face-to-face engagement would be much more engaging for all students.
- I agree that instructors should not be discussing things while facing the board, but it is also important that they clearly verbalize what they are writing while they are writing, so that students who are visually impaired are able to take accurate notes. This is particularly important in scientific courses where an accurate verbalization of mathematical expressions and verbal descriptions of illustrations are critical to the visually impaired student's ability to follow along in class.

Use large visual and tactile aids. Use manipulatives to demonstrate content. Make visual aids as large as is feasible (e.g., use large, bold fonts on uncluttered overhead displays and use a computer to enlarge microscope images).
- Large visual and tactile aids help students with limited vision, as well as those who are visual and tactile learners. Students and instructors should also be aware of the availability of photocopy machines and technology that can produce materials in a larger size when needed.

INFORMATION RESOURCES AND TECHNOLOGY

Ensure that course materials, notes, and other information resources are engaging, flexible, and accessible for all students.

Select materials early. Choose printed materials and prepare a syllabus early to allow students the option of beginning to read materials and work on assignments before the course begins. Allow adequate time to arrange for alternate formats, such as books in audio format or in braille, which, for textbooks, can take longer than a month.
- It is important for the faculty to be organized so that students can buy their textbooks and prepare for the class. I typically contact professors the week before, or the first week of, the quarter to arrange course accommodations. I have found if I contact professors earlier, they have either not completed their syllabuses or are still grading finals from the previous quarter.
- I took a Usability Engineering course for which no textbooks were originally required. On the first day of class, however, it was announced that course textbooks were not going to be made available for purchase through the bookstore, and instead, students would need to make their own arrangements. The timing of the announcement did a huge disservice to students. Many were without textbooks until the fourth week of the quarter because of the variability of shipping options from online distributors.

Use multiple, redundant presentations of content that use multiple senses. Use a variety of visual aids and manipulatives.
- I had a biology teacher who brought in models of animals and plants that helped illustrate concepts.
- Professors who augment their lectures by writing information on the board or in overhead visuals are very helpful to some students.

Provide all materials in accessible formats. Select or create materials that are universally designed. Use textbooks that are available in a digital, accessible format with flexible features. Provide the syllabus and other teacher-created materials in a text-based, accessible electronic format. Use captioned videos and provide transcriptions for audio presentations. Apply accessibility standards to Web sites.

- Simply stated, students with disabilities benefit from access to the same software, textbooks, Web sites, and other materials their nondisabled peers use.
- While taking a program management course, which had a heavy emphasis on Microsoft Project, I used the Web-based software tutorials provided by the textbook publisher. This was a really helpful tool.
- My experience has taught me that accessible design happens or does not happen at the publishing house, which bundles CD and Web resources with books. Faculty may choose accessible resources but still teach in an inaccessible way.
- I have found that even when accessibility standards are applied to departmental Web sites, they are frequently not imposed on course Web sites, which are thrown together during the first week of the quarter.
- In many classes at larger colleges and universities, TAs are responsible for managing course Web sites and class materials. I think it is critical that an instructor work closely with the TA to address accessibility standards and ensure consistent accessibility of materials.
- Instructors sometimes link Web media content, such as Web-based video clips. To accommodate students with hearing impairments, instructors may want to determine beforehand if the clip is captioned or if transcripts are available.

Accommodate a variety of reading levels and language skills, when appropriate, given the goals of the course. Present content in a logical, straightforward manner and in an order that reflects its importance. Avoid unnecessary jargon and complexity and define new terms when they are presented. Create materials in simple, intuitive formats that are consistent with the expectations and needs of students with a diverse set of characteristics.

- Faculty need to remind themselves that there are students in the class for whom English is not a first language and that opportunities to reduce language complexity will benefit everyone.
- Deaf students who use American sign language as their primary language may find jargon and complex vocabulary especially confusing. Just as important, sign language interpreters may have a difficult time interpreting such vocabulary to a deaf student. A valuable universal design strategy in this situation is for the instructor to give the interpreters as well as the students a list of complex terms, vocabulary, and concepts to be used in the class. Ideally this is done before the beginning of the course so that interpreters have time to strategize the best way to convey content to deaf students and all students have an opportunity to plan ahead.

Ensure the availability of appropriate assistive technology. If computer or science labs are used, ensure that assistive technology for students with disabilities is available or can be readily acquired.

- My campus had a lab with a number of software and hardware products. Although I am most comfortable using accessible technology on my own personal machine, where my preferences can be saved, I have used text-to-speech software with headphones in the campus labs.

FEEDBACK

Provide specific feedback on a regular basis.

Provide regular feedback and corrective opportunities. Allow students to turn in parts of large projects for feedback before the final project is due. Give students resubmission options to correct errors in assignment or exams. Arrange for peer feedback when appropriate. Solicit feedback from students regarding course effectiveness.

- I took a Systems Analysis course in which we received all our grades at the end of the quarter. This was a source of frustration and hindered my learning. I received no feedback during the course that could have been used to improve my work.
- For any report writing in technical fields, professors should be aware of the revision process and apply it appropriately.
- There is a benefit to group work and collaboratively building on the ideas of your peers, but peer feedback should not reduce the need for faculty to review student work. Instructors should keep in mind that some student feedback can be valuable, but frequently other students don't take the exercise seriously and provide meaningless feedback.
- Professors should encourage discussion and actually incorporate student feedback and comments into their course design and content.
- One professor asked for feedback in the middle of the quarter, not just about his own performance but also about how students felt the class was progressing. I did not see a notable change in his style, but the intent was greatly appreciated.

ASSESSMENT

Regularly assess student progress using multiple accessible methods and tools, and adjust instruction accordingly.

Set clear expectations. Keep academic standards consistent for all students, including those who require accommodations. Provide a syllabus with clear statements of course expectations, assignment descriptions, and deadlines, as well as assessment methods and dates. Include a straightforward grading rubric.

- It is helpful if a syllabus and grading rubric are presented to students on day one of a class and posted in an accessible format on a course Web site. Academic standards should be consistent for all students, including those with disabilities.

Provide multiple ways to demonstrate knowledge. Assess group and cooperative performance as well as individual achievement. Consider using traditional tests with a variety of formats (e.g., multiple choice, essay, short answer), papers, group work, demonstrations, portfolios, and presentations as options for demonstrating knowledge. Give students choices in assessment methods when appropriate. Allow students to use information technology to complete exams.

- I have a great deal of respect for professors who choose written answers over multiple-choice answers. It shows that they are willing to evaluate our unique thoughts, not just what we crammed in the night before.
- I think choices in assessment methods can work, but grading fairness is a huge issue if several methods are offered.

Monitor and adjust. Assess students' background knowledge and current learning regularly, informally (e.g., through class discussion), and/or formally (e.g., through frequent, short exams), and adjust instructional content and methods accordingly.

- I like it when instructors show an interest in how students are grasping content and adjust their teaching accordingly.

Test in the same manner in which you teach. Ensure that a test measures what students have learned and not their ability to adapt to a new format or style of presentation.

- It is helpful when the instructor provides some advance indication of which type of test the students should expect.

Minimize time constraints when appropriate. Plan for variety in students' ability to complete work by announcing assignments well in advance of due dates. Allow extended time on tests and projects, unless speed is an essential outcome of instruction.

- Just as a professor should use good judgment in giving appropriate time to complete an assignment, the student should be able to budget time to meet a variety of deadline assignment "styles."

ACCOMMODATION

Plan for accommodations for students whose needs are not met by the instructional design.

Know how to arrange for accommodations. Know campus protocols for getting materials in alternate formats, rescheduling classroom locations, and arranging for other accommodations for students with disabilities. Make sure that assistive technology can be made available in a computer or science lab in a timely manner. Ensure that the course experience is equivalent for students with accommodations.

- I don't expect a professor to be an expert about my disability; that's my job. What I do expect is that the professor will have a professional conversation with me and facilitate arrangements for my accommodations.
- One instructor offered to teach me verbal concepts of synoptic meteorology that other students learned by completing weather maps. When I asked him a few months before the beginning of the class what he thought might be the best way for me to participate in this highly visual work, he offered me the approach of weekly one-on-one meetings. I very much appreciated his willingness to go out of his way to help me learn the material in a manner that was effective for me.

- I have been very accommodating to instructors and willing to do whatever it takes, within reason, to succeed in class. I think I am successful with this because I provide the professor with my own accommodation ideas rather than asking them how they might suit my needs.
- If students take an exam in a classroom setting, they are allowed to ask the faculty and TAs questions. This is harder to do when a student is taking an exam in a disability services testing facility. To remedy this inequality, professors have included in the exam packet delivered to disability services written instructions and announcements that they plan to make to the entire class. One chemistry professor graciously called the disability services office in the middle of my exam to give me the opportunity to ask any questions. It meant a lot that he took my needs into account and made this extraordinary effort.
- In a Physical Oceanography class I took, the directions of the various currents and explanations for these directions were discussed in class, described in a textbook, and illustrated with maps. To reinforce understanding of the material, students were given the homework assignment of completing a map of the ocean currents. The instructor and I modified this assignment to accommodate my blindness, and instead I was quizzed orally about the locations and directions of the various currents. This arrangement provided me with an equivalent way of demonstrating my knowledge about the subject.

CONCLUSION

Students with disabilities do not always agree on the best practices for UDI. Overall, however, they make it clear that universal design strategies represent good teaching practice and minimize the need for specific accommodations. Important considerations are to create an environment that is welcoming and accessible to all students, employ a variety of teaching strategies, and ensure that each one is accessible to all students. Others are to make effective use of accessible information technology, make sure that course materials can be provided in accessible formats, ensure that products and environments are physically accessible and safe for everyone, interact often and in a variety of ways with students, assess students in multiple and accessible ways, and be prepared to provide accommodations to make learning activities fully accessible to students with disabilities. The disabled student services office, the instructor, and the student all have specific roles to play to ensure equal access to instruction for all students. All students benefit when universal design strategies are employed. Universally designed instruction is good instruction.

REFERENCES

Burgstahler, S. (2007). *Equal access: Universal design of instruction.* Seattle: University of Washington. Retrieved November 1, 2007, from http://www.washington.edu/doit/Brochures/Academics/equal_access_udi.html

Disabilities, Opportunities, Internetworking, and Technology (DO-IT). (2006). *DO-IT Prof: A project to help postsecondary educators work successfully with students who have disabilities.* Seattle: University of Washington. Retrieved November 1, 2007, from http://www.washington.edu/doit/Brochures/Academics/prof.html

DO-IT. (2007a). *AccessCollege: Systemic change for postsecondary institutions*. Seattle: University of Washington. Retrieved November 1, 2007, from http://www.washington.edu/doit/Brochures/Academics/access_college.html

DO-IT. (2007b). *DO-IT Admin: A project to help postsecondary campus services administrators work successfully with students who have disabilities*. Seattle: University of Washington. Retrieved November 1, 2007, from http://www.washington.edu/doit/Brochures/Academics/admin.html

The content of this chapter was developed under grants from the U.S. Department of Education Office of Postsecondary Education (grant numbers P333A990042, P333A020044, and P333A050064). However, this content does not necessarily represent the policy of the Department of Education, and you should not assume endorsement by the federal government.

7

The Benefits of Universal Design for Students with Psychiatric Disabilities

Al Souma
Deb Casey

The authors of this chapter discuss barriers to the learning process for students with psychiatric disabilities and suggest ways that applying universal design (UD) strategies can reduce these barriers as they enhance learning for all students. They offer practical suggestions for classroom teaching, assessment, and alternative assignments.

As coordinators of accommodations for students with disabilities, it has been our observation that most faculty are dedicated to teaching students theoretical and practical content without discrimination. However, they are continually challenged to create environments in which all students can achieve academic success. Accommodation requests to increase physical and sensory access in the classroom for students with disabilities are generally provided without objection. Examples of these accommodations include adjusting the height of a table for a wheelchair user, bringing in an oversized chair for a person large in stature, hiring an interpreter for a student who is deaf, and moving the location of a class when a student with mobility impairment is unable to access a classroom with entrance barriers. Requests for the removal of such physical and sensory barriers for individuals with disabilities are typically seen by faculty as reasonable.

During our tenure at various colleges and universities, however, we have spent many hours in consultation, workshops, and meetings with colleagues who question the justification for accommodations for students with disabilities that do not lend themselves to immediate visual identification, commonly referred to as invisible disabilities. Examples of invisible disabilities include learning disabilities, brain injuries, attention-deficit disorders, and psychiatric disabilities. Over the past decade, the number of students with invisible disabilities in postsecondary education has increased (Blacklock, Benson, Johnson, & Bloomberg, 2003; Matusow-Ayres, 2002; Weiner & Weiner, 1996). This trend increases the need for faculty members to learn strategies for effectively teaching these students. Universal design (UD) of instruction holds promise for addressing this need, while simultaneously improving the learning environment for other students.

In this chapter, we discuss barriers to the learning process for students with psychiatric disabilities and suggest UD strategies faculty members may employ that benefit students with psychiatric disabilities and others who have diverse learning abilities. Our experience suggests that a UD approach benefits students with and without disabilities, creates a productive and inclusive experience for everyone, and minimizes the need for additional accommodations for students with disabilities. Applying UD strategies in class provides "alternative teaching methods for individuals with different backgrounds, learning style abilities, and disabilities" and gives students flexible methods to learn materials and reflect knowledge (CAST, 2006, p. 2). The examples in this chapter affirm the application of UD principles for diverse learners.

PSYCHIATRIC DISABILITIES ON CAMPUS

Colleges throughout the country are reporting a marked increase in students with mental health disabilities, also referred to as psychiatric disabilities (Eudaly, 2002). These broad terms are used to describe a variety of mental health issues that vary in intensity and duration. A specific condition may have a biochemical origin, environmental origin, or a combination of both. A recent survey reveals a rise in the number of students taking psychiatric medication, from 9% in 1994 to 24.5% in 2003–04 (Gallagher, 2004). Learners with psychiatric disabilities may face educational challenges (Souma, Rickerson, & Burgstahler, 2003) that include those related to one or more of the following functional limitations:

- difficulty screening out environmental stimuli;
- difficulty sustaining concentration and stamina;
- difficulty handling time pressures and multiple tasks;
- difficulty interacting with others;
- fear of approaching authority figures, such as instructors or teaching assistants;
- difficulty responding to change;
- difficulty responding to negative feedback;
- severe test anxiety.

Students with psychiatric disabilities with whom we have worked have used one or more of the following accommodations:

- tape recorders;
- note-takers;
- consistent feedback from faculty members;
- extended test-taking time;
- testing in a quiet room;

- testing in alternative formats;
- written assignments to replace oral assignments;
- oral assignments to replace written assignments.

A negative aspect of providing traditional accommodations for specific students is the implication of an inherent dysfunction in the way these individuals learn without consideration of problems in the way the content is taught. In addition, accommodations often have the unintended consequence of singling out individual learners.

As educators critically assess the manner in which their instruction is delivered and learning is assessed, they may begin to appreciate the issues faced by students with psychiatric disabilities as learning differences. As explained by experts at the Center for Applied Special Technology, "Recent research in neurosciences shows that each brain processes information differently. The way we learn is as individual as DNA or fingerprints" (CAST, n.d.).

UNIVERSAL DESIGN AND INSTRUCTION

A model that shows promise in designing effective teaching, learning, and work-based learning environments in the academic setting is UD. This approach puts high value on full inclusion, accessibility, and usability for all students (Bar & Galluzzo, 1999; Burgstahler, 2007; Pliner & Johnson, 2004; Silver, Bourke, & Strehorn, 1998). Through the application of UD principles in classroom and clinical environments, faculty help all students without having to make major modifications to curriculum or clinical experiences for individual students.

UD emerged in the architectural field, and for over a decade it has been studied in the fields of education and technology (Burgstahler, 2007; CAST, 2006; Kalivoda, 2003; Pliner & Johnson, 2004). Researchers and practitioners have shown how academic content and materials developed in alternative formats, as well as diverse teaching strategies, can offer a host of benefits to students because they allow learners to customize and engage with instructional content in ways suited to their diverse learning styles and abilities (Abell, Bauder, & Simmons, 2004; Brown & Augustine, 2000; Casey-Powell, 2007). The conceptual framework of UD offers faculty and students new teaching and learning possibilities, as well as inclusive academic support provisions for students with disabilities.

Characteristics of universally designed instruction (PACE, 2002) include these:

- The essential components of the course are clearly defined.
- Prerequisite courses, knowledge, and skills are identified.
- Expectations are communicated clearly.
- The physical environment is accessible and conducive to learning.
- The climate encourages and supports interaction.
- Instructional methods recognize student diversity.
- Technology enhances instruction and increases accessibility.
- A variety of mechanisms for demonstrating knowledge are available.
- Feedback is clear, prompt, and frequent.
- Good study habits are encouraged and supported.

UD is designed to benefit students with disabilities, as well as those for whom English is a second language, nontraditional students, students uncomfortable with computer technology, and international students. "All learners, but especially those with learning disabilities, attention deficits, developmental disabilities, or affective difficulties, may encounter barriers when instructional materials are not designed in a flexible manner" (CAST, 2006). "Universal design education goes beyond accessible design for people with disabilities to make all aspects of the educational experience more inclusive for students, parents, staff, faculty, administrators, and visitors with a great variety of characteristics" (Burgstahler, 2007). Applying UD principles to teaching, assignments, and assessments promotes the greatest amount of learning and offers all students opportunities to express their knowledge without adaptation or retrofitting of lectures, assignments, or assessment practices. The end result is to reduce the need for traditional accommodations for students with psychiatric and other disabilities.

Examples of best practices for instructors dedicated to meeting the needs of all students are consistent with UD. Chickering and Gamson (1987) suggest the following best practices for instruction:

- encouraging student-faculty contact
- encouraging cooperation among students
- encouraging active learning
- giving prompt feedback
- emphasizing time on task
- communicating high expectations
- respecting diverse talents and ways of learning

UNIVERSAL DESIGN STRATEGIES THAT BENEFIT STUDENTS WITH PSYCHIATRIC DISABILITIES

The rising numbers of students with invisible disabilities in postsecondary education increases the importance of employing teaching practices that address the diverse needs of these students. The adoption of UD strategies benefits all students, but it may particularly benefit students with psychiatric disabilities and reduce their need for accommodations. In this section we point out how UD strategies might benefit students with psychiatric disabilities.

Classroom Teaching Strategies and Universal Design

Typical content delivery methods in the classroom require students to listen and take notes simultaneously, grasp key concepts quickly, listen attentively to long periods of verbal input, and negotiate interpersonal social relationships with other students. Some or all these activities may prove especially challenging for a student with a psychiatric disability (Draper & Jennings, 2003). Table 7.1 includes strategies that apply UD principles for the benefit of a student with a psychiatric disability in the classroom.

TABLE 7.1   Classroom Teaching: Universal Design Practices That Benefit Students with Psychiatric Disabilities

Issue Faced by a Student with a Psychiatric Disability	Universal Design Strategies That Benefit This Student and Others
Student may not be aware of accommodation options available.	Include course syllabus statement of accommodation (e.g., "If you need accommodations based on a documented disability, please contact Disability Support Services.").
Student may not be able to take notes while listening to a lecture.	Consider posting class notes on a Web site, or assign students to post notes; be sure that they are in a text-based accessible format.
Student may feel isolated from instructor and peers.	Strengthen faculty and student interactions by learning the names of students, encouraging office visits, personalizing feedback on student assignments, and mentoring.
	Encourage healthy student relationships by creating learning communities or study groups and modeling healthy exchanges when talking to students.
Student may not initially grasp key concepts introduced later in the lecture.	Present new concepts at the beginning of class using blackboards/whiteboards, and review them before the lecture.
Student may struggle to absorb information delivered in a single learning modality.	Consider the use of visual aids, hands-on learning, and electronic aids that underscore main ideas. Simulations, role-playing, structured exercises, and challenging discussions can also enhance learning.
The delivery of information is affected by the instructor's manner and pace of speech, as well as how the instructor is physically positioned in the classroom.	Face the class, speak in a direct manner, and make eye contact. Pace speech in a manner that promotes comprehension and observation of student facial expressions of understanding and confusion.
Student may need guidance when preparing for exams.	Consider holding optional review sessions for students before exams or after the completion of chapters, major topics, or important concepts.

Testing Strategies and Universal Design

Faculty members typically assess student learning with quizzes, unit tests, midterms, and final exams. A student's complete course grade might be based on the results of one or two written exams. Exams often include true/false, multiple-choice, matching, and/or short-answer essay formats. Unfortunately, some students may have a grasp of course content not measured by one or more of these exam formats. Students who think more globally may have a wider perspective on a topic but may not be able to identify, for example, the year a particular bill was signed into legislation. Similarly, a student may not remember what year Social Security was implemented under President Roosevelt but understand clearly what led up to this historic event.

Other challenges posed by standard exams for students with psychiatric disabilities may occur when a student is experiencing sleep deprivation, panic attacks, or unpleasant side effects of a new medication regimen. The student may be forced to miss an exam completely due to a medical emergency. UD strategies can be effective in assessing the knowledge of students with a wide variety of learning styles and abilities, including those with psychiatric disabilities. Offering a variety of alternative assessment strategies allows a student to express ideas and concepts in ways best suited to each student. Table 7.2 illustrates a number of ways diverse learners, including those who have psychiatric disabilities, can be assessed.

Class Assignments and Universal Design

The traditional oral method of teaching challenges students who are unable to focus on lectures 100% of the time. Faculty members may want to consider offering assignments inside and outside the classroom that apply UD principles. Through activities that include some degree of peer-to-peer or hands-on interaction, students with psychiatric disabilities can focus more directly and engage in ways that are more meaningful to them. In-class writing assignments to be passed in by the end of a class session cause a tremendous amount of anxiety for some students. Students with psychiatric disabilities report that their level of anxiety greatly increases when they can-

TABLE 7.2   Testing Strategies: Universal Design Practices That Benefit Students with Psychiatric Disabilities

Potential Learning Style of a Student with a Psychiatric Disability	Types of Assessments to Complement Student Learning Styles
Expressive learner. A student may exhibit test anxiety during paper-and-pencil testing. This learner may perceive test-taking as overwhelming, and a test may be too narrow in focus to allow the student to express comprehension.	Alternative methods of expressing knowledge include portfolios, student verbal presentations, written research assignments completed at home, peer- and self-evaluations, or individual creative projects agreed on by student and instructor.
	Group presentations as an alternative to, or in addition to, written exams can also be built into an assessment.
Team or group support learner. Group learning is effective for a student who needs to discuss course content to learn material and demonstrate learning.	Case study analysis by individuals or groups may be an effective assessment strategy.
Collaborative learner. A student may work well in peer-to-peer teaching and learning activities.	Instructors may employ group-testing strategies in which grades are determined, in part, by the collective efforts of students.
Reflective learners. A student may work well writing independently and in self-reflective experience of course content.	Journaling about how theories apply to concepts taught in class may be an effective assessment method.
Technology-competent learner. One-to-one computer time may be most effective for a student who works better alone and/or without distraction.	Web-based assessment programs provide an interactive option for testing learning and conceptual understanding of processes and procedures.

TABLE 7.3   Class Assignments: Universal Design Practices That Benefit Students with
Psychiatric Disabilities

Issues Faced by a Student with a Psychiatric Disability	Alternative Assignments
Auditory teaching is a passive activity that may not engage the student.	In-class debating Case studies and discussion Brainstorming Cooperative learning projects
Producing written work in class may not reflect a student's best work.	In-class writing that can be taken home and refined.

not take an assignment home to rework and better represent their thinking. Over the years, students have informed us that their reason for dropping a class was related to having to complete in-class writing assignments, citing anxiety about spelling, sentence structure, and other issues. Table 7.3 gives examples of UD strategies for assessment that might benefit a student with a psychiatric impairment.

CONCLUSION

Universally designed teaching practices can have a positive academic impact on students with psychiatric disabilities as they enhance the learning environment for other students. The UD approach recognizes that all learners have unique skills, interests, and learning styles. UD strategies presented in this chapter include those for presenting information in the classroom, assessing student knowledge, and designing class assignments. Such applications of UD can lead to the need for fewer individual accommodations for students with psychiatric or other disabilities. Clearly, UD holds promise for creating a positive and healthy institutional climate of inclusion, promoting access and success, and demonstrating a commitment to nondiscrimination.

REFERENCES

Abell, M., Bauder, D., & Simmons, T. (2004). Universally designed online assessments: Implications for the future. *Information Technology and Disability, 10*(1). Retrieved June 1, 2007, from http://www.rit.edu/~easi/itd/itdv10n1/abell.htm

Bar, L., & Galluzzo, J. (1999). *The accessible school: Universal design for educational settings.* Berkeley, CA: MIG Communications.

Blacklock, B., Benson, B., Johnson, D., & Bloomberg, L. (2003). *Needs assessment project: Exploring barriers and opportunities for college students with psychiatric disabilities.* Minneapolis: University of Minnesota, Office of Multicultural & Academic Affairs, Disability Services.

Brown, P. J., & Augustine, A. (2000). *Summary of the findings of the 1999–2000 screen reading field test: Inclusive comprehensive assessment system.* Newark: University of Delaware, Education Research and Development Center. Retrieved February 1, 2006, from http://www.rdc.udel.edu/reports/t000071.pdf

Burgstahler, S. E. (2007). *Universal design of instruction: Definition, principles, guidelines, and examples.* Seattle: University of Washington. Retrieved October 1, 2007, from http://www.washington.edu/doit/Brochures/Academics/instruction.html

Casey-Powell, D. A. (2007). Students with psychological disabilities in allied health sciences programs: Enhancing access and retention. In J. L. Higbee, D. B. Lundell, & I. M. Duranczyk (Eds.), *Diversity and the postsecondary experience* (pp. 87–102). Minneapolis: University of Minnesota, Center for Research on Developmental Education and Urban Literacy.

The Center for Applied Special Technology (CAST). (n.d.). *What is universal design for learning?* Wakefield, MA. Retrieved February 6, 2007, from http://www.cast.org/research/udl/index.html

The Center for Applied Special Technology (CAST). (2006). *Universal design for learning. Frequently asked questions.* Wakefield, MA. Retrieved October 1, 2007, from http://www.ode.state.or.us/initiatives/elearning/nasdse/udlfaqs.pdf

Chickering, A. W., & Gamson, Z. F. (1987). *Seven principles for good practice in undergraduate education.* Washington, DC: American Association for Higher Education (ERIC Document Reproduction Service No. ED282491).

Draper, M. R., & Jennings, J. (2003). *Factor analysis and concurrent validity of a university counseling center presenting problems checklist.* Austin: University of Texas–Austin Counseling and Mental Health Center, The Research Report of the Research Consortium of Counseling and Psychological Services in Higher Education. Retrieved on April 1, 2007, from http://www.utexas.edu/student/cmhc/research/rescon.html

Eudaly, J. (2002). *A rising tide: Students with psychiatric disabilities seek services in record numbers.* (Monograph No. 8N). Washington, DC: George Washington University HEATH Resource Center.

Gallagher, R. (2004). *National survey of counseling centers directors.* Alexandria, VA: International Association of Counseling Services.

Kalivoda, K. S. (2003). Creating access through universal instructional design. In J. L. Higbee, D. B. Lundell, & I. M. Duranczyk (Eds.), *Multiculturalism in developmental education* (pp. 25–34). Minneapolis: University of Minnesota, Center for Research on Developmental Education and Urban Literacy.

Matusow-Ayres, H. (2002). More students with psychiatric problems may be enrolled in your classes. *Student Affairs Today, 4*(3), 10–16.

Pliner, S., & Johnson, J. (2004). Historical, theoretical, and foundational principles of universal design in higher education. *Equity of Excellence in Education, 37*, 105–113.

Post-Secondary Academic and Curriculum Excellence (PACE). (2002). *Universal design: Applications in postsecondary education.* Little Rock, AR: University of Arkansas. Retrieved on April 17, 2007, from http://www.ualr.edu/pace/udcd/intro.html

Souma, A., Rickerson, N., & Burgstahler, S. (2003). *Psychiatric disabilities in postsecondary education: Universal design, accommodations, and supported education.* Seattle: DO-IT, University of Washington. Retrieved October 1, 2007, from www.ncset.hawaii.edu/institutes/mar2004/papers/pdf/Souma_revised.pdf

Silver, P., Bourke, A., & Strehorn, K. (1998). Universal instructional design in higher education: An approach for inclusion. *Equity and Excellence in Education, 31*(2), 47–51.

Weiner, E., & Weiner, J. (1996). Concerns and needs of university students with psychiatric disabilities. *Journal of Postsecondary Education and Disability, 12*(1), 2–8.

8

The Contribution of Universal Design to Learning and Teaching Excellence

Adele Darr
Richard Jones

The authors of this chapter discuss the evolution of the Center for Learning and Teaching Excellence at Arizona State University to include universal design (UD) in its professional development offerings. The content may be useful to other schools as they institutionalize the UD content into the offerings of teaching and learning centers.

The Center for Learning and Teaching Excellence (CLTE) acts as a clearinghouse for information to support faculty and foster excellence in teaching at Arizona State University (ASU). In addition to its comprehensive Web site, the CLTE has a library of books, journals, and monographs that focus on the improvement of teaching and learning. Topics include the use and assessment of active learning and learner-centered strategies, such as cooperative learning, case teaching, and the use of technology in the classroom. Established in the 1980s, the CLTE has evolved to provide comprehensive services to faculty as they work with students. Although the authoritative structure of the CLTE has varied through the years, it currently reports to the academic provost's office. The CLTE is located in a central building on the main campus, with plans for satellite offices on the other three campuses of ASU. Over the past two years, universal design (UD) concepts have been infused into the majority of the components of the CLTE. According to its own Web site (CLTE, n.d.), the CLTE's mission is

> to assist faculty in achieving their full potential as teacher/scholars in support of enhanced student learning. To realize this mission we:
>
> • provide a physical location and resources so faculty can broaden their pedagogical exploration and reflection.

- design, promote and host activities so individuals responsible for teaching may form professional and collaborative connections across the academic enterprise.
- focus on the individual, providing value-added consultation to teaching corps, departments, and colleges.
- serve as a clearinghouse for research on instructional strategies that enhance teaching and learning and increase student success.

CLTE is committed to reflective practice in understanding learning objectives, constructing learning activities, and assessment of student learning.

The CLTE actively pursues several goals to promote the advancement of this mission. The first goal is to assist faculty, programs, and departments in assessing and developing instructional approaches. UD is an integral part of the discussion in development of these instructional approaches (i.e., designing a multimodal approach to teaching). According to Ron Mace, UD is "the design of products and environments to be usable by all people, to the greatest extent possible, without the need for adaptation or specialized design" (Mace, n.d.).

The next goal includes providing instructional assistance to new faculty members. Always crucial to promoting UD concepts is the inclusion of new faculty in discussions and in the design of their courses. The CLTE also provides workshops designed to enhance specific instructional practices, a fundamental part of which is UD. Collaborating with other campus units to secure grant money for developing new courses, exploring innovative teaching methods, and researching effective instruction encourages the creation of multimodal teaching strategies that are accessible for all students within a campus unit, regardless of level of ability.

The CLTE serves as a clearinghouse for information about activities, events, resources, and projects that may enhance teaching and learning. Included in resources are written materials and contact persons who are knowledgeable about applying UD to courses. In on-site and online courses faculty are encouraged to reflect on their use of instructional technologies and evaluate their course materials, utilizing CLTE checklists that include UD principles. The CLTE provides handouts and materials on how to develop inclusive environments within the classroom, as well as videos providing hands-on examples of UD applications. The Disability Resource Centers on all of the ASU campuses are very involved with the CLTE and assist in providing workshops as well as updated information for faculty.

The CLTE was developed to assist experts in academic fields in the dissemination of knowledge to the greatest number of students. All faculty are invited to attend the workshops offered. New faculty are targeted through e-mail messages and personal invitations. Materials relating to the CLTE and UD are distributed at all new faculty orientations. Future faculty, who often begin their teaching careers as teaching assistants (TAs), are also invited through announcements to TAs. The CLTE Web site, a resource for all workshops and presentations, has been redesigned recently to focus more on UD. This focus on UD and student-centered learning can be seen in all the CLTE materials.

Student-centered learning is a general philosophy with the goal of developing a learning experience that, as much as possible, matches content with each student's abilities and interests. This philosophy has led to the CLTE's presenting workshops each semester, such as Enhancing Learning-Centered Education with Technology; Large Lecture Series: Faculty Panel; Course and Syllabus Design; Effective Discussions: Give Them Something to Talk About; Good Technology, Sound Pedagogy: Learning by Doing; Responding to Writing: The Good, the Bad, and the Ugly; Enhancing Teaching with Presentation Graphics; Interactive PowerPoint; Student Response System/Clickers in the Classroom; Learning Styles; Universal Design in Teaching; and Learning and Critical Thinking for Student Learning (CAST, n.d.; Spencer & Logan, 2005).

One of the workshops offered for faculty is Universal Design in Teaching and Learning. Participants learn how students with differing abilities, cultural and linguistic backgrounds, and ways of learning benefit from curricula that are universally designed—in other words, *all* students benefit from courses designed using a universal approach. This workshop introduces faculty to practical UD principles that can be applied to either existing or new courses. Participants learn to apply UD principles to teaching and learning activities in their courses and are engaged in the development of learning activities that employ UD principles.

These workshops represent an underlying belief in multifaceted instruction with student-centered learning and the use of technology to enhance learner and teacher effectiveness. These concepts are essential to the use of UD for learning and to reaching the CLTE goals. UD becomes the matrix for the application of instructional skills in the classroom setting, utilizing an educational philosophy that incorporates the best teaching strategies and techniques into a system that can be used by anyone who wishes to teach everyone.

The philosophy of UD for learning incorporates a student-centered focus inclusive of students with disabilities. The use of technology is not only a student learning accommodation but also an instructional strategy for all students. Applications of UD incorporate multiple means of representation to give learners various ways of acquiring information and knowledge. Representation may occur in written formats, field experience, illustrations, discussion, and other products. Providing multiple means of engagement to tap into learners' interests and offer appropriate challenges can increase motivation to learn. Assisting students to find an area of interest and then pursue it provides motivation for them to increase their learning.

When developing mechanisms of evaluation, the teacher can apply UD by offering learners alternatives for demonstrating what they know. A classic example is the teacher who requires a final project that is presented in one of three formats: a written paper, a PowerPoint presentation, or a class discussion. Each format evaluates the student's learning, but the choices account for individuality among the students.

CONCLUSION

In order to design instruction for the entire population of students, it is important to understand the diversity, problems, tools, and abilities of students. Students and faculty who can benefit from the application of UD in learning and teaching experiences include those with and without disabilities. Incorporating UD within those learning opportunities in a center that supports educational enhancement for all faculty is an absolute necessity for establishing an inclusive campuswide educational environment.

REFERENCES

The Center for Applied Special Technology (CAST). (n.d.). *What is universal design for learning?* Retrieved September 7, 2007, from http://www.cast.org/research/udl/

Center for Learning and Teaching Excellence. (n.d.). *Mission statement.* Tempe: Arizona State University. Retrieved on November 26, 2007, from http://clte.asu.edu/about/mission/

Mace, R. (n.d.). *About universal design (UD).* Raleigh: North Carolina State University, The Center for Universal Design. Retrieved March 26, 2006, from http://www.design.ncsu.edu/cud/about_ud/about_ud.htm

Spencer, S. S., & Logan, K. R. (2005). Improving students with learning disabilities ability to acquire and generalize a vocabulary learning strategy. *Learning Disabilities: A Multidisciplinary Journal, 13,* 87–94.

9

Universal Course Design
A Model for Professional Development

Kirsten Behling
Debra Hart

Universal Course Design (UCD) addresses the diversity of students' learning styles in today's college classrooms. UCD provides faculty with concrete strategies to vary the development of course curriculum, instruction, assessment, and the environment in which they teach so that all students have equal access to the course. The University of Massachusetts–Boston's Equity and Excellence in Higher Education project used the concept of UCD in its work with 15 community colleges and universities to help over 100 faculty members redesign their courses. In this chapter, the authors discuss UCD as a professional development strategy for faculty to better educate their increasingly diverse students.

> I am struck by the fact that, in the body of work that describes students with disabilities in postsecondary education, there is a substantial focus and reliance on accommodating the disability, the things that are "wrong" with the student, but little or nothing on how college faculty can adjust the way they teach to better reach the increasingly diverse student body.
> *—College graduate and self-advocate with disabilities*

College offers all students exciting opportunities, including meeting new friends, living independently, exploring current interests, and paving the road toward a career. Many of today's college students are returning after years in the workforce or the military, do not speak English fluently, are not fully prepared for coursework, or have a disability. Experiences with the increasing diversity of today's student body forces the realization that no two students learn alike (Center for Teaching and Learning, 2001; Davis, 1999; Gay, 2000; Harrison, 2006; Indiana State University, 2003; Meacham, McClellan, Pearse, & Greene, 2003). Some students learn best through lecture, others do extremely well with visual stimulation (e.g., graphics, videos, demonstrations), and others excel at hands-on learning (e.g., lab work, internships, experiments). To ensure that the highest-quality education is available to all students, college faculty should know how to broaden their course curriculum and instruction and assessment methods. There are few professional development opportunities for faculty that address this need.

For eight years, Equity and Excellence in Higher Education (E&E), a project of the University of Massachusetts–Boston/Institute for Community Inclusion, has worked with fifteen institutions of higher education providing professional development on how to teach *all* students effectively. The project has assisted faculty in diversifying their college courses by implementing the principles of Universal Course Design (UCD).

The authors of this chapter discuss the concept of UCD as a professional development tool for faculty at institutions of higher education to use proactively to reach all learners. The chapter highlights the importance of UCD in providing faculty with both the strategies and the confidence to diversify their teaching. Specifically, we (1) define UCD; (2) describe what a UCD core team is and how it can be used to increase faculty knowledge and build confidence in implementing UCD strategies; and (3) discuss the process used to successfully implement UCD in institutions of higher education and share examples of faculty work.

DEFINING UNIVERSAL COURSE DESIGN

UCD is built on the body of literature on universal design for learning (UDL) and universal design of instruction (UDI). The Center for Applied Special Technology (CAST) developed the UDL framework to create greater access to and flexibility in all aspects of learning, primarily for students in K–12 public education. Specifically, CAST developed three principles of UDL:

1. To support recognition learning and provide multiple flexible methods of presentation.
2. To support strategic learning and provide multiple flexible methods of expression and apprenticeship.
3. To support affective learning and provide multiple flexible options for engagement (Hall, Strongman, & Meyer). When operationalized, these three principles have been shown to be effective in reaching the diverse learning styles of all students, including those with disabilities.

The University of Washington's Disabilities, Opportunities, Internetworking, and Technology (DO-IT) Center developed strategies for UDI. Similar to CAST's concept of UDL, UDI expands on the seven principles of universal design for products and architecture, which was developed by architect Ron Mace, and applies them to academics. The DO-IT Center (Burgstahler, 2007) lists strategies for the application of UDI in eight areas:

1. Class climate
2. Interaction
3. Physical environments and products

4. Delivery methods
5. Information resources and technology
6. Feedback
7. Assessment
8. Accommodation

The DO-IT Center has applied the principles of universal design to higher education, advising faculty and disability support personnel about the benefits of rethinking the design of college courses to be more inclusive of all students (Burgstahler, 2007).

Building on the work of CAST and DO-IT, the E&E project developed UCD to be more responsive to course design and instructional and assessment methods, including the environment in which students are taught, and to acknowledge the culture from which the student comes. On the basis of past work with higher-education professionals, the E&E project recognized the need to create a concept specific to higher education, paying attention to course design, instruction, assessment, the environment, and the culture of each student. The academic, social, and conceptual differences among elementary, secondary, and postsecondary schools often make it difficult for college faculty to relate easily to the K–12 focus common to UDL.

The DO-IT Center's work applies directly to postsecondary educators, offering examples and practical tips for rethinking the design of a college course. UCD mirrors much of this UDI initiative but simplifies it from eight distinct categories in the DO-IT model to four categories by renaming "physical environments and products" as "environment"; combining class climate, delivery methods, and feedback under the label "instruction"; and eliminating the accommodation planning item. (Accommodation planning occurs throughout the four categories of UCD, but instead of addressing the needs of one student, UCD addresses the needs of the majority of students. Although UCD does not eliminate the need for all accommodations, it does dramatically reduce the number of requested accommodations.) Further, UCD adds a focal area on culturally responsive pedagogy as it relates to all aspects of course design.

Having spent the previous six years working with more than 100 college faculty, the E&E project staff recognized the following key characteristics of college teachers: (1) faculty who are interested in becoming more effective teachers often claim a lack of resources and time for achieving this goal; (2) the easier a concept is to understand and to implement, the more likely faculty will adopt it; and (3) faculty are more willing to use UCD strategies if they can recognize how doing so affects a wide group of students, including those from culturally, socioeconomically, and academically diverse backgrounds. As a result, the E&E project developed UCD to be a simple idea that is easy to conceptualize and implement.

E&E staff define UCD as the design of college course curricula, instruction, assessment, and the environment to be usable by all students to the greatest extent possible without the need for accommodations (Equity & Excellence in Higher Education Project, 2007). In addition to the definition of UCD, concrete tools were designed to address the three common characteristics (cited above) that many college faculty display when introduced to universal design. These tools include (1) an easily accessible

Web site (www.eeonline.org), (2) a readily available peer support team (i.e., a UCD core team), and (3) real-life examples from a variety of academic disciplines to refer to when integrating UCD into a particular course.

Forming a Universal Course Design Core Team

The UCD core team composition varies from campus to campus, but it is typically composed of individuals who are responsible for supporting faculty. A UCD core team usually contains a college librarian; one representative each from the disability services office, the information technology (IT) department, the Center for Teaching and Excellence (or its equivalent), and the Office of Cultural Diversity;, and other individuals chosen by the team to guide the faculty in their efforts to incorporate UCD strategies into their courses. These individuals are selected for the core team because of their knowledge of specific campuswide services, their expertise, and their relationship to campus departments and students with which faculty are often unfamiliar. Some universities have added more members once the initial team is developed. The primary role of the UCD core team is to teach faculty about UCD strategies and to offer ongoing technical assistance through monthly meetings while faculty rework at least one component of their courses. Before faculty members join the UCD core team, the team itself completes a semester-long orientation on UCD. Training for the UCD core team is done by someone who is familiar with universal design and has access to a list of UCD resources. Once the team is trained, the team works through the semester as a peer-support group guiding five or more faculty members who are committed to learning about and infusing UCD into their courses.

The UCD core team meets with faculty monthly to assist them as they learn about and experiment with UCD strategies. Faculty members can choose to focus on a specific strategy (e.g., How do I lecture less and use other strategies more in my history course?), a specific tool (e.g., How do I post my notes on my course Web site?), or a specific course topic or assignment (e.g., How can I change the final assignment to be more universally designed without reducing the rigor of my course?). The UCD core team can help a faculty member by brainstorming different UCD strategies, identifying on- and off-campus resources to assist with a particular idea, and offering support to struggling teachers.

Faculty participating in the UCD core team are expected to fulfill certain requirements in exchange for the semester-long training and technical assistance they receive. Each faculty member must

- attend monthly UCD meetings;
- make at least one significant UCD addition to a course;
- disseminate their work to colleagues via word of mouth, faculty meetings, poster presentations;
- become mentors for a new group of faculty entering the UCD core team the following semester.

During the first meeting with the UCD core team, faculty members are told that they must make at least one significant change to a course over the semester with the assistance of the team. This requirement is meant to be flexible so as to let teachers choose which aspect of their course(s) they want to focus on and what tools to use. Following are three examples of how faculty effectively utilized UCD strategies in their courses.

- A history professor wanted to change his didactic style. He began with a small step: having his students spend the last 15 minutes of class working in groups to review the main points covered in class. By augmenting his lectures with group work, he gave his students more than one opportunity to engage with the course material. He has turned this UCD strategy into a daily occurrence and extended it to 20 minutes so that each group can share their ideas with the rest of the class.
- A biology professor was interested in using digital photography to document steps of a lab experiment. Through the UCD core team, he connected with the IT representative and another faculty member who had experience with digital cameras and gathered enough information to begin documenting his labs with digital photos. The IT representative helped him find extra digital cameras on campus and attended the first lab to show students how to take pictures and download them onto their computers. Students would then label each picture accordingly and turn it in as a lab report in addition to or in place of a traditional text-based report. The availability of digital cameras allowed students to choose how to document the lab process according to their learning preferences, thus demonstrating the flexibility and variability of UCD instructional methods.
- A French professor came to the team frustrated over the poor grades the students in her Introduction to French course received on their midterm exams. A team member from the Cultural Diversity Office referred her to a French student. Together the professor and the student collaborated on different assessment options that reflected French culture (students had the option of writing a French pop-cultural journal article or creating and acting out a radio interview between the DJ and the French president on the status of the national football team). At the next team meeting, the professor reported that the implementation of UCD resulted not only in better midterm grades but also a new enthusiasm in the course among her students and an increased appreciation of French culture.

Participating faculty are required to disseminate their experiences to their colleagues. The manner in which they do this can vary. Some colleges have created poster sessions at faculty fairs; other faculty members have given presentations and workshops at local and national conferences and departmental meetings. Ideally, each institution strives to create a collection of examples of universally designed work for new faculty who are just beginning to learn about UCD and to assist current faculty with new ideas for their courses. This collection can be shared through Web sites, binders, and videos.

At the end of the semester, faculty who have gone through the UCD training with the team evolve into mentors for the newest group of faculty joining the team the following semester. *The guidance of the UCD core team and evolution into mentorship are significant to sustaining the implementation of UCD principles on campus.* As they continue their work with UCD, many faculty still connect with the team or individual members of the team for advice and resources, but they have now become comfortable enough with the concepts of UCD to offer assistance to their colleagues. This innovative practice of using a campus-based core team to educate faculty about UCD and then turn those faculty into mentors for other faculty has proven to be an effective method for achieving sustainability of UCD on college campuses (The Equity & Excellence in Higher Education Project, 2007).

The constant presence of the UCD core team is vital to gaining faculty trust and increasing confidence around UCD. A comfortable and safe peer work group provides faculty with the opportunity to share successes and discuss problems. It can also be an opportunity to seek advice from faculty and staff from different departments, gain new ideas, and form relationships for future collaborative projects.

IMPLEMENTING UNIVERSAL COURSE DESIGN IN COLLEGE COURSES

As discussed earlier, there are four main components to which faculty should be attentive when incorporating the principles of UCD into their courses: (a) the course curriculum, (b) instruction, (c) assessment, and (d) the environment. Although faculty can concentrate on one component at a time, the authors strongly encourage them to consider all these components because they are typically interrelated. A series of steps can be followed to successfully add UCD to courses. The components, their corresponding steps, and examples of faculty implementation are discussed below.

(A) Steps for Adding Universal Course Design Strategies to a Course Curriculum

1. Determine the specific content, skills, and strategies to be learned.
2. Ask "How will my students access this information?"
3. Provide flexible media and materials to ensure access to information for all students, including those with sensory impairments.
4. Motivate and engage students based on their interests, cultural experiences, and applications.

Faculty approach this component of UCD differently, according to their course(s) and their comfort level with UCD. Most faculty begin by examining their course syllabus (see Table 9.1 for tips on how to create a UCD syllabus). They use the UCD tip sheet to ensure that the syllabus itself is accessible for all learners before zeroing in on one particular topic. A nursing professor at a university in Massachusetts revised her syllabus to include UCD strategies. She describes how she went a step further.

> The first day of class, I asked students to tell me about their experiences with nursing and what their favorite style of teaching has been. Interestingly enough, most said a combination of group work and hands-on activities. Once I found that out, I restructured my primary method of teaching and found that the students were more engaged, and I became more confident about my teaching style as a result. I have made sure to ask students to tell me a little about themselves and how they learn in every class I have taught since.

In another example a statistics professor at a community college in New Hampshire describes how he engages students in his courses.

TABLE 9.1   Tips for Reaching All Students with a Universal Course Design Syllabus

Tip	Traditional Method	Universal Course Design Method
Present information in at least two different formats.	Write the course schedule in paragraph or table form.	Highlight due dates on a graphic calendar.
Give students as many resources as possible.	List required texts.	List places where students might find the text.
Provide lots of background information but be brief.	List your name and contact information.	Give students a brief overview of who you are and why you are teaching this topic.
Build in flexibility.	State your office hour times and location.	Show your schedule on a calendar graphic. Provide a map of your office on campus. Give directions from the classroom to your office.
Go digital.	Hand out your syllabus in paper format at the beginning of the course.	Distribute the syllabus on a course Web site, in an e-mail, on a CD, and in other formats.
Less is better.	Put *everything* that students will need to know about the course on your syllabus.	Too much text and information is overwhelming. Give only the facts of the course. Make a separate handout with extra information. Post it online or pass it out when appropriate.

Source: Equity and Excellence in Higher Education: Universal Course Design (2005). Universal Course Design Instructional Strategies. Retrieved on November 2, 2007, from www.eeonline.org.

[I] begin my courses by asking students to tell me what their career interests are. When we're working with statistical data sets, I tell them they can either use the data set that I have assigned or find another data set that corresponds with their career interests. About 70% have done the latter and, as a result, are better able to relate what they are learning to their future careers. In fact, I have a few students who are using the analysis that we do in papers for other classes.

By using the third principle of making a course curriculum universally designed (i.e., provide flexible media and materials to ensure equal access to information and to learning), a history professor restructured his class on the civil rights movement.

[I] began by framing the topic with an essential question and then provided multiple ways for my students to answer the question, depending on how they chose to interact with the resources available to them. The resources that I provided included reading a historical text, going online and viewing and listening to historic first-person accounts of what happened, watching a captioned video in class and/or on the course Web site, and listening to or reading the transcript from a Skype call with a guest speaker who participated in the civil rights rallies. Interestingly, I found that the students tended to choose a resource that paralleled their primary learning style. In addition, I was thrilled that my students became much more engaged, both in and out of class. It was very inspiring.

One of the key factors to gaining faculty trust is to apply UCD in small steps. It is much more feasible to apply a UCD strategy to one course topic at a time than to change an entire course right away.

(B) Steps for Adding Universal Course Design Strategies to College Instruction

1. Use multiple and flexible methods of presentation.
2. Provide multiple models of correct performance, multiple opportunities to practice, and flexible opportunities to demonstrate skills.
3. Provide culturally responsive choices of content, tools, and learning context.

Instruction is often the most obvious place to begin incorporating UCD strategies. Many college faculty teach the way they were taught (Adams, 1992; Ambrose & Ambrose, 1995; Ehrmann, 1995; Felder, 1993; Webb, 2007). We often forget that the majority of college faculty were not taught how to be good teachers (Adams & Marchesani, 1992; Ambrose & Ambrose, 1995; Felder & Brent, 2003; Selden, Assad, & Greenburg, 1998). Yet most faculty want to be high-quality teachers, engage students, and watch students grow into professionals. Because of this, many teachers will readily absorb information and suggestions for applying UCD.

The E&E project created a table of UCD instructional strategies based on the ideas and tools that faculty created and used through their work with the project. Table 9.2 is a fluid document that continues to grow as faculty develop new ideas for ensuring equal access to their courses. It is organized into four columns, the first of which lists strategies that take less than 15 minutes to implement. These strategies are for those who are curious about UCD and want to try something quickly. The third column has strategies that take between 15 and 60 minutes to implement and may require more experience with specific kinds of technology. The second and fourth columns contain suggestions for appropriate times to use these strategies. Items included in the table are not exhaustive; they are only ideas to help the novice UCD user get started. Many faculty try a UCD instructional strategy, evaluate its effectiveness, and then alter their approach to teaching based on the results achieved with that strategy. This is a quick and often straightfo rward method for incorporating UCD strategies into a course. For example, a professor at a university in Vermont has been primarily using lecture to teach human development to 100 students at a time. After attending a UCD core team meeting, he reevaluated the effectiveness of his lectures.

After meeting with the UCD core team and starting to understand what UCD is and how it can positively affect my teaching, I noticed that after 20 minutes of lecturing my students' eyes began to look dazed, and they stopped taking notes. So I asked the team for some help in figuring out what instructional methods I could use. They suggested I give students an outline of what would be covered in class right before it began. Once I did this the students seemed to be grateful because I tend to wander with my lectures, so it kept them and me on track. I have also been really curious about podcasting and have read a lot about its use on college campuses. I connected with the instructional technologist here, who helped me to begin recording my lectures with an MP3 player. After class, I have been putting the audio file on my Web site for students to download onto their iPods. Students told me that they were really pleased with the podcasts and were better able to study for my exams.

An occupational therapy professor at a university in New Hampshire recognized the difficulty that students were having with studying for an upcoming exam regarding correct arm positions. She came up with the following solution, which provides students with multiple models of correct performance:

> While I was demonstrating the correct positioning of the therapist's arm, I had a student videotape what my hands were doing. I then put the video clips on my class Web site for students to access when they were studying. Each clip was only about 20–30 seconds long. The students were thrilled with the new study materials in addition to their texts and the pictures I passed out in class, and they reported that without those clips, they wouldn't have been able to pass their comps. The best part is that since then they have asked their other OT professors to do the same. I love the fact that the students are driving UCD implementation.

TABLE 9.2   Universal Course Design Instructional Strategies

Less Than 15 Minutes to Implement	When to Use This Strategy	15–60 Minutes to Implement	When to Use This Strategy
Organizing the Class/Clearly Stating Ideas with Universal Design			
Provide an agenda or flowchart at the beginning of class, highlight the order of topics and connections, and state the purpose.	Direct Interactive	Design an activity so that it builds on a previous one.	Direct Experiential Independent Interactive
Engage Students through Universal Design			
Seek personal experiences of students with the subject or topic and then integrate those experiences into the course.	Direct Indirect Experiential Independent Interactive	In a nonresponsive class, plan for student-owned course time, when students are working in teams or give presentations (student-directed learning).	Direct Indirect Experiential Interactive
Encourage Student Ownership of Knowledge through Universal Design			
Ask students to develop their own definitions of key topics rather than providing the definition—compare/contrast with "professional" or "textbook" definitions.	Direct Indirect Independent	Assist students in determining how they learn (kinesthetic, auditory, visual, etc.) by using a learning styles inventory.	Direct Indirect Independent
Universally Designed Videos/Pictures/Audios			
Show all video presentations with closed captioning on.	Direct Experiential	Search for video clips on the Internet (use keywords such as "MPEG" or "video clips" in your search).	Direct Experiential

TABLE 9.2   Universal Course Design Instructional Strategies *(continued)*

Less Than 15 Minutes to Implement	*When to Use This Strategy*	*15–60 Minutes to Implement*	*When to Use This Strategy*
Universally Designed PowerPoints/Overhead Presentations			
Distribute PowerPoint handouts and reflection sheets with prompts for information discussed in class.	Direct Experiential Independent	Incorporate charts, diagrams, or graphic representations of course material.	Direct Experiential Independent
Universally Designed Course Texts and Handouts			
Make texts available ahead of schedule to allow students to work at their own pace.	Direct Experiential Independent	Use graphic representation, maps, digital photos, videos, case studies, online journals, and so on.	Direct Experiential Independent
Universally Designed Instructional Delivery in the Classroom			
All differentiated activities should be equally engaging and challenging.	Direct Experiential Independent Interactive	Incorporate interdisciplinary teaching into class, work with professors and students from other disciplines, bring in guest speakers (or have students bring in guest speakers).	Direct Experiential Independent Interactive
Universally Designed Online Instruction and Use of Learning Management Systems (Blackboard, WebCT, and Moodle*)			
Provide guidelines for students regarding how to submit assignments, participate in discussions, and so on.	Direct	Create and monitor online debates between groups.	Direct Interactive
Universally Designed Office Hours			
Provide all contact information (including TTY number) on the syllabus at the beginning of the semester.	Direct	Hold office hours in an accessible location or online through e-mail, chat rooms, and video conferencing.	Direct Indirect Interactive
Using Technology to Increase Access for All Learners			
Use Mimio or Smartboard to record notes on the whiteboard and then post them on the course Web site, or e-mail them to students.	Direct Indirect Experiential Interactive	Use concept maps and graphic organizers to make explicit the links between practicum and the class topics and to depict the same written information in a different format.	Direct Experiential
Universally Designed Classrooms			
Make sure that the space is comfortable for students, accessible, noise-controlled, and allows for preferential seating.	Experiential Interactive	Make sure that workstations are at least 29 inches high, 20 inches deep, and 36 inches wide, with aisles 42–48 inches wide.	Experiential

Source: Equity and Excellence in Higher Education: Universal Course Design (2005). Universal Course Design Instructional Strategies. Retrieved on November 2, 2007, from www.eeonline.org.

*Moodle is a free course management system designed to help educators create effective online learning communities. Retrieved January 23, 2008, from http://moodle.org

Another professor recognized the cultural diversity of learners in her class and rethought the texts, examples, and resources she had planned to use to demonstrate her points.

> I teach an introductory writing course to incoming freshmen. Most of my texts are written by white male authors. Well, on the first day, I looked around the classroom and saw at least three different ethnic groups represented, and that was without probing for more detailed background information like religion, age, and sexuality. So I went back to my office and began to research not only other books that were written by people from Chinese and Indian cultures but also what those cultural beliefs were toward autobiographical writing. I found some really interesting things and decided to allow my students to choose which book they wanted to read. It led to some fascinating discussions, a lot of increased knowledge about other cultures, and a new appreciation for diverse authors. I plan to do this in each of my classes from now on.

(C) Steps for Adding UCD Strategies to College Assessment

1. Create two or more assessment choices for students to choose from to coincide with their favored learning styles.
2. Provide ongoing evaluation of what is working and what is not.
3. Change assessment methods according to the effectiveness of the instruction format.
4. Measure student performance across multiple levels.

Final papers and written exams have been used for decades to measure students' knowledge. They work well for students who have effective writing skills, who like the structure of 20-page papers, and who thrive on the pressure of getting an exam done on time. For students who do not typically succeed with these types of assignments, however, papers and exams can inhibit the accurate demonstration of what they have learned (Agran, 2006; Harrison, 2006; McGuire & Scott, 2006). By providing students with a choice of means to demonstrate their knowledge, faculty have increased the odds that students will actively connect with the material and accurately demonstrate what and how they learned. Table 9.3 includes UCD Assessment Strategies. For example, an adaptive technology professor at a Rhode Island college recognized the diverse learning styles in her classroom and decided that giving a typical final exam would not accurately reflect what her students had learned.

> About a third of the way through the semester, after observing my students, I decided to add another option to the final exam. They could take the final exam or develop a Web site in groups of three using a wiki. ["A wiki is software that allows users to create, edit, and link Web pages easily" (Wikipedia, 2008).] The Web site was supposed to reflect what they had learned in class, incorporate their own experiences and provide a cultural perspective on assistive technology. About 65% of my students chose to develop a Web site. The Web sites were great! Very informative, very different, and good resources for students to use in the future.

A professor at a university in Massachusetts learned the value of assessing student understanding according to the effectiveness of her instructional format throughout the course, not just at the end of it.

> I now stop and say, "Did anybody understand what I just said because I think that was confusing." By the looks on their faces you can see whether or not students seem not only to be engaged but also to understand what you're talking about. When I see

TABLE 9.3   Universal Course Design Assessment Strategies

Less Than 15 Minutes to Implement	When to Use This Strategy	15–60 Minutes to Implement	When to Use This Strategy
Create activities and assignments that directly relate to the material covered in class; address the students' responses.	Direct Experiential	Provide students with study tips; don't ask questions on material not covered on the exam.	Direct Indirect
Form discussion groups for review purposes.	Direct Interactive	Create a clear rubric of what constitutes an "A" paper and what doesn't; give examples of previous student work and distribute to the class.	Direct Experiential Independent
Encourage students to include their notes in their lab reports.	Direct Indirect Experiential	Build graphic organizers that represent ideas required in the assignment for students to reference or use as templates.	Direct Interactive
Extend time to complete fieldwork assignments, or permit required fieldwork/ internship hours, to be completed in shorter blocks, over a longer period of time.	Indirect Experiential Independent	Give students opportunities to demonstrate their knowledge in alternative formats (e.g. presentations, papers, videos, newspaper articles, case studies, photo essays).	Indirect Experiential Independent
Provide the option of attending lab or forming a group of five or more and doing the lab in the manner that they see fit (allow creativity and dismiss the group from coming to school).	Indirect Experiential Interactive	Create tiered assignments: a series of related tasks of varying complexity related to the key skills that students need to acquire.	Direct Experiential
Encourage students to use various forms of nontechnical tools (e.g., graphs, color coding, maps, diagrams) and technology (e.g., concept map tools, spell-checking software, PowerPoint slides, digital cameras) as they develop themes or ideas for their assignments.	Indirect Experiential Independent	Have students create informative topic-specific Web sites; allow them to provide the information in a manner that works best for them.	Indirect Experiential Independent

Source: Equity and Excellence in Higher Education: Universal Course Design (2005). Universal Course Design Instructional Strategies. Retrieved on November 2, 2007, from www.eeonline.org.

confusion, that's the point at which I stop and realize that whatever I just said didn't come across correctly, or it was not interpreted, and I find a new way to say it and a new way to engage the student. This is something that the UCD core team has really helped me to develop.

One professor at a university in New Hampshire made sure to assess her students' performance across several levels by providing multiple opportunities for them to demonstrate their knowledge.

I am not the kind of professor who banks a student's grade on the final paper or exam. I really think that students can show us what they've learned in a variety of ways throughout the semester. If I wait until that last day when they may or may not be having a good day or test well, then that is not fair to them. It also gives me an inaccurate picture of how well I got the message across. Therefore, I provide multiple opportunities throughout the semester. Some of them are more formal (little quizzes, reflections, group presentations), others are informal (show me how to set up this lab, tell me what we should be looking for, etc.). That way, I have a full picture of what they've learned and how effective my instructional methods were.

(D) Steps for Adding Universal Course Design Strategies to the Environment

1. Create a campuswide climate that is safe, accessible, caring, and nurturing to all students from all cultures.
2. Build a personalized learning environment.
3. Use physical space to enhance student participation and engagement.

UCD draws attention to the teaching environment. If the classroom is inaccessible physically, students will be less engaged. Faculty should avoid teaching in classrooms where students can hide behind columns, cannot hear the professor speak, can barely see the board, and cannot break into groups easily. Faculty also need to be cognizant of the cultural differences between themselves and their students. In some cultures, active participation is looked down on; in others, working in groups is a newer concept (Center for Teaching and Learning, 2001; Meacham, McClellan, Pearse, & Greene, 2003). Some students may not speak English as a first language and may have a difficult time communicating in class discussions; others may have a disability that requires them to participate in another manner. Being sensitive to cultural differences will create a safe and personalized learning environment for all students. One education professor at a university in Maine describes her efforts.

I have a wide range of diversity in my classroom, including many foreign students, some of whom are refugees. There are some more mature students who are coming back to school after some time off, as well as some students with disabilities. When I began the class, I asked everyone to share one thing about their culture that they valued the most. It was a good learning experience for the students and a great one for me. It helped me to restructure the participation component of my course. Rather than require everyone to speak in each class, I asked them to participate in a manner that worked best for them. Some sent me e-mails ahead of time because they were shy, their culture didn't promote public speaking, or they couldn't speak. Some summarized their thoughts and posted them on the Web site. I had one student who drew cartoons of the day's topics and shared them with the class. It was a great experience for me and for my students, and as a result we all became more culturally aware.

Another professor, at a university in Vermont, felt that her students' participation was inhibited by the rows of desks in the classroom.

I don't like rows because it makes it really difficult for me to freely interact with all students. So, I try and get to class a half an hour early to rearrange the chairs into a large circle. My students can't hide and, in fact, have taken a more active role in the conversation during the class. I don't require them to speak, but this way I know that everyone can see and hear me.

SUSTAINING UNIVERSAL COURSE DESIGN ON A COLLEGE CAMPUS

Each college campus that is working to incorporate UCD into its courses will approach UCD differently, depending on a variety of factors. The E&E project has worked with fifteen community colleges and universities to successfully embed UCD on their campuses; twelve of those were established with the direct assistance of the project, and three were established with no project contact. Ten of those teams have been meeting for more than three years, while the other five have been meeting for more than two years. Membership in the UCD core team remains consistent as faculty rotate through each semester. Some teams have recruited faculty to join the team on a full-time basis and offer guidance to new faculty.

Each team has approached the effort to embed UCD on their campus differently, based on campuswide politics, goals, and a willingness to adopt UCD. For example, one rural institution has decided to integrate the principles of UCD at a system level, requiring all faculty to create universally designed syllabi for each course they teach. At another university, the team started small by recruiting faculty from the education department. After each semester, each faculty member was responsible for recruiting another to join the team the following semester. As a result, the entire education department has been trained on UCD principles, and those faculty are now recruiting others from a variety of other departments.

UCD sustainability depends in large part on the development of a UCD core team. The UCD core team drives the introduction of UCD, from a campuswide workshop to individual faculty experiences. However, many other steps can influence the degree of success a college will have in bringing UCD to its campus. Those factors include (a) initiating UCD from within, (b) listening to students' needs, (c) minimizing the use of the word "disability" when discussing the benefits of UCD, (d) gaining administrative support, and (e) relying on faculty mentors.

(A) Initiating UCD from within. A primary lesson learned in this project is that it is difficult for an outsider (i.e., someone not working for a specific university) to stimulate and direct a systematic change effort on a particular campus. Outsiders are just that; in this context, they are people who come in, provide professional development for

faculty about what they could be doing better, and then leave. In addition, one-shot optional workshops are not well attended. Faculty members who do attend them might question the presenter's credibility, doubt the person's familiarity with their particular campus atmosphere, or dismiss the innovation as a concept that will not work at their institution.

(B) Listening to students. Students can provide insight into their own learning experiences. After all, students are the reason that faculty need to examine their teaching, so why not ask them what they need? Faculty can also be encouraged to customize conversations with their students by asking questions specifically about their course and instructional style. Examples of these questions include:

- In addition to lecturing, what are some other teaching methods that you would like me to consider (e.g., group work, hands-on activities)?
- Would it be helpful to offer a choice of assignments rather than require everyone to do the same thing?
- Based on your learning style (visual, auditory, kinesthetic), what have I done to help you learn better, and what could I do to improve your learning?

(C) Minimizing the use of the word disability. Most faculty are not fully aware of the disability-related laws that govern access to college courses. Instead, they rely on disability services to "take care" of any disability-related needs that arise. When a student presents documentation from the disability services office, faculty will usually provide the necessary accommodations; however, few will make an effort to naturally weave those accommodations into their course structure so that all students benefit. Additionally, including the word *disability* in the titles of workshops tends to reduce attendance of faculty because they feel it is not relevant to them (The Equity and Excellence in Higher Education Project, 2007).

A successful strategy for attracting faculty to a UCD workshop is to advertise it as a professional development opportunity for improving instruction to benefit *all* students. Begin workshops by asking faculty a series of questions, including the following:

- Who is taking your class?
- Are all students right out of high school?
- Are they all proficient English speakers?
- What cultures do they come from?
- Do you have students with disabilities in your class?

Within the training, help faculty realize that efforts made to diversify instruction will help *all* their students, including those with disabilities (Harrison, 2006). Support this statement with recent demographic statistics of the student body (e.g., average student age, ethnicity, where they are from, the number who list English as a second language, the number who self-identify as having a disability). This information, coupled with asking faculty about their own experiences as learners (e.g., What was your favorite college class? Why? What methods of instruction did the professor use?), can highlight the need to ensure that all learners have equal access to their course.

(D) Getting administrative support. Administrative support can entice faculty to attend professional development opportunities. An authority figure who is respected by others and is viewed as promoting good teaching can be an effective advocate. University presidents, deans of faculty, and department chairs are examples of people who have given their support to faculty participating in UCD activities. Methods of support can range from financial support of UCD workshops, promotion of all UCD activities, written letters of acknowledgment, and small faculty stipends or technology that faculty are interested in using.

(E) Relying on faculty mentors. Faculty mentors, in combination with the UCD core team, are the linchpins for successful adoption of UCD. Once faculty experience the semester-long UCD training and technical assistance, they are equipped with the knowledge and confidence to advise their peers who are part of the next semester's group as well as those who are just learning about UCD for the first time. Using this method over the course of three years, a college campus can produce 30 or more UCD mentors in a variety of disciplines. This network of UCD experts is crucial for spreading the word, educating colleagues, pushing for departmental adoption of UCD strategies, and encouraging systematic policy changes within the college atmosphere.

CONCLUSION

The goal of UCD is to increase access for all students to college curriculum, instruction, assessment, and the environment. In the absence of UCD, students with learning styles similar to those of the professor will be most successful, whereas those who learn differently, come from different cultural backgrounds, have different levels of academic preparedness, and/or have disabilities will be at a disadvantage.

E&E project activities give professors simple, intuitive strategies for diversifying their courses. These strategies are not designed to water down the academic experience of students but rather to make that experience possible for *all* students. The project provides faculty with the tools necessary to become good and confident teachers (Equity and Excellence in Higher Education Project, 2007) and to ensure sustainability of UCD on college campuses.

Experiences through the E&E project suggest that UCD increases student engagement in a course. It levels the playing field for all students so that each student, regardless of learning style, cultural background, academic preparedness, or disability, has equal access to the course curriculum, instruction, assessment, and the environment in which the course is taught.

REFERENCES

Adams, M. (1992). *Promoting diversity in college classrooms: Innovative responses for the curriculum, faculty, and institutions.* San Francisco: Jossey-Bass.

Adams, M., & Marchesani, L. S. (1992). Dynamics of diversity in the teaching-learning process: A faculty development model for analysis and action. In M. Adams (Ed.), *New directions for teaching and learning (No. 52): Promoting diversity in college classrooms: Innovative responses for the curriculum, faculty, and institutions* (pp. 9–18). San Francisco: Jossey-Bass.

Agran, M. (2006). Self-determination: Achieving a say-do correspondence. *TASH Connections, 32* (5/6). Retrieved November 2, 2007, from http://www.tash.org/express/06mayjun/agran.htm

Ambrose, H., & Ambrose, K. (1995). *A handbook of biological investigation* (5th ed.). Winston-Salem, NC: Hunter Textbooks.

Burgstahler, S. (2007). *Equal access: Universal design of instruction.* Seattle: University of Washington. Retrieved November 1, 2007 from http://www.washington.edu/doit/Brochures/Academics/equal_access_udi.html

Center for Teaching and Learning. (2001). Teaching for inclusion. In *Students with learning disabilities* (chap. 14). Retrieved November 2, 2007, from http://ctl.unc.edu/tfi14.html

Davis, B. G. (1999). *Diversity and complexity in the classroom: Considerations of race, ethnicity, and gender.* Retrieved November 1, 2007, from http://www.hcc.hawaii.edu/intranet/committees/FacDevCom/guidebk/teachtip/diverse.htm

Ehrmann, S. C. (1995). Asking the right question. *Change, 29*(2), 20–27.

Equity and Excellence in Higher Education Project, University of Massachusetts (2007). U.S. Department of Education, Office of Postsecondary Education.

Felder, R. (1993). Reaching the second tier: Learning and teaching styles in college science education. *Journal of College Science Teaching, 23*(5), 286–290.

Felder, R., & Brent, R. (2003). Learning by doing. *Chemical Engineering Education, 37*(4), 282–283.

Gay, G. (2000). *Culturally responsive teaching: Theory, research, and practice.* New York: Teachers College Press.

Hall, T., Strongman, N., & Meyer, A. (2003). *Differentiated instruction and implications for URL implementation.* Wakefield, MA: National Center on Accessing the General Curriculum. Retrieved November 1, 2007, from http://www.cast.org/publications/ncac_diffinstructudl.html

Harrison, E. (2006). Working with faculty toward universal designed instruction: The process for dynamic course design. *Journal of Postsecondary Education and Disability, 19*(2).

Indiana State University. (2003). *Promoting diversity.* Retrieved November 1, 2007, from http://indstate.edu/cirt/pol/taga/promoting.htm

McGuire, J., & Scott, S. (2006). Universal design for instruction: Extending the universal design paradigm to college instruction. *Journal of Postsecondary Education and Disability, 19*(2).

Meacham, J. A., McClellan, M., Pearse, T., & Greene, R. (2003). Student diversity and educational outcomes: Student perceptions. *College Student Journal, 37*(4), 627–642.

Selden, S., Assad, A., & Greenburg, J. (1998). *Essays on quality learning: Teachers' reflections on classroom practice.* College Park: University of Maryland.

Webb, S. (2007, May 25). Community college faculty: Must love to teach. *Science Careers.* Retrieved June 14, 2007, from http://sciencecareers.sciencemag.org/career_development/previous_issues/articles/2007_05_25/caredit_a0700074/(parent)/68

Wikipedia. (2008). Wiki. Retrieved November 1, 2007, from http://en.wikipedia.org.wiki/wiki

The content of this chapter was developed under a grant from the U.S. Department of Education Office of Postsecondary Education (grant number P333A050051). However, this content does not necessarily represent the policy of the Department of Education, and you should not assume endorsement by the federal government.

10

Small Victories
Faculty Development and Universal Design

Susan Yager

Many college and university faculty receive "accommodations," of a sort, in the placement of their classrooms, setting of teaching and office hours, and so on, but they may not think pro-actively about accessible course design and accommodations for students with disabilities. Time constraints and institutional pressures may be factors preventing faculty from imple-menting universal design principles in their teaching. Faculty development centers, as well as teaching and learning centers, can play a significant role in educating faculty on this issue by building faculty awareness, celebrating incremental change, consistently applying principles of both good teaching and universal design, and modeling inclusive practices.

In the fall semester of 1993, I was pregnant with my second child and teaching Eng-lish at Iowa State University, a large, research-intensive university. I had become accus-tomed to teaching on the third floor of one of the university's oldest buildings, an impressive ivy-covered hall with windows that actually opened. It was a fine place to teach, until the pregnancy left me short of breath on my walks up to the third floor. There was an elevator, but it was small and slow enough to have been part of the building's original equipment. I asked a department administrator to move me in the spring to a classroom in the more modern main English building—and never again was assigned a room in the older hall. Years later, I learned that this courtesy of a new classroom assignment was similar to the reasonable accommodation process for per-sons with disabilities. It was easy for me, and it should be an easy process at both the logistical and curricular levels for anyone on campus who has a disability.

At many colleges and universities, faculty are among those most likely to find accommodations easily available, whether what is needed is a certain teaching sched-ule, carefully scheduled committee meetings, a laptop as part of a startup package, or a classroom accessible by elevator. These preferences can be built into the faculty's daily lives—arranged by design. In contrast, students, who often must take specific required courses, have far greater restrictions on their time and mobility. Students with disabilities may need coordination of services and support from staff and faculty who are aware of the necessity for accommodations. However, their need for accommodations can be minimized when faculty apply universal design principles in teaching and professional work. It is one of the functions of the Center for Excellence in Learning and Teaching (CELT), Iowa State University's faculty development center, to build faculty awareness of students' diverse needs and to provide ongoing support to instructors to enhance teaching and learning. One major element of this support is to encourage instructors to understand and implement universal design principles to maximize the learning of all students.

Universal design, true to its name, involves the application of broad-based principles of inclusiveness and accessibility at every stage of a process, whether that process is designing a building, creating a transit system, or teaching a course. An impressive example of universal design in architecture is an entrance to the main library at the University of Arizona–Tucson. Stairs flank a central ramp, which puts access by foot or by wheel at the literal heart of the library entrance. That no one is inconvenienced by this design underscores the fact that everyone is welcome in the building. Attractive and accessible buildings include such elements as wide doorways, automated water faucets and towel dispensers in bathrooms, and automatic doors. These elements of universal design, necessary to some, are efficient for all. In the same way, universal design in the classroom emphasizes inclusiveness of learning styles and preferences, as well as awareness of physical and social differences. (By contrast, my pregnancy-related relocation to a different classroom was an accommodation for a specific circumstance.) Universal design contributes to the learning of all students, not just those with a documented need for accommodation. To the extent that universal design is successfully applied, individual accommodations should become less frequent.

CONSTRAINTS ON FACULTY AWARENESS

Three constraints may impede the use of universal design: time, exposure to information about universal design and its principles, and institutional and professional situations. Time, of course, is the universal constraint. In an era of increasing demands and diminishing resources, time to reflect is increasingly precious, and schedules are unrelentingly full. Textbooks and supplies are ordered in a hurry; films and videos may be ordered without being previewed; or older media and technology that are already on campus are pressed into service. This haste may result in classroom materials or plans that are incompatible with universal design. Such materials could include, for example, videotapes that have no captioning; personal-response units without large, easily pressed buttons or braille accommodation; or in-class or out-of-class assignments that do not consider the needs of students with physical or social disabilities. Some people may consider universal design to be a simple matter of thinking globally, thinking about diversity in learning materials and experiences, and just looking ahead, and indeed these are all components of thoughtful course design. However, for harried faculty who are ordering next term's books under this term's pressures, nothing is really simple.

Level of exposure to information is a second element that may prevent faculty from thinking in terms of universal design. It can also be, I believe, a major impediment to instructors' implementing active, student-centered learning. Almost by definition, successful academics thrived, as students, under traditional teaching methods. Thus, insofar as human beings tend not to think beyond the dimensions of their own experiences, faculty will likely use teaching methods that worked well for them, although these methods may not work well for a variety of students. Without systematic reflection on how their own learning preferences may differ from others', faculty have little impetus to redesign, or consciously universally design, their teaching. As a result, when students do require accommodation, particularly if faculty have little advance notice, a temporary solution must be constructed. Such a quick fix solves the immediate problem but leaves thoughtful redesign of the course for another, perhaps ever-deferred, day.

A greater concern than the constraints of time and experience may be the limitations imposed by the structure of academe, especially the structure of large research universities. At these institutions, a set amount of faculty time is devoted to classroom work and office hours, with much of the remainder devoted to disciplinary research. Students' lives outside the classroom may therefore remain mysterious to busy faculty members. For workers in such large institutions, the divide between the provost's office and that of the dean of students is a sharp one, so faculty often know little about student affairs or other offices that support students. Again, the cause is relative lack of experience: Who would seek out the office of disability resources if it were not necessary? Where research is the primary concern of faculty, teaching sometimes receives less attention, and the university as it exists beyond the provost's purview may receive less still. Certainly, many faculty do interact with student affairs offices, but many others occupy a narrow academic channel, never coming in contact with supporting offices until a classroom accommodation requires it.

THE ROLE OF FACULTY DEVELOPERS

Given these challenges, faculty development centers or centers of teaching and learning can play a significant role in promoting universal design among faculty. These centers can help to build a culture in which universal design is a part of teaching and professional practice rather than accommodations as an emergency add-on or afterthought. Faculty development offices can provide a number of functions and services to help promote universal design and shape institutions that pay attention to the issue. For example, the professionals might

- build partnerships between academic and student-support units
- build faculty awareness at both the grassroots and institutional levels
- celebrate small successes, applauding progress in thinking about and acting on universal design principles

- at the same time work for larger, more systemic changes
- promote the realization that the principles of good teaching and the principles of universal design are congruent
- practice critical self-awareness so as to model and promote principles of universal design themselves

Building partnerships is perhaps the simplest of these tasks, although it takes commitment and persistence. At Iowa State, strong partnerships have been forged between the Office of the Dean of Students, which includes the disability resources office, and CELT, which is part of the provost's office. For example, staff have worked together to publicize Disability Awareness Weeks on campus and to support an expert speaker on campus offering workshops on universal design. CELT and the staff of the Office of the Dean of Students have participated in one another's programming in order to cement and publicize the tie between universal design and good teaching. For example, when students or staff watch a student affairs video on finding campus accommodations, they will see and hear CELT's message, and when CELT organizes its annual orientation for new faculty, information from the Office of the Dean of Students is included. Clear and ongoing communication—via orientation as well as CELT's Web site, weekly e-mails, and the biannual CELT newsletter—is vital to this partnership effort because the population of instructors, teaching assistants, and students continually changes. Because the university has legal obligations to community members who have disabilities, CELT's communication efforts also function as a reminder of the legal, ethical, and professional responsibilities we have in common.

Perhaps the most important component of building these partnerships—and this may be felt more strongly at a large research university than elsewhere—is to maintain mutual understanding and respect between faculty and professional staff, including Office of the Dean of Students personnel and advisors. CELT's mission statement, which was recently revised to refer to all those involved in student learning on campus, makes explicit the notion that professional staff and faculty are partners in the teaching effort.

Because CELT exists to forge connections among campus educators, CELT staff members strive to overcome the isolating effect of self-contained and independent departments and offices. This goal requires working for awareness and for change at both the grassroots and institutional levels. At the grassroots level, for example, CELT staff have worked to make instructors aware of the assistive technology lab on campus, a resource supported by the Iowa Vocational Rehabilitation Service. Having met the professional staff of that lab and learned of the creative and innovative assistive technologies available for students, CELT staff promoted the lab via its campus newsletter. More effective, and an important follow-up, was talking with individual faculty about how the lab could help meet their students' needs. A film professor whose classes were very long, for example, needed a writing board for a student who uses a wheelchair. It needed to be large enough to cover the arms of the chair and comfortable enough for the student to use for the entire class. Fulfilling this request was a simple matter for the assistive technology professionals, but the key element was making the connection. Faculty development personnel can publicize and promote campus resources but must be ready to make these connections and to spread the word about both accommodation and universal design. Faculty developers must let instructors know that help is available and that they are not to blame for needing such assistance or for not having foreseen every pedagogical circumstance.

EFFECTIVE INSTITUTIONAL SUPPORT

Faculty awareness also needs to be built in a top-down or institutional manner, again through some of the communication channels mentioned above. For example, as recently as 2002, Iowa State had no campuswide practice regarding whether or how course syllabi should convey information for students with documented disabilities. In 2003, a set of sample statements published by the Disability Resources Office was promoted by the Office of the Dean of Students and by CELT through publicity, workshops, and orientation for new faculty. Several slightly different statements were offered, varying in formality and tone, from which instructors may choose. The first such statement was probably the most widely used; it read simply:

> If you have a documented disability and anticipate needing accommodations in this course, please make arrangements to meet with me soon. Please request that a Disability Resources staffer send a SAAR [Student Academic Accommodation Request] form verifying your disability and specifying the accommodation you will need.

In 2004, the associate provost issued a reminder to deans, associate deans, and department chairs that such statements should be included on course syllabi, and by 2005, it was rare on campus to see a syllabus without one. A key element here was that while the change had strong institutional support, no explicit policy or directive brought it about; rather, constant reminders, widespread and ongoing communication, and instructor autonomy as to the wording and style of the statement helped to create a new expectation for course syllabi.

Although it may seem like a small matter, this change in culture regarding the course syllabus deserves to be celebrated. Because of this now institution-wide practice, every instructor is thinking at least once per course preparation about the needs of students with disabilities. Since each of the sample statements describes both the student's and the instructor's role in providing necessary accommodations, instructors are reminded of the possibility that a quiet room, an un-timed test, a captioned video, or a comfortable lap desk may be necessary for students in the upcoming class. As instructors consider the likelihood that some students will have unusual needs, universal design principles enter into the instructors' conscious course planning, even if it may be years before a student with a disability enrolls in one of their classes.

In addition to celebrating culture changes such as this, CELT has celebrated its successes by bringing faculty to conferences to recognize their efforts in promoting universal design and good teaching, and to call the institution's attention to that work. There are both indirect and direct ways to recognize good faculty work in implementing universal design. For example, CELT's annual Teaching Tips workshop features excellent faculty and can provide recognition and praise for teachers who have made strides in this area. Sharing stories on a one-to-one or small-group basis (i.e., "Professor X tried this technique, and it worked well") can both get the word out and provide public approbation for faculty, thereby rewarding efforts toward implementing universal design. More discreetly but still quite effectively, faculty developers who are appointed to teaching award committees or similar bodies can affect how the institution recognizes and rewards such efforts.

WORKING TOWARD SYSTEMIC CHANGE

At the same time, however, faculty developers must continue to work toward larger, systemic improvements. For example, Iowa State spent a year examining various brands of personal-response units, or "clickers," that instructors can use to receive instant feedback in classes. These were first brought to campus by forward-looking professors who received grants or whose departments provided them. More recently, as the various kinds and features of personal-response systems have proliferated, the university considered whether to support a single brand. Faculty developers, who have a natural interest in the pedagogical value of these systems, played a significant role in reminding faculty and support staff that not all students would find these easy to use: Larger keypads, raised numbers, or audible feedback may sometimes be necessary. In my rather limited experience, sales demonstrators have not thought about universal design as an issue in creating these systems. A consistent, persistent reminder communicated both to company representatives and to campus decision-makers can keep universal design in everyone's consciousness.

Classroom design is another area in which faculty developers may influence institutional change. As a new faculty developer, I had the opportunity to participate with faculty, students, and staff on a committee charged with imagining the optimal, if not the ideal, classroom. The imagined room would be wider than it was deep, full of light and air, and attractive. It would have excellent acoustics, good sight lines from every angle, and room enough to have students gather in groups. Equipped with both high- and low-tech equipment, such a classroom would be flexible, accessible, and learner-friendly. We waxed eloquent about the need for aisles by which students could easily reach the seats and faculty could easily reach the students, even in a large lecture hall.

Such a committee and its recommendations report may seem like an exercise in futility, but in this case the ideal was at least partially realized. A short time after the committee wrapped up its work, the university set out to replace an aging lecture hall, one with steep steps and a narrow focus on the speaker's lectern, with a new, more student-friendly classroom. This renovation offered an opportunity to act on the committee's ideas, and part of the role of the faculty development office was to help bridge the ideal and the possible. Working with such diverse groups as faculty users, planning and maintenance personnel, and the project's architects, the CELT staff helped to create a large hall that, while only 12 rows deep, seats more students than the original facility did. It contains tiered rows of alternately fixed and turnable chairs, allowing for unprecedented comfort and ease of student interaction during large-format classes. The room is accessible by elevator at three levels, giving mobility-limited students a number of seating options. Generous space between seats and rows as well as two broad aisles allow all students ease of access within the classroom and encourage the instructor to move around. The room's instructional technology is also designed for diverse student needs. For example, the hall is equipped for distance captioning, which allows students with difficulty hearing to read the instructor's spoken words on a computer with only a second's delay.

I do not mean to imply that the faculty development office was the sole, or even leading, actor in building this redesigned lecture hall. Many units, from academic departments to the instructional technology experts to classroom equipment and furnishings managers, played a role in its construction. (Indeed, a second classroom was being redesigned in a very similar fashion at about the same time, independently of this project, and more classrooms of this type have been built since then.) The faculty development role was one of mindfulness, continually keeping the principles of universal design in the forefront and bearing witness, as it were, to the benefit to all students of a well-designed—universally designed—teaching space.

If I have learned anything about universal design as a faculty developer, it is that universal design *is* good teaching: It helps instructors to think of students as individuals and promotes planning for learners with differing strengths and abilities. Universal design is also a boon to students with strong tendencies or preferences that might impede learning but do not rise to the level of a documented disability. Universal design offers what one might call a diverse approach to diversity, a habit of thought that creates options rather than limitations.

And yet, like the cobbler whose children went shoeless, faculty developers need to look to their own areas of responsibility as well. Are we adhering to universal design principles ourselves? Are our sessions frequently at the same times of day, the same days each week? Do we offer large-group, small-group, ongoing, and one-time events? In our conversations about teaching and learning, do we include diverse voices among our teaching assistants and undergraduates? Faculty developers must practice critical self-awareness if we are to model and encourage the use of universal design principles ourselves.

If faculty developers persist in efforts to communicate about, encourage, and practice the implementation of universal design, we can play a significant and central role in making universal design a part of campus cultures nationwide. As colleges and universities seek ways to diversify their campuses for reasons of fairness and justice, as well as for such pragmatic reasons as student recruitment and retention, faculty developers can serve their institutions and their colleagues by keeping this issue central across campus.

11

A Case Study Approach to Promote Practical Application of Universal Design for Instruction

Sally S. Scott
Joan M. McGuire

The confluence of classroom diversity, a changing professoriate, and expectations for collaborative learning environments has provided an environment in higher education that is ripe for examining innovative approaches to working with faculty as they rethink their teaching strategies and methods. This chapter provides an overview of the use of case studies as a strategy to support faculty reflection and application of universal design for instruction. The table entitled Principles of Universal Design for Instruction provides faculty with a framework for considering a range of inclusive practices. Case study methodology assists faculty in moving from general principles to guided practice in implementing inclusive teaching strategies.

The first decade of the twenty-first century is notable for postsecondary education for several reasons. First, the trend toward an increasingly diverse student population continues to grow. In 1995, 11% of undergraduate students enrolled in college were black, 8% were Hispanic, and 72% were Caucasian. In 2004, 14% were black, 11% were Hispanic, and 64% were Caucasian (Chronicle of Higher Education, 2006). The 2003–04 undergraduate demographic profile includes 43% of enrolled students who were of nontraditional age (i.e., 24 years of age and over), 45% who were attending college part-time, and 11% who indicated they had a disability (in 1978, this figure was 2.3%) (Chronicle of Higher Education, 2006; Henderson, 1999). Diversity in college classrooms brings an array of experiential backgrounds, learning styles, and learning needs.

Other noteworthy trends include projections for faculty retirements and a shift in philosophy about college teaching. Morrison (2003) has stated that within the next decade more than 20% of college and university faculty will retire. With this change will come a new cadre of instructors, who will incorporate more information technologies into their instruction at a time when the paradigm of college teaching is changing from providing instruction (the teaching paradigm) to producing learning (the learning paradigm) (Fink, 2003).

Finally, the development of the construct of universal design (UD) and the articulation of its guiding principles underlie the possibility of creating environments and products that are usable by the greatest number of people, without a need to retrofit accommodations to ensure equitable use (Center for Universal Design, 2007). The UD paradigm, from the field of architecture, is now being proposed as a model for implementation in creating accessible and inclusive learning environments. One such adaptation, universal design for instruction (UDI), is specifically targeted for college faculty, with the assumption that faculty are content experts who can refine their pedagogical skills to enhance instructional accessibility (McGuire & Scott, 2006). In keeping with theory development and application, the nine principles of UDI in Table 11.1 (Scott, McGuire, & Shaw, 2001) serve as guidelines for practice in intentionally developing and refining instruction using the UDI paradigm.

With the confluence of classroom diversity, a changing professoriate, and expectations for collaborative learning environments comes the opportunity to examine innovative approaches to working with faculty as they rethink their approaches to teaching. Whether it be through institutional structures, such as centers focused on teaching and learning, or through a more decentralized departmental or individual model, the time is prime for using UDI as a tool of reflection to support faculty endeavors.

The purpose of this chapter is to provide an overview of the use of case studies as a strategy that can be instrumental in supporting faculty reflection on and application of UDI.

CASE STUDIES AND PROFESSIONAL DEVELOPMENT

Case studies are an approach to training and professional development that have a long tradition in the fields of law, business, and medicine. The approach is characterized by the presentation of a compelling story that poses a dilemma that is realistic to participants. Participants identify issues embedded in the case and generate possible solutions or courses of action (Wasserman, 1994). The case method guides participants through a reflective process that draws on professional knowledge and experience to solve realistic professional problems and complexities (Lynn, 1999). A component of the case study methodology can include teaching notes that "address issues that might be raised, alternative methods for discussion (such as the use of leaderless small groups), ideas about background and follow-up readings to enrich analysis, and ways to link the case with other teaching-improvement activities" (Hutchings, 1993, p. 13). The use of case study methods has been widely recommended in the professional development of teachers. Shulman (1992) observed that the case study approach is particularly well suited to training instructors in the "day-to-day ambiguities of the

TABLE 11.1   The Nine Principles of Universal Design for Instruction

Principle	Definition	Example(s)
Principle 1: Equitable use	Instruction is designed to be useful to and accessible by people with diverse abilities. Provide the same means of use for all students, identical whenever possible, equivalent when not.	Provision of class notes on line. Comprehensive notes can be accessed in the same manner by all students, regardless of hearing ability, English proficiency, learning or attention disorders, or note-taking skill level. In an electronic format, students can utilize whatever individual assistive technology is needed to read, hear, or study the class notes.
Principle 2: Flexibility in use	Instruction is designed to accommodate a wide range of individual abilities. Provide choice in methods of use.	Use of varied instructional methods (lecture with a visual outline, group activities, use of stories, or Web board–based discussions) to provide different ways of learning and expressing knowledge.
Principle 3: Simple and intuitive	Instruction is designed in a straightforward and predictable manner, regardless of the student's experience, knowledge, language skills, or current concentration level. Eliminate unnecessary complexity.	Provision of a grading rubric that clearly lays out expectations for exam performance, papers, or projects; a syllabus with comprehensive and accurate information; a handbook guiding students through difficult homework assignments.
Principle 4: Perceptible information	Instruction is designed so that necessary information is communicated effectively to the student, regardless of ambient conditions or the student's sensory abilities.	Selection of textbooks, reading material, and other instructional supports in digital format or on line so students with diverse needs (e.g., vision, learning, attention, English as a second language) can access materials through traditional hard copy or with the use of various technological supports (e.g., screen reader, text enlarger, online dictionary).
Principle 5: Tolerance for error	Instruction anticipates variation in individual student learning pace and prerequisite skills.	Structuring a long-term course project so that students have the option of turning in individual project components separately for constructive feedback and for integration into the final product; provision of online "practice" exercises that supplement classroom instruction.
Principle 6: Low physical effort	Instruction is designed to minimize nonessential physical effort in order to allow maximum attention to learning. *Note:* This principle does not apply when physical effort is integral to essential requirements of a course.	Allowing students to use a word processor for writing and editing papers or essay exams. This facilitates editing of the document without the additional physical exertion of rewriting portions of text (helpful for students with fine motor or handwriting difficulties or extreme organization weaknesses while providing options for those who are more adept and comfortable composing on the computer).
Principle 7: Size and space for approach and use	Instruction is designed with consideration for appropriate size and space for approach, reach, manipulations, and use regardless of a student's body size, posture, mobility, and communication needs.	In small class settings, use of a circular seating arrangement to allow students to see and face speakers during discussion (important for students with attention-deficit disorders or who are deaf or hard of hearing).

TABLE 11.1   The Nine Principles of Universal Design for Instruction *(continued)*

Principle	Definition	Example(s)
Principle 8: A community of learners	The instructional environment promotes interaction and communication among students and between students and faculty.	Fostering communication among students in and out of class by structuring study groups, discussion groups, e-mail lists, or chat rooms; making a personal connection with students and incorporating motivational strategies to encourage student performance through learning students' names or individually acknowledging excellent performance.
Principle 9: Instructional climate	Instruction is designed to be welcoming and inclusive. High expectations are espoused for all students.	A statement in the class syllabus affirming the need for class members to respect diversity in order to establish the expectation of tolerance and encourage students to discuss any special learning needs with the instructor; highlighting diverse thinkers who have made significant contributions to the field; sharing innovative approaches developed by students in the class.

Source: S. Scott, J. McGuire, & S. Shaw. (2001). *Principles of universal design for instruction.* Storrs: University of Connecticut, Center on Postsecondary Education and Disability. Copyright 2001 by S. Scott, J. McGuire, & S. Shaw. Reprinted with permission.

classroom" (p. xiii). In structure, cases may be of varied length, format, and level of detail, ranging from a brief paragraph to multipage descriptions. Wasserman (1994) observed that good cases, regardless of length, are "based on problems or 'big ideas' that warrant in-depth discussion" (p. 13). Cases in teaching may focus, for example, on such topics as the relationships of instructional strategies to student outcomes, examination of teacher assumptions in the classroom, or cultural factors affecting student learning. Darling-Hammond and Baratz-Snowden (2007) described case study methods as a means of assisting instructors in building a schema for their decision-making and continued professional growth. Through a process of analyzing teaching situations, applying strategies, and considering alternatives, instructors are provided with a model to "seek out and add knowledge of specific techniques throughout their careers" (p. 115). This schema allows instructors to progress from "novice" decision-makers in the classroom to "expert" instructors, with a broader and more flexible repertoire of responses in the classroom.

USING THE INSTRUCTIONAL CYCLE TO PROMOTE REFLECTION

A review of the literature on effective instructional practices (Algozzine, Ysseldyke, & Elliott, 1997–1998; Brophy & Good, 1986; Kame'enui & Carnine, 1998) identifies three integral phases of the instructional cycle: (a) planning instruction, (b) delivering instruction, and (c) assessing learning outcomes. During the planning phase, learning goals and outcomes are determined, as are standards for performance and instructional methods and materials. Delivering instruction includes presenting information and monitoring the extent to which the content is understood or acted on by students. In the third phase of the cycle, assessing learning outcomes, activities occur to determine the extent to which students have met the instructional goals. The temporal phases of the cycle are closely linked, since the assessment phase should inform the first two phases. In our approach to using case studies with faculty, we have found that using the instructional cycle framework adds a dimension that faculty can readily identify with and apply in their reflection on their own teaching. A minicase, questions for reflection, and teaching notes are presented for each of the three phases of the instructional cycle.

SAMPLE MINICASES, QUESTIONS FOR REFLECTION, AND TEACHING NOTES

Phase 1: Planning Instruction

Peter Miller is a faculty member in the psychology department in a four-year state university. He teaches a required undergraduate course that meets for two hours every week. In this blended course, which includes lectures and use of the Web CT/Vista platform, he posts the class syllabus, assignments, and links to readings and articles. He finds the Web CT discussion board convenient because he can reach all the students in his class and respond to student queries at any time. He typically has forty to fifty students per semester in his class. The student population is varied and includes traditional- and nontraditional-age students. This semester he has been contacted by one of the students in his class who discloses that she has a language-based learning disability. The letter from the disability services office states that the student is entitled to reasonable accommodations under the Americans with Disabilities Act. According to the student's disability documentation, she is eligible for extended time on tests and use of a note-taker.

Questions for Reflection and Teaching Notes

What are the issues for Dr. Miller as he prepares to teach this course?
The class is diverse, comprising traditional- and nontraditional-age students who may vary in their skills with the use of a Web-based teaching platform. There is also a student with a language-based learning disability who may be reluctant to post questions and responses online because of weaknesses in her writing skills. Dr. Miller incorporates lectures into his teaching, with implications for note-taking, an area for which one student uses accommodations.

Which of the principles of UDI are most important for him to consider?
Given the diverse students in this class, principles 1 (equitable use), 2 (flexibility in use), and 6 (low physical effort) are particularly relevant.

Using the principles of UDI as a guide, what strategies do you suggest for Dr. Miller in planning an inclusive course?
Dr. Miller could plan to send a "Welcome" e-mail message before the first class begins that includes a link to the class Web site, a description of sections and their purpose on the class home page, and a link to the university's technical support for using Web CT/Vista (principle 1). Topics and dates for which discussion board postings are required could be identified in advance on the course syllabus, so that the student

with the learning disability could develop a draft and seek editing assistance before posting (principle 2); PowerPoint notes for class lectures could be posted in advance so that *all* students have the opportunity to come to class with a working outline (principle 6). While Dr. Miller does not currently use an online test format for the course, it is possible to permit extended test time online, should he modify the course in the future (principle 1).

Phase 2: Delivering Instruction

Mr. Stegman teaches a satellite summer course offered by ABC Community College to students in the nursing program. The course spans four weekends and is held in a public school classroom. Each session is a full day of lessons and activities. The room is small and has no air conditioning. Although the class has only seventeen students, he finds that many of them are distracted by the physical challenge of being in a small room in the summer heat. He has talked to the administrative personnel about the physical size and space of the classroom, but he has not received much sympathy. The budget is tight at the college, and the registrar is not always able to get air-conditioned rooms for summer classes. Mr. Stegman has talked to a faculty colleague about the impact of the classroom conditions on student learning. She told him to ignore the problem; if students are less engaged because of physical elements beyond his control, there is nothing he can do about it.

Questions for Reflection and Teaching Notes

What are the issues for Mr. Stegman as he considers how he is delivering instruction?
The physical environment of the classroom and the length of the daily schedule for delivery of the course content are major concerns.

Which of the principles of UDI are important for him to consider?
Principles 4 (perceptible information), 7 (size and space), and 8 (community of learners) are relevant in this case.

Using the Principles of UDI as a guide, what strategies do you suggest for Mr. Stegman in revising his course delivery?
Given the challenges of the learning space and schedule, creating a sense of community among students is particularly important. Before the first class, Mr. Stegman could contact students to acknowledge the rigor of the class schedule and encourage them to share ideas about the instructional environment (e.g., building in enough time for lunch, varying the structure of a class day) (principle 8). With advance planning, Mr. Stegman could vary the environment for delivering instruction by scheduling several class meetings in alternative, more user-friendly settings. For example, they could use the college's library, which is air-conditioned and has space allocated for instruction, including seminar rooms for small-group work (principle 7). On specific dates, class time could be structured so that small groups work on tasks (e.g., content-specific research questions, problem-based activities) outside of the allocated classroom, then come together to debrief and brainstorm about the topic (principles 4 and 7).

Phase 3: Assessing Learning Outcomes

Professor Mancini is planning assignments for her History 206 class. She usually assigns the class a set of readings, two quizzes, a midterm exam, and a final exam. It is a fairly large class, so all tests are in multiple-choice format. She feels this works well, since students have to be able to recall a large amount of declarative knowledge. However, she realizes that not all students are equally comfortable with multiple-choice questions. Though she is aware that some students perform better on other test formats, such as oral presentations, she is uncomfortable changing the test format due to the size and nature of the class.

Questions for Reflection and Teaching Notes

What are the issues for Dr. Mancini as she considers her assessment of learning outcomes?
While Dr. Mancini would like to be sensitive to students' test-taking abilities and preferences for test format, she also knows that factual learning is critical to the course objectives and that efficiency in the amount of time required for grading is essential.

Which of the principles of UDI are most related to these issues?
Principles 1 (equitable use), 2 (flexibility in use), and 5 (tolerance for error) are germane to the issues.

Using the principles of UDI as a guide, what strategies do you recommend for Dr. Mancini to make her assessment of student learning more inclusive of diverse students?
Dr. Mancini might consider an alternative to the two quizzes that she has previously structured as multiple-choice. Students could use class notes as well as chapter summaries they have developed while taking the quiz in class. This would reinforce students' class attendance and completion of reading assignments and accommodate diverse abilities in recalling facts (principle 2). Dr. Mancini could also design a multiple-choice test option for which students could explain their selection of the answer, affording a flexible alternative based on the rationale for item choice (principle 5). She could also set a threshold for dropping an item based on the percentage of the class answering incorrectly (e.g., 75% or more missing an item) (principle 1).

DISCUSSION

The case study method is well suited to the challenges of supporting college faculty in enhancing their knowledge and practice of inclusive instruction. While the principles of UDI provide faculty with a framework for considering a range of inclusive practices, case studies are a complementary approach to assisting faculty in building a schema for implementing UDI. Guiding faculty through the process of applying the principles in the classroom and providing a forum for faculty dialogue and exchange with colleagues around realistic dilemmas promote faculty growth in moving along a continuum, from novice to more expert instructional decision-makers. As Shulman (1986) concurred, the development of instructional decision-making should entail the "careful confrontation of principles with cases, of general rules with concrete documented events—a dialectic of the general with the particular" (p. 13).

Moving from general principles to guided practice in instructional problem solving allows faculty to consider unique classrooms and specific context considerations affecting instruction, such as campus missions or academic disciplines. The engaging format and flexible structure of cases make this approach adaptable to a number of different professional development strategies and settings. While it is important to be in tune with campus opportunities for training as they arise, we have found presemester professional development days, new faculty orientation, and teaching assistant orientation sessions to be prime settings for case study training and discussions. Often, departmental-level training in the form of brown-bag lunches focus on teaching, and online discussion boards provide engaging platforms for case study dialogue.

The use of a case study approach to promoting the application of UDI should be tempered by the awareness that finding ways to engage faculty in a process of examining their views and approaches to teaching comprises a major challenge (Saroyan, Amundsen, McAlpine, Weston, Winer, & Gandell, 2004). It is not unusual for faculty to view themselves as content experts and scholars rather than teachers. To effectively engage in a collaborative process of exploring the use of UD principles in instruction requires acknowledgment that a professor's "area of expertise is a matter of professional self-identity" (Saroyan et al., 2004, p. 16). It is also important to understand the broader context of the institution and its culture. Promoting a philosophy of proactively designing and using inclusive instructional strategies to benefit a wide range of learners, including students with disabilities, will be successful only if a systemic process is developed, with the clear support of top-level administrators (Saroyan et al., 2004; Seldin, 1995).

In the recent report of the Secretary of Education's Commission on the Future of Higher Education (U.S. Department of Education, 2006), the quality of student learning in our colleges and universities is described as inadequate and, in some cases, declining. The Commission has called for "a robust culture of accountability and transparency," including the measurement of student learning outcomes (pp. 20, 23). Research initiatives to examine the results of inclusive instructional strategies grounded in the paradigm of UD must be undertaken to avoid the danger of false claims regarding the efficacy of UD and its applications. Precision in clearly articulating the theory and its principles, as well as rigor in investigating the work of faculty in creating accessible instruction, hold great promise as higher education seeks to address the learning needs of a diverse student population. As noted, the use of case studies that incorporate principles and focus on practice has received a great deal of attention as an approach for training instructors. We believe that this methodology is well suited for advancing the dialogue about UD and its application to instruction. With a diverse audience of participants (e.g., faculty, disability services professionals, administrators, graduate students) and systematic data collection that includes qualitative comments based on reflection about the case study process, another tool for promoting inclusive teaching may contribute to efforts to refine teaching in more engaging ways.

REFERENCES

Algozzine, B., Ysseldyke, J., & Elliott, J. (1997–1998). *Strategies and tactics for effective instruction.* Longmont, CO: Sopris West.

Brophy, J., & Good, T. L. (1986). Teacher behavior and student achievement. In M. Wittrock (Ed.), *Third handbook of research on teaching* (pp. 328–375). Chicago: Rand McNally.

Center for Universal Design. (2007). *About universal design: Universal design history.* Raleigh: North Carolina State University, The Center for Universal Design. Retrieved November 8, 2007, from http://www.design.ncsu.edu/cud/about_ud/udhistory.htm

Chronicle of Higher Education. (2006). *Almanac Issue 2006–2007.* Washington, DC: Author.

Darling-Hammond, L., & Baratz-Snowden, J. (2007). A good teacher in every classroom: Preparing the highly qualified teachers our children deserve. *Educational Horizons, 85*(2), 111–132.

Fink, L. D. (2003). *Creating significant learning experiences.* San Francisco: Jossey-Bass.

Henderson, C. (1999). *College freshmen with disabilities: Statistical year 1998.* Washington, DC: American Council on Education.

Hutchings, P. (1993). *Using cases to improve college teaching: A guide to more reflective practice.* Washington, DC: American Association for Higher Education.

Kame'enui, E. J., & Carnine, D. W. (1998). *Effective teaching strategies that accommodate diverse learners.* Upper Saddle River, NJ: Merrill.

Lynn, L. (1999). *Teaching and learning with cases: A guidebook.* Chappaqua, NY: Seven Bridges Press.

McGuire, J. M., & Scott, S. S. (2006). Universal design for instruction: Extending the universal design paradigm to college instruction. *Journal of Postsecondary Education and Disability, 19*(2), 124–134.

Morrison, J. (2003). *U.S. higher education in transition* [Electronic version]. *On the Horizon, 11,* 6–10. Retrieved July 26, 2005, from http://horizon.unc.edu/courses/papers/InTransition.asp

Saroyan, A., Amundsen, C., McAlpine, L., Weston, C., Winer, L., & Gandell, T.(2004). Assumptions underlying workshop activities. In A. Saroyan & C. Amundsen (Eds.), *Rethinking teaching in higher education: From a course design workshop to a faculty development framework* (pp. 15–29). Sterling, VA: Stylus.

Scott, S. S., McGuire, J. M., & Shaw, S. F. (2001). *Principles of universal design for instruction.* Storrs: University of Connecticut, Center on Postsecondary Education and Disability.

Seldin, P. (1995). Improving college teaching. In P. Seldin et al., *Improving college teaching* (pp. 1–12). Bolton, MA: Anker.

Shulman, J. (Ed.). (1992). *Case methods in teacher education.* New York: Teachers College Press.

Shulman, L. (1986). Those who understand: Knowledge growth in teaching. *Educational Researcher, 15*(2), 4–14.

U.S. Department of Education. (2006, September). *A test of leadership: Charting the future of U.S. higher education.* Washington, DC: Author.

Wasserman, S. (1994). *Introduction to case method teaching: A guide to the galaxy.* New York: Teachers College Press, Columbia University.

12

Engaging Higher Education Faculty in Universal Design
Addressing Needs of Students with Invisible Disabilities

Andrea M. Spencer
Olga Romero

As the higher-education population has become more diverse, faculty struggle to adapt peda-gogy to meet students' varied learning needs. Some of these needs go unrecognized, as with students with invisible learning disabilities. However, anxiety, confusion, and the prospect of failure for these students may be reduced through the implementation of basic principles of universal design (UD). However, the process of change in higher education can be limited by the level of faculty familiarity and experience with UD and the support available for stu-dents with disabilities. This chapter describes the early stages of the Higher Education Dis-ability Support–Universal Design Principles (HEDS-UP) project, which is federally funded to initiate change within higher education institutions through professional development on UD principles and strategies.

Dramatic increases in the number of students with learning disabilities in postsec-ondary institutions (U.S. Department of Education, 2000) have begun to affect higher education. It has been estimated that up to 9% of students in higher education have disabilities and that, of those, 5% report having learning disabilities (Wolanin & Steele, 2004). As they move from secondary to postsecondary school, students must assume primary responsibility for informing schools of their disabilities and propos-ing accommodations that will support their learning (Stodden & Conway, 2003), as legal mandates differ at these two educational institutions. Without the support they relied on in high school, many of these students struggle to adjust to the expecta-tions of higher education faculty and staff (Heiman & Kariv, 2004). However, within institutions of higher education, faculty familiarity and experience with various types of disabilities and practices and willingness to provide accommodations vary widely (Vogel, Leyser, Wyland, & Brulle, 1999).

A recognition of these challenges for both faculty and students with learning disabilities led to the Higher Education Disability Supports–Universal Design Principles (HEDS-UP) project, a federally funded project to improve the quality of higher education for undergraduate and graduate students with learning disabilities at two institutions: a large public university on the West Coast (IHE-1) and a small private graduate school of education on the East Coast (IHE-2). The project design includes the development of three training modules to be disseminated widely among colleges and universities and focused on the understanding and application of UD principles in higher-education coursework. Although the creation of professional development training modules was a relatively straightforward goal, it became evident that the process of implementation would involve many levels of institutional engagement. To successfully change attitudes and practice, faculty would need enhanced knowledge of disabilities, academic accommodations, and UD.

The challenge of changing institutions of higher education and adopting strategies to support change (Hellstrom, 2004; Smith & Parker, 2005; Van Loon, 2001) suggests that the process of infusing principles of UD within higher education environments is no small undertaking. In recent years, colleges and graduate schools have experienced dramatic increases in diversity in terms of race, ethnicity, language background, socioeconomic status, and physical and learning disabilities. Though most aspects of diversity are fairly visible, learning disabilities are less so.

Some faculty at higher education institutions recognize individual differences in receptive and expressive learning profiles but make incorrect assumptions about lack of motivation, poor readiness for academic expectations of the institution, and generally low ability level. They may identify specific areas of performance deficit, such as writing skills, as an ongoing concern but may attribute the problem to an insufficiently selective admissions process, lack of resources for tutorial support, or job and family pressures that impinge on the academic performance of some undergraduate and graduate students. Faculty may also feel unprepared to work effectively with students with learning disabilities.

The HEDS-UP project team recognized the need to design and implement professional development experiences for faculty that would go beyond the initial stated project focus to become embedded in the curriculum and pedagogy of the institution. Organizational learning and transformation were seen as necessary to ensure that UD principles become a primary means of supporting all learners.

UD principles are grounded in the concept that products and physical environments should be designed to meet the needs of diverse individuals, including those with disabilities. Educational applications of UD principles have been described in chapter 2. When working with faculty, project staff described UD principles as providing (1) multiple means of representing information by faculty, (2) multiple means of expression and practice of knowledge and skills by students, and (3) multiple strategies for engaging learners that tap into learners' interests and motivation (CAST, 2006).

Berger and Van Thanh (2004) identified a multidimensional model of organizational change with colleges that addresses systemic, bureaucratic, collegial, symbolic, and political organizational behaviors. The project team considered each of these elements in initial planning stages, deciding to begin the process by building on collegial relationships that were highly valued by faculty, although not necessarily immune to bureaucratic or political issues. The project team recognized the importance of professional autonomy and a collaborative style in working toward institution-wide incorporation of UD principles. They recruited representatives of general and special education departments and students with disabilities as members of the project team. An interdisciplinary team and the use of technology as a tool for teaching and learning can facilitate the slow process of transformation within institutions (Tetreault & Rhodes, 2004). A work in progress, the change process has involved wide participation from the beginning.

STUDENT AND FACULTY PERSPECTIVES

Many students in higher education can be very vocal about their instructional and programmatic needs. But students with invisible learning disabilities may hesitate to raise questions or concerns that could expose them to uncomfortable scrutiny of classmates or professors. Our student interns, two capable young women with learning disabilities, told us that many students prefer to try to compensate for all learning challenges themselves, without the assistance of faculty or the Office for Students with Disabilities. In order to clarify student perceptions, student surveys were conducted at a large state university on the West Coast (IHE-1) and a small urban college dedicated to teacher preparation (IHE-2) in the Northeast. The goal was to provide a better understanding for the project team—and eventually for faculty members—of the needs and preferences of students with learning disabilities in undergraduate and graduate school courses.

The survey contained nineteen questions that asked students about themselves as learners, their educational history, learning challenges they experience, and the degree to which their courses or course content are accessible to them via universally designed pedagogical methods. In addition, students were asked to identify strategies they used to manage their own learning difficulties.

Since students were drawn from the general graduate student population, it was important to understand how many individuals considered themselves to have a specific learning challenge. Of the 102 students who responded to this question, 19% believed they had one or more significant learning problems. Seven percent (7%) had received special education services in elementary and secondary school, but only 4% had registered with the disability office at their institutions.

Survey respondents reported that the most frequent difficulties encountered included unclear expectations from instructors, writing papers and journals, managing time, and reading (Figure 12.1). When asked what would make courses more effective and accessible, the most frequent responses were more focused assignments and presentations that are more challenging and inspiring. Students also recog-

FIGURE 12.1   Survey of Students' Perceived Needs as Learners

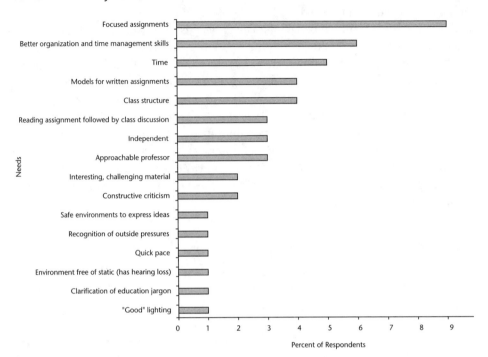

nized a need to develop better organization and time-management skills for themselves. Other needs related to preferred modes of learning (e.g., visual presentations, hands-on experiences, small-group interactive projects, and independent work), clarity of the syllabus and class structure, reading (e.g., time to complete readings, having reading assignments followed by class discussion), writing (e.g., models for written assignments, time for writing), and support from instructors (e.g., encouragement, approachable instructors, constructive criticism). Nearly three-fourths of student respondents felt that professors were comfortable in addressing the needs of students with learning difficulties.

Faculty surveys were carried out at both IHE-1 and IHE-2. Specific student learning difficulties perceived by respondents included conceptual difficulties, writing difficulties, problems understanding assignments, time management, rate of production, and processing difficulties. Faculty at both institutions saw their primary strategies for working with students with learning challenges as offering a range of assignments for students to choose from, scaffolding instruction, providing organizational aids, making themselves available, and being patient. The most frequently reported modification was allowing students extra time to complete assignments. Other modifications included reviewing sample assignments and rubrics in class, allowing students to submit multiple drafts of assignments, providing individual support, distributing handouts to detail steps in the process of preparing assignments, e-mailing lesson plans to students a week in advance, and having students work on collaborative projects. Instructors reported that they used video and Web-based resources as a way of providing multiple types of input for students. However, despite having an array of strategies for helping students overcome learning challenges, faculty saw themselves as limited by insufficient familiarity with student needs and time to devote to them. They also expressed concerns about equity of assessment and their limited knowledge of the range of possible instructional accommodations.

Questions were raised at both sites concerning support for students with learning challenges. However, there were clear differences in the types of questions and concerns expressed by faculty at the two institutions. IHE-1 faculty respondents were less likely to question the presence of students with disabilities in their teacher education program and seemed to accept personal responsibility for providing support to individual students more readily. IHE-2 faculty members, in contrast, were more likely to have questions about whether or not students with disabilities can meet the expectations of a graduate program. They seemed to see support as an institutional charge rather than a faculty responsibility. Taken together, these two groups of faculty may represent the continuum of familiarity with and attitudes about serving students with disabilities that is evident to a greater or lesser degree in many institutions of higher education. Creating institutional change is important in both circumstances if the higher education experience is to be sufficiently supportive to students with disabilities.

STRATEGIES FOR DEEPENING UNDERSTANDING

Though initial surveys and focus groups provided information about student and faculty needs and perspectives, project staff recognized that the change process required a deeper level of understanding before it would be reasonable to expect faculty buy-in. At IHE-2, a whole-faculty presentation began the process in the spring of an academic year. An overview of UD principles and shared data from student and faculty surveys prompted lively discussion. More questions arose. Faculty members recognized that a number of their students were struggling with several aspects of their graduate school programs, and they were intrigued with the possibilities of UD to mitigate those struggles. They could see the benefits of simplifying syllabi, providing visual materials and graphic supports for verbal presentations, offering students choices of assignments, and encouraging students to become more aware of their own learning styles. All these ideas had potential for making courses more accessible to all students, including those with invisible disabilities. Some voiced concerns about the integrity of course content and fairness to all students (similar to those described by Scott, 1997). Several expressed an interest in being part of the development process the following academic year.

In the second year of the project, the IHE-2 special education faculty reserved a monthly meeting for a UD workshop. The project team then organized large- and small-group presentations of UD principles to be shared with colleagues from different programs. Between presentations and the informal conversations among faculty, a new common language began to emerge—an essential communicative element of the change process. References to UD now seem to bubble up in a variety of curriculum and committee discussions.

Building on the interest level generated by the first presentation to the whole faculty, smaller workshops in the fall provided focused professional development on UD principles and formed the basis of discussion for user groups that shared ideas about UD and provided feedback to each other in informal settings. Monthly (voluntary) department meetings focused discussions on implications of UD for instruction across a variety of course and fieldwork expectations. Faculty members examined their syllabi, looking at details such as visual organization and clarity of expectations and began to work toward a goal of posting all syllabi online within one semester. Instructional presentations were videotaped, shared, and critiqued.

Smaller workshops offered hands-on opportunities for faculty, who brought their syllabi, class assignments, and activities and worked directly with the project team to make their own course materials more accessible to students with disabilities. A key realization was that small changes could have an important impact. Faculty who initially felt overwhelmed by the prospect of redesigning their whole course structure became enthusiastic about making small revisions based on UD principles within the context of their own course content and teaching styles.

PATHWAYS TO PRACTICE

Recognizing that experience is often the best teacher, the project team worked together to analyze and experiment with aspects of instruction, syllabus design, and assignments to make them more congruent with UD. After videotaping and analyzing class instruction, redesigning a syllabus, and developing alternative multimedia materials to support course instruction, the project team shared their experiences in an informal workshop for the special education department. Emphasis was on small, manageable action research projects focused on making changes in syllabus format, clarity of assignments, and instructional strategies and seeking student feedback about the value of course adaptations. Among experienced faculty there was an understandable reluctance to change formats and practices, but for others, shared examples of small modifications were key motivators. "I can't wait to try [additional strategies] in my course next semester!" was an attitude that a number of department members expressed.

Following the workshop, an evaluation included a query about modifications that faculty had already made in their courses to increase accessibility for all students, including those with invisible disabilities. Even participants who confessed that they were not very familiar with UD principles began to recognize and share UD strategies they already implemented in their teaching, such as improving the format of the syllabus and color-coding different sections, posting an agenda for each class session, providing students with choices for fulfilling assignment requirements, and regularly collecting feedback from students. A review of the workshop evaluation reflected not only a high level of participant interest in the topic but also their desire to hear and be shown more about the practical applications of UD principles. Responses of faculty included comments such as "We need to form small groups where we look at each other's teaching very closely" or "We need more of this in our department! We're just talking about it for the first time."

Other survey respondents asked questions like "How do we include adjuncts and share this information?" or "We need to explore the tension between the time it takes to implement UD and the amount of time we actually have." Some made suggestions: "Maybe more people should volunteer to be videotaped while teaching or to have a small group look at one's syllabus" and "It would be useful to have discussions with faculty across programs about accommodations they've made."

The format of course syllabi has been traditionally left to faculty, and it was with some trepidation that the issue of more uniform syllabus design was brought forward. Individuals with learning disabilities and others communicated frustration with the degree of variation in syllabi. One graduate student said, "Some syllabi are pages long, with multiple parts; others are a simple outline. It always takes me a week or two just to orient myself to the syllabus."

Although sensitive to anything that might appear to be a mandate for a particular syllabus format, faculty were responsive to concerns raised by students and began to think together about ways to make syllabi more consistent, while considering some of the pitfalls for students with learning disabilities in both online and hard-copy syllabi. One of the modifications being piloted is a standard and accessible Web-based template. The goal is to create a standard visual format students can expect every time they take a course. The standard format offers options for individuals who need to deal with new information in small chunks by providing weekly assignments that can be accessed one at a time, as well as a complete syllabus to give students a perspective on the whole course from beginning to end. Since some students with learning disabilities prefer stepwise processing and report a higher need for self-orientation, planning, and monitoring their learning (Heiman, 2006), these adjustments appear likely to produce increased learning efficiency and are relatively easy to implement.

Related features of the campus software system were also explored as tools for supporting learners with disabilities. For example, the software allowed instructors to use an actual calendar to list due dates for assignments. But the same information could easily be provided in list form for those who did not find the calendar user-friendly. Other options included listing all individual grades and absences so that students had access to the instructor's information and thus a better idea of how they were doing in the course at any time during the semester. After the trial period, students will be polled to see if, in fact, the new syllabus format helps them navigate the syllabus more easily. The computer information systems department will make the necessary technology adjustments to the format according to students' responses.

In addition to online syllabi, computer-based resources provide numerous opportunities to adapt instructional materials using text-to-speech functions, speech output, modification of font size, and captioned video materials for students who have reading problems, are blind, or have visual, mobility, or hearing impairments. Auditory amplification through use of earphones for computer-based work or classroom presentations also supports students with hearing impairments. The accessibility of Web-based resources allows students with mobility impairments to work nearly anytime and anywhere. The current availability of flash drives reduces the physical effort required to carry course materials and assignments from place to place. While the HEDS-UP project has focused on students with learning disabilities, as long as specific accessibility issues are addressed (e.g., providing all content on a Web site in text format), the implementation of UD principles improves the quality of higher education for individuals with many different disabilities, including those with multiple disabilities.

As part of the creation of a "UD frame of mind" in both institutions, rubrics are being developed that allow faculty to apply UD to their teaching in a systematic way. These rubrics apply to instructional strategies, syllabus design, assignments, and assessments (see Table 12.1). Faculty have participated in the design process at each level, reviewing and testing rubrics to make sure they include critical elements of teaching and learning in a way that can be useful to faculty for self- and peer evaluation.

Video clips of instructors edited by the faculty provide a tool for self-evaluation using the rubric for instruction. Videotapes were analyzed privately and thoughtfully by each faculty member, thus reducing the anxiety of individuals as they viewed and edited their own tapes. The editing process provided many opportunities for reflection and analysis that produced surprising realizations: "I was explaining the concept while writing on the whiteboard, my back to the class—thus presenting problems for anyone with a hearing impairment! I also lost the ability to monitor group understanding of the concept I was describing." Once edited, the video clips provided a great stimulus for discussion, which in turn led to recognition by other faculty: "I turn away while I'm talking all the time too!" Equally important, the group began to share ideas for addressing common teaching behaviors that might present obstacles for students with learning and other disabilities.

Using rubrics to develop and examine syllabi, class presentations, and assignments have led teachers to small increments of change. One strategy that emerged from faculty analysis of instructional practices facilitated the note-taking process in class—a difficult task for English-language learners, students with auditory processing problems, and students who process information slowly. In one graduate class, two note-takers volunteered to take notes during each session on a rotating basis. All class members participated. Their notes were collected, copied, and shared with the group. It quickly became evident that this note-sharing system highlighted very different learning styles, some organized and linear, others with intriguing graphics to support understanding. This strategy can be expanded. Notes can be scanned and made available digitally, taking steps to ensure that all content presented is offered in a text-based, accessible format. Using electronic versions of notes, students can highlight salient information and reorganize notes or listen to notes by means of text-to-speech software.

Students were enthusiastic about the opportunity to share and compare note-taking strategies to enhance their understanding of class presentations and course concepts. In the sharing process, they became more aware of a primary UD principle: the importance of multiple ways of sharing information. The collegial process provided a context that emphasized shared creativity, and it produced practical approaches to making course content accessible to students with diverse learning abilities and varied cultural and educational backgrounds.

TABLE 12.1   A Rubric of Universal Design Principles as Applied to Higher Education Assignments and Assessments

Universal Design Principle	Assignments and Assessments	Score
1. Equitable use	Assignments and assessments demonstrate competency through a combination of oral, written, or graphic products and live and video demonstration.	3
	Assignments and assessments demonstrate competency through at least two of the following: oral, written, or graphic products and live and video demonstration.	2
	Assignments and assessments demonstrate competency through only one of the following: oral, written, or graphic products and live or video demonstration.	1
2. Flexibility in use	Assignments and assessments allow the student a broad range of choice of topic, product, and research strategies.	3
	Assignments and assessments allow the student some choice of topic, product, and research strategies.	2
	Assignments and assessments do not allow the student a choice of topic, product, and research strategies.	1
3. Simple and intuitive	Assignments and assessments are described in simple terms with differential levels of structure and performance requirements based on student need.	3
	Some assignments and assessments are described in simple terms with some differential levels of structure and performance requirements based on student need.	2
	Assignments and assessments are not described in simple terms or with differential levels of structure and performance requirements based on student need.	1
4. Perceptible information	All assignments and assessments allow for alternative products, including oral presentations, artistic expression, and use of assistive technology (e.g., spelling check, word prediction, and text-to-speech software).	3
	Some assignments and assessments allow for alternative products, including oral presentations, artistic expression, and use of assistive technology (e.g., spelling check, word prediction, and text-to-speech software).	2
	Assignments and assessments do not allow for alternative products, including oral presentations, artistic expression, and use of assistive technology (e.g., spelling check, word prediction, and text-to-speech software).	1
5. Tolerance for error	All assignments and assessments emphasize feedback to improve performance with options for corrective revisions.	3
	Some assignments and assessments emphasize feedback to improve performance with options for corrective revisions.	2
	Assignments and assessments do not emphasize feedback to improve performance with options for corrective revisions.	1

TABLE 12.1   A Rubric of Universal Design Principles *(continued)*

Universal Design Principle	Assignments and Assessments	Score
6. Low physical effort	Assignments and assessments emphasize tasks that require low levels of physical effort.	3
	Some assignments and assessments emphasize tasks that require low levels of physical effort.	2
	Assignments and assessments require tasks with high levels of physical effort.	1
7. Size and space for approach and use	All assignments and assessments take into account the accessibility of resources, including library, technology laboratory, meeting areas, and online interaction, and so on.	3
	Some assignments and assessments take into account the accessibility of resources, including library, technology laboratory, meeting areas, online interaction, and so on.	2
	Assignments and assessments do not take into account the accessibility of resources, including library, technology laboratory, meeting areas, online interaction, and so on.	1
8. Instructional climate	Assignments and assessments require inclusion and integration of varied research, thought, and opinions.	3
	Some assignments and assessments require inclusion and integration of varied research, thought, and opinions.	2
	Assignments and assessments do not require inclusion and integration of varied research, thought, and opinions.	1
9. Community of learners	Assignments and assessments require collaborative and cooperative planning, implementation, and analysis of knowledge and skills related to the course.	3
	Assignments and assessments require some collaborative and cooperative planning, implementation, and analysis of knowledge and skills related to the course.	2
	Assignments and assessments do not require collaborative and cooperative planning, implementation, and analysis of knowledge and skills related to the course.	1

Source: Adapted from *Principles of Universal Design for Instruction* by Sally Scott, Joan McGuire, and Stan Shaw, Center on Postsecondary Education and Disability, University of Connecticut. Copyright 2001. Adapted and reprinted with permission.

The number of faculty who have participated in large or small workshops continues to increase, and individual faculty members seek out project team members for suggestions about modifying assignments that seem to be especially difficult for students to understand or complete successfully. References to UD as a strategy for program improvement have appeared in diverse contexts at the college. The project team and members of the special education staff report new questions from their colleagues, such as "I'd like to make my Science for Teachers course more accessible for students. Can we have lunch and talk about some ideas?" These experiences represent important changes among a faculty that had virtually no exposure to UD for instruction before the project began.

The rubric for evaluating assignments has prompted faculty to consider principles of UD in planning for choices among assignments, use of various media, simplicity and clarity of directions, and varied levels of structure to ensure that students understand and can respond to faculty expectations without undue confusion and stress. Though no one expects that rubrics will be applied to each assignment, they have provided a common framework for discussions in faculty study sessions across departments. Although the rubrics are constantly being modified according to feedback from faculty, they have been shared with colleagues in other institutions, with the proviso that they are a work in progress.

These early attempts at incorporating UD principles into higher-education institutions at graduate and undergraduate levels has produced a number of insights as the project team works toward development and dissemination of three professional development modules. The challenge is designing learning experiences for faculty that will, in and of themselves, provide a model of pedagogy that emphasizes multiple means of representation, multiple means of expression and practice, and multiple means of engagement.

Project staff will meet with the Program Review and Curriculum committees to propose that the principles be adopted as part of the existing guidelines used in course creation, course revision, and program review. The goal is to ensure that all new courses will incorporate UD tools as a way to better serve every student enrolled in a course, not just students with disabilities. Additional workshops for faculty from all college divisions will continue to heighten awareness of what UD can do to solve the problems and increase the possibilities for students with invisible learning disabilities and others.

Initial ideas about creating change through a collegial model of organizational transformation have so far seemed to engage faculty. In an attempt to institutionalize the use of UD principles, efforts are expanding beyond the initial instructional focus to begin to implement systemic changes. The Admissions Committee at one institution has already implemented a change in procedures to ensure that applicants with writing difficulties have the opportunity to complete a required on-site writing sample using word processing and related tools (e.g., spelling check, grammar check), instead of handwriting an essay as in the past. The Integrated Master's Project Committee is considering alternatives to traditional options for culminating projects that would better accommodate diverse learners.

CONCLUSION

Although the process of institutional change is sometimes slow, both faculty and students express excitement about new opportunities not only for success in teaching and learning for students with visible and invisible disabilities, but also for students whose individual learning profiles reflect the rich diversity of higher education in the twenty-first century. Capturing small increments of progress in many different courses, fieldwork experiences, and interactions with students presents ongoing challenges. The project team has focused on qualitative changes in educational practice in terms of the variety of modifications and accommodations introduced by faculty and the effect that such changes have on student performance. In quantitative terms, the number of faculty involved in training and small-group work on course adaptations and modifications also provides a measure of change within the institution. As is true in any new learning situation, the learning curve is different for different faculty members and institutions. Our project team has concluded that awareness and change happens most effectively from the ground up. Institutions that wish to spread awareness of the needs of students with disabilities and that want their faculties to embrace UD as a guide for practice must provide multiple forums in which faculty can interact, share experiences, express frustrations, and ultimately, become more willing to examine their own teaching practices through a new lens. Progress will be gradual; it will ebb and flow, but it will happen.

REFERENCES

Berger, J. B., & Van Thanh, D. (2004). Leading organizations for universal design. *Equity and Excellence in Education, 37*, 124–134.

Center for Applied Special Technology (CAST). (2006). *Universal design for learning.* Retrieved November 5, 2007, from http://www.cast.org

Heiman, T. (2006). Assessing learning styles among students with and without learning disabilities at a distance-learning university. *Learning Disability Quarterly, 29*, 55–63.

Heiman, T., & Kariv, D. (2004). Coping experience among students in higher education. *Educational Studies, 30*(4), 441–455.

Hellstrom, T. (2004). Between a rock and a hard place: Academic institutional change and the problem of collective action. *Higher Education, 48*, 511–528.

Scott, S. S. (1997). Accommodating college students with learning disabilities: How much is enough? *Innovative Higher Education, 22*(2), 85–99.

Smith, D. G., & Parker, S. (2005). Organizational learning: A tool for diversity and institutional effectiveness. *New Directions for Higher Education, 131*, 113–125.

Stodden, R. A., & Conway, M. A. (2003). *Supporting individuals with disabilities in post-secondary education.* Honolulu, HI: Center on Disability Studies, National Center for the Study of Postsecondary Educational Supports, National Center of Secondary Education and Transition.

Tetreault, M. K., & Rhodes, T. (2004). Institutional change as scholarly work: General education reform at Portland State University. *Journal of General Education, 53*(2), 81–106.

U.S. Department of Education. (2000). *Twenty-first annual report to Congress on the implementation of public law 101-476: The Individuals with Disabilities Education Act.* Washington, DC: Author.

Van Loon, R. (2001). Organizational change: A case study. *Innovative Higher Education, 25*, 285–301.

Vogel, S. A., Leyser, Y., Wyland, S., & Brulle, A. (1999). Students with learning disabilities in higher education: Faculty attitude and practices. *Learning Disabilities Research & Practice, 12*(3), 173–187.

Wolanin, T. R., & Steele, P. E. (2004). *Higher education opportunities for students with disabilities: A primer for policymakers.* Washington, DC: The Institute for Higher Educational Policy.

13

Incorporating Universal Design into Administration Courses
A Case Study

Karen A. Myers

For universal design to be understood and utilized by faculty and student affairs profession-als, educational preparation programs must address this concept through disability aware-ness, pedagogical practices, and experiential learning. As a result, future educators will be prepared to utilize universal instructional design (UID) in their classes, and future student affairs professionals will be prepared to use universal design in their programs and services. In her student affairs and higher education preparation programs, the author incorporates UID into her classes and teaches universal design to current and future higher education fac-ulty and student affairs practitioners. In this chapter, the author addresses her academic plan for infusing UID into professional preparation programs and discusses courses and modules used in professional development efforts.

> People will forget what you said, people will forget what you did, but people will never forget how you made them feel.
> —*Bonnie Jean Wasmund*

It is my goal as an educator to foster understanding and appreciation of human dif-ferences while helping people recognize the importance of civility and inclusion. One way to demonstrate this philosophy is to apply universal instructional design (UID), which can create an environment that fosters inclusion. Teaching UID to stu-dents who will be developing their own courses and teaching their own classes is a rewarding experience. Teaching universal design while utilizing UID, thus mod-eling what is being taught, is an exhilarating experience. As a professor in a gradu-ate higher education/student affairs preparation program, I am in the "exhilaration" stage and thrilled to be there. Educating future teachers and practitioners in how to use universal design in their classes, curriculum, services, programs, and daily work can be accomplished through a variety of methods and techniques with a multimodal approach. By eliminating barriers in the classroom and providing equal access for all students to all information, I employ "pedagogical curb cuts" (Ben-Moshe, Cory, Feldbaum, & Sagendorf, 2005), also known as UID. In this chapter, I address my academic plan for infusing UID into professional preparation programs, focusing on competency-based learning, instructional practices, and in-class and online delivery methods. I also discuss courses and modules related to disability.

BACKGROUND

Anecdotal evidence suggests that universal design has not been a significant part of the curriculum in the program in which I teach or at my current institution as a whole. My only student who was familiar with the concept prior to my class was the university's disability services provider. As I conduct campuswide seminars on disability issues, it is becoming apparent to me that few faculty and teaching assistants have even heard of UID. Although it has been presented, written about, and discussed in our country for many years (e.g., Silver, Bourke, & Strehorn, 1998), UID appears to be a well-kept secret on many college campuses.

This chapter relates primarily to my institution, a religious-affiliated private research university in the Midwest with an enrollment of 11,800 (approximately 7,500 undergraduate students and 4,300 graduate students). Founded in 1818, the institution offers degrees in the fields of law, medicine, natural and health sciences, social sciences, business, education, aviation, technology, and the humanities. The Higher Education graduate program is housed in the Department of Educational Leadership and Higher Education in the College of Education and Public Services. Degrees offered in the program are a master's in Student Personnel Administration and a Ph.D. or Ed.D. in Higher Education Administration. The Higher Education faculty and the Educational Leadership faculty (both in the same department) form a collaborative team, working together to educate students to become highly qualified elementary, secondary, and postsecondary teachers and administrators. In support of its mission, the university welcomes diversity in its faculty, staff, and students—diversity in racial, religious, and ethnic backgrounds and beliefs. It fosters a community of learners and promotes social justice and service to others. This philosophy of inclusion is a natural fit with the intentions of universal design.

DESCRIPTION OF IMPLEMENTATION

My teaching responsibilities at this institution include courses in higher education curriculum, organization, and administration in higher education; student personnel administration; student development theory; higher education culture; and college teaching. Given this unique opportunity to educate future postsecondary faculty and practitioners, I made a conscious decision at the outset to incorporate universal design into every course I taught. Not only do I educate students about universal design, but I also make every effort to model UID by using these strategies in all my classes. My latest venture has been developing and teaching a course called Disability in Higher Education and Society.

In each of my classes, I assess learning styles with a learning style inventory, and students provide me with their expectations of the course via e-mail during the first week of the term. Armed with this valuable information, I can use UID as planned or modify my strategies to fit the learning styles, needs, and expectations of the students.

I first discussed the idea of incorporating UID in every class with the department chairperson, not only to inform him about UID but also to gain his support. Building on informal communication with colleagues in the department and at other institutions and with current graduate students, I developed an academic plan as to how I would utilize, model, teach, and, in the process, spread the word about universal design. As a result of intentional communication with the director of the university's Center for Teaching Excellence (CTE), I now partner with the Center, utilizing its expertise in my college teaching course. In turn, I present campuswide workshops on disability awareness, policies, rights and responsibilities, communication, and UID. I model UID in the workshops with the use of large-print handouts, open-captioned videos, and multiple delivery methods and instructional strategies. I provide coaching (i.e., guiding) and scaffolding (i.e., incorporating hints and tips) to the participants as they apply UID techniques and processes to various scenarios. When participants leave the educational setting, they should be able to reflect on their performance in the educational experience workshop, reflect on what they have learned about UID, articulate that knowledge in their own work and provide reasons for their decisions, and explore new opportunities to use UID as they apply various strategies and observe their effects.

THE PLAN

For ten years, I consulted on disability issues and dabbled in universal design. As director of disability services and an adjunct faculty member in a student affairs graduate program at a midwestern regional institution, I developed a course on disability in higher education at the urging of my graduate students. They wanted to learn more about communicating with students with disabilities, a topic their curriculum did not provide. The course addressed disability law, policies, procedures, responsibilities, language, communication, disability types and models, and universal design. It emphasized barrier-free facilities and classrooms. Years later, as director of disability services at a large public research institution on the West Coast, I contributed to a book chapter on integrating disability into professional preparation programs (Evans, Herriott, & Myers, in press). This opportunity motivated me to revise and update the original course to address two essential topics: viewing disability through a social construct lens and utilizing UID through modeling, teaching, and experiential exercises.

An insatiable desire ensued among my colleagues to spread the word about incorporating disability issues into the higher education curriculum. The disability course and sample modules of it were shared at national, state, and local venues. In my role as chair of the disability committee for the American College Personnel Association (ACPA)–College Student Educators International, I collaborated with the commission for professional preparation programs to cultivate interest in the infusion of disability information into graduate programs nationwide. This collaboration led to a national research project (described under The Research Project) addressing disability knowledge and disability education of graduate students in professional preparation programs.

My next step was to offer a three-week online noncredit course, Disability and Student Development, through ACPA's E-Learning Series. I designed, developed, and implemented this online course using UID, with a component of the course addressing universal design. My coinstructor and I insisted on modeling UID throughout the entire course. During course preparation we learned about the accessibility capabilities of Blackboard, an online course development program, and of JAWS, screen-reader software commonly used by people who are blind. This online course served as a precursor to the national seminar, Enhancing Learning for Students with Disabilities: The Intersection of Disability Studies and Student Development Theories, which was offered in spring 2006 at the National Center for Higher Education in Washington, DC. The 3-day seminar was one of the most edifying experiences of my career. It was there that I gleaned essential information to be used in my new course, which was offered as a result of my research project conducted in winter 2006.

THE RESEARCH PROJECT

Rationale. The number of college students with disabilities has tripled in the last two decades to approximately 9% of the undergraduate population (U.S. Census Bureau, 2000), and the numbers continue to climb. Nondiscrimination laws have opened the doors of higher education to students with disabilities who may never have considered college a viable option. These students are engaging in graduate and undergraduate programs, accessing student services, participating in campus clubs and organizations, living in residence halls, working in libraries and labs, and participating in institutional events. Despite the fact that legislation that prohibits discrimination against people with disabilities was enacted years ago (e.g., Section 504 of the Rehabilitation Act of 1973 and the Americans with Disabilities Act of 1990), knowledge of disability issues and sensitivity about inclusion are lacking on our campuses and in our communities. It is essential to educate future faculty, practitioners, and university administrators in this area.

Purpose. The purposes of this study were to determine (1) how much graduate students know about disability inclusion and (2) if students are interested in enrolling in a course designed around disability issues.

Methodology. I developed a questionnaire to assess graduate student interests and needs regarding the infusion of a disability course or disability modules into existing program curricula. The survey asked seven questions, including one that identified the student's current degree program. The final question was open-ended, allowing the participants to list any other courses they would like added to their curriculum.

Chairpersons and program coordinators of selected graduate programs were asked, via e-mail, to send the questionnaire to their students. Students received an introductory e-mail message from me explaining the purpose of the survey.

I sent surveys to 29 higher education/student affairs professional preparation programs throughout the United States (with names obtained from the ACPA Web site) and to four selected colleges (approximately 20 graduate programs) within my home institution. Of the 784 respondents, 67% were enrolled in master's programs and 33% in doctoral programs. Fifty-seven percent (57%) of the respondents expressed interest in enrolling in the proposed disability course. Of these, 24% preferred an online course, 32% preferred a classroom course, and 44% would take either. Seventy-one percent (71%) of the respondents saw a need for this type of course in their degree programs. Regarding course requirements, 57% said that it should be an elective course; 27% believed it should be a module within an existing course, and 13% reported that it should be required. When asked about their knowledge of disability issues in higher education, 53% believed that students with disabilities do not fully participate in higher education and 62% said they do not know what steps to take to ensure that students with disabilities can fully participate in higher education. These responses revealed an interest in and need for some type of disability education.

THE COURSE AND MODULES

Given the results of this study, I was allowed to develop and offer an experimental course through our higher education graduate program. The three-credit hybrid course, Disability in Higher Education and Society, meets for 24 hours face to face and 21 hours online using Blackboard. After two semesters, the course was officially approved and is now required for the master's program in Student Personnel Administration. In preparation for the course, I enrolled in a seven-week noncredit online course on Competency Assessment in Distributed Education (CADE). The CADE model is a "backward design approach from competencies to evidence to tasks . . . [which] makes the assessment of student competencies within designed tasks explicit from the start" (Association of Jesuit Colleges and Universities, 2004, p. 1). With the disability course as the CADE assignment, my first task was to develop strategic, procedural, and factual knowledge competencies. Strategic knowledge competencies are complex thinking strategies and processes that students will utilize during the class and in their lives beyond the classroom. One strategic knowledge competency for the disability course is the following: "Students will learn strategies to create an environment that fosters inclusiveness." This strategic competency is complemented by the following procedural knowledge competency: "Students will learn techniques for incorporating universal design into academic and student services environments." Evidence of student mastery for this strategic competency is that students are able to use techniques for structuring educational settings in accordance with suggested universal design methods. Through the CADE process, I was able to develop competencies; evidence for student mastery; instructional tasks to reveal the evidence; course modules; instructional strategies using the Cognitive Apprenticeship model; and a timeline for designing, developing, and implementing the hybrid course.

Additional preparation for me included participation in an online seminar, Low-Tech Strategies to Incorporate Technology into Teaching, offered through the university's CTE. Based on the seven principles for good practice in undergraduate education of Chickering and Gamson (1991), the seminar addressed best practices for using technology, such as streaming videos, PowerPoint with audio, and Web-based discussion boards, both in and out of the classroom. It was particularly helpful to those of us who were technology novices and timid about using it in our classes. This seminar gave us confidence and encouragement—so much so that I incorporated a podcast into my syllabus this semester. Now *that* is progress.

Instructional resources that are well received by students in the course and in classes utilizing modules, are the videos, handouts, and online materials offered by the Disabilities, Opportunities, Internetworking, and Technology center at the University of Washington (DO-IT, n.d.a). The AccessCollege site encourages students to utilize DO-IT's online resources, such as the Faculty Room, Student Services Conference Room, Board Room, Student Lounge, and the Center for Universal Design in Education. Some assignments entail the use of the Web site's streaming videos, access information, and readings (DO-IT, n.d.b).

The Disability in Higher Education and Society course and modules utilize UID in the following ways: course notes and readings in accessible online formats; large-print handouts; multimodal course instruction, delivery methods, and resources; open-captioned videos; individual and group work; and an online discussion board. Prior to the first day of class, students complete an online learning inventory. Survey results provide valuable information to me and to the students themselves. Knowing students' learning styles, I prepare the course accordingly, modifying existing lesson plans and developing new plans to meet the their needs. Adjusting to a variety of learning styles in teaching the course content is an excellent way to apply UID. And UID can be used comfortably by faculty who, like me, employ a constructivist model of teaching, in which students are encouraged and expected to construct their own meaning and take responsibility for their own learning.

Modules addressing disability and UID have been incorporated into other courses offered at the university (e.g., Law in Higher Education, Curriculum in Higher Education, Student Personnel Administration, Counseling and Diversity) and for professional development (e.g., CTE seminars, Student Development brown-bag sessions, and university leadership institutes). Especially useful in the student affairs sessions are DO-IT's universal design for student services materials (DO-IT, 2002–2006).

GAUGING SUCCESS

Formative and summative evaluations are used throughout the course. At the end of each class session, students respond in writing to the following questions: "When were you most engaged in today's class? When were you least engaged in today's class?" From time to time, I also use "Three Checks and a Wish," a quick and easy assessment idea suggested by one of my students (R. Von der Hyde, personal communication, March 2006). Students write down three lessons learned that session and one topic they wish could be covered by the end of the course or be improved when the course is offered again. Both of these exercises give me immediate feedback to which I can respond in a timely fashion. They allow me to keep my finger on the pulse of the class and, accordingly, make changes in current and future courses. Students are asked to complete an online midterm evaluation, which I use for my own edification and to make curricular adjustments, as I deem necessary.

Students also complete an online final evaluation conducted by the academic department. I use these final assessment results to improve or modify the course the next time it is offered. Seminar and workshop participants (faculty, staff, and students) also provide feedback via evaluation forms at the end of the session. I use constructive criticism to improve and enhance future presentations.

LESSONS LEARNED

My UID modeling and universal design instruction have so far received high marks from learners. Students, faculty, and staff appear genuinely interested in the topic and are pleased to know they can participate proactively in the universal design movement. They enjoy applying what they have learned to the scenarios presented to them in classes and other instructional sessions, and they enthusiastically collect examples and samples of universal design techniques and strategies.

The CADE course, a pedagogically based workshop, supports both faculty and curriculum development. Through presentations, readings, timely feedback, and discussions with the instructor and classmates, the course provides the unique opportunity to develop the hybrid course and modules using the backward design approach, which focuses first on the learner and the learner's competencies and then on evidence and instructional tasks. Much time was spent pondering this question: "What do you want students to be able to do beyond the classroom?" This type of thinking shifts attention from learning outcomes for the class to learning outcomes for life.

Future plans at this institution include providing face-to-face and online seminars in UID for faculty and teaching assistants. These will be offered through CTE workshops for student affairs administrators and practitioners on utilizing universal design in student services. Also planned are meetings or sessions on universal design for university administrators and continued courses and modules on universal design infused into the higher education curriculum.

To gain more expertise in the UID field, I attended a 3-day train-the-trainer workshop on UID through the University of Minnesota's Pedagogy and Student Services for Institutional Transformation (PASS IT) program. As a result of that workshop, I organized a campus UID Community of Practice, a small group of faculty who are interested in teaching and modeling UID principles. I accompanied four members of the Community of Practice to subsequent UID PASS IT training, and the group continues to develop and conduct UID educational initiatives to transform institutional student services and pedagogy.

It has been my experience that faculty, staff, and students are more receptive now to the idea of designing their courses, programs, and services for all students utilizing UID, rather than focusing exclusively on students with disabilities. Marketing universal design seminars, classes, and other training options by relating them to diversity or multicultural inclusion rather than disability inclusion puts more people in the seats. By focusing on inclusion of *all* students, we are taking the spotlight off persons with disabilities and putting it where it should be: on society as a whole. We are asking society (e.g., members of the campus community) to make change by incorporating universal design into their lives, work, classes, and services. We are not asking persons with disabilities to change to fit our agendas; rather, we are asking the institution to create an environment that fosters total inclusion. With universal design, we all benefit.

REFERENCES

Americans with Disabilities Act of 1990. 42 U.S.C.A. § 12101 *et seq.*

Association of Jesuit Colleges and Universities. (2004). *Competency assessment in distributed education.* Washington, DC: Author.

Ben-Moshe, L., Cory, R., Feldbaum, M., & Sagendorf, K. (Eds.). (2005). *Building pedagogical curb cuts: Incorporating disability in the university classroom and curriculum.* Syracuse, NY: Graduate School, Syracuse University.

Chickering, A., & Gamson, Z. (Eds.). (1991). *Applying the seven principles for good practice in undergraduate education.* San Francisco: Jossey-Bass.

Disabilities, Opportunities, Internetworking, and Technology (DO-IT). (n.d.a). DO-IT publications, videos, and training materials. Seattle: University of Washington. Retrieved November 1, 2007, from http://www.washington.edu/doit/Brochures/

DO-IT. (n.d.b). *AccessCollege: Postsecondary education and students with disabilities.* Seattle: University of Washington. Retrieved November 1, 2007, from http://www.washington.edu/doit/Resources/postsec.html

DO-IT. (2002–2006). *Applying universal design to specific student service units.* Seattle: University of Washington. Retrieved November 1, 2007, from http://www.washington.edu/doit/CUDE/apply_ud.html

Evans, N., Herriott, T., & Myers, K. (in press). Integrating disability into the diversity framework of our professional preparation and practice. In A. Mitchell & J. Higbee (Eds.), *Making good on the promise: Student affairs professionals with disabilities.* Washington, DC: ACPA and University Press of America.

Section 504 of the Rehabilitation Act of 1973, as amended. 29 U.S.C. § 794 *et seq.*

Silver, P., Bourke, A., & Strehorn, K. C. (1998). Universal instructional design in higher education: An approach for inclusion. *Equity and Excellence in Education, 2,* 47–51.

United States Census Bureau. (2000). *Disability.* Retrieved November 1, 2007, from http://www.census.gov/hhes/www/disability/disability.html

PART 3

Universal Design of Student Services, Physical Spaces, and Technological Environments in Higher Education

In Part Three, the authors share perspectives and strategies for applying universal design principles to student service units, such as career services, admissions, tutoring centers, and housing and food services; physical spaces, such as classrooms; and technological environments, such as Web-based lectures. The following chapters detail how the authors' efforts have led to the desired outcome, namely, that all students and their associates (e.g., parents), including those with disabilities, feel welcome and are able to participate effectively in institutional offerings.

Universal Design in Higher Education

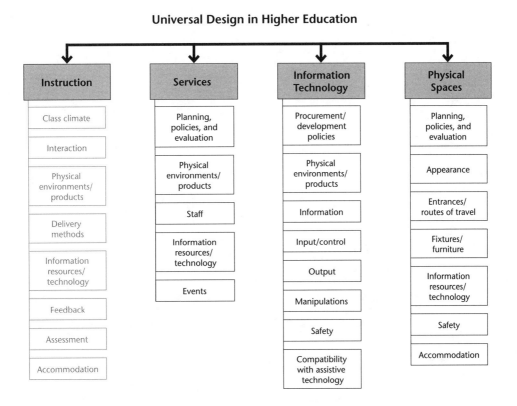

Source: S. Burgstahler (2007). Applications of Universal Design in Education. Seattle: University of Washington. http://www.washington.edu/doit/Brochures/Academics/app_ud_edu.html

14

Universal Design of Student Services
From Principles to Practice

Sheryl E. Burgstahler

This chapter includes strategies, a process, and resources for applying universal design to student service units in institutions of higher education. The result is services that are more welcoming and useful for all students.

Here is a math problem: In an ongoing effort to improve services, a registration officer invited a group of nine university students to discuss their experiences registering for courses. One of the participants requested a sign language interpreter for the meeting. Later, the office accountant looked at the interpreting bill and remarked, "Wow, $80 for one student! That's expensive." The registration officer said, "Oh, no, the cost was only $8 per person; ten of us participated in the discussion." The registration officer's response embodies a view that considers the interpreting service to be of value to each participant in the group—interpreting what others are saying for the benefit of the deaf student and interpreting what the deaf student is saying for the benefit of others.

The student service officer described in this example clearly values equity and social integration. If access and inclusion issues are dealt with in a systemic way throughout the unit, everyone who interacts with the service's staff and resources will have a positive experience. Universal design (UD) holds promise as a paradigm for setting goals, developing a process, and then implementing inclusive practice within student service units.

STUDENT SERVICES AND UNIVERSAL DESIGN

Institutions of higher education offer a range of student services that may include libraries, admissions and registration offices, student housing, career centers, computer labs, tutoring and learning centers, food services, and student organizations. As campuses are becoming more diverse with respect to such characteristics as gender, age, race, ethnicity, culture, physical and sensory abilities, learning styles, reading ability, and native language, the accessibility and usability of student services to a diverse audience increases in importance.

If a student service goal with respect to diversity is that everyone who needs to use the service can do so comfortably and efficiently (Burgstahler, 2007, p. 1), staff would want to ensure that everyone feels welcome and can

- get to the facility and maneuver within it;
- communicate effectively with support staff;
- access printed materials and electronic resources;
- fully participate in events and other activities.

UD holds promise for making a student service welcoming, accessible, and usable for everyone. As explained in Parts One and Two of this book, UD has a rich history in architecture and commercial product development and, more recently, in instructional design. Ronald Mace coined the term *universal design* and defined it as "the design of products and environments to be usable by all people, to the greatest extent possible, without the need for adaptation or specialized design" (Mace, n.d.). In its application to postsecondary campus units, UD means that services are designed not for the average user but for people with a broad range of abilities, disabilities, ages, learning styles, native languages, cultures, and other characteristics. It is important to keep in mind that students (as well as staff) may be diverse with respect to such skills as reading, vision, hearing, mobility, and communication. Preparing a service that will be accessible to them will make it more usable by everyone and minimize the need for special accommodations, as discussed in earlier chapters of this book.

Although there is no federal mandate to apply UD to a student service in higher education, civil rights laws cannot be ignored. For example, virtually all postsecondary institutions are covered entities under Section 504 of the Rehabilitation Act of 1973 and the Americans with Disabilities Act of 1990. These laws prohibit discrimination against individuals with disabilities. With respect to student service units, no otherwise qualified students with disabilities should be excluded from the participation in programs or activities or be denied access to resources offered to others solely by reason of their disabilities (U.S. Department of Justice, 2005). Being proactive in making a campus unit accessible to students with a wide variety of disabilities goes a long way toward the ultimate goal of UD.

Reports of applying accessible and universal design to student service units, though not plentiful, are beginning to appear (e.g., Kroeger & Schuck, 1993; Sheppard-Jones, Krampe, Danner, & Berdine, 2002; Uzes & Connelly, 2003; Wisbey & Kalivoda, 2003). These publications suggest a growing interest in the application of UD to student services. The following sections in this chapter include a process, guidelines, and resources that may help student service units apply UD.

A PROCESS FOR UNIVERSAL DESIGN OF A STUDENT SERVICE

UD is a process as well as a goal. Keys to applying UD principles when designing a new student service or upgrading an existing one are to plan ahead and keep the diversity of the campus population in mind at each design phase. The following steps outline a process for the application of UD to a student service unit (Burgstahler, 2007, pp. 1–2). They are adapted from the more general process presented in chapter 1 and are also summarized in Figure 14.1.

1. *Identify the service.* Select a student service (e.g., library, tutoring center, career services office). Consider the purpose of the campus unit, specific services and resources provided, facility constraints, budget, and other issues that affect the range and delivery of services provided.

2. *Define the universe.* Describe the overall population and then consider the diverse characteristics of those who might potentially use the service (e.g., students and other visitors with diverse characteristics with respect to gender; age; size; ethnicity and race; native language; learning style; and abilities to see, hear, manipulate objects, read, and communicate).

3. *Involve consumers.* Involve people with diverse characteristics (as identified in Step 2) in all phases of the development, implementation, and evaluation of the service. Also, gain perspectives of students through diversity programs such as the campus disability services office.

4. *Adopt guidelines or standards.* Review research and best practices to identify specific strategies for the delivery of an effective service (e.g., best practices for housing and food services, career services, a tutoring center, or other services as identified in Step 1). Create or select existing universal design guidelines and standards for the service (e.g., DO-IT, n.d.a). Integrate universal design practices with other best practices within the field of service.

5. *Apply guidelines or standards.* Apply universal design strategies in concert with other best practices, both identified in Step 4, to the overall design of the service, all subcomponents of the service, and all ongoing operations (e.g., procurement processes, staff training) to maximize the benefit of the service to students with the wide variety of characteristics identified in Step 2.

6. *Plan for accommodations.* Develop processes to address accommodation requests (e.g., arrangements for a sign language interpreter) from individuals for whom the design of the service does not automatically provide access.

7. *Train and support.* Tailor and deliver ongoing training and support to student service staff.

8. *Evaluate.* Include universal design measures in the evaluation of the service; evaluate the service with a diverse group of students; and make modifications based on their feedback. Provide ways to collect ongoing input from service users (e.g., through online and printed instruments and communications with staff).

The following section suggests UD guidelines and practices that can be identified as part of Step 4 and then applied to create a welcoming, accessible, and usable student service.

FIGURE 14.1   A Process of Universal Design for Student Services

GUIDELINES FOR APPLYING UNIVERSAL DESIGN TO STUDENT SERVICES

The application of UD can help administrators ensure that everyone can comfortably use all aspects of the provided service. A checklist of UD strategies for student service units is maintained at the Disabilities, Opportunities, Internetworking, and Technology (DO-IT) Center (Burgstahler, 2007; DO-IT, n.d.a). It was developed, tested, and applied in collaboration with more than 20 postsecondary institutions nationwide as part of the DO-IT Admin project to improve the accessibility of student service units (DO-IT, 2007). DO-IT Admin was funded by a 3-year grant from the Office of Postsecondary Education (OPE) of the U.S. Department of Education. When project collaborators field-tested a checklist for the UD of any student service (Burgstahler, 2007), they learned that student service organizations expressed an interest in having discreet checklists tailored to the unique characteristics of their specific units. In response, the original checklist (DO-IT, n.d.a) was modified and unique lists were created for

- Recruitment and undergraduate admissions
- Registration
- Financial aid
- Advising
- Housing and residential life
- Tutoring and learning centers
- Computer labs
- Libraries
- Career services

Although no single checklist can capture all the issues to address in the design or redesign of a campus service, these publications provide a good starting point for administrators who wish to implement UD. All checklists are working documents; practitioners are encouraged to propose revisions to DO-IT and to modify them for their own use. Included below are categories of UD applications that are common to most of the student service checklists.

- *Planning, policies, and evaluation.* Consider diversity issues as you plan and evaluate services.
- *Physical environments and products.* Ensure physical access, comfort, and safety in an environment that is welcoming to visitors with a variety of abilities, racial and ethnic backgrounds, genders, and ages.
- *Staff.* Make sure staff are prepared to work with all students.
- *Information resources and technology.* Ensure that publications and Web sites welcome a diverse group, content is accessible to all visitors, and technology in the service area is accessible to everyone.
- *Events.* Ensure that everyone can participate in events sponsored by the organization.

Under each guideline, specific strategies for implementation are suggested. Table 14.1 provides examples of these strategies.

As reflected in the checklist, an essential skill for student service staff is to be able to communicate effectively with all students. The following suggestions provide some general guidance in this regard (Honolulu County Committee on the Status of Women, 1998):

- Don't single out a person's sex, race, ethnicity, or other personal traits or characteristics (such as sexual orientation, age, or a disability) when it has no direct bearing on the topic at hand. In other words, don't create or promote stereotypes based on unavoidable human characteristics.
- Be consistent in your description of members of a group: Don't single out women to describe their physical beauty, clothes, or accessories or note a disabled person's use of an aid, or refer to the race of the only minority in a group unless it is at that individual's request.
- Keep in mind that inclusive language is for general cases. Direct requests by individuals take precedence over general rules.

Specifically, administrators should make sure that staff members are trained to support individuals with diverse abilities, respond to specific requests for accommodations in a timely manner, and know who to contact if they have disability-related questions. To provide guidance in this area, the DO-IT checklist in the publication *Equal Access: Universal Design of Student Services* (Burgstahler, 2007), includes communication hints, which are also listed in Table 14.2.

In the OPE-funded project called AccessCollege, staff conducted a nationwide survey of student service personnel (DO-IT, n.d.b). Data analysis resulted in further refinements to the checklists. Furthermore, AccessCollege team members report that

TABLE 14.1   Universal Design of Student Services

Universal Design Guidelines	Examples of Universal Design Applied to a Student Service
1. *Planning, policies, and evaluation.* Consider diversity issues as you plan and evaluate services.	• Include students with disabilities in planning and review processes and advisory committees. • Consider accessibility issues in procurement processes. • Address disability-related issues in evaluation methods.
2. *Physical environment.* Ensure physical access, comfort, and safety within an environment that is inclusive of people with a variety of abilities, racial and ethnic backgrounds, genders, and ages.	• Be sure there are ample high-contrast, large-print directional signs to and throughout the office. • Keep aisles wide and clear for wheelchair users and protruding objects removed or minimized for the safety of users who are visually impaired.
3. *Staff.* Make sure staff are prepared to work with all students.	• Ensure that all staff members are familiar with disability-related accommodations, including alternate document formats and procedures for responding to requests for accommodations, such as sign language interpreters.
4. *Information resources and technology.* Ensure that publications and Web sites welcome a diverse group and content is accessible to everyone.	• In key publications, include a statement about a service commitment to access and procedures for requesting disability-related accommodations. • Ensure that Web resources adhere to accessibility guidelines or standards. • For student service unites that use computers as information resources, ensure that commonly used assistive technology is available.
5. *Events.* Ensure that everyone can participate in events sponsored by the organization.	• Ensure that events are located in wheelchair-accessible facilities and that information about how to request disability-related accommodations is included in promotional materials.

Source: S. Burgstahler. (2007). Equal access: Universal design of student services. Seattle: University of Washington.

measurable change toward UD of a student service requires ongoing staff training, encouragement, and systematic monitoring but that UD can be implemented in steps.

RESOURCES

The combined efforts of teams of postsecondary institutions who collaborated in DO-IT's three OPE-funded projects resulted in the creation and maintenance of five Web sites, with content tailored to the interests of specific stakeholder groups:

1. The Faculty Room
2. The Student Services Conference Room
3. The Board Room
4. The Student Lounge
5. The Center for Universal Design in Education

TABLE 14.2   Hints for Communicating with Individuals Who Have Disabilities

Treat people with disabilities with the same respect and consideration with which you treat others. There are no strict rules when it comes to relating to people with disabilities, but here are some helpful hints.

General
- Ask people with disabilities if they need help before providing assistance.
- Talk directly to the person, not through the person's companion or interpreter.
- Refer to a person's disability only if it is relevant to the conversation. If so, mention the person first and then the disability. "A man who is blind" is better than "a blind man" because it puts the person first.
- Avoid negative descriptions of a person's disability. For example, "a person who uses a wheelchair" is more appropriate than "a person confined to a wheelchair." A wheelchair is not confining—it's liberating!
- Do not interact with a person's guide dog or service dog unless you have received permission to do so.

Blind or Low Vision
- Be descriptive. Say, "The computer is about three feet to your left," rather than "The computer is over there."
- Speak all the content presented with overhead projections and other visuals.
- When guiding people with visual impairments, offer them your arm rather than grabbing or pushing them.

Learning Disabilities
- Offer directions/instruction both orally and in writing. If asked, read instructions to individuals who have specific learning disabilities.

Mobility Impairments
- Sit or otherwise position yourself at the approximate height of people sitting in wheelchairs when you interact.

Speech Impairments
- Listen carefully. Repeat what you think you understand and then ask the person with a speech impairment to clarify and/or repeat the portion that you did not understand.

Deaf or Hard of Hearing
- Face people with hearing impairments so they can see your lips. Avoid talking while chewing gum or eating.
- Speak clearly at a normal volume. Speak louder only if requested.
- Use paper and pencil if the person does not read lips or if more accurate communication is needed.
- In groups, raise hands to be recognized so the person who is deaf knows who is speaking. Repeat questions from audience members.
- When using an interpreter, speak directly to the person who is deaf; when an interpreter voices what a person who is deaf signs, look at the person who is deaf, not the interpreter.

Psychiatric Impairments
- Provide information in clear, calm, respectful tones.
- Allow opportunities for addressing specific questions.

Source: S. Burgstahler. (2007). *Equal Access: Universal design of student services.* Seattle: University of Washington.

Of specific relevance to this chapter is the Student Services Conference Room, which includes a collection of documents, checklists, and videos to help student service administrators and staff make their offerings welcoming, accessible, and useful to everyone. Also relevant here is the Center for Universal Design in Education, which disseminates information on all aspects of UD applied to educational settings. Consult any of these Web sites by selecting "*AccessCollege*" from the DO-IT home page at http://www.washington.edu/doit/.

CONCLUSION

UD holds promise for making student service units welcoming, accessible, and usable for all students. The authors of the next chapter are students with disabilities (Scott Ferguson, Eric Patterson, and Lacey Reed) and student service practitioners (Alice Anderson, Rebecca Cory, Pam Griffin, and Patricia Richter). They share their experiences and recommendations with respect to UD of student services. In chapter 20, Terry Thompson discusses the application of UD to a specific service area, campus computer labs.

REFERENCES

Americans with Disabilities Act of 1990. 42 U.S.C.A. § 12101 *et seq.*

Burgstahler, S. (2007). *Equal access: Universal design of student services.* Seattle: University of Washington. Retrieved November 1, 2007, from http://www.washington.edu/doit/Brochures/Academics/equal_access_ss.html

Disabilities, Opportunities, Internetworking, and Technology (DO-IT). (n.d.a) *Resources for student services staff.* Seattle: University of Washington. Retrieved November 1, 2007, from http://www.washington.edu/doit/Conf/staff_resources.html

DO-IT. (n.d.b). Survey on universal design of student services. [Unpublished raw data.]

DO-IT. (2007). *DO-IT Admin: A project to help postsecondary student services administrators work successfully with students who have disabilities.* Seattle: University of Washington. Retrieved November 1, 2007, from http://www.washington.edu/doit/Brochures/Academics/admin.html

Honolulu County Committee on the Status of Women. (1998). *Do's and don'ts of inclusive language.* Honolulu, HI: Author. Retrieved November 1, 2007, from http://honolulu.hawaii.edu/intranet/committees/FacDevCom/guidebk/teachtip/inclusiv.htm

Kroeger, S., & Schuck, J. (1993). *Responding to disability issues in student affairs.* San Francisco: Jossey-Bass.

Mace, R. (n.d.). *About universal design (UD).* Raleigh: North Carolina State University, The Center for Universal Design. Retrieved November 1, 2007, from http://www.design.ncsu.edu/cud/about_ud/about_ud.htm

Section 504 of the Rehabilitation Act of 1973, as amended. 29 U.S.C. § 794.

Sheppard-Jones, K., Krampe, K., Danner, F., & Berdine, W. (2002). Investigating postsecondary staff knowledge of students with disabilities using a Web-based survey. *Journal of Applied Rehabilitation Counseling, 33*(1), 19–25.

United States Department of Justice. (2005). *A guide to disability rights laws.* Washington, DC: U.S. Department of Justice, Civil Rights Division. Retrieved November 1, 2007, from www.ada.gov/cguide.pdf

Uzes, K. B., & Connelly, D. O. (2003). Universal design in counseling center service areas. In J. Higbee (Ed.), *Curriculum transformation and disability: Implementing universal design in higher educa-*

tion (pp. 241–250). Minneapolis: Center for Research on Developmental Education and Urban Literacy, University of Minnesota.

Wisbey, M. E., & Kalivoda, K. S. (2003). Residential living for all: Fully accessible and "liveable" on-campus housing. In J. Higbee (Ed.), *Curriculum transformation and disability: Implementing universal design in higher education* (pp. 215–230). Minneapolis: Center for Research on Developmental Education and Urban Literacy, University of Minnesota.

The content of this chapter was developed under grants from the U.S. Department of Education Office of Postsecondary Education (grant numbers P333A020044 and P333A050064). However, this content does not necessarily represent the policy of the Department of Education, and you should not assume endorsement by the federal government.

15

Applications of Universal Design to Student Services
Experiences in the Field

Alice Anderson
Rebecca C. Cory
Pam Griffin
Patricia J. Richter
Scott Ferguson
Eric Patterson
Lacey Reed

In this chapter, four administrators describe how universal design was implemented in student services units on their campuses, and three students with disabilities share their experiences in using campus services. Access issues and solutions include those related to planning, policies, and evaluation; facilities; staff training; information resources; computer software; and campus events. Practitioners may find these insights useful as they design student services in higher education.

Student services are an important part of any institution of higher education. As campuses strive to become more competitive and respond to the pressure to address a spectrum of needs for students as whole, well-rounded people, administrators have created a variety of services to support them. These include residential life programs, counseling centers, and career centers, as well as niche services like minority student centers and support services for gay, lesbian, bisexual, and transgender students. One-time special programs, such as campus orientation or commencement, and initiatives for first-year students are also common in higher education. The application of universal design strategies holds promise for making all these programs and services welcoming, accessible, and usable for everyone.

The coauthors of this chapter share examples of challenges faced by students with a variety of disabilities as they access student services, as well as how some administrators have implemented universal design in aspects of their student service units. Student coauthors provide the perspectives of students with disabilities that affect sight, mobility, speech, learning, and social interaction. Other coauthors include members of a team of disability services and student life professionals from a diverse set of colleges and universities around the country. These professionals work together to develop and promote practices that advance the implementation of universal design. They are part of the AccessCollege team, which is directed by the Disabilities, Opportunities, Internetworking, and Technology (DO-IT) Center at the University of Washington (UW). To meet their goal of preparing postsecondary faculty and administrators to fully include students with disabilities in their courses and service units (DO-IT, 2007a), AccessCollege team members offer training in universal design and accommodations to faculty and staff on their campuses.

The topics discussed in this chapter are organized around a checklist that is included in the publication *Equal Access: Universal Design of Student Services* (Burgstahler, 2007b). This checklist was developed and updated in two projects funded by the U.S. Department of Education (DO-IT, 2007 a, b) and continues to be improved by the AccessCollege team in an iterative process. To validate the checklist, a large group of disability student services and career services personnel were asked to respond to a survey distributed nationwide. Initial analysis of the results shows that all areas of access referred to in the checklist are considered "important" or "highly important" by the majority of respondents (DO-IT, n.d.).

The coauthors of this chapter hope that their experiences will inspire other campuses to take concrete steps to ensure that student services benefit all students. Their comments are organized around the five subcategories of the current student services accessibility checklist:

1. Planning, policies, and evaluation
2. Physical environments and products
3. Staff
4. Information resources and technology
5. Events

PLANNING, POLICIES, AND EVALUATION

This section of the checklist asks the user to think about diversity while planning, creating policies, and evaluating programs. When universal design is used to inform the policies of an institution, the result is accessibility and usability for people with a wide range of characteristics.

One way universal design can inform institutional planning policies is by considering accessibility in the procurement process. Purchasing inaccessible products places a burden on some students. For example, a student who is blind said, "[I had a] programming instructor who expected me to use a software utility that was not accessible with screen readers and keyboard commands. I was frustrated." This student was unable to work independently with that software because accessibility was not considered when the software package was purchased. When an institution implements a policy requiring forethought about accessibility in the procurement process, it promotes access and usability for all members of the campus community. UW has such a policy: Its purchasing officers added a requirement in contracts for Web design stating that the resulting product must meet accessibility standards.

Policies that ensure timely responses to requests for accommodations can also make the campus more welcoming. For example, a student who is blind noted, "It frequently takes more time for students with disabilities to acquire [accessible] material." Encouraging faculty to prepare reading lists and order materials in advance is one step toward ensuring equal access for students with print-related disabilities (e.g., students who are blind, students with dyslexia).

Institutions can be proactive by implementing policies that require accessibility. For example, at Kutztown University in Pennsylvania, the administration implemented a policy for on-campus events (Kutztown University, 2006):

> Meetings, events, programs and activities that are open to the public or the Kutztown University campus community must be held in an accessible location. There may be attendees who need reasonable accommodation. The Room Scheduler system was remodeled so that currently inaccessible spaces will require a second approval before they can be scheduled. For other accommodations, the sponsor of an event, meeting or program will include on the promotional/invitational material a statement that asks for special needs to be made known ahead of time in order to allow a reasonable accommodation.

To implement this policy, the campus revamped the online room reservation system to indicate the level of accessibility of any space and removed from the automatic system the option to reserve spaces that are inaccessible to some people. This means that when someone reserves a room through this system, they are automatically reserving an accessible space. To reserve one of the inaccessible spaces on campus, an event planner must communicate with a staff member in the room reservation department. Before the space can be reserved, the event planner must confirm that the guest list is known and no one on the list requires a physically accessible space. This reservation system makes accessibility the default and inaccessibility the exception, thus ensuring that a space is accessible to everyone planning to attend an event. Additionally, reminding event planners to include a statement that invites requests for accommodations in their materials sends the message that people with disabilities are welcome. This example recognizes that universal design requires both proactive steps and a process for arranging accommodations when needed.

PHYSICAL ENVIRONMENTS AND PRODUCTS

The second section of the checklist reminds users that universal design principles can be implemented to make the facilities and the campus's social and cultural environment more welcoming to and usable by all campus community members, including people with disabilities. Discussions of physical access to campus are often limited to providing access for individuals who use wheelchairs. Universal design of physical spaces considers the wide variety of ways in which people may wish to use the space and the difficulties they may encounter when attempting to do so. For example, the design and layout of physical spaces should be intuitive, so that people who are visually impaired or have difficulty orienting themselves in space can easily find their way. One student on the autism spectrum gave this example about his campus:

> My community college has a road system that does not circle the campus in a way that is easy to follow. Roads around a college campus should be intuitive. That means it should be easy to find your way at each place along the way, even if you can't read the signs. The road was not marked clearly by a continuous line system or signs. In several places you could not tell which way to go to get back to the main entrance, or how to exit to get off campus. You would get stuck in a parking area and not know how to get out. This made it very difficult for people with processing or directional disabilities to figure out where to go. I use the Access bus, and often a new driver would get lost. It was almost impossible for the dispatcher to give them directions over the phone because the roads were not marked.

In this case, self-advocacy of the student, with the help of his mother, brought some resolution, explained as follows:

> The administration has posted some signs now that my mom and I brought it to their attention. They did not realize how difficult the old system was for people with disabilities. When they are finished with the major construction project they are working on, they have promised to paint a continuous line on the roadway that circles the campus.

The accessibility of routes of travel also affect students with visual impairments. As one student who is blind explained:

> On my campus, some areas are not very safe and accessible for students with visual impairments . . . especially when I have had to try and cross the parking lot in order to get to the library. I was relieved when my trainer from the State Commission for the Blind helped me find an accessible route.

The student also noted, "When people park their service vehicles on the walkways, this makes it harder for me to get to the library or science building without running the risk of ending up in the parking lot." Vigilance to remove physical barriers from campuses can help meet universal design goals for a welcoming and accessible environment. A student with a mobility impairment reminds us:

> Accessible restrooms are really important. Not only does there need to be enough room for a wheelchair to navigate, there also needs to be enough room for an assistant, if needed. The handles on the door need to be universally accessible too. Often the dispensers are mounted on the wall, too close to the hand bars, which make it hard to grab the hand bars without banging your knuckles.

An easy way to improve to the usability of all physical spaces is to install window blinds to reduce glare, especially on computer screens. Window blinds help students with visual impairments, but others benefit as well. As pointed out by one student, "The reduction of sensory input will allow autistic workers to concentrate with fewer sensory problems. This also includes the ability to control other light and sound in the workspace."

Additionally, the availability of quiet spaces can benefit visually impaired students who use talking computers, as well as students with learning disabilities or attention-deficit disorders that make it difficult to focus. One student confirms the value of a space free of distractions: "I started utilizing the academic support center to do my studying. It is a quiet area with seats next to power outlets, so I can plug in my laptop."

Student service administrators should consider visual and auditory stimuli when planning student spaces. The reduction of sensory input may help many students pay attention to the task at hand. For example, a career center that is planning to incorporate computer workstations for students to use when searching for jobs may want to provide adjustable lighting at each station and reduce distractions through the use of cubicles or some other space dividers instead of open desks.

Additional space considerations to be considered by student service administrators include issues related to transportation and food services. One student offers these comments: "Student services organizations should be close to bus stops and train stations, so people with disabilities can get to and from the office using transit." That student also noted:

> It is important that cafeterias be accessible so that people with disabilities can see, reach, and choose the food, and then pay for it. Food choices also need to be accessible. Hardly anyone thinks about that. Offering food and drinks that are easy to open and eat are an important accessibility issue.

Student service offices can take a proactive stance in the improvement of facilities to make the campus appear accessible and welcoming. For example, the campus Webmaster and other staff of Information Technology Systems and Services at the University of Minnesota–Duluth (UMD) collaborated to create an accessible campus map. Now students, faculty, staff, and campus visitors can look up this map on the Web to find accessible building entrances and elevators on campus. The map helps people plan their route of travel prior to a journey. It is especially helpful to individuals with mobility impairments—both permanent and temporary—and to those who fatigue easily or are carrying large items across campus.

The admissions office is often the first point of contact between a prospective student and the college or university; therefore, making it accessible is crucial for a campus that welcomes all prospective students. In the process of redoing the reception space in one admissions office, it became apparent that a person could not see over the reception counter from a seated position. With the assistance of the facilities management office, admissions staff replaced the counter with a modular desk that accommodates a variety of counter heights. Now those who are seated and those who are standing can get the attention of staff behind the desk and use the surface to fill out forms. In allowing comfortable use by people with a broad range of physical sizes and abilities, this option is a good example of universal design.

Universal design can be applied to telephone communications as well. UMD worked with an outside contractor to install the first public videophone stations in northern Minnesota. The videophones provide a video-to-video connection, through which people who are deaf or hard of hearing can communicate by using American sign language or another means of visual communication. To call a hearing person, a deaf person can use a video relay service, in which an interpreter translates between sign and spoken word. With these systems in place, people who are deaf or hard of hearing can communicate easily and naturally with others; this contributes to a campus environment of access and inclusion.

STAFF

The next section on the checklist focuses on ensuring that staff members are prepared to help all students. One way to create a more welcoming campus is to have staff with diverse characteristics as role models for the student body. Colleges may consider ways to recruit people with disabilities in order to diversify their staff. Such steps require flexibility on the part of existing staff, but taking the time to hire a diverse staff can provide the institution with new perspectives and depth of skills. As one student pointed out:

> Because many people on the autism spectrum have high skill levels and positive attitudes toward work, it is important to consider them beyond the first impression when hiring because their abilities tend to make up for any minor social issues or lack of work experience.

Preparing staff to work with individuals with disabilities is as important as having an accessible physical environment. Staff should be ready to greet all community members who enter their offices (or contact them via phone or e-mail) and to respond to requests for accommodations. Because the quality of customer service provided to visitors is a critical component of creating a welcoming environment for students with disabilities, a list of communication hints is included in *Equal Access: Universal Design of Student Services* (Burgstahler, 2007b) and in chapter 14 of this book. Students with disabilities emphasize the need for college and university staff who are able to focus on their diverse interests and skills, not just their disabilities. One way to help students know that staff are open to working with people with disabilities is to include a statement in key publications that conveys the following:

> Our goal is to make all materials and services accessible to everyone. Please inform staff of accessibility barriers you encounter and request accommodations that will make activities and information resources accessible to you.

As one student reported:

I think it is important for student services staff to publicly state their commitment to accessibility because that assertion may be difficult for people on the autism spectrum to understand if not in writing. A physical copy of information will help them more easily make use of resources.

In an effort to improve the ability of staff to work with students with disabilities, one campus streamlined the process of arranging a sign language interpreter by creating an accessible Web-based form for interpreter requests. All staff on campus were informed of the new process and thus empowered to retain an interpreter more easily. Sharing information and streamlining processes for obtaining accommodations are examples of universal design that contribute to a welcoming and accessible campus.

INFORMATION RESOURCES AND TECHNOLOGY

The fourth section of the checklist focuses on ensuring that publications and Web sites welcome diverse groups, that information resources are available in accessible formats, and that technology in the service area is accessible to all visitors. Equal access to information is a key aspect of a universally designed campus. One visually impaired student explains:

For a Web site to be accessible to people who are visually impaired, it needs to have text descriptions for each link and graphic. The more information available and accessible online, the better it is for me. Many classes have their syllabus online. In one class I took, the professor posted his notes online, including the test reviews, and that worked great.

Providing information in an accessible electronic format allows students to access it in their preferred way: by using a screen reader or braille, reading it on screen in the preferred size, or printing it in standard or large print.

An additional way to make Web sites and campus publications more accessible is to include pictures of people with disabilities engaged in campus life. Students often look through campus publications for images with which they can identify. Making sure that they find images of individuals with disabilities, and that those individuals are engaging with others on campus, can help to cultivate a welcoming environment. Alternative text in electronic versions of these publications should describe these visuals in such a way that individuals who are blind and using text-to-speech systems can access the visual content as well.

At the University of Wisconsin–Madison, the registrar's office is continually challenged to provide enrollment information, transcripts, and tuition rates in an accessible format for students with disabilities. To achieve their accessibility goals, they have implemented an online system using commercial software along with software built by the Division of Information Technology on campus. The registrar's office, along with the disabilities services office, wrote questions to include in the annual Students with Disabilities Survey to assess the accessibility of the online registration tools. As a result of the survey, problems with online registration were identified and addressed by the Division of Information Technology, thus improving the tools' accessibility to all students, regardless of levels of ability, mobility, age, or gender, and to those with slow network connections, older hardware, diverse software platforms, and small mobile devices.

Administrators should consider space issues for all potential service users, not just the average user. One student notes that she often works with an assistant and needs room for both of them to work at the computer at the same time. Many standard workstation spaces are too small to do this. Providing adequate space for both right- and left-handed users is also important.

UMD created an assistive technology (AT) team to ensure timely responses to AT requests from students. The team focuses on providing hardware and software solutions that allow people with disabilities to access the current information technology. The team is composed of representatives of key campus constituents: disability services, information technology, the library, and human resources. Together, they respond to requests for AT and have access to a budget from which to purchase software and pay technicians to install it. The team works with all campus computer labs to ensure that adjustable tables and at least one large monitor are available to students. To take the technology to the next level, the AT team participated in UMD's Transformational Leadership Program (TLP) to teach staff how to identify and prioritize opportunities for improvement, measure the effectiveness of current services and programs, analyze what can be done better, implement new solutions, and institutionalize improvements. This curriculum, taught by the TLP, is based on the process improvement methodology used at 3M, a corporate sponsor of UMD research and process improvement initiatives. These methodologies are incorporated in a checklist that focuses on the universal design of computing environments and can be found in the publication *Equal Access: Universal Design of Computer Labs* (Burgstahler, 2007a).

UW integrated an Access Technology Lab (ATL) into the largest general-use computer lab on campus. This strategy addressed the needs for a centralized resource for AT and universal design consultation *and* for students with disabilities to be able to work side-by-side with their peers. The ATL serves all UW students, faculty, and staff through this main facility and by supporting satellite workstations located in some departmental computing labs. These satellite stations are equipped with the most commonly used AT. When additional AT is needed for a specific student in a departmental lab, ATL staff arrange to purchase appropriate products using central funds allocated for this purpose. They also provide technical support to the department staff.

EVENTS

The final section of the universal design of student services checklist emphasizes the importance of ensuring that everyone can fully participate in the campus community. Wheelchair-accessible facilities, wide aisles, and adjustable-height tables are some important considerations in making events accessible to all participants. Campus safety is another important consideration for large and small events. One student reminds us:

Autistic individuals may need to see visually where to go in an emergency. Maps and evacuation plans must be able to be followed, otherwise confusion may occur regardless of verbal instructions or practiced drills.

One institution that wanted to make its Welcome Week more welcoming to all new students used universal design principles to examine current practices and make more aspects of the orientation accessible. First, campus signage was examined to ensure that accessible entrances to buildings were easy to find and that there were large-print and braille signs in all buildings. Next, they arranged the schedule for Welcome Week to be simple and predictable: academics in the morning, exploration of clubs and employment in the afternoon, and major social events in the evening. Each required session was repeated multiple times to allow students options to plan their own schedules and eliminate the likelihood of fatigue. Finally, all students were given a guide to Welcome Week, available in print, alternate formats, and on line, allowing participants to access at their convenience the schedule of activities and session handouts. These universally designed improvements to the traditional Welcome Week activities created a more welcoming, accessible, and navigable program for all students.

CONCLUSION

Universal design can be applied to any product or environment. This chapter provides concrete examples of universal design actions that institutions of higher education have taken to improve their student services. These implementation strategies make campuses more welcoming and accessible to everyone. As the universal design of student services checklist was being field-tested, student service administrators requested checklists tailored to the unique needs of their service areas. In response, checklists were created for recruitment and undergraduate admissions, registration, financial aid, advising, libraries, computer labs, career services, and housing and residential life (DO-IT, 2007c). They can be located, along with other useful information, in the Student Services Conference Room at http://www.washington.edu/doit/Conf.

REFERENCES

Burgstahler, S. (2007a). *Equal access: Universal design of computer labs*. Seattle: University of Washington. Retrieved November 1, 2007, from http://www.washington.edu/doit/Brochures/Technology/comp.access.html

Burgstahler, S. (2007b). *Equal Access: Universal design of student services*. Seattle: University of Washington. Retrieved November 1, 2007, from http://www.washington.edu/doit/Brochures/Academics/equal_access_ss.html

Disabilities, Opportunities, Internetworking, and Technology (DO-IT). (n.d.). Survey on universal design of student services. [Unpublished raw data.]

DO-IT. (2007a). *AccessCollege: Systemic change for postsecondary institutions*. Seattle: University of Washington. Retrieved November 1, 2007, from http://www.washington.edu/doit/Brochures/Academics/access_college.html

DO-IT. (2007b) *DO-IT Admin: A project to help postsecondary campus services administrators work successfully with students who have disabilities*. Seattle: University of Washington. Retrieved November 21, 2007, from http://www.washington.edu/doit/Brochures/Academics/admin.html

DO-IT. (2007c). *Resources for student services staff*. Seattle: University of Washington. Retrieved November 1, 2007, from http://www.washington.edu/doit/Conf/staff_resources.html

Kutztown University. (2006). *Kutztown University policy 2006-305: Accessible meetings, events, programs*. Retrieved November 1, 2007, from http://www.kutztown.edu/admin/AdminServ/human/human305.htm

The content of this chapter was developed under a grant from the U.S. Department of Education Office of Postsecondary Education (grant number P333A050064). However, this content does not necessarily represent the policy of the Department of Education, and you should not assume endorsement by the federal government.

16

Universal Design of Physical Spaces
From Principles to Practice

Sheryl E. Burgstahler

When universal design (UD) is applied to physical spaces, they are welcoming, accessible, and usable for people with a wide range of characteristics. History, strategies, and processes for applying UD to physical spaces in higher education are discussed in this chapter. This content can help administrators design inclusive learning environments.

Let's start with a test. When a student has only one choice for a place to sit in an auditorium, and it is *not* next to his friends, is it (1) because *he* uses a wheelchair or is it (2) because the *space* was not designed to be flexible? When a student cannot tell that an emergency alarm is blaring, is it (1) because *she* is deaf or (2) because the designer of the emergency *alarm system* neglected to provide a visual along with the audio warning signal? The second responses to these questions resonate with the universal design (UD) paradigm, because they suggest that a disabling condition may reside in the environment rather than within an individual.

Designers who apply UD to physical spaces anticipate the wide variety of abilities and other characteristics potential users might have, and they make design decisions that both serve the needs of the broadest audience and are reasonable under the given circumstances. When an existing space is not suitable for a specific user, UD advocates consider how the environment might be improved so that, even if an accommodation must be provided to address the current situation, the accessibility barrier may be removed for future users.

The field of UD can guide institutions of higher education as they strive to make their physical environments functional and comfortable for all students, employees, and visitors. To put the practice of UD in higher education into context, highlights from the history of UD of physical spaces are shared in the next section.

HISTORY OF UNIVERSAL DESIGN OF PHYSICAL SPACES

Many people have worked toward the goal of making physical spaces welcoming, accessible, and usable. Following are some of the most noteworthy.

Pioneering Work

Marc Harrison, professor of industrial engineering at the Rhode Island School of Design (RISD), was a pioneer in what eventually became known as UD. His experiences through years of rehabilitation after sustaining a brain injury as a child gave him insight and inspiration in his design of physical spaces that could be used efficiently by everyone, including those who have disabilities or are elderly. At the end of his career, he was part of a large team of RISD faculty and students that, in 1993, became engaged in the Universal Kitchen project to design kitchens that are efficient, user-friendly, and accessible to people with a wide range of abilities. The motivation for the project is described as follows (Rhode Island School of Design, n.d., p. 1):

> Spurred by the knowledge that routine kitchen tasks force people to bend, stoop, reach and lift—repeatedly compensating for weak design in uncomfortable ways— the team began with research. Making a succession of dinners together in typical kitchens, they used careful time/motion studies to document how inefficiencies in kitchen design require more than 400 discrete steps to make a simple dinner. Ultimately, the goal was to redesign the kitchen environment and help as many potential users as possible function independently—from the young to the old.

The Universal Kitchen team disassembled common elements of a kitchen (e.g., stovetops, ovens, refrigerators, dishwashers), studied ergonomics and human factors, and researched demographic trends. They generated thousands of innovative ideas, such as continuous wet surfaces, pop-up burners, countertop waste channels, retractable appliance cords, and modular refrigeration components. Each component, designed to be custom selected and arranged, included flexible features such as heights and depths that could be manually or automatically adjusted to an individual's "comfort zone" (Rhode Island School of Design, n.d., p. 1) Prototypes of the Universal Kitchen were exhibited at the Hagley Museum and Library in New York City (n.d.), and it and similar projects were shown in other venues (e.g., Rhode Island School of Design, n.d.). The exhibitions served to increase interest in the design of environments within which people of all ages and abilities can function independently and comfortably. Together, they demonstrated that many accessibility barriers could be blamed on weak design, an observation in sharp contrast to the more traditional view that products and environments were inaccessible due to the limitations of specific individuals. Instead of looking for disabling conditions in the individual, these designers looked for disabling conditions in physical spaces.

Development of a Definition and Principles of Universal Design

The term *universal design* was coined by Ronald Mace, an internationally known architect, product designer, educator, and wheelchair user. He ultimately defined UD as "the design of products and environments to be usable by all people, to the greatest extent possible, without the need for adaptation or specialized design" (Mace, n.d., p. 1). After four years of practicing conventional architecture, Mace helped create the first building code for accessibility in the United States. It became mandatory in North Carolina in 1973, served as a model for other states, and contributed to the passage of the federal Architectural Barriers Act of 1968. This act mandates that "buildings and facilities that are designed, constructed, or altered with Federal funds, or leased by a Federal agency, comply with Federal standards for physical accessibility" (U.S. Department of Justice, 2005, p. 19).

In 1989, Mace established the Center for Accessible Housing, currently known as the Center for Universal Design, at North Carolina State University. Under Mace's direction, the Center became a leader in UD research and practice with respect to products and the built environment. Its staff created the seven principles of UD described in chapter 1. Projects that Mace directed include the creation of universally designed house plans, thermostats, toilets, faucets, bathing units, and other products. At Designing for the 21st Century: An International Conference on Universal Design held in New York in 1998, Mace delivered his last speech before his death later that year. In it he shed light on the differences between assistive technology, barrier-free design, and UD. He explained that barrier-free design, or accessible design, is predominantly focused on removing architectural barriers for people with physical disabilities through adherence to building codes and regulations, such as architectural standards mandated by the Americans with Disabilities Act of 1990 (ADA). In contrast, he said, UD defines the "user" more broadly (Reagan, 1998, p. 1):

> It's a consumer market driven issue. Its focus is not specifically on people with disabilities, but all *people*. It actually assumes the idea that everybody has a disability and I feel strongly that that's the case. We all become disabled as we age and lose ability, whether we want to admit it or not. It is negative in our society to say "I am disabled" or "I am old." We tend to discount people who are less than what we popularly consider to be "normal." To be "normal" is to be perfect, capable, competent, and independent. Unfortunately, designers in our society also mistakenly assume that everyone fits this definition of "normal." This just is not the case.

Public Awareness and Advocacy for Removal of Environmental Barriers

A barrier-free movement began that included veterans injured in World War II and other individuals with disabilities and their advocates. It gained momentum during the civil rights movement of the 1960s and resulted in the enactment of public policies and legislation mandating accessible design, including the Architectural Barriers Act of 1968 (U.S. Department of Justice, 2005). More general civil rights legislation followed. Section 504 of the Rehabilitation Act of 1973 states that "no qualified individual with a disability in the United States shall be excluded from, denied the benefits of, or be subjected to discrimination under any program or activity" (U.S. Department of Justice, 2005, p. 17) that receives federal financial assistance, which includes the vast majority of institutions of higher education. Further, Section 504 regulations address "reasonable accommodation for employees with disabilities; program accessibility; effective communication with people who have hearing or vision disabilities; and accessible new construction and alterations" (U.S. Department of Justice, 2005, p. 17).

Patricia Moore, an industrial designer and gerontologist, contributed to greater awareness of the need for UD of the built environment with her book *Disguised: A True Story* (Moore & Conn, 1984). In the book, Moore reported her experiences undertaking activities of everyday life when she disguised herself as an elderly woman and artificially limited her physical and sensory abilities. She encountered many barriers including lights that could not be turned on, directions that could not be seen, steps that could not be negotiated, knobs that could not be turned, and doors that could not be pushed by people with limited strength, sight, hearing, and motor skills. The popularity of Moore's book, her appearances on television talk shows, and related articles in magazines and newspapers increased public awareness of the extent to which the traditional built environment is inaccessible to many people.

Moore emphasizes that the solution to inaccessible design is *not* to design multiple sets of products (e.g., one for those who are young, healthy, and physically fit; one for the elderly; one for those with a specific type of disability) but rather to design products that are flexible, making them suitable for people of all ages and abilities.

Many other educators and architects have promoted accessible, usable, and universal design. For example, since the mid-1970s, James Pirkl, chair of the Department of Design at Syracuse University, has sensitized his students to the needs of people who are elderly and/or who have disabilities. In 1985, he pioneered the concept of transgenerational designs, in which products and environments are designed to be compatible with physical and sensory changes associated with aging (Cooper-Hewitt National Design Museum, 1998).

The Baby Boomers

Patricia Moore predicts that the free market system will build demand for accessible products and environments because of "the graying of America": "an unprecedented demographic bulge in the United States, in which senior citizens comprise the fastest-growing segment of our society" (Moore & Conn, 1984, p. 158). In her book (p. 160), she quotes Canadian social critic Joel Garreau as somewhat cynically describing the situation in this way:

> Greed is a far more reliable and universal agent of change than is the urge to do good for your fellow man. The future of any great idea is always made more bright when it's found to be profitable.

The increasing size of the aging population—many members of which experience varying levels of physical, sensory, and cognitive limitations—and the desire of senior citizens to continue to live in single-family housing as long as possible have kindled interest in addressing issues beyond basic wheelchair accessibility to promote UD of physical spaces. One example is universal smart home design, which is defined as "the process of designing products and housing environments that can be used to the greatest extent possible for people of all ages, abilities and physical disabilities" (Schwab, 2004). As Gordon Mansfield, former deputy secretary of the Department of Veterans Affairs and chair of the Architectural and Transportation Barriers Compliance Board, explains (Mansfield, n.d.):

Universal design is an approach to design that acknowledges the changes . . . everyone [undergoes] during his or her lifetime. It considers children, the elderly, people who are tall or short, and those with various disabilities. It addresses the lifespan of human beings beyond the mythical "average" person.

The Americans with Disabilities Act

In 1990, the ADA extended the requirements of Section 504 and increased public awareness of accessibility issues. The ADA "prohibits discrimination on the basis of disability in employment, State and local government, public accommodations, commercial facilities, transportation, and telecommunications" (U.S. Department of Justice, 2005, p. 1). The ADA requires that covered entities follow specific architectural standards in new construction and alterations of their facilities (United States Access Board, 2002). Some state laws mandate even higher standards for accessibility. Although the practice of ADA compliance focuses on a narrow range of issues (typically by employing barrier-free or accessible design), the ADA and other civil rights legislation have promoted the idea that product and facility designers should be proactive in considering users with a range of abilities rather than simply focusing on the average user.

UD goes beyond legal compliance for accessibility by addressing a broader range of user characteristics. Strategies and processes for applying UD are presented in the next sections of this chapter.

UNIVERSAL DESIGN GUIDELINES FOR PHYSICAL SPACES

UD addresses issues not only for individuals with disabilities but also for those who are short and tall, are poor readers, are left-handed, speak a variety of native languages, and have other characteristics that are not defined as disabilities. As in other applications of UD described in chapter 1, UD of physical spaces can be measured on a continuum. For example, whereas including a ramp next to steps into a building is an example of accessible design, developing a sloping entrance into that building for all visitors to use is closer to the UD ideal because it does not unnecessarily segregate people who belong to specific groups. UD encompasses both accessible design, which primarily focuses on complying with standards so as to avoid creating barriers for individuals with physical disabilities, and usable design, ergonomics, and human factors, which more subjectively measure the capacity of a product or space to allow an individual to perform a task efficiently, safely, and comfortably (Iwarsson & Stahl, 2002).

The Center for Universal Design at North Carolina State University provides guidelines and technical assistance regarding UD in housing, commercial and public facilities, and outdoor environments. Other organizations have applied the principles of UD to create guidelines and checklists for the UD of specific physical spaces. For example, the American Association of Retired Persons (n.d.) has created checklists for UD of residential spaces that include strategies for entrances, interior circulation, storage, bathrooms, and kitchens. They suggest that a universally designed home include such features as an entry with no steps; main rooms on one level; thresholds that are flush with the floor; wide doorways and hallways; nonslip surfaces; lever door handles and faucets; grab bars by toilets; rocker light switches; appliances with large print on the controls; and lighting for walkways, closets, and work areas.

The author's review of existing guidelines and checklists for accessible and universal design and formative review by postsecondary administrators led to a list of examples of strategies for the application of UD to physical spaces on postsecondary campuses. Table 16.1 shows examples of these strategies (Burgstahler, 2007, pp. 2–4).

TABLE 16.1   Universal Design of Physical Spaces

Categories	Examples of Universal Design Applied to a Physical Space
Planning, policies, and evaluation. Consider diversity issues as you plan and evaluate the space.	• Include people with diverse characteristics, including various types of disabilities, in planning processes. • Consider accessibility issues in procurement processes. • Address disability-related issues in evaluation methods.
Appearance. Design the space to foster a campus climate that is inclusive of all students, staff, faculty, and visitors.	• Create an environment that is appealing to those with a broad range of cultures, ages, abilities, and other characteristics.
Entrances, routes of travel. Make physical access welcoming and accessible to people with a variety of abilities, sizes, and ages.	• Ensure convenient, wheelchair-accessible parking spaces and routes of travel to facilities and within facilities. • Shelter entryways. • Install outdoor lights with motion sensors near entrances. • Provide sensors to automatically open exterior doors. • Use lever handles rather than knobs for doors. • Use gently sloping walks that are integrated into the design rather than steps and ramps that segregate individuals with physical disabilities. • Ensure that there are ample high-contrast, large-print directional signs to and throughout the physical space.
Fixtures, furniture. Provide fixtures and furniture that can be used by all employees, students, and visitors.	• Install levers for sink handles. • Use front-mounted, easy-to-operate controls on appliances and other equipment, with labels in large, high-contrast print. • Position electrical outlets and light switches (with dimmers) to be reached from standing or seated positions. • In classrooms, use furniture and fixtures that are adjustable in height and allow flexible arrangements for different learning activities and student groupings.
Information resources, technology. Ensure that information and technology is accessible to everyone.	• Position publications to be reachable from standing and seated positions. • Make sure directional and information kiosks are reachable from standing and seated positions.
Safety. Design the space to minimize the risk of injury.	• Use nonslip walking surfaces. • Install emergency systems that incorporate audio and visual warnings.
Accommodation. Develop a system for staff to address accommodation requests by individuals for whom the space design does not automatically provide access.	• Include procedures for requesting disability-related accommodations in signage, publications, and information kiosks.

Source: S. Burgstahler. (2007). *Equal access: Universal design of physical spaces.* Seattle: University of Washington.

The strategies were reviewed by and updated with formative feedback from members of a team of administrators who engaged in AccessCollege, a comprehensive project to make all aspects of postsecondary institutions welcoming, accessible, and usable (DO-IT, 2007). Team members participating in AccessCollege, which is funded by the U.S. Department of Education Office of Postsecondary Education, represent a diverse set of institutions of higher education in more than twenty states.

Although UD guidelines are typically used to create a fully inclusive environment, UD considerations also can be applied where segregated spaces are desirable. For example, facilities typically include restrooms for men and for women. However, considering the diversity of a population that might use a large facility, there may be situations that require a restroom to accommodate mixed-sex groups and other individuals. Examples include a man who would like to accompany his young daughter to the restroom, an individual with a physical disability whose personal assistant is of the opposite sex, and someone whose physical characteristics and gender identity are not associated with a single sex. Consideration of such situations have led designers to offer male, female, and "family" restrooms in airports and other large facilities; this third option can be used by individuals whose needs are not met by a typical women's or men's restroom. Depending on the size of its student body and of other groups that use its facilities, a campus may choose to offer one or several family or "gender-neutral" restrooms.

A PROCESS FOR UNIVERSAL DESIGN OF PHYSICAL SPACES

Key considerations to address when applying UD to a physical space at an institution of higher education are to plan ahead and to keep in mind the diversity of the campus community at all stages of a project. The following steps, adapted from the more general process presented in chapter 1 of this book, can be used when designing a new space or an upgrade of an existing space (Burgstahler, 2007, pp. 1–2). They are also summarized in Figure 16.1.

1. *Identify the space.* Select a physical space (e.g., a student union building, dormitory, theater, athletic facility, classroom, or science lab). Consider the purpose of the space, location, dimensions, budget, and other issues that affect design.
2. *Define the universe.* Describe the overall population and then consider the diverse characteristics of potential members of the population who might potentially use the space (e.g., students, staff, faculty, and visitors with diverse characteristics with respect to gender; age; size; ethnicity and race; native language; learning style; and abilities to see, hear, manipulate objects, read, and communicate).
3. *Involve consumers.* Consider and involve people with diverse characteristics (as identified in Step 2) in all phases of the development, implementation, and evaluation of the space. Also, gain the perspectives of potential users through diversity programs such as the campus disability services office.
4. *Adopt guidelines or standards.* Review research and practice to identify the most appropriate practices for the design of the type of space identified in Step 1. Iden-

tify universal design strategies to integrate with these best practices in architectural design.

5. *Apply guidelines or standards.* Apply universal design strategies in concert with other best practices identified in Step 4 to the overall design of the physical space (e.g., aesthetics, routes of travel) and to all subcomponents of the space (e.g., signage, restrooms, sound systems, fire and security systems).

6. *Plan for accommodations.* Identify processes to address accommodation requests by individuals for whom the design of the space does not automatically provide access (e.g., cafeteria staff members should know how to assist customers who are blind).

7. *Train and support.* Tailor and deliver ongoing training and support to staff who manage the physical space. Share institutional goals with respect to diversity and inclusion and practices for ensuring welcoming, accessible, and inclusive experiences for everyone using the space. Explain the reasoning behind design decisions, so that design integrity is maintained over time (e.g., make sure that staff know not to configure furniture in such a way that it creates physical barriers to wheelchair users).

8. *Evaluate.* Include universal design measures in periodic evaluations of the space, evaluate the space with a diverse group of users, and make modifications based on feedback. Provide ways to collect ongoing input from facility users (e.g., through online and printed instruments and signage that requests suggestions).

These steps can be adapted to any campus space. For example, the following steps could be taken to universally design a science lab.

FIGURE 16.1   A Process of Universal Design for Physical Spaces

1. *Identify and describe the science lab.* Consider the purpose of the space, location, dimensions, budget, and other issues that affect its design.
2. *Define the universe.* Consider all the students, faculty, staff, and others who might use the science lab and list their potential characteristics with respect to gender, size, age, race and ethnicity, physical and sensory abilities, and native language.
3. *Involve consumers.* Consider the perspectives of students and other individuals that reflect the diversity identified in Step 2. Include them in an advisory role and seek their perspectives in other ways, such as by viewing the video *Working Together: Science Teachers and Students with Disabilities* (Burgstahler, 2006c), in which high school students with a wide range of abilities recommend teaching strategies to science teachers.
4. *Adopt design guidelines or standards.* These includes guidelines, standards, and checklists for applying UD to a science lab. Consult publications, Web sites, and practitioners for ideas on UD strategies to employ. For example, in chapter 17 of this book, author Elizabeth Goldstein shares design suggestions that could be applied to a science lab. Other resources also provide specific guidance, such as the following (Burgstahler, 2006a, b, c):
   - Address safety procedures for students with a variety of sensory and mobility abilities, including the provision of visual lab warning signals.
   - Make laboratory signs and equipment labels in large print, with high contrast.
   - Make sure that the lab is accessible to a wheelchair user.
   - Maintain wide aisles and keep the lab uncluttered.
   - Incorporate an adjustable-height work surface for at least one workstation.
   - Install a mirror above the location where demonstrations are typically given.
   - Use lever controls instead of knobs.
   - Install flexible connections to water, gas, and electricity.
   - Buy lab products that can be used by students with a variety of abilities (e.g., plastic lab products instead of glass, tactile models, large-print diagrams, nonslip mats, support stands, beaker/object clamps, handles on beakers/equipment, surgical gloves to handle slippery items, and video camera with computer/TV monitor to enlarge microscope images).
   - Apply these UD practices in concert with other best practices used for the design of science labs.
5. *Apply design guidelines or standards.* Apply UD strategies in concert with other best practices identified in Step 4 to the overall design of the science lab (e.g., floor plan) and to all subcomponents of the space (e.g., signage, work stations, emergency systems).
6. *Plan for accommodations.* Make sure faculty members and lab assistants understand processes for addressing accommodation requests by individuals for whom the lab environment or activities are not fully accessible.
7. *Train and support.* Tailor and deliver ongoing training and support regarding access issues to faculty, staff, and lab assistants.

8. *Evaluate*. Include UD measures in the evaluation of the lab space, making efforts to gather input from individuals with diverse abilities. Provide ways for users to offer input (e.g., signage that requests suggestions from lab users for making the facility more accessible and comfortable to visitors).

CONCLUSION

To some degree, most institutions of higher education understand their legal obligations to offer courses and services in physically accessible spaces; however, efforts must be made to ensure that more inclusive UD strategies are routinely applied. The pioneers and founders of UD envision a world in which products and environments are designed to be welcoming, accessible, and usable by people with a wide range of abilities. Developments in the areas of accessible design, ergonomics, human factors, and UD can provide guidance to administrators who wish to create inclusive environments for everyone who might use campus spaces. In the next chapter of this book, Elisabeth Goldstein shares examples of the application of UD to specific campus spaces.

REFERENCES

American Association of Retired Persons. (n.d.). What is universal design? Retrieved November 1, 2007, from http://www.aarp.org/families/home_design/universaldesign/a2004-03-23-whatis_univdesign.html

Americans with Disabilities Act of 1990. 42 U.S.C.A. § 12101 *et seq.*

Architectural Barriers Act of 1968. 42 U.S.C. §§ 4151 *et seq.*

Burgstahler, S. (2006a). *Equal access: Science and students with sensory impairments.* Seattle: University of Washington. Retrieved November 1, 2007, from http://www.washington.edu/doit/Brochures/Academics/equal_access_sci.html

Burgstahler, S. (2006b). *Making science labs accessible to students with disabilities.* Seattle: University of Washington. Retrieved November 1, 2007, from http://www.washington.edu/doit/Brochures/Academics/science_lab.html

Burgstahler, S. (2006c). *Working together: Science teachers and students with disabilities.* Seattle: University of Washington. Retrieved November 1, 2007, from http://www.washington.edu/doit/Brochures/Academics/working.teachers.html

The Center for Universal Design. (n.d.). *Welcome.* Raleigh: North Carolina State University. Retrieved November 1, 2007, from http://www.design.ncsu.edu/cud/

Cooper-Hewitt National Design Museum. (1998). *Unlimited by design.* New York: Author. Retrieved November 1, 2007, from http://cooperhewitt.org/exhibitions/archive/unlimited/background.htm

DO-IT. (2007). *AccessCollege: Systemic change for postsecondary institutions.* Seattle: University of Washington. Retrieved November 1, 2007, from http://www.washington.edu/doit/Brochures/Academics/access_college.html

Hagley Museum and Library. (n.d.). *The Marc Harrison collection.* Wilmington, DE: Author. Retrieved November 1, 2007, from http://www.hagley.org/A2193D.HTM

Iwarsson, S., & Stahl, A. (2002). Accessibility, usability and universal design—positioning and definition of concepts describing person-environment relationships. *Disability and Rehabilitation, 25*(2), 57–66.

Mace, R. (n.d.). *About universal design (UD).* Raleigh: North Carolina State University, Center for Universal Design. Retrieved November 1, 2007, from http://www.design.ncsu.edu/cud/about_ud/about_ud.htm

Mansfield, G. (n.d.). In AT and universal design. *AT Network*. Retrieved November 1, 2007, from http://www.atnet.org/index.php?page=at-and-universal-design

Moore, P., & Conn, C. P. (1984). *Disguised: A true story*. Waco, TX: World Books.

Reagan, J. (Ed.) (1998). A perspective on universal design. Presented at Designing for the 21st Century: An International Conference on Universal Design on June 19, 1998. Retrieved November 1, 2007, from http://www.design.ncsu.edu/cud/about_us/usronmacespeech.htm

Rhode Island School of Design. (n.d.). *Sponsored research: Universal kitchen*. Providence, RI: Author. Retrieved November 1, 2007, from http://www.risd.edu/sponsored_research_unikit.htm

Schwab, C. (2004). A stroll through the universal-designed smart home for the 21st century. *The Exceptional Parent, 34*(7), 24–28.

Section 504 of the Rehabilitation Act of 1973, as amended. 29 U.S.C. § 794.

United States Access Board. (2002). *ADA accessibility guidelines for buildings and facilities*. Washington, DC: Author. Retrieved November 1, 2007, from http://www.access-board.gov/adaag/html/adaag.htm

United States Department of Justice. (2005). *A guide to disability rights laws*. Washington, DC: U.S. Department of Justice, Civil Rights Division. Retrieved November 1, 2007, from www.ada.gov/cguide.pdf

The content of this chapter was developed under grants from the U.S. Department of Education Office of Postsecondary Education (grant numbers P333A990042, P333A020044, and P333A050064). However, this content does not necessarily represent the policy of the Department of Education, and you should not assume endorsement by the federal government.

17

Applications of Universal Design to Higher Education Facilities

Elisabeth Goldstein

Universal design principles can be readily applied to buildings and classrooms on campus. Specifically, universal design can be used to make gathering spaces, classrooms, labs, and student centers more accessible to students and the greater campus community through methods that promote equality, flexibility, and usability while simultaneously facilitating instruction, interaction, and learning. The author of this chapter explores the ways that a number of campuses have applied universal design to their spaces.

In the United States, each building project is required to follow accessibility guidelines mandated by the Americans with Disabilities Act of 1990 (ADA), which directs the minimum accessibility requirements for the built environment. Universal design is a concept developed by architect Ron Mace as "the design of products and environments to be usable by all people, to the greatest extent possible, without the need for adaptation or specialized design" (Mace, 2007, p. 1). Designing with the barrier-free considerations of universal design goes beyond making the built environment accessible to individuals with disabilities and makes it inclusive and equitable for everyone.

Promoting universal design of higher education campus grounds and facilities is particularly important since a widely diverse group of people (students, faculty, administration, alumni, visitors), with varying ages and physical and sensory abilities, makes up the campus community. A college campus is similar to a small city. Whether the campus is located in a rural or urban setting, there are spaces dedicated to housing, working, learning, retail, recreation, and social gathering that are available to all members of the campus community. The main function of the campus built environment is to provide places for all to learn, work, and live successfully. When designing campus grounds and facilities, one should be mindful of how its varied user groups travel throughout the campus, approach buildings, and work and live inside them.

FIGURE 17.1   Signage points to a wheelchair-accessible entrance that is located in a different location from the main building entrance. (Courtesy of the author.)

BUILDING ENTRANCES

The entry sequence to a building may be its most important feature. Approaching a building is an inherently communicative experience because it gives the first impression one has of the site and orients the visitor to the spaces within the rest of the facility. Building entrances are a high priority for universal design considerations. Entrances that meet accessibility codes are often located as an alternate entrance to a more prominent, noncompliant entrance. This design may technically provide access for all types of people to enter a building, but they will not share a common entry experience (Figure 17.1). An accessible entrance may be difficult to find if it is not located near the main entrance, and if a wheelchair user must separate from a group of friends or business colleagues to use an alternate entrance, it may make that person feel lower in status than the rest of the group (Bain, 1989). Those who do not use wheelchairs also benefit from a shared accessible entrance. Stairs are difficult to navigate for those using crutches (Figure 17.2), pushing strollers, and moving equipment or carrying luggage. While codes are useful to dictate a minimum threshold width and the rate of incline for a ramp, the designer and client institution should consider how the site conditions, building context, and desired user experience will allow for an optimally designed, barrier-free entrance for all user groups.

Erb Memorial Union Amphitheater, University of Oregon–Eugene

The Erb Memorial Union Amphitheater on the University of Oregon campus provides a good example of universal design because it is accessible for people of all abilities without providing separate travel routes for differently abled individuals. The amphitheater is sited within a plaza in front of the Erb Memorial Union Building (EMU), which is the student commons building and is centrally located on the University of

FIGURE 17.2   A student on crutches travels down a building's entry stair. (Courtesy of the author.)

Oregon campus. The EMU was built in 1950 and designed to be a place where students could gather and freely exchange ideas. In the 1970s, when the university experienced significant growth in enrollment, the EMU went through a series of renovations that changed the flow of traffic through the building, detracted from the aesthetics and accessibility of the spaces, and made it difficult for students to gather. In the late 1990s, to commemorate the Associated Student Government's 100th anniversary, the student body donated funds to restore the EMU to better fulfill its original mission and build a new gathering space in the form of an outdoor amphitheater.

The University of Oregon hired landscape architects Cameron McCarthy Gilbert & Scheibe and included groups of students, faculty, and staff in the design process (University of Oregon Planning Office, n.d.):

> [The amphitheater] was expressly designed with universal access in mind, and all of its areas are accessible by those in wheelchairs. Its main space is moved as far north as possible to take full advantage of the sun and to bring the activities as close as possible to the intersection [of two main arterials through campus].

One strength of the amphitheater's design is its placement into the site as the entrance for the EMU. The amphitheater itself is a physical symbol of the university's mission to provide a venue for the freedom of expression, and its location at the center of campus enhances the function of the building as a student commons. But it is the way that its paths are woven through the site and connect to the building that supports the university's mission to provide equality of opportunity. The amphitheater is formed by a series of stairs that wrap around a plaza and define its edge. While the amphitheater stairs can be used to reach the street from the plaza, they are deemphasized as a means of travel and are often used by those who want to sit and survey the action on the stage and plaza below.

The circulation through this space is mainly dictated by a sidewalk that follows the curve along the outside of the amphitheater and leads pedestrians to and from the EMU building. The sidewalk forks to form two gently sloping paths. The inner path slopes downward, providing access to the lower floor of the EMU as well as access into the plaza itself. The outer path slopes upward, bringing pedestrians to the upper level of the EMU. The gentle, even slope of the paths allows wheelchair users and those who are moving wheeled items to travel along the same route of travel as those who are not traveling with wheels.

These paths are also a barrier-free means of travel for pedestrians with visual impairments. Because the paths curve around the amphitheater with a broad turning radius, an individual with limited sight is not confronted with an abrupt change in direction of travel. There are no protruding objects within the path or along its edges to create unpredictable barriers along the path, and its edges are accentuated by raised curbs so that the transition from the pedestrian path to the spaces beyond is easily detectable. In addition, the wide paths, gradual level changes, wide turning radius, and low landscaping beds offer expansive and clear sightlines of the plaza and amphitheater, which are a benefit to pedestrians with hearing loss (Kirschbaum et al., 2001).

By making the pathways accessible to everyone and creating an accessible main entrance, the designers allow all user groups to have the same opportunity to experience the plaza, enter two levels of the EMU facility, and engage in the activities that occur within the amphitheater.

CLASSROOMS

Classrooms on a college campus are typically used by multiple instructors throughout the day; they teach a variety of subjects and employ different pedagogical styles. Consequently, they should be flexible and user-friendly to a broad audience. Classroom types range from small seminar-style rooms to lecture halls with a large seating capacity. With the increased use of media-enhanced tools and interactive learning models, the demands for flexibility in classrooms of all sizes are significant. A classroom designer must keep all potential instructors and students in mind and consider how to support the full range of activities that will occur within the space in order to create an inclusive classroom environment. A traditional classroom model is to place rows of fixed seats facing in one direction toward an instructor who lectures in front of a chalkboard. The more the classroom is designed to be fixed in place, the less accommodating it is to the wide variety of user groups who will use the space for learning. Also, the rigidity of a traditional classroom can make implementation of different methods of instruction difficult.

Large lecture hall–type classrooms typically utilize a tiered seating configuration to ensure clear sightlines and gain spatial efficiency within the building. With this type of seating configuration, a wheelchair user or someone who has difficulty navigating stairs must sit in a designated area of the classroom determined by the location of an accessible entrance. Ideally, the lecture hall should have entrances that allow wheeled access to the teaching area and multiple, if not all, seating levels of the classroom. Also, it is recommended that a total of at least 4% of the classroom seating area be available for wheelchair stations throughout the classroom, offering a choice of sight-lines that is comparable to those provided for people who do not use wheelchairs (Allen et al., 1996).

LeBaron Hall Auditorium, Iowa State University–Ames

As part of a campuswide project to upgrade classrooms, Iowa State University reno-vated LeBaron Hall Auditorium, a tiered lecture hall with large seating capacity, to facilitate an interactive learning atmosphere that is often difficult to achieve in a tra-ditional classroom of its size. The design team included architects from Baldwin & White, KI furniture manufacturers, and specialists in educational studies, space man-agement, and technology services. The design team established goals for this class-room that included improving contact between the faculty member and students, facilitating active learning through group interaction, and promoting a social and collaborative atmosphere among students. They recognized that to achieve these goals, an inclusive classroom environment must be created that supports movement and encourages interaction and participation.

The renovated LeBaron Hall Auditorium has 363 seats and continues to use a tiered seating configuration, but the room was reconfigured to be wider than it is deep, so students seated in the back rows are not far from the front of the room. Sightlines were improved, so that students are more inclined to engage in classroom activities. There are wheelchair stations on the first, third, and sixth tiers, and an elevator out-side the classroom allows for access to all three levels. Each of the six seating tiers has two rows of seats, and the horizontal walkways between these rows are wide. These walkways allow for wheelchair passage and easy navigation by students and instruc-tors moving around the classroom as they participate in group activities (Figure 17.3). The wide spacing between the rows also accommodates a unique design feature of the seats themselves. The seats have a swivel function, with no "spring back to front" fea-ture, that allows students sitting in one row to easily turn their seats to face the row behind them to engage in a group activity (see Figure 17.3).

Positive feedback from instructors and students using this classroom confirm that the classroom promotes an inclusive environment and active learning experience. Dr. Corly Brooke, professor and director of the Center for Excellence in Teaching and Learning, reports, "The best thing it does for my students is create community in the classroom. I can see all the students, and I can get them interacting easily" (Twetten, 2006, p. 22.8). Students describe this classroom as their favorite and feel a close con-nection with their instructor.

Adjustable Height Furnishings, University of Connecticut School of Business–Hartford

The classrooms at the University of Connecticut School of Business demonstrate another creative way to rethink the concept of a "tiered classroom." Instead of pro-posing the construction of a tiered floor, the designers at Schoenhardt Architecture

FIGURE 17.3 Iowa State University, LeBaron Hall. Seats swivel so that students may face each other to work in groups. (Courtesy of Iowa State University.)

+ Interior Design worked with Steelcase Furniture Systems to apply a tiered furniture model to the classrooms (Figure 17.4). The floor remains level while the chairs and tables incrementally increase in height toward the back of the classroom. The chairs and tables are on wheels, are fully adjustable, and are wired for power and data access. This tiered furniture model offers a low-cost design solution to maximize clear sight-lines in the classroom without compromising the accessibility and flexibility of the space to its users. Students who use wheelchairs can access any space within the classroom and choose a table height that is most appropriate for them. The adjustability of the tables and chairs also allows students of any size to find a work area that fits them best (Steelcase Furniture Systems, n.d.).

FURNISHINGS, EQUIPMENT, LIGHTING, AND SOUND

To accommodate the wide range of sizes of people, designers should lay out spaces and choose equipment and furnishings to accommodate the "tallest and the smallest" persons on the anthropometric scale of human measurement (e.g., dimensions that fall within the 5th percentile for women and the 95th percentile for men). It is recommended that seat widths and aisle and row depth are designed to accommodate the largest male, and vertical reach height for equipment and controls are within reach for the smallest female (Allen et al., 1996).

Because it is difficult to find one type of classroom seat that will be comfortable for everyone, it is ideal to select a seat that can adjust to the user in a variety of ways (e.g.,

FIGURE 17.4   University of Connecticut, adjustable-height furnishings. The floor remains flat while the height of each row of tables and chairs rises incrementally toward the back of the room. (Copyright Steelcase Inc. 2007.)

adjustable seat height, arm height, arm length). If it is not possible to provide adjustable seating within the context of the classroom design, providing chairs in a range of sizes may be a feasible solution.

Using tables for work surfaces in classrooms is recommended over tablet arms attached to chairs because the configuration of tablet arms can limit seating choices for left-handed students versus right-handed students, and tablet arms limit the amount of space available for one to sit comfortably in a seat. Also, tablet arms typically do not have enough surface area to support the materials students need to do their work in class. Each workspace should allow enough room (36" wide × 30" deep) for a student to use a computer or to spread out study materials (Niemeyer, 2003). Table heights should adjust from 28 inches to 34 inches above the finished floor, and it is best to find tables that have T-shaped or L-shaped legs that are positioned at the farthest ends of the table to provide sufficient leg room.

Universal design considerations should also be applied to furnishings used by the instructor. These furnishings should include an adjustable-height podium, a table at least 60 inches wide by 24 inches deep, and adjustable-height seating (Allen et al., 1996).

Lighting and sound quality directly influence how well students and instructors are able to receive and communicate information. Outside noise, uneven sound, and poor lighting can easily interfere with one's ability to concentrate and participate in classroom activities. People with vision and hearing loss can be particularly sensitive to the quality of light and sound in their environment. Classrooms should be located within a building so that they are isolated from areas that will bring unwanted noise into the classroom, such as mechanical systems, elevators, restrooms, and vending areas. It is important that each person in the classroom have the opportunity to hear consistent and clear sound at appropriate decibel levels. Thus, the ceiling should be designed with hard-surfaced materials to reflect sound downward, rather than acoustical tile, which absorbs sound and produces an uneven sound distribution throughout the room (Allen et al., 1996). It is ideal to install a wireless microphone to offer the instructor flexibility to move around the classroom while lecturing without compromising sound projection quality. Assistive listening systems should be available for people with hearing loss (Allen et al., 1996; Niemeyer, 2003).

Flexibility is the key to lighting a classroom space. The more technology is used in classrooms, the more types of lighting options are needed. A zoning system should be implemented so that if, for example, students are viewing a media presentation, lights may be turned off in the projection area while lights remain available for the instructor and students to review or take notes. Lighting should also be flexible enough to spotlight a sign language interpreter for students who are deaf or hard of hearing while the rest of the lights are dimmed. Chalkboards or whiteboards should be uniformly lit across the writing surface. It is also useful to control the lights in sections along the board to allow for a section to be lit while a projection screen is in use (Allen et al., 1996).

Instructors have varying familiarity and comfort with the equipment and technology that is available to them in a classroom, so along with providing a variety of lighting and media options for a classroom, the control systems should be user-friendly and have standard layouts between all classrooms on campus. Also, the number of control switches should be minimized, clearly labeled, illuminated for use in the dark, and operable from a seated position (Allen et al., 1996).

Technology-Enabled Active Learning Classroom, Massachusetts Institute of Technology, Cambridge

In 2001, the Massachusetts Institute of Technology Physics Department built a 3,000-square-foot classroom to implement a new teaching model of hands-on active learning for introductory physics courses (Figure 17.5). The technology-enabled active learning classroom (TEAL) is designed so that the instructor and students can easily move between lecture, lab experiment, and discussion sections of the class. By increasing the technology capability of the classroom and the range of instructional activities that this classroom was modeled to support, the TEAL classroom inherently applies barrier-free design principles.

Characteristic of an "in-the-round" design, the instructor's workstation is placed in the center of the room and is surrounded by thirteen round tables that seat nine students each. There is a networked laptop computer on the table for every three students. Thirteen whiteboards and eight video projectors and screens are arranged around the perimeter of the classroom. The instructor's lecture, class notes, images,

FIGURE 17.5   MIT, TEAL Physics Classroom. Round tables are arranged around a central instruction area with whiteboards and projection screens placed along the perimeter of the room, so that all have equal sightlines of presentation materials. (Courtesy of Mark Bessette of the MIT TEAL/Studio Physics Project.)

and live video can be projected onto each screen, affording everyone a direct sight-line to the presentation materials. With presentation and lab materials accessible by a computer at their workstations, students with visual impairments have an opportu-nity to enlarge the materials on their computer screen for large-print viewing and to utilize audio functions as needed (Keller, 2005). Since students are required to work together to complete lab assignments, chairs are adjustable and mobile to facilitate students working in groups around the computers and using the whiteboard dedi-cated to their work area.

The classroom affords the instructor flexibility in how she presents a lecture and guides an interactive lab demonstration using the technology the classroom offers. The option of using a wireless microphone allows the instructor to lecture from differ-ent parts of the room where mobile lab demonstration stations are set up. The design team placed a storage and preparation room adjacent to the classroom for lab mate-rials and equipment so that demonstration stations could be prepared in advance of the lectures without having to transfer them a great distance. Because the tech-nology and equipment allow everyone a direct sightline to class presentations and because the classroom must allow teaching stations and lab demonstrations to move easily around the room, its floor remains at one level. Also, the flexibility of mobile teaching stations and the equitably interactive experience the students have with the presentation and lab materials facilitate greater retention of the physics curriculum. To determine the effectiveness of this classroom model, tests were given before and after the semester to students in the TEAL classroom and to students taking the same course in a traditional classroom. The students who used the TEAL classroom scored significantly higher on these exams, particularly on questions evaluating conceptual understanding of the subject matter (Anthony, 2004).

Learning Studios, Estrella Mountain Community College, Avondale, AZ

"Radical flexibility" of the classroom environment was the driving design concept for the Learning Studios Project at Estrella Mountain Community College in Arizona. The design team proposed that the more a classroom offers flexibility in space, furnishings, and technology, the greater the potential for students to be engaged and actively learning and retaining information. This vision of radical flexibility was translated by the design team into a classroom that is "changeable on the fly." Each Learning Studio is 900 square feet and accommodates 32 students. The studios are equipped with wireless laptops, data projectors, mobile teaching stations, folding tables on wheels, adjustable ergonomic chairs on wheels, adjustable lighting, and combination whiteboards/projection surfaces. None of the furnishings is fixed in place, so all items can be arranged in the configuration that is most appropriate for the instructor to engage students in a particular learning activity (Figure 17.6). The classroom can easily transform from large- to small-group configurations and enables faculty to implement a variety of teaching styles, even within one class period. Tables are easily collapsible so that they can be moved aside when not in use. With approximately 30 square feet, instead of the traditional 20–25 square feet allocated per student, there is more room for students to spread out their study materials, move their chairs, and comfortably organize a discussion group around a whiteboard or laptop (Figure 17.7).

The ability for a group of students to arrange seats and position a computer and whiteboard anywhere in the classroom benefits students who are deaf or hard of hearing by allowing the workgroup to sit in a circle or horseshoe configuration for better sightlines within the group. A workgroup also has an opportunity to position itself at a distance from the mix of noise coming from other workgroups, which can also make communication easier for students with hearing loss (Keller, 2005). With movable furnishings and equipment, the instructor is also able to easily maneuver throughout the room and transport a mobile teaching station without having to navigate through narrow aisles or fixed furniture.

Estrella Mountain Community College has found that the "radical flexibility" of the Learning Studios lowers barriers to student participation and offers students a greater feeling of control, which adds to their sense of comfort and well-being while building a sense of identity and belonging to the class. Instructors also reported that the learning studios improved peer-to-peer support and permitted more relaxed, less intimidating group collaboration (Lopez & Gee, 2006). Eighty-seven percent (87%) of the faculty surveyed indicated a preference for the learning studios over traditional

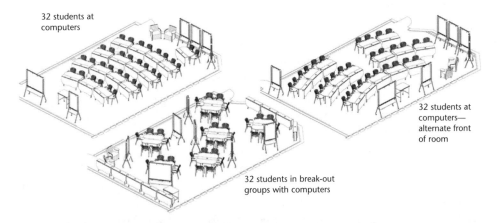

32 students at computers

32 students at computers— alternate front of room

32 students in break-out groups with computers

FIGURES 17.6 & 17.7 Estrella Mountain Community College, Learning Studios. "Radical Flexibility" of the furnishings and equipment allow the room to be configured in a variety of ways to support a range of instructional activities. (Top image courtesy of Herman Miller, Inc. Copyright 2006 Zeeland, MI. Bottom image by Ralph Campbell, copyright 2005 Maricopa Community Colleges.)

learning environments, and students viewed the learning studios as more "inviting and comfortable" than traditional classrooms, which were characterized as "oppressive, restrictive, and intimidating" (Herman Miller, 2006; Lopez & Gee, 2006). Due to this positive feedback, Estrella Mountain Community College has implemented twenty-two learning studios in a new academic building on campus.

LESSONS LEARNED

All the case studies presented in this chapter have in common a collaborative design process that embraces thinking beyond traditional models for building entrances, classrooms, and classroom furnishings, as well as beyond the federal requirements for the built environment mandated by the ADA. Design teams included not only architects and campus administration but also students, faculty, learning and teaching experts, furniture manufacturers, and technology providers. An integrated design process allowed each constituency to contribute a unique perspective to the design program and respond collectively to the needs and concerns of others.

Although it may be impossible to accommodate every person and think of every scenario regarding the use of a space, establishing universal design goals at the beginning stages of a project will positively influence its success in accommodating the widest variety of people. If universal design goals are established on the front end of a project, each design decision can be evaluated in this context, and inform decisions throughout, to create an optimal barrier-free design that is incorporated into and respects the architecture. This approach can avoid accessible design solutions that are "tacked on" as an afterthought and subsequently do not achieve higher levels of functionality, such as equal paths of travel or experience between differently abled people.

The following guidelines provide a good place to start for campus leaders who want to apply universal design to higher education facilities.

Planning and Design

- State universal design goals at the beginning of a design project.
- Let a variety of perspectives inform design decisions by involving students, faculty, staff, and people who are differently abled on the design team.
- Consider possibilities that are beyond traditional models for campus grounds, facilities, and classrooms.

Building Entrances

- Design all main and/or most-traveled entrances of the building to be wheelchair-accessible.
- Design travel paths that do not abruptly change direction or transition unpredictably.
- Keep travel paths clear of protruding objects.

Classrooms

- Locate wheelchair-accessible routes and work areas so that one has a choice of sightlines that is comparable to those provided for people who do not use wheelchairs.
- Provide wide aisles and a generous allocation of space per student.
- Consider how the size and shape of the classroom will affect how furnishings and equipment are configured to facilitate interaction and provide clear sightlines.
- When possible, keep the floor of the classroom at one level.

Furnishings and Equipment

- Provide mobile and adjustable furniture so that it can be located and sized as needed.
- Provide adjustable-height tables (as opposed to tablet arm desks) to give students room to spread out study materials, accommodate leg room as needed, and facilitate use by right-handed and left-handed students alike.
- Consider how students will use computers, view projection screens, and work at whiteboards. Access to computers, for example, can help students customize the information they receive and communicate with their zoom and audio functions.

Sound and Lighting

- Isolate the classrooms from areas that may provide unwanted noise, such as mechanical rooms, elevators, restrooms, and vending areas.
- Allow lighting to be controlled in zones, so that areas can remain lit (i.e., for note-taking or to view a sign language interpreter) when other lights are dimmed for projection screen viewing.
- Standardize control system layouts throughout the campus.
- Minimize the number of control switches and make sure they are clearly labeled, illuminated for use in the dark, and operable from a seated position.

CONCLUSION

The built environment directly affects how people feel and behave. Welcoming, comfortable, and barrier-free classrooms, facilities, and overall campus design can positively influence how well students interact and learn, as well as promote a sense of well-being, physically and psychologically, within the campus community. Applying universal design to physical spaces can support an institution's goal of creating a welcoming, inclusive, and usable environment for all students, faculty, staff, and campus visitors.

REFERENCES

Allen, R. L., Bowen, J. T., Clabaugh, S., DeWitt, B. B., Francis, J., Kerstetter, J. P., & Rieck, D. A. (1996). *Classroom design manual* (3rd ed.). College Park: University of Maryland Academic Information Technology Services.

Anthony, R. (2004). TEAL Teaching: Technology enabled active learning (TEAL) is transforming physics education. *Massachusetts Institute of Technology Spectrum, Winter.*

Bain, B. (1989). *The entry experience: Preferences of the mobility impaired, changing paradigms.* Proceedings of the Environmental Design Research Association. Raleigh: North Carolina State University.

Herman Miller, Inc. (2006). *Rethinking the classroom.* Zeeland, MI: Author. Retrieved November 7, 2007, from http://www.estrellamountain.edu/awareness/download/06/RethinkingTheClassroom.pdf

Keller, E. (2005). *Strategies for teaching students with vision impairments*, Retrieved November 7, 2007, from http://www.as.wvu.edu/~scidis/vision.html

Kirschbaum, J. B., Axelson, P. W., Longmuir, P. E., Mispagel, K. M., Stein, J. A., & Yamada, D. A. (2001). *Designing sidewalks and trails for access, Part II of II: Best practices design guide.* U.S. Department of Transportation: Federal Highway Administration.

Lopez, H., & Gee, L. (2006). Estrella Mountain Community College: The learning studios project. In D. G. Oblinger (Ed.), *Learning spaces.* Boulder, CO: Educause.

Mace, R. (2007). *About universal design (UD).* Retrieved November 7, 2007, from http://design.ncsu.edu/cud/about_ud/about_ud.htm

Niemeyer, D. (2003). *Hard facts on smart classroom design: Ideas, guidelines, and layouts.* Lanham, MD: Scarecrow Press.

Steelcase Furniture Systems. (n.d.). *Case study: University of Connecticut School of Business Graduate Learning Center.* Grand Rapids, MI. Retrieved November 7, 2007, from http://www.steelcase.com/na/files/96f8baadda344caf9f39a24c63a9178b/Full%20version%20of%20this%20story.pdf

Twetten, J. (2006). Iowa State University: LeBaron Hall Auditorium. In D. G. Oblinger (Ed.), *Learning spaces.* Boulder, CO: Educause.

University of Oregon Planning Office. (n.d.). *Association of University Architects 1998 Case Study Awards Program.* Retrieved November 7, 2007, from http://planning.uoregon.edu/recognition/AUA98_3.html

18

Universal Design of Technological Environments
From Principles to Practice

Sheryl E. Burgstahler

When universal design (UD) is applied, technological environments are accessible and usable for people with a wide range of abilities. The author of this chapter shares highlights of the history of the application of UD to information technology as well as strategies for applying universal design to technological environments in colleges and universities.

Have you ever used a software application and found yourself stuck, unable to accomplish what you set out to do? Do you blame yourself for not knowing enough about the product or about computers in general? Someone who embraces universal design (UD) would instead look first to the product itself and ask how it might be made more intuitive and provide hints when users make incorrect selections. This chapter covers issues related to the UD of technology on postsecondary campuses. This topic is of particular importance because of the explosive development of information technology (IT) (e.g., hand-held computing devices, Web sites, software applications, multimedia, telecommunications devices), which has changed the way stakeholders in postsecondary institutions teach, learn, share information, and provide services. Depending on how it is implemented, IT can either level the playing field or further widen the gap in educational attainment between individuals of minority groups (e.g., individuals with disabilities, people from poor communities) and those of the majority.

Specialized software and hardware called assistive technologies are used by some individuals with disabilities to operate standard IT (Closing The Gap, 2007). Head control, speech input, Morse code input, and dozens of alternative keyboard and mouse options make it possible for individuals with mobility impairments to fully operate computers. In addition, people who are blind can use text-to-speech technology to access the functions, navigation, and content of software products. This technology reads aloud the text on the screen. However, it cannot read the content of graphic images unless they are described in a text-based format (e.g., in alt text). Speech output is also desirable for individuals who prefer to listen to content read aloud, are English language learners, or have a specific learning disability that affects their ability to read printed text.

To create products that are fully accessible to and usable by everyone, IT developers must consider the wide range of abilities of potential users and the assistive technologies they may employ, as well as their native language, age, and other characteristics. In other words, they must practice UD. The goal of UD is to enhance a product's usability for the broadest audience without diminishing its function. Such an approach reflects the definition of UD established by Ron Mace of the Center for Universal Design: "the design of products and environments to be usable by all people, to the greatest extent possible, without the need for adaptation or specialized design." (Mace, n.d., p. 1) Examples of universally designed IT are video presentations with captions, transcriptions offered along with audio clips, office equipment with large control buttons that can be reached from a seated position, operating systems that include an option to enlarge characters on the screen, and hand-held computing devices that are compatible with assistive technologies. UD not only minimizes the need for assistive technology but also is compatible with commonly used assistive technology devices.

In many cases, including a UD feature in an IT product is easy to do, results in cost-savings to consumers, and benefits other people in addition to those for whom the feature was originally designed. For example, today it is required that television sets include decoder chips that allow the display of captions whenever they are provided by a video presentation. This built-in feature is inexpensive compared to the decoder device that, in the past, had to be purchased separately in order to make captions appear on television screens. Designed for individuals who have hearing impairments, the built-in feature has also benefited people in noisy or noiseless environments (e.g., a sports bar, an airport, a conference exhibit, a library) and English language learners. It also promotes the inclusive goal of UD, as it allows individuals with a wide range of characteristics to use the same product.

A decision to adopt accessible or universal IT design practices in higher education is sometimes motivated by legal mandates. For example, almost all institutions of higher education are covered entities under both Section 504 of the Rehabilitation Act of 1973 and the Americans with Disabilities Act of 1990 (ADA). These laws prohibit discrimination on the basis of disability. Neither one specifically mentions IT, but they are generally interpreted to require that postsecondary institutions make IT accessible to people with disabilities unless it would pose an undue burden to do so; when an institution develops or selects IT that is not usable by individuals with disabilities, the subsequent expense of providing access to an individual with a disability is not generally considered an undue burden when this cost could have been significantly reduced by considering accessibility at the time of product development or selection (Patrick, 1996; Waddell, 2007). Legislation has also been interpreted to mean that the institution should have a plan in place for ensuring that technology is accessible (Waddell, 2007, p. 3):

The courts have held that a public entity violates its obligations under the ADA when it only responds on an ad-hoc basis to individual requests for accommodation. There is an affirmative duty to develop a comprehensive policy in advance of any request for auxiliary aids or services. . . . The bottom line, according to OCR [Office for Civil Rights] is that effective communication imposes a duty to solve barriers to information access that the entity's purchasing choices create. Whenever existing technology is "upgraded" by a new technology feature, it is important to ensure that the new technology either improves accessibility or is compatible with existing assistive computer technology.

UNIVERSAL DESIGN GUIDELINES FOR INFORMATION TECHNOLOGY

Coordinated efforts to create IT that is usable by a broad audience began with a focus on accessibility. In the 1980s, cooperation between key stakeholders, including the IT industry, consumers, researchers, and government, led to the development of guidelines for more accessible design (Vanderheiden & Vanderheiden, 1992). Organized by IT function, these guidelines address issues related to sensory, physical, cognitive, and language abilities, as well as seizure disorders. Each guideline is phrased as an objective followed by examples of how the objective might be achieved (Vanderheiden & Vanderheiden, 1992, Part III, Sections 1–5):

1. *Output/Displays* includes all means of presenting information to the user. [The design should] maximize the number of people who can
   - O-1 hear auditory output clearly enough.
   - O-2 not miss important information if they can't hear.
   - O-3 have line of sight to visual output and reach printed output.
   - O-4 see visual output clearly enough.
   - O-5 not miss important information if they can't see.
   - O-6 understand the output (visual, auditory, other).

2. *Input/Controls* includes keyboards and all other means of communicating to the product. [The design should] maximize the number of people who can
   - I-1 reach the controls.
   - I-2 find the individual controls/keys if they can't see them.
   - I-3 read the labels on the controls/keys.
   - I-4 determine the status or setting of the controls if they can't see them.
   - I-5 physically operate controls and other input mechanisms.
   - I-6 understand how to operate controls and other input mechanisms.
   - I-7 connect special alternative input devices.

3. *Manipulations* includes all actions that must be directly performed by a person in concert with the product or for routine maintenance; e.g., inserting [a] disk, loading [a] tape, changing [an] ink cartridge. [The design should] maximize the number of people who can
   - M-1 physically insert and remove objects as required to operate a device.
   - M-2 physically handle and/or open the product.

      M-3 remove, replace, or reposition often-used detachable parts.

      M-4 understand how to carry out the manipulations necessary to use the product.

4. *Documentation* primarily [focuses on] operating instructions. [The design should] maximize the number of people who can

      D-1 access the documentation.

      D-2 understand the documentation.

5. *Safety* includes alarms and other protections from harm. [The design should] maximize the number of people who can

      S-1 perceive hazard warnings.

      S-2 use the product without injury, due to unperceived hazards or [the] user's lack of motor control.

More recently, federal agencies have taken steps to ensure the accessibility of their IT. Section 508 of the Rehabilitation Act of 1973 mandates that any IT they develop, maintain, procure, or use must be accessible to people with disabilities (U.S. Department of Justice, 2005). According to the Department of Justice (2005, p. 18), accessible IT

> can be operated in a variety of ways and does not rely on a single sense or ability of the user. For example, a system that provides output only in visual format may not be accessible to people with visual impairments and a system that provides output only in audio format may not be accessible to people who are deaf or hard of hearing.

The 1998 amendments of Section 508 directed the U.S. Access Board to produce minimum accessibility standards for the IT of federal agencies. In 2007, the board was conducting a review to update its accessibility standards for technology covered by Section 508 (U.S. Access Board, 2007). This includes computers, Web pages, software, video and multimedia, telecommunications products, and office equipment. Section 508 standards promote the integration of flexibility and inclusive features within mainstream IT products. Although they apply only to IT products of federal agencies, the Section 508 standards have been voluntarily adopted by some states, educational institutions, and other organizations as one way to meet their obligations under the ADA (Information Technology Technical Assistance and Training Center, n.d.).

Besides the technology itself, accessible UD strategies can be applied to a computer lab, library, or other physical environment in which technology is located, as described in chapter 16. For example, computers available in a career services office can be placed on adjustable-height tables to accommodate individuals of different sizes and those who use wheelchairs of various dimensions. Additionally, universally designed computing areas are located in wheelchair-accessible facilities, have wide aisles that are clear of obstructions, employ high-contrast and large-print signage, situate at least part of a service counter at a height accessible from a seated position, make lighting adjustable by the individual, and have window blinds available to reduce glare on computer screens (Burgstahler, 2006).

Following are some specific UD recommendations for IT commonly used in higher education.

Universal Design of the Web

The World Wide Web emerged in the 1990s and has grown to be ubiquitous in post-secondary settings. Early on, articles about accessible design (e.g., Laux, McNally, Paciello, & Vanderheiden, 1996; Nielsen, 1996; Rowland & Smith, 1999) and UD (e.g., Burgstahler, Comden, & Fraser, 1997; Waters, 1997) of Web pages began to appear.

The World Wide Web Consortium (W3C), which develops and maintains protocols to ensure interoperability of the Web, has always been committed to UD. According to the "inventor" of the Web, Tim Berners-Lee, "The power of the Web is in its universality. Access by everyone regardless of disability is an essential aspect" (Berners-Lee, n.d.). W3C's vision of the Web is that of an inclusive environment that allows for the expression of cultural nuances and language differences (World Wide Web Consortium, 2007b). In 1997, W3C announced its Web Accessibility Initiative (WAI) to develop guidelines for the accessible design of Web sites. The WAI (Web Accessibility Initiative, 2005b) promotes universal as well as accessible design pointing out that

> Web accessibility also benefits people *without* disabilities. For example, a key principle of Web accessibility is designing Web sites that are flexible to meet different user needs, preferences, and situations. Such flexibility benefits people with disabilities, but also those *without* disabilities, such as people using a slow Internet connection, people with "temporary disabilities" such as a broken arm, and people with changing abilities due to aging.

In 1999, the Web Content Accessibility Guidelines 1.0 (WCAG 1.0) were published as a W3C recommendation (World Wide Web Consortium, 1999). WAI employs large numbers of volunteers to review, implement, promote, and update its guidelines, which are widely regarded as the international standard for Web accessibility.

The U.S. Access Board adopted much of the WAI's early work when it developed the Section 508 accessibility standards for IT of the federal government. Both WAI guidelines and Section 508 standards demonstrate that developers can create pages that are accessible to everyone by avoiding certain types of inaccessible formats and creating alternative methods for carrying out the functions or accessing the content delineated by inaccessible formats. Web pages can be tested for accessibility by using special validator programs and by accessing the pages with a variety of monitors, computer platforms, and Web browsers and with sound and graphics capabilities turned off and a keyboard alone (World Wide Web Consortium, 1999).

The WAI is currently near the end of an international process to develop WCAG 2.0. The WCAG 2.0 draft (World Wide Web Consortium, 2007b, p. 1) includes recommendations for making Web content

> accessible to a wider range of people with disabilities, including blindness and low vision, deafness and hearing loss, learning disabilities, cognitive limitations, limited movement, speech difficulties, photosensitivity and combinations of these. Following these guidelines will also make Web content more usable to users in general.

The draft guidelines are organized around four principles that lay the foundation necessary for anyone to access and effectively use Web content. These principles (World Wide Web Consortium, 2007b) state that Web content be

- *Perceivable*—Information and user interface components must be presentable to users in ways they can perceive.
- *Operable*—User interface components and navigation must be operable.
- *Understandable*—Information and operation of user interface must be understandable.
- *Robust*—Content must be robust enough that it can be interpreted reliably by a wide variety of user agents, including assistive technologies.

The draft guidelines are technology independent in that the success criteria for each guideline can be applied across a wide range of existing and emerging Web technologies. According to WAI, it is essential that different components of Web development and interaction work together in order for the Web to be accessible to people with disabilities. These components include the following (Web Accessibility Initiative, 2005a):

- content in a Web page or Web application including text, images, and sounds, as well as markup that defines structure and presentation;
- user agents such as Web browsers and media players;
- assistive technology such as screen readers, alternative keyboards, and switches;
- users' knowledge, experiences, and adaptive strategies for using the Web;
- developers, designers, coders, authors, and others, including those with disabilities;
- authoring tools used to create Web sites;
- evaluation tools such as Web accessibility evaluation tools and HTML validators.

Some quick tips (Web Accessibility Initiative, 2007) for ensuring Web accessibility are as follows:

1.1 Provide text alternatives for any nontext content, so that it can be changed into other forms people need, such as large print, braille, speech, symbols, or simpler language
1.2 Provide synchronized alternatives for synchronized media
1.3 Create content that can be presented in different ways (for example, simpler layout) without losing information or structure
1.4 Make it easier for users to see and hear content, including separating foreground from background
2.1 Make all functionality available from a keyboard
2.2 Provide users with disabilities enough time to read and use content
2.3 Do not design content in a way that is known to cause seizures
2.4 Provide ways to help users with disabilities navigate, find content, and determine where they are
3.1 Make text content readable and understandable
3.2 Make Web pages appear and operate in predictable ways
3.3 Help users avoid and correct mistakes

4.1 Maximize compatibility with current and future user agents, including assistive technologies

W3C (World Wide Web Consortium, 2007a, p. 1) continues to expand the reach of the Web to

- *Everyone* (regardless of culture, abilities, etc.),
- *Everything* (applications and data stores, and on devices ranging from power computers with high-definition displays to mobile devices to appliances),
- *Everywhere* (from high- to low-bandwidth environments),
- *Diverse modes of interaction* (touch, pen, mouse, voice, assistive technologies, computer to computer),
- *Enable computers to do more useful work* (through advanced data searching and sharing).

In spite of international efforts to make the Web accessible to everyone, many Web sites of postsecondary institutions remain inaccessible to faculty, staff, students, and visitors with disabilities (Hackett & Parmanto, 2005; Kelly, 2002; Schmetzke, 2001, 2003; Thompson, Burgstahler, & Comden, 2003). Contributing to this problem are Webmasters' and administrators' lack of awareness of the barriers erected by their Web sites, of legal obligations to provide accessible content, of guidelines for designing accessible sites, and of the benefits of UD for all Web users. Much work remains to be done to ensure that Web resources maintained by institutions of higher education are accessibly designed; even greater efforts are needed to ensure that these resources are universally designed.

Universal Design of Telecommunications, Software, and Other Products

The design of standard telecommunications equipment can potentially erect barriers to individuals attempting to use it. A person who is hard of hearing cannot understand people speaking on a telephone without an amplification feature. A person who is deaf needs a nonaudio alternative to communicate with someone calling on a standard telephone. An individual who cannot use a voice for communication needs alternatives to speech communication. An individual without full hand function may not be able to operate some telephones without assistive technology. A person who is blind cannot access the content of the visual presentation of a videoconference unless audio options are available.

Many laws at the federal level have promoted the development and use of accessible telecommunications products. Their purposes include protecting the civil rights of individuals with disabilities, establishing procurement requirements for specific agencies, and mandating accessibility standards for the manufacture of products. For example, the Americans with Disabilities Act of 1990 requires that public programs and services provide accessible, "effective communication," regardless of what medium is typically used for that communication (U.S. Department of Justice, 2005). It mandates a nationwide system of telecommunications relay services (in which a human being is involved in translation), which make it possible for standard voice telephone users to talk to people who have difficulty hearing or speaking. Section 255 of the Telecommunications Act of 1996 requires that manufacturers of telecommunications equipment and providers of telecommunications services ensure that such products and services are accessible to people with disabilities, if readily achievable (U.S. Department of Justice, 2005). Section 508 standards for telecommunications products procured, developed, or used by the federal government are similar to the Section 255 design standards for manufacturers (U.S. Department of Justice, 2005).

UD of telecommunications equipment goes beyond the minimum accessibility standards set forth in legislation. For example, without compromising the functions of a telephone, applying UD ensures that the telephone can be used by the broadest audience, including those whose first language is not English, individuals who have a wide range of sensory and physical abilities, and those who are elderly. Institutions of higher education can apply UD to the telecommunications infrastructure as well as to specific offerings, such as distance learning programs (see chapter 2).

As with telecommunications, Web sites, and other IT, the U.S. Access Board developed technical and functional performance criteria necessary for software to comply with Section 508. Additionally, comprehensive software design guidelines for educational software were developed by the National Center on Accessible Media (2000). As discussed in chapter 2, the Center for Applied Special Technology (CAST) is a leader in expanding "learning opportunities for all individuals, especially those with disabilities, through the research and development of innovative, technology-based educational resources and strategies" (CAST, n.d.b). CAST (n.d.a, p. 1) defines UD for learning (UDL) as

> a framework for designing curricula that enable all individuals to gain knowledge, skills, and enthusiasm for learning. UDL provides rich supports for learning and reduces barriers to the curriculum while maintaining high achievement standards for all.

Although UD has the potential to increase product markets and help institutions meet their legal obligations under legislation such as the ADA, and accessibility guidelines and standards are available to help developers create accessible IT, companies rarely take the full spectrum of user diversity into account when they develop their products and they often unintentionally erect barriers to product use (Golden, 2002; National Council on Disability, 2004). Some designers are unaware of accessibility issues; others may consider the market too small to address. A research study, undertaken by the National Council on Disability (2004) to analyze the market for universally designed mainstream IT products, documented consumer needs and UD processes, facilitators, and barriers. It was found that rapid changes in technology often cause decreases in accessibility and that even when accessibility features exist, sales associates for these products are often unaware of them. Additional findings of this study include the following:

- Section 508 has clearly had an impact on increasing accessibility and UD efforts by industry.
- A sizeable market for universally designed products and services exists.

- UD principles can be easily incorporated into the current design practices of manufacturers.
- UD processes can be incorporated gradually as part of an organized, deliberate rollout of a UD initiative.
- Products designed to be accessible are often not fully effective because developers do not understand the needs of users with disabilities, and people with disabilities are not integrated into design and testing processes.

The authors of this report (National Council on Disability, 2004, p. 20). concluded

> People with disabilities want to use the same products that everyone else uses. Implementation of universal design satisfies this desire of people with disabilities, while also providing more cost-effective products for all users. While it is impossible to satisfy the needs of all users, products and services that come closer to accommodating a variety of physical and cognitive differences will benefit both users and companies.

With the aging of the "baby boom" generation and other demographic factors, the authors suggest that

> Good business practice dictates that designers and engineers avoid unintentionally excluding large populations of consumers from accessing and using the electronic and information technology they develop and manufacture.

Employing a UD process is "one solution to accommodating people with disabilities that also improves the usability of the products for the rest of the population" (National Council on Disability, 2004, p. 8). Technology vendors should keep in mind that as more people use computers, they represent a wide range of language proficiency, cultures, ages, abilities, and technology expertise. Consumers and consumer advocates, including those in the field of higher education, can find opportunities to increase industry awareness of IT accessibility and usability issues through vendor interaction and procurement policies. For example, imagine if all library procurement officers, as they communicated with database vendors, routinely emphasized the libraries' commitment to equitable access for all patrons and their goal to procure accessible products and then inquired about current product accessibility features and the company's future plans in this regard. Such efforts would put companies on notice that institutions of higher education expect universally designed products to be available.

STEPS TOWARD ACCESSIBLE INFORMATION TECHNOLOGY IN HIGHER EDUCATION

Making an institution-wide commitment to using accessible IT is an important step, but translating that commitment into action takes significant effort. Myriad issues must be considered when cultivating a campus culture that promotes UD of IT: vision, leadership, legal issues, technical standards, development and procurement policies, procedures, support and training, accountability, and enforcement (Bohman, 2007). Generalizing to all IT, the key steps of the WAI's *Implementation Plan for Web Accessibility* (2002) has resulted in the following process:

1. *Establish responsibilities.*
   - Establish a coordination team with a communication plan.
   - Identify a high-level champion or spokesperson for accessible IT.

2. *Conduct an initial assessment.*
   - Find out whether the institution is subject to external requirements regarding IT accessibility.
   - Conduct an initial assessment of the accessibility of campus Web sites and other IT.
   - Assess current awareness of the need for IT accessibility by survey or interviews within the institution.
   - Assess expertise of campus IT developers with regard to accessible design.
   - Assess suitability of current software to support development of accessible Web sites and other software.
   - Estimate resources required to address the needs identified in the initial assessment.

3. *Develop institutional policy.*
   - Find out whether the institution has an existing policy that mandates IT accessibility.
   - Establish an institutional policy on IT accessibility.

4. *Develop initial and ongoing promotion plans to increase awareness of the institution's IT accessibility policy.*

5. *Provide training.*
   - On a regular basis, offer a range of training options to meet the needs of administrators, technical support staff, and others with relevant roles in the institution.
   - Integrate training within mainstream IT training (e.g., Web design classes).

6. *Develop accessible Web sites/software.*
   - Make UD a priority throughout the development process.
   - Provide development teams with resources and software tools that promote accessibility.

7. *Promote IT accessibility awareness.*
   - Incorporate the organization's IT accessibility policy into key documents where appropriate.
   - Enforce the organization's policy on IT accessibility.

8. *Monitor IT accessibility.*
   - Specify the evaluation process to be used for IT accessibility.
   - Conduct ongoing monitoring of the accessibility of the organization's IT.
   - Invite and respond to user feedback on campus IT.
   - Periodically review all aspects of the implementation plan for effectiveness.

CONCLUSION

Although legislation, guidelines, promising practices, and resources are available, the inaccessible design of IT on postsecondary campuses continues to create barriers to some members of the community. Authors of the next two chapters of this book share specific strategies for applying UD to technological environments in institutions of higher education. In chapter 19, Alice Anderson and Mike Litzkow describe campuswide efforts to adapt an electronic tool so that it can deliver online lectures that are accessible to students who are blind. In chapter 20, Terry Thompson discusses issues to address when designing an accessible computer lab.

REFERENCES

Americans with Disabilities Act of 1990. 42 U.S.C.A. § 12101 *et seq.*

Berners-Lee, T. (n.d.). *W3C Web accessibility initiative.* Retrieved November 1, 2007, from http://www.w3.org/WAI/

Bohman, P. (2007). Cultivating and maintaining Web accessibility expertise and institutional support in higher education. *ATHEN Access Technologists Higher Education Network, 2.* Retrieved November 1, 2007, from http://athenpro.org/node/55

Burgstahler, S. (2006). *Equal access: Universal design of computer labs.* Seattle: University of Washington. Retrieved November 1, 2007, from http://www.washington.edu/doit/Brochures/Technology/comp.access.html

Burgstahler, S., Comden, D., & Fraser, B. (1997). Universal access: Designing and evaluating Web sites for accessibility. *CHOICE: Current Reviews for Academic Libraries, 34 Supplement,* 19–22.

Center for Applied Special Technology (CAST). (n.d.a). *CAST transforming education through universal design for learning.* Wakefield, MA: Author. Retrieved November 1, 2007, from http://www.cast.org

CAST. (n.d.b). R & D projects. Wakefield, MA: Author. Retrieved October 1, 2007, from http://www.cast.org/research/projects/index.html

Closing The Gap. (2007). Resource directory. *Closing The Gap, 25*(6), 33–195.

Golden, D. C. (2002). Instructional software accessibility: A status report. *Journal of Special Education Technology, 17*(1), 57–60.

Hackett, S., & Parmanto, B. (2005). A longitudinal evaluation of accessibility: Higher education Web sites. *Internet Research, 15*(3), 281–294.

Information Technology Technical Assistance and Training Center. (n.d.). *State IT database.* Atlanta, GA: Author. Retrieved November 1, 2007, from http://accessibility.gtri.gatech.edu/sitid/stateLawAtGlance.php

Kelly, B. (2002). An accessibility analysis of UK university entry points. *Ariadne, 33.* Retrieved November 1, 2007, from http://www.ariadne.ac.uk/issue33/web-watch/

Laux, L. F., McNally, P. R., Paciello, M. G., & Vanderheiden, G. C. (1996). Designing the World Wide Web for people with disabilities: A user centered design approach. *Proceedings of the Second Annual ACM Conference on Assistive Technologies, Association for Computing Machinery, Special Interest Group on Accessible Computing,* Vancouver, BC, 94–101.

Mace, R. (n.d.). *About universal design (UD).* Raleigh: North Carolina State University, Center for Universal Design. Retrieved November 1, 2007, from http://www.design.ncsu.edu/cud/about_ud/about_ud.htm

National Center on Accessible Media. (2000). *Accessible digital media: Design guidelines for electronic publications, multimedia and the Web.* Boston: Author. Retrieved November 1, 2007, from http://ncam.wgbh.org/cdrom/guideline/

National Council on Disability. (2004). *Design for inclusion: Creating a new marketplace.* Washington, DC: Author. Retrieved October 1, 2007, from http://www.ncd.gov/newsroom/publications/2004/online_newmarketplace.htm#afbad

Nielsen, J. (1996, October). Accessible design for users with disabilities. *Alertbox: Current Issues in Web Usability.* Retrieved November 1, 2007, from http://www.useit.com/alertbox/9610.html

Patrick, D. L. (Correspondence to Senator Tom Harkin, September 9, 1996). Retrieved November 1, 2007, from http://www.usdoj.gov/crt/foia/cltr204.txt

Rehabilitation Act of 1973. 29 U.S.C. § 79 *et seq.*

Rowland, C., & Smith, T. (1999). Web site accessibility. *The Power of Independence, Summer,* 1–2.

Schmetzke, A. (2001). *Accessibility of the homepages of the nation's community colleges.* Stevens Point: University of Wisconsin–Stevens Point. Retrieved November 1, 2007, from http://library.uwsp. edu/aschmetz/Accessible/nationwide/CC_Survey2001/summary_CCC.htm

Schmetzke, A. (2003). *Web accessibility survey home page.* Stevens Point: University of Wisconsin–Stevens Point. Retrieved November 1, 2007, from http://library.uwsp.edu/aschmetz/Accessible/websurveys.htm

Section 508 of the Rehabilitation Act of 1973, as amended. 29 U.S.C. § 794d.

Thompson, T., Burgstahler, S., & Comden, D. (2003). Research on Web accessibility in higher education. *Journal of Information Technology and Disabilities, 9*(2). Retrieved November 1, 2007, from http://www.rit.edu/%7Eeasi/itd/itdv09n2/thompson.htm

United States Access Board. (2007). *Update of the 508 standards and the Telecommunications Act guidelines.* Retrieved November 1, 2007, from http://www.access-board.gov/sec508/update-index.htm

United States Department of Justice. (2005). *A guide to disability rights laws.* Washington, DC: U.S. Department of Justice, Civil Rights Division. Retrieved November 1, 2007, from www.ada.gov/cguide.pdf

Vanderheiden, G. C., & Vanderheiden, K. R. (1992). *Guidelines for the design of consumer products to increase their accessibility to people with disabilities or who are aging (Working Draft 1.7).* Madison, WI: Trace Research and Development Center. Retrieved November 1, 2007, from http://trace. wisc.edu/docs/consumer_product_guidelines/toc.htm

Waddell, C. D. (2007). Accessible electronic & information technology: Legal obligations of higher education and Section 508. *ATHEN Access Technologists Higher Education Network, 2.* Retrieved November 1, 2007, from http://athenpro.org/node/54

Waters, C. (1997). *Universal Web design.* Indianapolis, IN: New Riders.

Web Accessibility Initiative. (2002). *Implementation plan for Web accessibility.* Cambridge, MA: World Wide Web Consortium. Retrieved November 1, 2007, from http://www.w3.org/WAI/impl/Overview

Web Accessibility Initiative. (2005a). *Essential components of Web accessibility.* Cambridge, MA: World Wide Web Consortium. Retrieved November 1, 2007, from http://www.w3.org/WAI/intro/components

Web Accessibility Initiative. (2005b). *Introduction to Web accessibility.* Cambridge, MA: World Wide Web Consortium. Retrieved November 1, 2007, from http://www.w3.org/WAI/intro/accessibility.php

Web Accessibility Initiative. (2007). *WCAG 2.0 quick reference* [Draft]. Cambridge, MA: World Wide Web Consortium. Retrieved November 1, 2007, from http://www.w3.org/WAI/WCAG20/quickref/

World Wide Web Consortium. (1999). *Web content accessibility guidelines 1.0: W3C recommendation 5-May-1999.* Cambridge, MA: Author. Retrieved November 1, 2007, from http://www.w3.org/TR/WAI-WEBCONTENT/

World Wide Web Consortium. (2007a). *About W3C: Future.* Cambridge, MA: Author. Retrieved November 1, 2007, from http://www.w3.org/Consortium/future

World Wide Web Consortium. (2007b). *Web content accessibility guidelines 2.0: W3C Working Draft 11, December 2007.* Cambridge, MA: Author. Retrieved January 8, 2007, from http://www.w3.org/TR/WCAG20/

This material is based on work supported by the National Science Foundation under Cooperative Agreement number HRD-0227995. Any opinions, findings, and conclusions or recommendations expressed in this material are those of the author and do not necessarily reflect the views of the National Science Foundation.

19

Problems and Solutions for Making Multimedia Web-Based Lectures Accessible
A Case Study

Alice Anderson
Mike Litzkow

Most instructional content authors use Web authoring tools, rather than manual hypertext markup language (HTML) to create Web pages. Authoring tools that easily create accessible content can assist developers who have neither the knowledge nor the will to make their Web pages accessible. This chapter describes the challenges and solutions encountered in developing a Web authoring tool that encourages the creation of accessible content and shares how making Web pages accessible adds significant value to applications created.

eTEACH is a freely available authoring tool used to create multimedia lectures delivered as streaming video that students view in a Web browser. Other tools in this category include Macromedia Breeze by Acrobat Connect Professional, SoftTV Presenter, MediaSite, and Microsoft Presenter. Using such tools to provide out-of-class lectures allows faculty to engage students in more active learning and problem-solving activities in class. However, some of these tools are intended more for creating marketing materials than educational materials. They are often limited as learning tools and lack features such as assessment, navigation, and accessibility.

Those who design multimedia content often overlook the need to reach students with disabilities; in fact, many consider it impossible. A unique feature of eTEACH is that it creates content that is accessible to students with a wide variety of disabilities. Closed captioning is included to meet the needs of students who are deaf or hard of hearing, and keyboard interaction capabilities are included for those with fine motor limitations. We believe eTEACH can make complex multimedia materials accessible and can help content creators turn the "impossible" into the easily doable. This chapter focuses primarily on how eTEACH addresses the needs of students who are blind.

Professors who create their own classroom materials generally do not have time to become experts in the complex issues involved in making Web-based multimedia lectures accessible. Learning to create their own accessible course materials using hand-coded HTML techniques is time-consuming for already overburdened faculty. Furthermore, even with training, few faculty members have the experience to apply those techniques to complex materials, such as interactive lectures involving video, audio, and slides. We believe that offering them tools that automatically create accessible materials is effective and saves valuable time.

eTEACH is a user-friendly authoring tool that makes the production of accessible multimedia content almost automatic. It allows professors to concentrate on their areas of expertise rather than on accessibility issues. Building accessibility into the authoring tool makes materials created with that tool accessible with little extra thought or effort.

BACKGROUND

The University of Wisconsin–Madison (UW–Madison) is a leading comprehensive research university and one of the largest Ph.D-granting institutions in the United States. Founded in 1848, UW–Madison currently enrolls more than 40,000 undergraduate, professional, graduate, and doctoral students and employs nearly 14,000 faculty and staff members.

Since 2000, the UW–Madison College of Engineering has used the Web as a tool for providing lectures in a large undergraduate class. Traditional lecture hall sessions with hundreds of students who meet weekly have been replaced with online rich-media presentations, as a result of a project funded by the National Science Foundation through the National Partnership for Advanced Computing Infrastructure. Before this change, students expressed dissatisfaction in their course evaluations, stating that the lectures and labs were disconnected. We developed eTEACH to enhance student learning through improved teaching methods and better integration between lectures and labs. These eTEACH lectures have replaced traditional lectures in classes in such diverse departments as Computer Sciences, Nuclear Engineering, Nursing, and Business Education on UW–Madison campuses, as well as several other campuses across the United States (eTEACH, 2006).

eTEACH lectures generally consist of streaming video and audio, which presents an instructor (a "talking head"), animated slides (usually generated with PowerPoint), an interactive table of contents, links to other Web-based assets, and self-assessment exercises (quizzes). Students choose where and when they will view these lectures. This system allows instructors more time to engage students actively in problem-solving activities during in-class meetings. Students taking courses delivered with eTEACH give feedback that is predominantly positive (Moses & Litzkow, 2005).

In contrast to traditional classroom lectures, which by nature are one-time events, eTEACH lectures become resources available at any time during a student's coursework (e.g., while working on homework problems or studying for an exam). Students using eTEACH watch short, Web-based, rich-media presentations that include the lecturer on video, animated slides, and other HTML and graphical elements at their convenience. We find that significantly less time is wasted in these pre-prepared lectures so that the presentations can be shorter than traditional classroom lectures. The lectures can be viewed at computer labs on campus, in dorm rooms via the campus network, or in private residences using dial-up or broadband connections. Students can now attend hands-on labs to work on engineering problems, thus allowing the professor to assist them directly in the problem-solving process. The new format reverses the traditional lecture/homework paradigm: Students do their homework in class with help from the instructor and view lectures out of class (Foertsch, Moses, Strikwerda, & Litzkow, 2002).

MAKING ᴇTEACH ACCESSIBLE TO SCREEN READER USERS

Too often we forget that computer users who are blind are unable to benefit from the functionality of a mouse because they cannot see where the cursor is located on the screen. To operate a computer, people who are blind must use a program called a screen reader. Screen reader software allows the user to hear, via a speech synthesizer, or to touch, via a braille display, the information that is available to other people by viewing the screen (Anderson & Ewers, 2001). Screen readers provide ways for the user to interact with buttons, dropdown lists, checkboxes, and other graphical elements normally selected with a mouse. The screen reader "speaks" in a synthesized voice to the user, who controls everything through keyboard commands. Experienced screen reader users become amazingly quick at these interactions, to the point where they exceed the speed of sighted users. Major screen readers in use today include the commercial products JAWS and Window-Eyes.

eTEACH is now in its third major version. Mike Litzkow, one of its authors, built the first two versions at UW–Madison's College of Engineering. A diverse team of individuals from UW–Madison's Division of Information Technology collaborated with Litzkow to build the third version. The third version represents the transition from a National Science Foundation-funded research project in engineering physics to an academic Division of Information Technology Innovation Award-funded product that belongs to our campus as a whole (Engage, 2007). In version two, we achieved accessibility for screen reader users by enhancing the user interface and applying a custom JAWS script designed specifically to support eTEACH. None of the changes to the user interface were visible to sighted users, and their experience was not altered in any way by the introduction of the accessibility features. The mechanisms used to achieve this end have been described elsewhere (Anderson, Bundy, & Litzkow, 2004).

While the mechanisms we built into version two were a step forward in accessibility, several problems and limitations remained. First, our content worked with only one screen reader (JAWS 5) and thus was not accessible to users of other screen readers or even different versions of the same screen reader. Second, the content worked with only one Web browser and on only one company's family of operating systems.

In short, many screen reader users would have to alter their computing environment significantly to access these materials. With the development of version three of eTEACH, we created a completely different set of mechanisms that are applicable across a wide variety of screen readers, browsers, and operating systems. When evaluating similar multimedia tools, we found the following problems:

- Buttons (e.g., pause, forward, stop) were not labeled.
- Hot keys conflicted with screen reader keystrokes.
- Presenter and screen reader volumes were inconsistent and could not be controlled separately.
- Slides were changing before a student was ready (i.e., slide changes were outside the screen reader's control).

We hope that the knowledge we have gained through creating eTEACH will be useful for developers of other tools who face similar problems. In addition, we hope to influence content creators to choose authoring tools that implement such accessibility features.

SPECIAL CHALLENGES FOR SCREEN READER USERS

A goal of eTEACH is to be usable by the broadest possible audience to the greatest extent possible, including people with disabilities who use assistive technology. This goal parallels the concept and principles of universal design (Burgstahler, 2007):

> Universal design in education . . . promotes the consideration of people with a broad range of characteristics in all educational products and environments. Universal design in education goes beyond accessible design for people with disabilities to make all aspects of the educational experience more inclusive for students, parents, staff, instructors, administrators, and visitors with a great variety of characteristics. These characteristics include those related to gender, race/ethnicity, age, stature, disability, and learning style.

With dedication to such lofty goals, well-known guidelines from the World Wide Web Consortium, and governmental standards for creating accessible Web-based materials, one might assume that making these lectures accessible to students who are blind would be fairly straightforward. One challenge, however, is that eTEACH incorporates video, which cannot be seen by users who are blind. Our experience is that making this material accessible is not easy, but it is possible.

The first thing we learned is that the presence of video is not the problem. Students who are blind have been sitting in classrooms beside sighted students and learning the same materials in lectures for years. Since eTEACH is intended to be a replacement for traditional classroom lectures, our goal was to make these lectures just as accessible to blind students as are face-to-face lectures. We believe we have achieved this goal.

We began by implementing the Web accessibility techniques suggested by standards and advocacy bodies, such as the Web Accessibility Initiative Web Content

Accessibility Guidelines (World Wide Web Consortium, 2007) and Section 508 of the Rehabilitation Act (U.S. Access Board, 2007). We then presented eTEACH to a student who is blind and is an expert at using the screen reader JAWS. Unfortunately, he was unable to grasp the material without guidance from a sighted person. We quickly discovered that viewing eTEACH lectures is a much more complex task than viewing simple Web pages, which contain static text, graphics, and links. All the media— video, audio, and images—contribute significantly to the "lecture experience" and often contain important parts of the information presented by the lecturer. Because audio and video are time-based media, and the PowerPoint slides and animations are synchronized with the audio and video, timing is a significant issue. For example, a play/pause button might be available, but if the access method is slow and awkward, the student who wants to pause the audio so that the screen reader can speak the text on a PowerPoint slide may be unable to do so before the slide changes. Also, students need to be able to navigate within a lecture using a table of contents or other controls. While JAWS was able to read the table of contents, it failed to recognize that the lines it was reading were links to other parts of the program. We also found that when page content changed dynamically, JAWS would return to the beginning of the page and start reading again from the top. From the perspective of the student who is blind, this meant that, with no explanation, JAWS would stop reading the contents of a slide at random and start describing the buttons and other controls on the page. Even for expert screen reader users, this was frustrating and confusing.

Even after extensive coaching by sighted users, our test student was unable to make much sense of the lecture material. We concluded that, even though we had already met accessibility guidelines and standards, including our campus Web accessibility policy (University of Wisconsin–Madison, 2006), considerably more work was necessary to make eTEACH lectures accessible to screen reader users.

Conducting the test with an experienced screen reader was the first time that the eTEACH code developer had seen a screen reader in use. He was impressed by the speed and facility with which the blind student could operate his computer with so little knowledge of the product. He became convinced that with appropriate changes, eTEACH lectures could be effective for teaching blind students, and he was determined to make that happen. Thus began a long and exciting journey into the world of those who "see" life in a different way. It was only after much coaching from real users who were blind and becoming a novice screen reader user himself that the developer was able to achieve his goal of making eTEACH accessible to people who use screen readers.

EXPERIENCES WITH SCREEN READERS

Early attempts to make eTEACH usable by screen reader users were frustrating. The major challenge lies in the dynamic nature of the page presented by eTEACH. We began by concentrating on adding alt attributes to images, putting labels on buttons, and applying other "standard" accessibility techniques. We learned that every screen reader reacted to dynamic changes on the page in a unique way, often by returning to the top of the page. When we tried presenting the correct answer to a quiz question in a pop-up window, screen readers would sometimes start reading the contents of the new window somewhere in the middle—completely skipping the "correct" or "incorrect" answer cues. It was impossible to predict where the screen reader would begin reading when it returned from the pop-up window to the main window. Results depended on the particular version of the screen reader, the particular version of the browser, the size of the browser window, and other factors we could not identify. This unpredictable behavior made the lectures unavailable to people who are blind. We had disappointing results with several major screen readers, including JAWS and Window-Eyes.

Besides all the unpredictable reactions to dynamic content by the various screen readers, an even more fundamental problem was discovered. To comprehend a multimedia lecture, individuals who are blind use audio for three purposes:

1. to hear the words spoken by the lecturer
2. to hear what is written on the PowerPoint slides
3. to navigate and operate the various controls presented by the application

Users need to control when the program speaks, and they should be able to choose to hear either the slide first or the audio first and switch between the two at will. In addition, students who use screen readers need to hear the screen reader's audio description of the controls to control and navigate within the presentation.

The solution we ended up with dramatically reduces the dynamic nature of the page while preserving the fundamental linkage between slide content and professor commentary. To achieve this, we created a special Web page just for screen reader users. This is possible because the underlying data structure for eTEACH lectures is Extensive Markup Language (XML). All eTEACH Web pages are created from that XML code, using Extensible Stylesheet Language Transformations (XSLT). Thus, by creating a unique XSLT transformation for screen reader users, we are able to reformat the underlying material to make it screen reader-friendly. eTEACH automatically creates a link directing screen reader users to their special version of the page.

Our special screen reader format places the text for all slides on a single page. Each slide starts with an HTML heading that includes the slide number and title. Screen readers and their users are already accustomed to using page headings to navigate to content areas of interest, so this process is quite natural for them. Also, while different screen readers may use different keystrokes for navigating a page by headers, all of them can do it effectively. Following the text of each slide is a button that plays or pauses the lecturer's voice while that slide is visible to sighted users. Since the button only controls one slide's audio at a time, there is still a close association between the spoken audio and the slide content. By jumping directly to this button (another common screen reader feature), the user can choose to listen to the spoken audio first, listen to the slide text first, or alternate between the two. Some slides have additional Web resources associated with them. For example, the professor might have the students read background material from a particular Web site to enrich the lecture content. Those slides have an additional button to direct the user to a list of associated Web links and a button at the end of the list that returns the user to the starting point.

A table of contents makes it much easier for all students to navigate through lectures to find sections that are relevant to specific topics or assignments. However, it may be difficult for users who are blind to locate the table of contents. To address this problem, we created a hot key or shortcut—a key or combination of keys used together—that allows the screen reader to jump immediately to the table of contents (e.g., ALT plus C is used to copy text). The table of contents is formatted as a list of links. Experienced screen reader users find this approach natural because they are already adept at dealing with both lists and links. Clicking on one of these links takes the student directly to the start of the text for the appropriate slide. With this technique, users who are blind can find their way to a particular slide almost as quickly as sighted users.

Another initial eTEACH access problem for screen reader users is that it is difficult to manage the audio level of a spoken lecture. If this audio level is much different from the level at which the screen reader speaks, it becomes difficult to switch between these different uses of audio information. We provided two hot keys that raise and lower the volume of the spoken text. They allow the user to adjust the lecture volume to match the screen reader's volume. This small adjustment is important in real use. Otherwise, either the screen reader or the presenter would be much louder or softer, thus making comprehension difficult.

An important feature of eTEACH is its self-assessment (quiz) capability. These quizzes highlight important information and allow students to assess their level of understanding and become more engaged in the presentation material. However, the quizzes presented an additional challenge for screen reader users. Asking students to click on the best answer for a multiple-choice question and telling them whether or not they are correct in a pop-up window is not effective. Instead, we format the answers in an HTML list and then follow with a statement of the correct answer. Since screen readers and their users know how to traverse HTML lists, students can consider all the possible options before listening to the correct answer. Some questions have hints associated with them. These are formatted in such a way that students can either listen to them or skip directly to the answer choices. In addition, some questions contain review points available through buttons that return users to the particular slide in the lecture where the subject of the question was discussed. All screen readers have effective means of locating and activating buttons.

One key to making the Web accessible to students who are blind is to make pages that are not dynamic and that have carefully chosen formatting, which corresponds with common features of screen reader navigation techniques. In this way, blind users can quickly find slides they are interested in, read the text on those slides, listen to the professor speak about the slides, take the self-assessment quizzes, and use the included resource links. The complexity of these pages does require some initial learning, but students generally can navigate easily with less than an hour of practice. Since a typical college class may consist of forty or more lectures, and every lecture is formatted in exactly the same way, such practice quickly pays off.

UNSOLVED PROBLEMS

Although eTEACH automatically makes most lectures accessible to students who are blind, the professor may have to modify certain presentations that contain pictures in the PowerPoint slides. Blind students will not understand the significance of these images (or even realize they are there) unless the professor uses PowerPoint's feature to add "alternative text" (alt attributes) that describes the content of the image. Once this is done, the eTEACH tool can find the alt attributes and insert them into the normal slide text in a location that corresponds to the location of the image on the slide. Thus, the screen reader can properly read a slide that alternates between text and images. While this works well in many cases, we realize that sometimes the images (e.g., maps) will be too complex to describe. The critical need is to convince professors to add the alternative text, which should not be too difficult because it is a relatively easy way to customize a presentation to meet the needs of particular students. Professors who have not taken this step initially can easily add such descriptions after discovering they have students who are blind in their classes—a far better prospect than starting over with a different tool—and perhaps will discover that other students benefit from the availability of image descriptions.

CONCLUSION

We learned firsthand about the challenging accessibility issues faced by developers who care about accessibility. We found that none of the tested screen readers can effectively handle dynamic changes to the pages they are reading. In addition, their reactions to the same material vary greatly. However, software developers must predict how screen readers will convey their content to users who are blind to ensure that the presentation is useful. We believe that these problems severely limit the amount of accessible educational content available to students today and hope that Web technology developers and screen reader vendors continue to work on these problems; we applaud their efforts.

Most important is that many college faculty members are concerned with creating course content that is accessible to the widest possible variety of students. However, faculty members have demanding research and teaching loads and other time-consuming obligations that prevent them from becoming experts in this area. For this reason, we feel that the development of software tools that automate and support the creation of course materials is important in the effort to make such materials accessible. The development of such tools is more efficient and cost-effective than having many individual faculty members struggling to create accessible content on their own. We have shown that it is possible to make complex, interactive, Web-based lectures accessible to screen reader users and to create a tool that does not place an undue burden on faculty time. We developed ways to work around the limitations of current screen reader technology by using a variety of techniques that are not specific to any particular screen reader or browser.

REFERENCES

Anderson, A., Bundy, B., & Litzkow, M. (2004). *Making multi-media Web-based lectures accessible: Experiences, problems, and solutions.* Retrieved October 1, 2007, from http://www.csun.edu/cod/conf/2004/proceedings/193.htm

Anderson, A., & Ewers, N. (2001). *Introduction to the screen reader.* Video and transcript. Retrieved October 1, 2007, from http://www.doit.wisc.edu/accessibility/video/intro.asp

Burgstahler, S. (2007). *Universal design of instruction: Definition, principles, guidelines, and examples.* Seattle: University of Washington. Retrieved October 1, 2007, from http://www.washington.edu/doit/Brochures/Academics/instruction/

Engage. (2007). Accomplishments and portfolio: eTEACH. Retrieved October 1, 2007, from http://engage.doit.wisc.edu/accomplishments/eTeach/index.html

eTEACH (2006). eTEACH home. Retrieved October 1, 2007, from http://eteach.engr.wisc.edu/new Eteach/home.html

Foertsch, J., Moses, G., Strikwerda, J., & Litzkow, M. (2002). Reversing the lecture/homework paradigm using eTEACH Web-based streaming video software. *Journal of Engineering Education, 91*(267).

Moses, G., & Litzkow, M. (2005). In-class active learning and frequent assessment reform of nuclear reactor theory course. *Frontiers in Education*, 2005. FIE '05. Proceedings 35th Annual Conference, October 2005. Retrieved October 1, 2007, from http://ieeexplore.ieee.org/xpls/absprintf.jsp?arnumber=1612006

U.S. Access Board. (2007). *Guide to the Section 508 standards for electronic and information technology; software applications and operating systems* (1194.21). Retrieved October 1, 2007, from http://www.access-board.gov/sec508/guide/1194.21.htm

University of Wisconsin–Madison. (2006). *Policy governing World Wide Web accessibility at UW–Madison.* Madison: Author. Retrieved October 1, 2007, from http://www.wisc.edu/wiscinfo/policy/wwwap.php

World Wide Web Consortium (W3C). (2007). *Web accessibility initiative (WAI) Web content accessibility guidelines (WCAG).* Retrieved October 1, 2007, from http://www.w3.org/WAI/

20

Universal Design
of Computing Labs

Terry Thompson

The author of this chapter shares how administrators of computer labs can take concrete steps to make their facilities and resources welcoming, accessible, and usable by all students, faculty, and staff. The ultimate accessible computing environment is one that supports learning anywhere, anytime, and for anyone, allowing all students, including students with disabilities, to access needed technology resources without restrictions posed by time and space. This chapter includes case studies from three higher education institutions that have taken positive steps toward implementing universally accessible computing labs.

The evolving role of computer labs on college campuses has become a common topic of conversation among higher education information technology professionals. As wireless Internet access improves on campuses, and as students' personal technology becomes more portable, students might conceivably have less need for centralized computing facilities. However, computer labs at many colleges and universities seem to be defying these expectations and are frequently packed with students, often to capacity.

Why are computer labs so resistant to extinction? They continue to offer unique benefits. Computing labs typically provide a broader array of software applications than students would otherwise have access to, including highly specialized, discipline-specific products. They also provide a place for students to work alongside their peers and, in some cases, to collaborate on computing-related projects. Also, students can tap into the technical expertise of computing center staff and knowledgeable patrons.

Higher education computing labs provide a unique climate in which students can be productive, learn, and be nourished by the people and technologies that surround them. All students can benefit from this environment, including students with disabilities. However, some students in the latter group face significant barriers unless computing labs are built to support the needs of all users.

Human beings are incredibly diverse. Some use wheelchairs and may require extra space for moving between aisles, as well as extra desk height that allows them to approach a workstation. Some use alternative input devices, such as trackballs, speech recognition software, eye tracking systems, or other technologies collectively known as assistive technology (AT). Some perceive computer output using speech synthesis or braille devices rather than monitors. Some are unable to hear and may require visible alternatives (e.g., flashing computer screens) to inform them of sounds, such as computer alerts. Some, such as individuals with learning disabilities or individuals whose native language differs from the primary language spoken at the institution, may use software that combines speech output with visual highlighting of on-screen text. These are only a few examples of the types of technologies that people use to access computers.

Historically, the needs of students with disabilities have been accommodated by professionals who specialize in disabilities, usually within disabled student services (DSS) offices. DSS offices are typically responsible for ensuring that students with disabilities receive the accommodations necessary for access to college programs and services, including extended time on tests, note-takers, and sign language interpreters. Early AT labs rose out of this environment, in which DSS personnel found that the most effective way to provide access to computers for students who required AT or other accommodations was to do it themselves. This approach provided DSS staff with control over the choice and deployment of technologies and spared them the frustration that often arose from trying to persuade central computing groups to build accessible labs.

However, despite the benefits of this approach to DSS staff, these isolated labs rarely provided access that was truly equal to that of other students. Students were being forced to do their computing in segregated settings, without the benefits of working alongside and collaborating with their nondisabled peers. Often, the specialized software applications that were available in the mainstream computing facilities were not available in the DSS labs, and the labs were only open during normal business hours, whereas mainstream labs remained open 24/7.

There are legal reasons for rejecting a segregated model for the delivery of computing services. The Office for Civil Rights (OCR) of the U.S. Department of Education is charged with enforcing both Section 504 of the Rehabilitation Act of 1973 and Title II of the Americans with Disabilities Act of 1990, federal laws that prohibit recipients of federal funds and public institutions from discriminating against persons with disabilities. In 1999, in a letter that summarized their investigation of a complaint filed by a student who was blind against California State University–Long Beach (Scott, 1999), OCR stated the following:

> As universities have striven to provide effective communication to students with disabilities with respect to computer technology, traditionally the academic community has relied heavily on a single centralized unit on campus to house and maintain the specialized adaptive technology equipment. This practice has been seen as a method for enabling a small number of staff with adaptive technology expertise to serve a relatively large number of students with disabilities. However, such sole reliance

upon a single centralized location (when not limited to adaptive technology training, but instead used for instructing disabled students in course subject matter) may run counter to the strong philosophy embodied in [federal law] . . . . Thus OCR assumes in most cases computer access will be effectively provided to the student with the disability in an educational setting with his or her nondisabled peers and classmates at the various computer laboratory sites scattered throughout the campus.

Over the past decade, many higher education institutions have moved beyond the older DSS computing lab model to a more inclusive model in which mainstream labs provide the AT tools, customizable settings, and overall level of accessibility required for students with disabilities to attain equal access.

Universal design is an important concept to be applied as institutions make this transition. Universal design is a design process in which products and environments are designed to meet the needs of the broadest possible spectrum of users. Although human beings are incredibly diverse, in some contexts it's possible to describe, with some accuracy, an "average user." For example, in a college computer lab in the United States, an average user might be 5 feet 10 inches tall, male, English-speaking, and a user of a computer monitor for visual output and a keyboard and mouse for input. However, if a computer lab is designed to meet the physical and intellectual needs of these users only, many potential users would be excluded. Universal design breaks away from designing for average users. Instead, the objective is to design for the largest possible number of users, so that individuals with a broad range of abilities, disabilities, heights, ages, reading levels, learning styles, native languages, cultures, and other characteristics are welcome and can fully participate in and contribute to the learning environment.

To apply universal design to a computer lab setting, one needs to consider the various functions of the lab. What do students do there? How can the facility, environment, equipment, and staff be designed, deployed, and trained to support the broadest possible spectrum of users? The Disabilities, Opportunities, Internetworking, and Technology (DO-IT) Center at the University of Washington has published a brochure, *Equal Access: Universal Design of Computer Labs,* that includes a checklist of questions that can guide those responsible for college computing labs in ensuring that their labs adhere to principles of universal design (Burgstahler, 2006). The checklist organizes universal design considerations for computing labs into the following categories:

- Planning, policies, and evaluation
- Facility and environment
- Lab staff
- Information resources
- Computers, software, and AT

Considerations in each of these categories are equally important. For example, I once encountered a major research university in the United States that had equipped one of its computer labs with several accessible workstations, including a wide variety of AT and a height-adjustable desktop that could be raised or lowered with a single electronic switch. Unfortunately, the university had focused solely on making the technology accessible and had overlooked the fact that this newly accessible lab was located on an upper floor of an older building that was not accessible by elevator. This example underscores the need to consider the big picture when practicing universal design. Consider the needs of all possible users and do so with consideration of the full array of functions that lab users engage in when using the lab. As the example illustrates, a person's use of the lab starts prior to sitting down in front of a computer. It starts when the person is sitting or standing outside the building, wondering how to get inside. Actually, it starts even before that, when the student is enjoying the comfort of the dorm room and consulting the computing lab Web site for hours of operation and to see if there is documentation listing available AT. In order for all possible users to have access to this information, it must be presented in a way that is accessible. Accessible design of Web resources is covered in the "Accessible Content" section later in this chapter.

There are also policy and procedural considerations. For example, in a computing lab with only a small number of designated accessible workstations, who is allowed to use those workstations, especially if all other workstations in the lab are occupied? Some institutions have established policies that students without disabilities are allowed to use these workstations but must relinquish them if the stations are needed by students with disabilities. This can put disabled students in the awkward situation of having to ask people to move or of asking lab staff to do so on their behalf. Also, how do students qualify for access to these stations? Do they simply have to disclose their disabilities to lab staff, or is there a more formal process by which they become authorized users?

Issues like these are further complicated if software specifically designed for students with learning disabilities is included on "accessible" workstations. Often students whose disabilities are invisible are not eager to disclose those disabilities, to the point where they may be unwilling to sit at workstations that are promoted as being accessible because of the stigma that may create. The solution to these sorts of problems would seem to be this: Build a truly *universal* computing environment, in which any student can operate any computer in any lab on campus, with full access to all needed tools and resources, including AT. But is this even possible? The following case studies show how a few higher education institutions have worked toward this goal.

COLLEGE OF THE REDWOODS

College of the Redwoods is a 2-year public college in Eureka, California, with approximately 7,000 students. In 2001, the Board of Trustees at the college approved Policy No. 809, access to programs and facilities (College of the Redwoods, 2001). This policy includes the following requirement:

> Computer labs with more than ten stations for use by students shall have a minimum of three [accessible] stations or 10%, whichever provides greater accessibility for the disabled use. Computer labs with less than ten stations shall have at least one accessible station. Standards for accessible software can be found in the Transition Plan.

The details of what constitutes an accessible station are laid out in the *Computer Labs Accessibility Standards* (College of the Redwoods, 2004). An accessible station meets the following minimum standards: It has screen reading software for users who are blind, screen magnification software for those with low vision, speech recognition software for users who are unable to type, and either a 19-inch monitor or a 17-inch flat-panel screen for users with low vision and those who are distracted easily.

The standards document also defines an "enhanced standard," which must be followed for at least one computer station in each lab that has more than ten stations. The enhanced standard includes all minimum standards plus several additional peripherals and software products, such as a closed-circuit television (CCTV, a camera attached to the computer sending enlarged images to the screen for persons with low vision to read print documents); a scanner; and accompanying software. This configuration allows users who are unable to read print documents to scan them and have them read electronically. Word prediction software is also considered an enhanced standard; it allows users who type slowly or who have spelling challenges to select words from a list as they type and present them on an even larger monitor (21-inch monitor or 19-inch flat-panel display), which is also an enhanced standard.

The standards document also includes a set of guidelines that address physical barriers, calling for adjustable-height chairs, tables, and keyboard trays for *all* workstations; utility and equipment controls located within easy reach; and clear aisles that are at least 36 inches wide. Features such as these benefit individuals with disabilities but are beneficial to everyone else as well. Especially important in this implementation model is the inclusion of adjustable features. Universal design should not be misconstrued as "one size fits all." Customizability is a key to creating an environment that works equally well for all people and their many diverse qualities and characteristics.

OKLAHOMA STATE UNIVERSITY

Like the College of the Redwoods, Oklahoma State University (OSU) has created lab standards that document physical dimensions, required hardware and software for accessible workstations, and requirements for the number of accessible workstations that must be present within labs of various sizes (Oklahoma State University, n.d.). At OSU, roughly 5% of all workstations in central computing labs must be accessible.

OSU has also taken an even more significant step toward universal design of its campus computing environment: The most commonly used AT applications are available from any computer used to log in to the university computing network, including home computers. Available applications include screen readers, screen magnification software, and either of two scanning and reading applications (one for users who are blind and one for those with learning disabilities). Speech recognition software is also available universally, and stenography masks are available for students on request. Stenography masks enable students to dictate to the computer without being heard and provide a consistent acoustic environment so that students can use speech recognition in a variety of settings without loss of accuracy. Nevertheless, for convenience, most students install speech recognition software on their home computers, which the OSU license permits.

Negotiating suitable licenses with AT vendors is a key to universal deployment of AT. Examples of suitable licenses include unlimited site licenses (copies of the product can be installed and used on any computer in the organization without restriction) and concurrent user licenses (copies of the product can be installed anywhere, but usage must be tracked, and only a specified number of users can use the product simultaneously). OSU has had success in attaining licenses that meet their needs for campuswide accessibility.

Another key to universal accessibility of the campus computing environment is to ensure portability of user application files, including custom settings. As mentioned previously, customizability is a key concept in universal design. This is particularly true with AT, since users typically must configure AT software extensively to make it work best for their individual needs. Unless configuration data can be accessed over the network, users will be tethered to their individual workstations. At OSU, a single server has been set up as the AT server. This server holds AT applications and user data and handles license tracking and confirmation. For most AT applications, additional software components must be installed on client workstations, which then communicate with the AT server for license verification and user settings. From a user standpoint, this means they simply have to log in to the OSU network, and all their AT and custom settings are readily available.

OSU has developed an open-source software product, AT Loader, that facilitates the log-in process for users connecting remotely to the campus network. It provides an accessible self-voicing interface, so users with visual disabilities have access to log-in prompts and other information prior to their AT loading. It then establishes a secure connection to the OSU network, locates the users' needed AT software, confirms license availability, and loads the AT.

NORTH CAROLINA STATE UNIVERSITY

Like OSU, North Carolina State University (NCSU) is deploying AT on all workstations throughout its centrally supported student computer network, utilizing roaming profiles so that users can access their custom settings and application data from any computer on the network. The Information Technology Division (ITD) is responsible for providing the university's network infrastructure; it creates a base image that is used for installing the operating system and applications on workstations in centrally supported public computing labs, as well as in labs that are otherwise managed by individual colleges and departments across campus. The base image for both Windows and Mac environments includes a variety of AT, such as screen readers and screen magnification software for students with disabilities (Windows only), word prediction software and highlight-and-read applications for students with writing and reading challenges, and all the accessibility applications and settings that come bundled with each operating system (North Carolina State University, n.d.a).

As long as students continue to use public labs, accessibility efforts such as these will be required. However, as more and more college curricula are available to remote students through distance learning, the ultimate goal for access to computing resources is access anywhere, anytime, and for anyone. NCSU has made significant strides toward this goal through its Virtual Computing Lab (VCL) Project, a joint venture of ITD and the NCSU College of Engineering (North Carolina State University, n.d.b). The VCL provides on-demand 24/7 remote access to advanced computing lab facilities, including engineering, design, and scientific software applications across Windows, Mac, and Linux operating systems.

Accessibility was incorporated into design parameters in the early stages of the VCL Project, and the design team has worked with major AT vendors toward the goal of accessing remote computing applications using AT. This has been successfully demonstrated using all major Windows screen readers, at least one Windows screen magnification product, and various alternative input devices (Primlani & Bahram, 2005; Primlani, 2006). There are still significant challenges, but NCSU's emphasis on accessibility in the early stages of VCL development holds promise for the accessibility of virtual computing in the future.

ACCESSIBLE SOFTWARE

Providing AT for students is one part of creating an accessible computing environment, but AT in and of itself does not guarantee accessibility. AT must be able to work with available software. If software requires a mouse for operation of controls, or if it communicates important ideas using images exclusively, or if it is developed using nonstandard application program interfaces that fail to communicate with AT, then students with disabilities may be denied access, despite their being well equipped with AT.

Section 508 of the Rehabilitation Act, amended in 1998, requires accessibility of any electronic and information technology developed, procured, maintained, or used by the federal government. The Access Board was the federal agency charged with developing standards to support this legislation. The resultant Electronic and Information Technology Accessibility Standards (United States Access Board, 2000) establish standards for ensuring the accessibility of six categories of electronic and information technology: software applications and operating systems; Web-based intranet and Internet information and applications; telecommunications products; video and multimedia products; self-contained, closed products (i.e., standalone devices such as scanners, copiers, and information kiosks); and desktop and portable computers.

Clearly, many of these technologies are used in computing labs. Although the Section 508 legislation explicitly applies to the federal government, the supporting standards are an excellent resource for higher education institutions that are looking to ensure the accessibility of their computing facilities. In fact, many state governments and individual higher education institutions have adopted these standards or have developed their own standards that are based in part on the Access Board standards (e.g., Missouri Office of Information Technology, 2003; Oregon State University, n.d.). Without policies and/or procedures that require consideration of accessibility during the procurement process, institutions are more likely to procure inaccessible software, which can become an insurmountable barrier for students with disabilities and can be expensive to correct if institutions are required to do so as a result of legal action.

Section 504 of the Rehabilitation Act requires accessibility of programs and services, as long as making them accessible does not constitute a fundamental alteration in the nature of a program or activity or undue financial and administrative burdens. Many software applications in higher education are highly specialized products developed for specific disciplines. If there are only one or two products available that meet the academic needs of a program, and neither is accessible, then the academic program does not have to refrain from using the software. Rather, it must find other ways for a student to gain access to the content or functionality the product provides, perhaps through the assistance of a staff member. However, both "fundamental alteration" and "undue burden" are difficult to prove and require extensive well-documented deliberation with qualified experts for reaching such conclusions. Sometimes seemingly inaccessible software can be customized so that it is more accessible, or workarounds can be developed for students who are unable to access certain features.

When institutions deploy software applications that have accessible features, these features should be readily available by default, and lab staff should be aware of how to enable and support them. For example, most major media players support the display of closed captions if they're available, but steps may need to be taken to ensure that this feature is enabled by default. Similarly, recent versions of Microsoft Office ship with speech recognition capability, but this feature is not automatically installed. Also, all the major operating systems ship with integrated assistive technologies and other accessibility features, and, again, these features might not be installed or enabled by default.

ACCESSIBLE CONTENT

More and more educational content is distributed electronically, including content relevant to computer labs such as lab specifications, locations, hours of operation, help documents, and online applications for reserving specialized resources. The format for electronic distribution typically assumes one of two forms: Web pages in hypertext markup language (HTML) or document files designed to be read in specific software applications.

If content is delivered using HTML, accessibility is attained by complying with established accessibility standards. One of the six categories of the Section 508 standards described above is "Web-based intranet and Internet information and applications." This set includes sixteen standards that define Web accessibility. However, these standards were informed by a more comprehensive set of Web Content Accessibility Guidelines developed by the World Wide Web Consortium. Creating accessible Web content can be as simple as creating valid HTML documents with a clearly organized heading structure and providing alternate text for all images. However, Web accessibility becomes more challenging in relation to the complexity of the page. For example, as data tables, forms, and dynamic rich media content are introduced, making these resources accessible becomes more challenging but is still attainable.

Similarly, if content is distributed in the form of document files such as DOC (Microsoft Word), PPT (PowerPoint), or PDF (Adobe Acrobat Reader), steps are required of the author to ensure the accessibility of these documents. The National Center on Accessible Information Technology in Education (AccessIT, n.d.) at the University of Washington has developed a knowledge base of short articles on the accessibility of these and many other products. The articles summarize each issue and then link to additional resources for more extensive detail.

Several software products have been developed to facilitate the authoring of accessible Web content. Examples include Web accessibility checkers; tools for converting Word and PowerPoint files into accessible HTML documents; tools for adding closed captions to multimedia files; and equation editors that export to Mathematics Markup Language (MathML), the emerging XML standard for communicating mathematical notation in a way that is platform-independent and accessible to AT users.

In addition to deploying AT across campus as described above, NCSU deploys a variety of helpful accessibility-related tools for authors and instructors. Products in all the categories mentioned in the preceding paragraph are available to NCSU faculty, staff, or student either as universally deployed applications, via the standard lab image, or as downloadable applications available to any NCSU-authenticated user.

CONCLUSION

Earlier in this chapter, readers were asked to consider fundamental questions about the functions of the computer labs on their campuses: What do students do there? How can the facility, environment, equipment, and staff be designed, deployed, and trained to support the broadest possible spectrum of users? This chapter has explored a few strategies for addressing the latter question, with examples from three higher education institutions. Whether computer labs exist within designated physical spaces or as virtual spaces supporting learning anywhere, anytime, and for anyone, they exist because they provide unique learning opportunities for students. Universal design allows these spaces to be designed and deployed in ways that support the largest possible number of users, so that all students in higher education, regardless of individual qualities and characteristics, can share experiences and fully participate in, and contribute to, the learning process.

REFERENCES

AccessIT. (n.d.) *AccessIT knowledge base*. Seattle: University of Washington. Retrieved November 1, 2007, from http://www.washington.edu/accessit/kb.html

Burgstahler, S. (2006). *Equal access: Universal design of computer labs*. Seattle: University of Washington. Retrieved November 1, 2007, from http://www.washington.edu/doit/Brochures/Technology/comp.access.html

College of the Redwoods. (2004). *Computer labs accessibility standards*. Eureka, CA: Author. Retrieved January 19, 2007, from http://hightech.redwoods.edu/AccessibilityStandards.htm

College of the Redwoods, Board of Trustees. (2001). *Board of Trustees policy no. 809*. Eureka, CA: Author. Retrieved January 19, 2007, from http://www.redwoods.edu/district/board/policies/ar/AR80907.htm

Missouri Office of Information Technology. (2003). *Information technology standard.* Retrieved January 19, 2007, from http://www.oa.mo.gov/itsd/cio/standards/ITGS0003.pdf

North Carolina State University. (n.d.a). *Accessible IT@ NC State.* Raleigh: Author. Retrieved February 4, 2008, from http://www.ncsu.edu/it/access/

North Carolina State University. (n.d.b). *Virtual computing labs.* Raleigh: Author. Retrieved January 19, 2007, from http://www.eos.ncsu.edu/remoteaccess/vcl.html

Oklahoma State University. (n.d.) *Accessible computer labs deployment standards.* Stillwater: Author. Retrieved February 4, 2008, from http://access.it.okstate.edu/content/view/18/39

Oregon State University. (n.d.). *IT accessibility at OSU.* Corvallis: Author. Retrieved January 19, 2007, from http://oregonstate.edu/accessibility/

Primlani, S. (2006). *Accessible remote computing.* Presentation slides from Accessing Higher Ground: Accessible Media, Web and Technology Conference. Boulder, CO. Retrieved January 19, 2007, from http://www.colorado.edu/ATconference/Accessible_Remote_Computing/Accessible_Remote_Computing.htm

Primlani, S., & Bahram, S. (2005). Building an accessible next-generation virtual computing environment: Benefits, challenges and strategies. *Proceedings of Technology and Persons with Disabilities Conference, California State University, Northridge.* Retrieved January 19, 2007, from http://www.csun.edu/cod/conf/2005/proceedings/2314.htm

Scott, R. E. (1999). *California State University, Long Beach; Docket Number 09-99-2041.* Retrieved January 19, 2007, from http://www.rit.edu/~easi/law/lbeach.htm

United States Access Board. (2000). Electronic and information technology accessibility standards (section 508). *The Federal Register, 65,* 80499–80528. Retrieved January 19, 2007, from http://www.access-board.gov/sec508/standards.htm

This material is based on work supported by the National Science Foundation under Cooperative Agreement HRD-0227995 and grant number CNS-0540615. Any opinions, findings, and conclusions or recommendations expressed in this material are those of the author and do not necessarily reflect the views of the National Science Foundation.

PART 4

Institutionalization of Universal Design in Higher Education

In Part Four, the authors share strategies for institutionalizing universal design in all campus policies and procedures. The result is an institution with instruction, services, physical spaces, and technology that is welcoming, accessible, and usable for everyone.

Universal Design in Higher Education

Instruction	Services	Information Technology	Physical Spaces
Class climate	Planning, policies, and evaluation	Procurement/ development policies	Planning, policies, and evaluation
Interaction	Physical environments/ products	Physical environments/ products	Appearance
Physical environments/ products	Staff	Information	Entrances/ routes of travel
Delivery methods	Information resources/ technology	Input/control	Fixtures/ furniture
Information resources/ technology	Events	Output	Information resources/ technology
Feedback		Manipulations	Safety
Assessment		Safety	Accommodation
Accommodation		Compatibility with assistive technology	

Source: S. Burgstahler (2007). Applications of Universal Design in Education. Seattle: University of Washington. http://www.washington.edu/doit/Brochures/Academics/app_ud_edu.html

21

Indicators of
Institutional Change

Sheryl E. Burgstahler
Rebecca C. Cory

The authors of this chapter explore motivations for change to a universal design (UD) model, discuss the process of systemic change, and share indicators of an inclusive campus that were developed by representatives from campuses nationwide. These indicators and processes can be tailored to any campus to guide the implementation of UD.

Institutions of higher education face challenges addressing the needs of increasingly diverse student bodies with respect to gender, ethnicity, race, disability, socioeconomic status, and other characteristics. The experiences of many campuses suggest that change toward better serving these students occurs gradually (Pittendrigh, 2007; Williams, 2006). Although it may cause discomfort and conflict, change is central to the culture of higher education (Andresen, 1991) as institutions respond to new legislative mandates, demographic shifts, alternative technologies, funding realities, and new teaching and learning theories and practices (Englert & Tarrant, 1995).

Campus administrators who highly value equity and inclusion may accept universal design (UD)—"the design of products and environments to be usable by all people, to the greatest extent possible, without the need for adaptation or specialized design" (Mace, 2007)—as one approach for addressing diversity issues. Campuswide strategic plans can build on an administrative commitment to diversity and be implemented using principles of UD to inform all decisions made by faculty and staff as they develop and revise courses and programs. Alternately, if high-level institutional support for UD has not yet been garnered, interested parties can implement UD in their own areas of responsibility (e.g., postsecondary courses, physical spaces, services, technology, information resources), thus providing a model of UD for other campus units and continuing to seek high-level buy-in. Or change can be simultaneously instituted through both high-level commitments and grassroots work.

Characteristics of change can be viewed from many perspectives. One approach is to organize aspects of a specific change according to (1) the reasons for change, (2) the content of change, and (3) the process of change (Levy & Merry, 1986). The authors of this chapter use this organizational model to frame their discussion of change to a UD model in institutions of higher education.

THE REASONS FOR CHANGE TO A UNIVERSAL DESIGN MODEL

Why might a college or university adopt UD as a standard practice? A campus might embrace UD for reasons that are external to the institution (e.g., legislative mandates, institutional peer pressure), or the primary motivations for change may be internal to the institution (e.g., institutional values that embrace diversity, changing student demographics, cost). Campuses are likely to have both external and internal motivations for adopting UD.

Higher education policies and practices with respect to students with disabilities have evolved on a continuum, from exclusion to increased levels of access. In past years, institutions of higher education excluded many people with disabilities through discriminatory enrollment policies and the inaccessible design of courses, services, and physical spaces (Welsh, 2002). Some institutions considered inclusion of a student with a disability as an "act of charity" (Hebel, 2001, p. A23) Over time, institutions adopted an accommodation model, in which adjustments are made for specific individuals (e.g., moving a course to an accessible location for a wheelchair user, providing printed materials in an alternate format for a student with a visual impairment). The movement toward providing accommodations on a routine basis was in part due to external pressures from several stakeholder groups. These included college-bound veterans returning from World War II with injuries, students with disabilities who were mainstreamed in precollege environments, and parents who wanted more academic and career options for their children. These efforts eventually led to civil rights mandates for people with disabilities (Welsh, 2002).

Institutional acceptance of responsibility for providing accommodations to qualified students with disabilities increased postsecondary options for these students. However, there are several negative aspects of the accommodation-focused approach. The following paragraphs summarize factors—demographics, marginalization, equity, deficits and strengths, mandates and values, cost—that may justify an institution's change from an accommodation model in addressing the needs of students with disabilities to a UD model to ensure a welcoming, accessible, and inclusive educational experience for everyone.

Demographics

A focus on "typical students" often drives the design of campus environments and offerings. Typical students have been described as "white undergraduates from middle class or upper-middle class homes, ages 18 to 22, attending 4-year institutions full time, living on campus, not working, and having few if any family responsibilities" (Pascarella, 2006). These "typical" students might also be verbally precocious, able to afford laptop computers and MP3 players, healthy, and athletic. Courses, physical spaces, technological environments, and student programs and services are often designed to address the needs of students with a narrow range of characteristics presumed to be typical; adjustments are then made for others as they encounter access barriers. For some populations, such as gay, lesbian, bisexual, and transgender students; women; students from a racial or ethnic minority group; and students who have disabilities, a program or office is made available for services and support.

In contrast to the notion of a typical student, the literature on "millennial" students describes the current student population as the most diverse group of students ever to come through colleges and universities (DeBard, 2004; *The Chronicle of Higher Education Almanac,* 2007; Henderson, 2001; National Center for Education Statistics, 2005). In this population, the *majority* of students are part of a *minority* group. To meet their needs, institutions must find ways to be responsive and flexible, creating programs for a diverse audience rather than for a narrow category of "normals." UD considers a broad range of human characteristics during the planning stages of design, including youth and age, gender, height, degree of athleticism and mobility, native language, use of wheelchairs or walkers, and sightedness and lack of it. Considering the wide range of characteristics of a student body leads to the development of courses, technology, services, and buildings that are welcoming, accessible, and usable for everyone.

Marginalization

Accommodations serve to marginalize students because those with disabilities are asked to access campus offerings in different ways from those who do not have disabilities (Burgstahler & Cory, in press). For example, when the main entrance to a building is not wheelchair accessible due to the presence of stairs, it is socially isolating for the student who must separate from a group of friends who are using the stairs to use a ramp to enter the building (Mutua, 1997). In contrast, if UD was applied, the main entrance would be usable by all students and thus would support an integrated experience.

Equity

Adopting a UD model requires a change in thinking about where the problem lies when a product or environment is not accessible. The accommodation approach recognizes the mismatch between a person with a disability and the academic, service, physical, or technological environment. It then makes adjustments for that individual. The individual's inability to meet the requirements of the product or environment is seen as the "problem," and making an accommodation for this individual is viewed as the "solution." Since accommodations are afterthoughts, the experience of the person receiving an accommodation is not always equivalent to that of other individuals. For example, students who need extra time to take an exam often end up doing so in a side office or testing center instead of in the regular classroom. In this case they, unlike their nondisabled peers, may not have full access to the professor during the exam to ask questions about or request interpretations of test items. UD might lead to a situation in which professors give shorter, more frequent exams so that all students have the time they need to complete an exam.

Deficits and Strengths

The accommodation model tends to focus on deficits: A person with a disability is singled out for what he cannot do, and an accommodation is put in place to make up for his deficit. This deficit focus may underestimate the capacity of a person with a disability and create dependency on accommodations. For example, when a professor does not make handouts available in an accessible electronic format, a student who is blind may need to rely heavily on the disability services office to convert these materials into an accessible format. In contrast, a professor of a universally designed course might provide handouts in a text-based format on a class Web site so that the content is available to all students, including the student who is blind. In summary, UD reduces the deficits in the product or environment that make it unwelcoming, inaccessible, or unusable to some individuals.

Mandates and Values

To a great extent, campus responses to students, staff, faculty, and visitors with disabilities focus on legal obligations under Section 504 of the Rehabilitation Act of 1973 and the Americans with Disabilities Act of 1990 (ADA). Both were conceived as civil rights laws that would lead to a more inclusive world and open doors to education, employment, and community involvement for individuals with disabilities. When he signed the ADA (The U.S. Equal Employment Opportunity Commission, 2002), President George H. W. Bush said

> With today's signing of the landmark Americans with Disabilities Act, every man, woman, and child with a disability can now pass through once-closed doors into a bright new era of equality, independence, and freedom.

However, meeting minimum requirements under the ADA may still result in products, services, and environments that are fundamentally unusable by and not fully inclusive of some students. For example, a tiered classroom might have one location where a student in a wheelchair may sit, but when small group discussions take place, this student might not be able to move to a new tier to join a group. UD of the space would allow for this option. UD looks beyond compliance with legal mandates to create a campus that is fully inclusive.

Cost

Designing products and environments that are not fully accessible may be easier and less expensive initially but result in greater expense and effort for the institution further down the road. For example, designing the institution's online registration system to be fully accessible to individuals using assistive technology may ultimately cost less than providing personal assistance to every student for whom the online system is inaccessible.

THE CONTENT OF CHANGE IN A UNIVERSAL DESIGN MODEL

What would a universally designed campus look like? A team of disability service professionals from twenty states have been exploring answers to that question. These leaders, representing institutions of higher education nationwide, are members of the AccessCollege team funded by the Office of Postsecondary Education of the U.S. Department of Education (DO-IT, 2007). AccessCollege is an initiative of the Disabilities, Opportunities, Internetworking, and Technology (DO-IT) Center at the University of Washington. Through literature reviews, discussions, and an iterative process, the AccessCollege team developed a list of Campus Accessibility Indicators that describe the characteristics of an institution that is fully inclusive of individuals with disabilities (DO-IT, 2007).

The Campus Accessibility Indicators provide a starting point for campuswide conversations and can help administrators focus on key issues to address in creating an inclusive campus. These indicators promote systemic change for the inclusion of people with disabilities and move toward ensuring that all people fully experience campus opportunities. Although this list focuses on access for individuals with disabilities, discussions are under way to consider how it might be modified to better address issues for individuals from other underserved populations. The following Campus Accessibility Indicators (DO-IT, 2007, p. 2) continue to evolve based on feedback from researchers and practitioners, who are encouraged to adapt the current indicators to their own campuses and send DO-IT their suggestions for improving the list.

University conversations
1. The university-level mission statement is inclusive of people with disabilities.
2. Disability is included in discussions of diversity and special populations on campus.

Administrative empowerment
3. Policies, procedures, and practices are regularly reviewed for barrier removal and inclusivity.
4. Administrators, staff, faculty, and student leaders are trained, encouraged, and empowered to take action around disability and universal design issues.
5. People with disabilities are visible (even if their disabilities are not) on campus and include those in positions of power or authority.

Infusion of universal design in all campus offerings
6. Budgeting reflects the reality of the cost of universal design and of accommodating current and prospective employees, students, and visitors with disabilities.
7. Measures of student success are the same for all student populations; institutional research includes this data.
8. Campus marketing, publications, and public relations are accessible and include disability representation.
9. Campus Web sites, including Web-based courses, meet established accessibility and usability standards.
10. Relevant disability issues are addressed in curricula.
11. All campus facilities are physically accessible and universally designed.

Each Campus Accessibility Indicator can be rated on a continuum. For example, disability may already be a component of the curricula in some departments, such as rehabilitation counseling, law, education, and sociology. That is a start. However, a campus that is committed to UD would integrate diversity issues into curricula across campus. Just as themes from focused disciplines like women's studies and African American studies now show up in courses on media, design, history, and science, disability can fit into the curriculum of almost any academic discipline. For example, a professor of a course on

- software development could cover the application of UD to information technology;
- civil rights could cover the history of the disability rights movement;
- architecture could include not only ADA-compliant design but also the more inclusive UD practices;
- medical ethics could include a discussion of the quality of life of individuals with disabilities.

THE PROCESS OF CHANGE TO A UNIVERSAL DESIGN MODEL

How might an institution of higher education apply UD? Implementing UD throughout an institution may appear to be an overwhelming task. However, authors of his book have put forth strategies, processes, and resources that can help administrators implement UD in campus classrooms, student services, physical spaces, and technological environments. To institutionalize the UD process, administrators could work with divisions of the institution to tailor processes presented in earlier chapters of this book to their unique needs. High-level commitment and guidance for implementing UD aided by the resources and the responsiveness of campus units could result in significant institutional change. Without high-level buy-in, promoters of UD in higher education could join forces through voluntary working groups to initiate a grassroots effort to implement UD.

CONCLUSION

UD in higher education involves a paradigm shift from the accommodation model to an inclusion model. Instead of focusing on creating systems for typical students and modifying those systems for other students, UD promotes the design of systems for students with a broad range of characteristics. This requires a change in thinking: from viewing disability as a problem of the individual to seeing inclusion as the responsibility of the institution.

The authors of the remaining chapters in this section share specific strategies for institutionalizing UD on postsecondary campuses. In chapter 22, Cathy Jenner shares how her campus has systemically implemented UD. In chapter 23, Donald Finn, Elizabeth Evans Getzel, Susan Asselin, and Virginia Reilly discuss implementations of UD on their campuses. In the final chapter, Sheryl Burgstahler highlights promoters and inhibitors of UD in higher education.

REFERENCES

Americans with Disabilities Act of 1990, 42 U.S.C.A. § 12101 *et seq.*

Andresen, L. (1991). Teaching university teachers to teach—while they teach. *A Quarterly Experience, 26*, 14–17.

Burgstahler, S., & Cory, R. C. (in press). Moving in from the margins: From accommodations to universal design. In Gabel, S. L., & Danforth, S. *Disability and the politics of education: An international reader.* New York: Peter Lang.

The Chronicle of Higher Education almanac. (2007). Washington, DC: *The Chronicle of Higher Education, 54*(1), 3–96.

DeBard, R. (2004). Millennials coming to college. *New Directions for Student Services, 106* (Summer 2004), 33–45.

Disabilities, Opportunities, Internetworking, and Technology (DO-IT). (2007). *AccessCollege: Systemic change for postsecondary institutions.* Seattle: University of Washington. Retrieved November 1, 2007, from http://www.washington.edu/doit/Brochures/Academics/access_college.html

Englert, C. S., & Tarrant, K. L. (1995). Creating collaborative cultures for educational change. *Remedial and Special Education, 16*, 325–336.

Hebel, S. (2001). How a landmark anti-bias law changed life for disabled students. *The Chronicle of Higher Education, 47*(20), A23–A25.

Henderson, C. (2001). *College freshmen with disabilities: A biennial statistical profile.* Washington, DC: Heath Resource Center.

Levy, A., & Merry, U. (1986). *Organizational transformation: Approaches, strategies, theories.* New York: Praeger.

Mace, R. (2007). *About universal design (UD).* Raleigh: North Carolina State University, Center for Universal Design. Retrieved November 1, 2007, from http://www.design.ncsu.edu/cud/about_ud/about_ud.htm

Mutua, K. (1997, March). *The semiotics of accessibility and the cultural construction of disability.* Paper presented at the American Educational Research Association annual meeting, Chicago, IL.

National Center for Education Statistics. (2005). *Students with disabilities in postsecondary education.* Washington, DC: U.S. Department of Education.

Pascarella, E. T. (2006). How college affects students: Ten directions for future research. *Journal of College Student Development, 47*(5), 508–520.

Pittendrigh, A. (2007). Reinventing the core: Community, dialogue, and change. *The Journal of General Education, 56*(1), 34–56.

Section 504 of the Rehabilitation Act of 1973. 29 U.S.C. § 794.

The U.S. Equal Employment Opportunity Commission. (2002). *Remarks of President George Bush at the signing of the Americans with Disabilities Act.* Retrieved August 23, 2007, from http://www.eeoc.gov/ada/bushspeech.html

Welsh, P. (2002). A brief history of disability rights legislation in the United States. *Universal Design Education Online.* Retrieved November 15, 2007, from http://www.udeducation.org/resources/readings/welch.asp

Williams, D. A. (2006). Beyond diversity: Implementing a dynamic and evolving diversity change project. *Diverse Issues in Higher Education, 23*(14), 50.

The content of this chapter was developed under a grant from the U.S. Department of Education Office of Postsecondary Education (grant number P333A050064). However, this content does not necessarily represent the policy of the Department of Education, and you should not assume endorsement by the federal government.

22

A Change Process for Creating a Universally Designed Campus

Cathy Jenner

Using the categories outlined in the Project Management Body of Knowledge commonly used in product development in the private sector, the author of this chapter describes the project management process utilized by a two-year technical college to develop a comprehensive, cross-departmental system for increasing the academic success of students with disabilities. Challenges unique to the public social program sector in implementing universal design projects are examined.

UNIVERSAL DESIGN FOR LEARNING PROJECT

In 2002, Renton Technical College (RTC) received a grant from the U.S. Department of Education to increase the success (as measured by course completion rates) of students with disabilities in classrooms affected by the funded project. Degree completion rates for students with disabilities nationwide are considerably lower than those for students without disabilities, according to the U.S. Department of Education (Horn, Berktold, & Bobbitt, 1999). One of the initial project challenges was the comparatively small number of students who disclosed disabilities or sought help from the Special Needs Population Counselor, who provides services to students with disabilities. Although it has been estimated that 6% of all undergraduates nationwide report having a disability (Lewis, Farris, & Greene, 1999), not all of those with disabilities seek assistance from campus disability services. For example, RTC reports that only 1% of the student population disclosed disabilities to the Disability Services Office in 2001, prior to the project start date. This fact contradicted information bubbling up from the classroom instructors during the project's initial discovery period. Instructors almost unanimously reported that they were sure they had students in their classrooms with learning disabilities, attention-deficit/hyperactivity disorder, and other disabilities. Instructors were concerned that students who did not disclose their disabilities or otherwise seek help were unlikely to be getting the help they needed to be successful. Since students are not required to disclose disability-related information, the project sought alternate ways to deliver services to a broad audience of students who might need them. A review of current national innovative practices in teaching revealed that universal design for learning (UDL) might provide the best approach to the RTC project (Abell, Bauder, & Simmons, 2005; Pisha & Stahl, 2005).

PROJECT MANAGEMENT PRINCIPLES

Most projects face similar fundamental conditions, whether they are in the private sector or the public social program environment, which includes postsecondary institutions: There are products or tools to be developed, benchmarks to be set, deadlines to be met, and data to be collected. Factors exist in the social program environment, however, that often make project management less straightforward than in the private sector. Factors that introduce unique challenges include those related to (1) buy-in, (2) government-restricted funding, and (3) limited access to data. In 2002, RTC began a project that incorporated UDL into college classrooms using project management principles (Pisha & Stahl, 2005). The goal of this project was to increase success, as measured by course completion rates, of students with disabilities in classrooms affected by project activities. To do this, several tasks were identified in the project scope: (1) train all faculty on UDL and disability issues, (2) increase access to assistive and multimodal teaching technologies, (3) develop a system to identify students with learning challenges who need more intensive intervention from the student services department, and (4) find ways to provide support to instructors on how to teach these students more effectively.

The Project Management Body of Knowledge (PMBOK), a resource used extensively for project management, describes a project as a "temporary endeavor to create a unique product, service, or result" (Project Management Institute, 2004, p. 5). Project management is accomplished through the processes of initiating, planning, executing, monitoring, controlling, and closing. It is a one-time, multitask job that has a definite starting point once the use of resources, such as people, funds, and equipment, are identified and approved. A project has a definite ending point: when the result is transferred to the "customer" to become part of "business as usual." A project also has a clearly defined scope of work, a budget, and an implementation team. In the private sector, project management is typically used when a product is being developed or a specific change is being implemented, such as the opening of a new store or a change in computer services.

The first step in project management is to create a charter, which is a document written by the project sponsor that describes and authorizes the project at a global level. Once the charter is secured, the next step is to identify a project manager who is responsible for facilitating all aspects of the project. The project manager does not necessarily do the technical work but is responsible for removing business-level roadblocks and championing the project to people and groups outside the project team. The project manager also tracks progress, resolves conflicts among team members, and facilitates meeting financial and performance targets. As appropriate to the business, the project manager uses the tools or knowledge areas described in the PMBOK (Project Management Institute, 2004). These knowledge areas represent work to be done by the project manager and project team. They are *not* sequential steps; areas overlap and interrelate. Knowledge areas, according to the Project Management Institute (2004), include the following:

- *Integration management:* the broad oversight of the project, including developing the project scope and closeout
- *Project scope management:* keeping the project on track
- *Time management:* estimating and scheduling time on a project
- *Cost management:* estimating costs, budgeting, and reconciliation
- *Quality management:* planning, quality assurance, and control
- *Human resource management:* facilitating the selection and use of personnel
- *Communications management:* compiling and synthesizing information, communicating information to project team members
- *Risk management:* identifying and evaluating areas of risk
- *Procurement management:* planning purchases and acquisitions, contracting

Project management principles can be applied to developing new systems as well as concrete products. In *Start as You Mean to Go On: Project Management for Beginners* (Caan, Wright, & Hampton-Matthews, 1997), the authors suggest that projects often fall short of expected outcomes because they fail to incorporate sufficient structure into their initial planning. They go on to describe several approaches to project management that can be used to create a more productive process.

There are some obvious differences between the model described in the PMBOK and how projects may unfold in the public social program sector. Although a charter is often established, even if informally, managers who run projects in the public sector are often line supervisors in charge of coordinating entire departments, divisions, or programs, and they have many pressing responsibilities. They are not dedicated to discrete and temporary projects and are not typically trained in project management knowledge areas such as those cited in the PMBOK. In the PMBOK model, the project manager's primary responsibility is coordinating the project. Staff supervision, training, evaluation, and other managerial responsibilities are often left to other supervisors in a matrix management configuration.

Another challenge found in the public social program environment is the need for cooperation and buy-in of stakeholders. In private sector product development companies, buy-in is a given because personnel are there for the purpose of developing and/or implementing the product. However, in the public sector, projects are often added to current responsibilities and so they are unwelcome changes. This situation often causes resistance on the part of stakeholders and creates an additional challenge for the project manager.

An element of project management seen more frequently in the public than the private sector is funding restricted by outside agencies. In this case, funds from particular government or grant sources can only be used in specific ways or to support specific outcomes during specific time periods. Such restrictions can create challenges in planning, budgeting, and procuring.

Access to data is also considered in the social program sector in a way that is different from the private sector. For example, due to confidentiality, student data are frequently collected only for certain reporting purposes and are not always available to project teams. Few staff resources may be devoted to obtaining and analyzing data for specific projects. Yet without quantitative data, a project can go astray very quickly and ultimately fail to meet the reporting requirements of a funding source. A project manager in the public social program environment must carefully consider and incorporate these unique challenges in the project's risk assessment, or the project is likely to fail.

PROJECT MANAGEMENT PRINCIPLES IN ACTION

RTC project staff had little exposure to the concepts of UDL prior to receipt of the grant, but UDL offered a promising approach for helping undisclosed or undiagnosed students with disabilities by offering universally designed accessible learning strategies and environments to *all* students. What follows is a description of how RTC used the project management principles described in the PMBOK to implement a campus-wide change in teaching and service delivery.

Create a Charter

The charter was created by the dean of Basic Studies and a program administrator from the Washington State Board of Community and Technical Colleges, through the board's approval of the initial grant proposal. Buy-in from this group provided authorization to develop a comprehensive, cross-departmental system for increasing the academic success of students with disabilities.

Designate a Project Manager

The charter and external funding made it possible to hire a dedicated project manager. The fact that the new manager was allowed to focus solely on the project contributed to its success. However, having a dedicated project manager is less critical to a project's success than having a project manager who understands the knowledge areas described in the PMBOK and postsecondary campus dynamics and has sufficient time for the analytical and planning elements.

Integration Management

The project goal was to help students with disabilities to be more academically successful, even though the college did not have an accurate count of the numbers of students with disabilities. Because most classes do not have test or language prerequisites, the school is attractive to students who are not English-proficient or who have had difficulties in the precollege school system or other learning environments. The project team believed that because of its unique environment, RTC was likely to attract students with undisclosed or undiagnosed disabilities who may also have had problems in traditional learning environments. This belief developed through an informal discussion process with administrators and instructors and was confirmed by focus groups held at departmental meetings. The focus groups with instructors and deans told a compelling story: Instructors as well as students were struggling to address the wide variety of students' learning capabilities and skills. Instructors described being stretched too thin in their efforts to meet the diverse learning needs in their classrooms. Further interviews with college administrators, including the president, the vice president of instruction, and the vice president of student services, echoed these concerns but also revealed limitations in funding and staff resources, in addition to the institution's goal to increase student retention.

Out of the discovery process grew the project scope, a detailed description of the work to be done to complete the project. Several tasks were identified in the project scope: (1) training all faculty on UDL and disability issues, (2) increasing access to assistive and multimodal teaching technologies, and (3) developing a system to identify students with learning challenges who need more intensive assistance from the student services department, along with a way to support their instructors to teach them more effectively.

Risk Management

Anticipating and mitigating risks was particularly critical in creating the project design. One of the biggest risks in undertaking a campuswide change process was that instructors, administrators, and counselors might not cooperate. As mentioned earlier, the risk factor of buy-in in the public social program environment must be carefully addressed. Without a clear strategy to promote and check for collaboration and buy-in, even the most promising solutions cannot be implemented.

The initial discovery process made it abundantly clear that faculty and staff were already overtaxed and frustrated with lack of time, money, and other resources. Therefore, the project scope had to consider carefully what would best promote uptake of a new paradigm for helping students. The project began with a trial period. A small group of selected instructors and counselors piloted an attempt to help students with disclosed, undisclosed, and undiagnosed disabilities by increasing their disability awareness and using UDL principles in their classrooms. The plan was to share successful practices with all full-time instructors and staff on campus in an endeavor to make a campuswide change. A further analysis of risk revealed that this pilot could take several months, perhaps even years, to become effective enough to spread to multiple classrooms. During these months, it would be critical to ensure that the instructors and staff outside the pilot program had enough knowledge of the project to be receptive to implementing some new practices when the time came. It was also critical that administrators continue to support and promote the project as it unfolded. Therefore, one project task was to deliver ongoing trainings, meetings, and presentations to faculty and key staff and administrators in order to understand concerns and promote buy-in and uptake of the project.

Another risk was the potential for insufficient technical support for changes that would need to occur in the classroom and in student laboratories as new assistive and multimodal teaching technologies were brought on board. Addressing this risk demanded a strong collaboration with the information services department.

An additional risk was related to the project team's limited access to data. The community and technical college system collects data, most of which are specific to state and federal reporting requirements. At RTC, as at many colleges, limited staff resources are available to collect data outside of these reports. The project team had to come up with a plan for collecting and analyzing data on a continual basis in order to make informed changes in project services as needed. Collaboration with the research and development department was critical for collecting and comparing quantitative data, such as the completion rates of students with and without disabilities, as well as qualitative data on student and instructor responses to the changes created by the project.

Human Resource Management

Selection of people with the right skill set for the pilot team was critical to the project's success. It was determined that the initial group of instructors should be leaders in their departments: people who had demonstrated the ability to be innovative and persuasive with their peers. The project team selected these initial instructors with the help of the department deans, since they brought the potential to promote buy-in at the dean level. Also included in the pilot team were two counselors, the special needs populations counselor, the learning disabilities counselor, and the vice president of student services. In addition, information services support was needed to promote the use of technology for assisting students in the classroom and other places on campus. The project team collaborated with the director of information services to hire a technician to work intensively on the project and contribute long-term technical oversight. The project team also collaborated with the research and development department to collect and analyze data.

Project Scope Management

Many project tasks demanded completion of subtasks that were dependent on each other. For example, in order to create a more comprehensive system for identifying and helping students with learning challenges, it was necessary to increase access to assistive technology (AT). Therefore, one of the first subtasks was the research, procurement, and installation of AT. That, however, meant collaborating with the information services department in order to hire a computer technician. Dependencies like these were identified and inserted into the project plan.

Task 1: Training All Faculty on Universal Design of Learning and Disability Issues

The project manager worked with the director of Instructional Improvement to have experts in the area of UDL and disabilities offer workshops to faculty. In addition, shorter trainings were offered at departmental and other meetings. The online instructional newsletter of the Instructional Improvement Office was used to broadcast information on UDL and disability awareness. By 2005, three years after the project's start, 66 of 75 full-time instructors had attended workshops on targeted subjects.

Task 2: Increasing Access to Assistive and Multimodal Teaching Technologies

The project team wanted to create *universal* access to AT, not just access for students with disabilities. This approach addresses the concern that many students with disabilities do not disclose their disabilities and/or their disabilities are not diagnosed.

The team hired an AT consultant who identified several key pieces of AT: a screen reader, a screen magnifier, a speech-to-text program, a graphic organizer program, adjustable tables, and ergonomic keyboards. These products were installed in pilot classrooms, student labs, and libraries across campus. Workshops and training CDs were offered to help students learn about AT. Multimodal teaching tools, such as projectors, devices to capture and digitize board notes, and closed-caption televisions, were purchased for pilot classrooms. Each pilot instructor committed to increase multimodal teaching through technology or other strategies. After a few months of using these strategies, 134 students in the pilot classrooms were surveyed; 95% of them reported that the changes in their classrooms were positive.

Task 3: Development of a System to Identify Students with Learning Problems That Require More Assistance

It was initially expected that the project would replicate and expand an assessment process currently in place in some of the Basic Studies classrooms. In this assessment system, known as the Learning Disabilities Quality Initiative from the Washington State Board of Community and Technical Colleges, the instructor performs thorough individualized interviews and develops strategies for students. However, this approach quickly dissolved as it became clear that the technical classroom did not afford time for the in-depth individualized attention that is common in a Basic Studies classroom. An efficient group process was needed. This led to the development of a new system, which the pilot team called the Learning Assessment System (LAS).

The LAS included a learning styles inventory and a series of questions to help students discover their learning challenges. The questions were based on pilot instructors' experience with the issues that typically cause students to struggle, such as problems with attendance or child care. After students responded to these questions, suggestions for remediation were given based on the students' learning styles and learning challenges. Although it began as a paper-and-pencil tool, the LAS developed into a Web-based tool that gave automated individualized reports to students and a group report to instructors. "Scope creep" occurred with the LAS Web tool subtask. This common problem occurs when the original intent of a project "creeps" or broadens without intention. The Web tool began to incorporate many other features beyond the initial plan, including an e-mail messaging system and tracking of strategies. Eventually, the LAS Web tool was scaled back to its original scope to make it more manageable.

Quality Management

Because the project was cross-departmental, it was important that the project team be able to manage it at both broad and detailed levels. Therefore, three committees were convened: the project team, consisting of the dean of Basic Studies, the project manager who reported to the director of Instructional Improvement, and an administrative assistant to the project manager; the Advisory Committee, consisting of key RTC administrators and disability experts from the community; and the Campus Implementation Team, with representation from most departments on campus, including registration, library, student success, instruction, student services, information services, and financial aid. The purpose of the Campus Implementation Team was to help with planning and service design at a campuswide level. These committees met regularly to give feedback and ensure quality control of the project. To guard against the ever-present risk of lack of buy-in, these committees had a double purpose: to help with project oversight and to promote buy-in across departments. For example, the Advisory Committee helped promote buy-in by having administrators work with disability experts to gain more understanding of the issues and potential solutions. The Campus Implementation Team promoted buy-in by including the entire campus in project design and decisions.

Ongoing data analysis was built into the quality management plan. The project team considered not only course completion rates but also the results of student and instructor surveys and interviews. Analysis of a variety of data helped guide the project. One of the most useful applications of data involved student learning strengths and barriers collected from the LAS. Specifically, the instructors' group reports showed them, at a glance, how many visual, auditory, and kinesthetic learners were in their classes so they could better customize teaching delivery. They could also see what types of barriers each student faced so they could offer individualized help or referral. When the pilot instructors administered LAS surveys in their classrooms, more students began to disclose disabilities or were screened by the learning disabilities specialist for undiagnosed disabilities. The number of students disclosing disabilities went from 1% of the student population at the start of the project in 2001 to 5% in 2005. This substantiated the initial suspicion that there were many more students with learning challenges and disabilities than had disclosed them at registration. Because of its value in identifying and helping students with special needs, the LAS underwent further development and eventually became an automated Web-based tool used widely at RTC.

Time Management

Estimating the time needed to create a change in work behaviors is always a challenge. The project manager created a timeline to document overall goals, tasks, subtasks, major benchmarks, and due dates. As the project went along, the project manager compared progress to the initial timeline, making adjustments as needed. Keeping the project tasks moving along on time was a priority of the project manager. This was done through progress reporting and troubleshooting meetings with workers, where any barriers to success were identified. Plans to resolve problems were developed and sometimes facilitated by the project manager. This was a particularly important element of the project manager's role, since the project spanned many departments that did not interface on a regular basis. For example, one of the critical subtasks was the training of instructors on AT. This subtask spanned nine departments: seven instructional departments and the Instructional Improvement and Information Services departments. The project manager had to work with all department leaders to ensure that this subtask would be accomplished. Researching and procuring AT, installing it, getting the Information Services staff familiar enough to provide training, and then setting up trainings with all the departments took careful planning and time estimation. Completing these subtasks took about a year. The time needed to develop a system for identifying students with learning challenges was very difficult to estimate because the task contained so many unknowns, such as the best assessment tools and formats and the individuals to be involved in each level of assessment. In the first time projection, it was assumed that the process would replicate the assessment process occurring in the Basic Studies department. However, the time allotment was underestimated because the process did not transfer to the technical classrooms and a new system had to be developed.

Cost Management

Most of the effort of cost management involved estimating the cost of assistive and multimodal teaching technologies, consultants for training, and the Web tool. The remaining project costs were staff-related and fairly easy to estimate. The biggest cost management challenge was adhering to specific funding restrictions of federal and state government organizations. For example, many items must be purchased through specified government vendors, have funding caps, and/or must follow certain bid or contractual regulations. In some cases, certain purchases are prohibited entirely, without special permission, such as providing food for training events, something that is easily done in the private sector. All cost projections had to be carefully considered in accordance with state and federal guidelines.

Communications Management

The project manager ensures the continual flow of information between the project team and stakeholders. In this project, the pilot team met regularly to discuss progress, share information, and troubleshoot. In addition, monthly reports were delivered to faculty via the online instructional improvement publication, and presentations regarding the progress of the project were regularly given at meetings of all team members, the Board of Trustees, and the Advisory Committee. Surveys from the faculty and students helped inform the project. In fall 2006, survey results of the faculty at RTC on their knowledge of UDL were compared to those at two other colleges beginning to institute a similar project. Seventy-five percent (75%) of the RTC instructors interviewed said that they were currently using UDL in their classrooms, as compared to 25–28% at the other two colleges.

Procurement Management

Aside from the AT purchases, planning purchases and acquisitions and contracting were straightforward because the college has an established process for this. Purchasing AT was complicated by the fact that it was being loaded onto classroom computers that already had sophisticated software programs. The AT had to work with and not disrupt these programs. For example, one of the classrooms included in the pilot was computer-aided drafting (CAD). Sophisticated CAD programs were already on computers in the student lab, and any AT had to be able to coexist and augment that software. To make sure that no problems would occur in the lab, the AT specialist recreated the classroom environment on a special computer network set up for testing purposes, and then loaded the AT programs one at a time before reconfiguring the classroom computers.

TABLE 22.1   Course Completion Rates in Pilot Classrooms

School Year	Students without Disabilities	Students with Disabilities
2001–02	80.3%	65.2%
2005–06	94.6%	97.7%

TABLE 22.2   Course Completion Rates in Nonpilot Classrooms

School Year	Students without Disabilities	Students with Disabilities
2001–02	80.8%	78.6%
2005–06	93.6%	95.9%

PROJECT RESULTS AND RECOMMENDATIONS

At the end of the 2005–06 school year, the project outcomes were compared to the original charter of increasing the success of students with disabilities by comparing completion rates of students with and without disabilities in pilot and nonpilot classrooms before the project's start in 2002. Of the students *with disabilities* who took classes in pilot classrooms, 97.7% completed courses in 2005–06, up from 65.2% in 2001–02. These figures can be compared to an increase in the completion rate from 80.3% to 94.6% among students *without disabilities* in the same classes (Table 22.1). A comparison of nonpilot classes showed that students with disabilities had increases in completion rates somewhat similar to those of students without disabilities. The completion rate of students *with disabilities* increased from 78.4% in 2001–02 to 95.9% in 2005–06, while that of students *without disabilities* increased from 80.8% to 93.6% in the same time period (Table 22.2). Students with disabilities in pilot classrooms gained more completion-rate percentage points than did students without disabilities in these classes and more than students with or without disabilities in nonpilot classes.

CONCLUSION

Project management principles were successfully applied to a project to improve the quality of education through the use of UDL at RTC. The unique challenges that exist in the college environment, as in many public environments, were taken into consideration and mitigated successfully. The results of this project suggest that project management principles can be successfully applied in postsecondary institutions. Using these principles helps to provide a more replicable, accountable outcome. Since an experimental design was not used in this project, caution should be exercised in interpreting the results. Data analysis suggests that students with disabilities in classrooms where the instructors participated in the pilot experienced more academic success than other students. Success rates of *all* students with disabilities increased more than those of students without disabilities, possibly as a result of faculty training on UDL, disability issues, and teaching topics.

Based on experiences at RTC, project team members suggest that campuses interested in infusing UDI campuswide consider

- getting high-level administrative buy-in;
- conducting a needs assessment of faculty;
- gathering input from students;
- setting up a task force.

It is clear in the RTC case that successful implementation of universal design requires careful planning and ongoing processes.

REFERENCES

Abell, M. M., Bauder, D. K., & Simmons, T. J. (2005). Access to the general curriculum: A curriculum and instruction perspective for educators. *Intervention in School and Clinic, 41*(2). Retrieved October 1, 2007, from http://www.questia.com

Caan, W., Wright, J., & Hampton-Matthews, S. (1997). Start as you mean to go on: Project management for beginners. *Journal of Mental Health, 6*(5), 467–472. Retrieved November 7, 2006, from http://search.ebscohost.com/login.aspx?direct=true&db=a9h&AN=9711242339&site=ehost-live

Horn, L., Berktold, J., & Bobbitt, L. (1999). *Students with disabilities in postsecondary education: A profile of preparation, participation, and outcomes.* Washington, DC: U.S. Department of Education, National Center for Education Statistics.

Lewis, L., Farris, E., & Greene, B. (1999). *An institutional perspective on students with disabilities in postsecondary education.* Washington, DC: U.S. Department of Education, National Center for Education Statistics.

Pisha, B., & Stahl, S. (2005). The promise of new learning environments for students with disabilities. *Intervention in School and Clinic, 41*, 67–75. Retrieved December 18, 2006, from Questia database.

Project Management Institute. (2004). *A guide to project management body of knowledge* (3rd ed.). Newtown Square, PA: Author.

The content of this chapter was developed under grants from the U.S. Department of Education Office of Postsecondary Education (grant numbers P333A020003 and P333A050032-06). The work is funded at 98% by the DOE for the period of October 2002 to September 2008. However, this content does not necessarily represent the policy of the Department of Education, and you should not assume endorsement by the federal government.

23

Implementing Universal Design
Collaborations Across Campus

Donald E. Finn
Elizabeth Evans Getzel
Susan B. Asselin
Virginia Reilly

Beginning in the late 1990s, the Rehabilitation Research and Training Center at Virginia Commonwealth University (VCU) conducted structured faculty and student interviews to help identify areas of need for instructing students with disabilities. The findings led to the implementation of disability awareness workshops for faculty and subsequent identification of need for understanding how to best design and deliver instruction. Developing partnerships with established on-campus entities helped to extend the reach of the information to faculty. Outreach strategies included workshops and the distribution of print- and Web-based materials. The success of the VCU efforts led to a replication project at Virginia Polytechnic Institute and State University (Virginia Tech), a land grant university in the southwestern section of the state. The authors of this chapter outline the approaches to disability awareness and instructional techniques of the VCU and Virginia Tech projects, including their development, unique characteristics, and outcomes.

As greater numbers of students enter college with diverse learning and support needs, and as new technologies and teaching strategies emerge, faculty must continue building and expanding professional development activities. Helping to create instructionally accessible environments is a growing theme of professional development activities on college campuses across the country (Brinckerhoff, McGuire, & Shaw, 2002; Getzel & Finn, 2005; Scott & Gregg, 2000; Wilson & Getzel, 2001). Collaborative relationships between instructional faculty, staff, college administrators, and students with disabilities create an atmosphere where everyone's input is valued. This collaborative atmosphere can help determine the most effective instructional and support strategies and resolve issues that may arise when educating students with disabilities in higher education (Alfano, 1994; Brinckerhoff, McGuire, & Shaw, 2002; Getzel &

Finn, 2005; Scott & Gregg, 2000). A concerted effort is needed to respond effectively and efficiently to emerging trends in educating a diverse college population. Scott and McGuire (2005) emphasize that the impact of diversity on educational strategies in higher education cannot be overstated. They contend that as universities respond to changes in higher education, including more new faculty members and the use of emerging technologies on campus, instructional strategies will broaden to include more inclusive methods and techniques to reach all students.

Since the late 1990s, Virginia Commonwealth University (VCU) has worked on a campuswide approach to determine the professional development needs of faculty, staff, and administrators. Using an extensive evaluation process, VCU obtained input from these groups and from students with disabilities. Structured interviews were conducted to determine the professional development needs on the university's academic and medical campuses. The first evaluation focused on how students with disabilities at VCU are currently educated. Most of the instructional faculty and staff who were interviewed taught courses in which one or more students with disabilities were enrolled. Both faculty and administrators reported limited knowledge of disability-specific legislation and other related issues and were generally uninformed about resources, accommodations, and assistive and educational technology (Wilson & Getzel, 2001). As a result of this study, VCU implemented a training initiative designed to provide the university at large with the knowledge, awareness, and sensitivity necessary to interact with and serve VCU students with disabilities more effectively.

At the end of the 3-year implementation, a second university-wide evaluation was conducted to determine the outcomes of the training and technical assistance provided. Again, the evaluation process included instructional faculty and staff, administrators, and students with disabilities. Faculty and staff members wanted more training and information, especially on the integration of disability-related information, materials, and resources. In particular, universal design strategies emerged as a campuswide interest. Faculty members contributed professional development ideas, including guides on teaching students with disabilities and collaborating with other professionals on campus, more workshops or seminars through the VCU Center for Teaching Excellence (CTE), and ongoing communications via e-mail (e.g., sharing helpful Web sites). The two evaluations provided an invaluable tool for determining how to meet the expressed needs of instructional faculty and staff across the university.

The initial evaluation helped VCU to focus on specific information related to the educational learning needs of students with disabilities, the process for requesting accommodations at VCU, and campus resources. During the first series of professional development activities, universal design was introduced as a framework for instructing and assessing student learning in a more inclusive manner. In response to the evaluations, a team of faculty members from the VCU Rehabilitation Research and Training Center (RRTC) who specialize in the educational needs of college students with disabilities worked with CTE staff members to develop a 2-day workshop that focused on effectively instructing large classes. This workshop included a 2-hour segment that introduced participants to universal design philosophy, and the entire workshop demonstrated universal design techniques that faculty members could incorporate into their classes.

The team at VCU-RRTC formed a partnership with the CTE to disseminate disability-related information and resources through the CTE. The materials focus on universal design techniques, with the goal of ensuring that disability-related information is fully integrated into university-sponsored professional development activities. According to Getzel, Briel, and McManus (2003), several universities have found that incorporating universal design concepts into information that faculty and staff received through their center for teaching excellence (or similar entity) was an effective outreach method. Providing information on universal design enables teaching professionals to learn how adjustments in their instruction, curriculum, and use of technology can benefit all students. The VCU-RRTC team determined that establishing this partnership and evaluating its effectiveness could assist other universities and colleges across the country.

THE PARTNERSHIP WITH THE CENTER FOR TEACHING EXCELLENCE

At VCU, the CTE is the primary source of instructional support and information about the teaching and learning process for faculty. It incorporates a variety of approaches, including holding group workshops, authoring and distributing self-study materials, providing individual consultations, and offering PowerPoint presentations and other materials through its Web site. The VCU-RRTC team worked closely with the CTE director and associate director to identify outreach approaches to reach VCU's faculty members. The two primary approaches identified were face-to-face faculty workshops and the publication of a print newsletter. The team agreed that the best approach for introducing universal design instructional practices to faculty was to discuss the diversity of college learners. Using this approach establishes a context for discussing learner differences along a continuum of diversity that includes individuals with disabilities. This context gives faculty a new framework and sensitivity toward students with disabilities. It also helps to cultivate a receptive atmosphere to universal design concepts and practices as applied to classes (both face-to-face and online) and materials (print- and Web-based) (Getzel & Finn, 2005).

Collaborative Sponsorship of Workshops and Training

The initial outreach method resulting from the CTE-RRTC partnership was the presentation of universal design concepts at the annual winter and summer CTE institutes. These institutes are designed for instructional faculty and last for two to four days. Each institute operates under a theme, such as Effective Instructional Strategies for Large Classes, Integrating Technology into Instruction, and Teaching with Blackboard. The institutes attract faculty from across VCU who want to learn more about effective and innovative instructional methods. The VCU-RRTC team has offered presentations and brief workshops at a number of these institutes.

Print Material Developed through Collaboration

Another effective faculty outreach method is the collaborative effort of developing a newsletter for faculty, *VCU Teaching*. In its original form, *VCU Teaching* was a Web-based newsletter produced by the CTE with a limited readership. The new version is designed for online viewing the print distribution via campus mail semiannually to all faculty, including adjuncts. Currently, *VCU Teaching* reaches thousands of faculty members on both campuses. CTE staff write the bulk of the publication, but a column on universal design principles and effective practices for working with students with disabilities is written by VCU-RRTC faculty. This endeavor has provided excellent exposure of disability-specific information as well as an effective means for presenting topics of student diversity and universal design techniques on a regular basis.

The collaboration resulted in more original outreach publications about universal design and effective work with diverse groups of learners. Publications have included postcards, fact sheets, and newsletters offering concise universal design information and links to additional materials about VCU-RRTC services and upcoming workshops and events.

Online Resources

Because of time constraints and scheduling issues, the project team worked to develop a self-paced, Internet-based module introducing universal design to faculty. The module content and sequence were based on participant feedback and evaluation data from the face-to-face workshops delivered at VCU and other venues. The module begins with an overview of learner diversity, including subtopics of learning styles or preferences, international students, and disabilities. Next, the rationale for universal design is presented, along with examples of universally designed materials in the college setting. Tools for locating and creating universal design-friendly materials are introduced, along with an overview of assistive technology and software packages available for use by students and faculty. Consistent with universal design principles, the module design incorporates universally designed elements, including alt tags for all pictures and diagrams, easy-to-read Arial font, and minimal use of italic, bold, and underlined text. For further study, Internet-based resources are included with the Internet addresses written out to ensure recognition by screen readers. In the pilot stage, professors who completed the module confirmed that it was an effective method for introducing universal design and showing examples of universally designed materials. Additionally, they reported that the module prompted them to reexamine their classroom materials and instructional practices to help address the needs of diverse learners (Finn, 2005). Because of this module's success, future self-paced modules are being considered.

Direct Outreach Methods

In addition to the partnership with the CTE, VCU-RRTC team members conducted universal design outreach efforts across the VCU campuses. They tailored workshops and information sessions about universal design and methods for working effectively with diverse students for groups requesting subject-specific presentations and workshops. Those requesting presentations or workshops included faculty and administrators from the schools of education and social work and supervisors of graduate teaching assistants from schools across the academic campus. Universal design workshops were also developed for student groups, including medical residents who supervise first-year medical students, art education and special education majors, master's of social work students, and undergraduate honors-level students from various disciplines.

As the benefits of the partnership with the CTE emerged through evaluation results and other feedback, the VCU-RRTC team sought to determine the effectiveness of this type of partnership in another setting. The team decided to seek another university to collaborate with, offering resources and support to facilitate their replication effort. Because of previous collaborative projects and other associations with the director of Americans with Disabilities Act (ADA) services at Virginia Tech, team members approached the ADA director and her associates about establishing a replication site. Virginia Tech was chosen because its geographic and student population differences would help to determine the effectiveness of the VCU model in a different setting. Both universities are comparable in size, each serving more than 26,000 students, 500–600 of whom have disclosed their disabilities to the university. These are primarily individuals with learning disabilities, attention-deficit/hyperactivity disorder (ADHD), psychiatric disabilities, medical disabilities, and combinations thereof. However, VCU is an urban university in the heart of the city of Richmond, covering two campuses, whereas Virginia Tech is located in the rural southwestern part of the state and has a more homogeneous student population than VCU. After initial discussions, the ADA director formed a team to discuss the VCU model and determine the professional development needs at Virginia Tech.

PROJECT REPLICATION EFFORTS AT VIRGINIA TECH

University-wide Collaboration

The staff in the offices that provide services to students with disabilities and support faculty at Virginia Tech have a long-standing relationship. Universal design philosophy was commonly discussed and embraced by University ADA Services and the ADA Executive Advisory Committee; however, these groups have struggled to find ways to introduce this philosophy to the academic side of campus. The VCU initiative offered a systematic approach to facilitate campuswide understanding and acceptance of universal design principles. The director of University ADA Services at Virginia Tech and the VCU-RRTC faculty began talking about how the work at VCU could be continued at Virginia Tech (Finn, Reilly, & Asselin, 2005). These talks led to the formation of the Universal Design Faculty Initiative at Virginia Tech to assist faculty to teach all learners more effectively, especially those with disabilities.

Universal Design Planning Committee

The first and most important step was forming a committee of key leaders who would support and communicate the project's goals to the teaching faculty. The Universal Design Planning Committee consists of the director of University ADA Services, director of the Center for Excellence in Undergraduate Teaching (CEUT), the assistant provost and director of the Center for Academic Enrichment and Excellence, the director of Services for Students with Disabilities (SSD), and a teaching faculty member from the School of Education. Each of these members brings special expertise and the ability to publicize, grow, and manage a sustained effort.

The Universal Design Planning Committee informally polled a sample of teaching faculty to determine the most effective method for receiving information about teaching techniques; the overwhelming preference was for face-to-face professional development opportunities. This venue offers opportunities for interaction with a presenter and with peers to share experiences and to secure practical solutions to take back to the classroom. The planning committee worked with the VCU-RRTC team to plan a strategy based on the survey results to capture the interest of a diverse faculty population. A model that included elements of the approach used at VCU was developed for Virginia Tech; it included a plan for multiple mailings and events to reach faculty several times throughout the next year. The plan was to begin with "awareness" information about the basics of universal design in the fall, followed by more in-depth information in the spring to equip faculty with tools and ideas to adapt their own curricula.

Workshops

The first strategy was to invite faculty, particularly new members, to a Universal Design Workshop facilitated by a VCU-RRTC faculty member. Recruitment began at the fall Graduate Teaching Assistant Training and New Faculty Orientation, with members of the planning committee promoting the upcoming 2-hour Introduction to Universal Design workshop. The next step was campuswide outreach using an article about universal design written for the CEUT newsletter. Faculty members rely on this newspaper-style publication for announcements about workshops, study group opportunities, and pedagogical articles. The introductory workshop was marketed as providing approaches and information that would assist diverse learners, not only those with disabilities, Shortly after the CEUT newsletter was distributed, an adaptation of a postcard designed and used by the VCU project the previous fall was mailed to faculty members at Virginia Tech. The caption on the front of the postcard asked, "Are They Getting It?" and showed scenes of students in various learning settings. On the back, some practical universal design techniques were offered, along with an announcement about the upcoming workshop. In addition to these announcements, the workshop was also featured on the university Web site.

The multiple outreach methods were successful, as evidenced by the diversity of departments and schools represented at the 2-hour workshop presented in late September. Don Finn, a faculty member and replication project liaison from the VCU-RRTC, facilitated the workshop, called An Introduction to Universal Design: Strategies for Reaching ALL Students. Participants included representatives from veterinary medicine, education, engineering, and other administrative and academic departments. In addition to an overview of universal design, this presentation introduced various types of assistive technologies and software. Inspiration software was demonstrated as a tool for designing materials for effective instruction, including presentations and handouts. Several copies of Inspiration were given as prizes to encourage faculty to explore ways to integrate universal design–friendly materials and techniques into their instruction. Workshop attendees received practical information, and many were anxious to learn more.

Following the fall workshop, the Planning Committee designed a newspaper-style publication about the Universal Design Faculty Initiative. The CEUT director contributed the lead article about the philosophy, tenets, and benefits of universal design. Additional articles described the missions of and services offered by the partnering offices involved in the Virginia Tech Universal Design Faculty Initiative. A faculty perspective on universal design revealed teaching practices that exemplify universal design strategies, such as including accommodation statements for students with disabilities in syllabi, offering alternative assignments, and using a variety of methods and materials to supplement lectures.

The second workshop built on the materials and concepts introduced in the first workshop. It was taught by Dr. Sally Scott, codirector of the Universal Design for Instruction Project at the University of Connecticut, and provided hands-on group activities that allowed attendees to apply techniques for designing instructional materials and syllabi for their curriculum.

Faculty Study Group

At the end of the workshop, the planning committee announced the formation of a universal design faculty study group. Members of the group would meet at the CEUT, could apply for study group stipends, and would support each other in learning more about universal design in reevaluating and redesigning their instructional materials. The invitation resulted in a diverse group that included faculty from the colleges of Human Sciences and Education, Science, and Architecture and Urban Studies and representatives from the SSD. The study group was instrumental in helping the planning committee identify faculty needs for a final workshop.

Faculty-Designed Workshop

The faculty group explored student assessments and determined that a major challenge faculty faced was that the design and delivery of tests often inadvertently create barriers for students, particularly those with disabilities. The group reviewed examples of poorly designed tests from a collection on file at SSD. Faculty had sent these tests to SSD for administration to students served by the office. An examination of the tests provided a starting point for the inquiry. Could faculty apply universal design concepts to create more accessible instruments? The result was a collaborative effort between the study group and the Universal Design Planning Committee to develop a two-part workshop called All Tests Are Not Created Equal. Workshop recruitment was done through a modified version of a newsletter from the VCU project, *The Professor's Assistant,* which was mailed to faculty members in the early spring. Its lead article outlined research-based guiding principles of universal design (McGuire, Scott, & Shaw, 2003; Scott, McGuire, & Foley, 2003) and an overview of the benefits of integrating universal design concepts into the college curriculum (Finn & Thoma, 2006).

The All Tests Are Not Created Equal workshop was delivered by a VCU-RRTC faculty member, with the assistance of the study group members. The second part of the workshop included a breakout activity in which study group members worked with small teams of participants to examine test formats and recommend changes through implementing universal design principles covered in the presentation. Changes made to the tests included using consistent font size and style (e.g., Times or Arial were suggested), limiting the use of special text formatting (e.g., bold, italics, or underlining to highlight important words or concepts), revising wordy or vague questions, grouping questions by type (e.g., true/false, multiple-choice, short-answer), ensuring consistency of layout (e.g., alignment of choices for multiple-choice questions, consistent placement of blanks or locations for inserting answers), and determining which illustrations or diagrams would be useful and which could be eliminated.

Several faculty participants agreed to revise their tests by applying universal design principles with assistance from the study group. Following the workshop, study group members conducted research to determine the impact of revised assessments; this research was supported by a grant from the university Office of Multicultural Affairs (Asselin & Reilly, 2006). Initial data on test format changes were collected from students with and without disabilities. The data revealed that the changes were recognized by students, made the items clearer and easier to read, and enhanced student performance. The faculty participants reported that the changes were relatively easy to implement and they were pleased to offer more accessible assessment instruments.

OUTCOMES OF THE REPLICATION PROJECT AT VIRGINIA TECH

Faculty Awareness

Over the course of the replication project, nearly 200 faculty, administrators, and teaching assistants participated in the series of universal design workshops offered at Virginia Tech. Of the faculty members attending the initial workshop, 19 completed an informal follow-up survey regarding specific teaching practices that they employed (Finn, Reilly, & Asselin, 2005). The respondents were tenure-track faculty with 11 or more years of teaching experience, primarily with undergraduates. The group reported that of their overall enrollment, 5% or less were students with disabilities, with one-third reporting having less than 1%. Certain trends in teaching practices could be drawn from the responses. In general, these faculty participants provided a positive learning environment by inviting students to spend time with them to discuss accommodations and verify course expectations. They willingly offered lecture notes or outlines in advance of classes, and more than half reported checking their classrooms or labs for accessibility in size, space, and physical effort. Half the participants implemented other aspects of universal design by supplementing their lectures with multiple learning experiences and helping students make the connection to real-life situations.

Faculty Initiatives

An outcome that was particularly pleasing to the Universal Design Planning Committee was the level of faculty ownership and contributions to the initiative. The members of the initial CEUT-sponsored study group met to enhance their own awareness of universal design and to integrate universal design principles into their instruction. The study group then served alongside the Universal Design Planning Committee to contribute to the design and delivery of faculty workshops. A core group of these faculty members remained together for two years, making strides to implement, evaluate, and disseminate the results of their efforts. One of the group's first activities included a visit to the Assistive Technology Lab at Virginia Tech to see a demonstration of available software and hardware to increase accessibility of instruction. Several study group members submitted internal and external grant proposals to further their universal design research interests, with some presenting their findings at national, regional, and university-sponsored conferences. Some faculty members are analyzing data to compare student performance on tests, before and after universal design revisions are applied, to determine if the changes have an impact on student learning.

Next Steps

Like the VCU-RRTC project, the Universal Design Planning Committee is exploring more ways to reach the faculty at Virginia Tech, including offering print and electronic documents, arranging for additional face-to-face trainings, and creating online informational modules. Additionally, the group is seeking ways to build on current faculty training offered through the Faculty Development Institute on various aspects of instruction, such as Web accessibility, student assessment, and new software programs. Possible topics for this training include using assistive technologies and applying universal design principles to instruction.

Lessons Learned through the Replication Effort

Faculty who participated in workshops, individual projects, and interviews expressed the realization that universal design strategies are "good teaching practices" and appreciated the opportunity to enhance their own skills. We found that, given the information, faculty were more than willing to try out universal design strategies and were pleasantly surprised by the impact on student achievement.

The Universal Design Planning Committee recognized the importance of collaboration with various departments across the university that support students and faculty and enhance the emphasis on diversity in the mission of the university. The synergy created by the individuals in the committee extended their impact to faculty as well as students. Most important was the fact that faculty members who became involved in the Universal Design Faculty Training Initiative were able to provide input into the process and guide implementation of various professional development opportunities.

RECOMMENDATIONS FOR SUCCESSFUL FACULTY OUTREACH PROGRAMS

Project staff make the following recommendations to other campuses who wish to conduct similar activities on their campuses.

Use Evaluation Strategies to Understand the Learning Environment

At both sites, evaluation studies, or study groups, were used to obtain input from key individuals to assess the learning environment and the professional development needs of faculty and staff. Because universal design is based on the inclusive nature of learning, we recommend including students with disabilities in evaluation activities to obtain their perceptions of the learning environment.

Create Collaborative Partnerships

At both universities, partnering with individuals and administrative offices proved to be critical to the success of the projects, particularly because of the visibility and good reputations of these entities among the faculty. Networking efforts within the universities provided access to faculty members who otherwise may not have considered the benefits of applying universal design principles to their instruction.

Determine a Strategy for Implementation

It is important to develop a plan for implementation. Having evaluation or needs assessment results will offer a direction for planning professional development activities. Consideration of how the activities will be disseminated is equally important.

Develop Training Using Several Formats

Programs at seventeen colleges and universities that have developed professional development activities found that face-to-face, online, and print methods were effective strategies for infusing information and resources with universal design techniques (Getzel, Briel, & McManus, 2003). Offering different formats not only models the use of universal design techniques but also helps to address the challenge of faculty and staff finding time to participate in professional development activities.

Create Incentives for Faculty Participation

A primary lesson learned from the activities at both sites was that some faculty members need incentives and some type of recognition or reward for their commitment to improving instruction. Several incentive options were explored. At VCU and Virginia Tech, faculty members who attended workshops were eligible to receive Inspiration software. Both sites were also able to offer mini-grants to purchase equipment and software, as well as stipends for faculty to develop and incorporate universal design strategies into their coursework.

CONCLUSION

Providing university-wide professional development activities infused with universal design strategies to create learning environments for all students, especially students with disabilities, has shown promising results at VCU, Virginia Tech, and other universities and colleges across the country (Getzel, Briel, & McManus, 2003). However, achieving positive results requires an ongoing commitment between highly visible university departments and academic faculty. Additionally, faculty should receive outcomes research that demonstrates the impact of universal design on student learning. Further study is needed on the long-term impact of these collaborative relationships and on outcomes for students with disabilities who take courses designed using universal design principles. Innovative practices should be shared among institutions of higher education in order to add to the growing body of knowledge in the field of disability and higher education.

REFERENCES

Alfano, K. (1994). *Recent strategies for faculty development.* (ERIC Document Reproduction Service no. ED371807). Los Angeles: ERIC Clearinghouse for Community Colleges.

Asselin, S., & Reilly, V. (2006). *Improving the learning climate for students with disabilities.* Blacksburg: Virginia Tech, Office of Multicultural Affairs.

Brinckerhoff, L. C., McGuire, J. M., & Shaw, S. F. (2002). *Postsecondary education and transition for students with learning disabilities* (2nd ed.). Austin, TX: Pro-Ed.

Finn, D. E. (2005). *Measuring the effectiveness of online faculty development: Exploring factors related to the integration of universal design concepts by community college professors.* Unpublished doctoral dissertation, Virginia Commonwealth University.

Finn, D. E., Reilly, V., & Asselin, S. (2005, August). *A collaborative model: Helping college faculty implement principles of universal design.* Paper presented at the annual international conference of the Association on Higher Education and Disability, Milwaukee, WI.

Finn, D. E., & Thoma, C. A. (2006, January). What is a universal design approach to learning? *The Professor's Assistant: An Informational Publication for University Instructors at Virginia Tech.*

Getzel, E. E., Briel, L. W., & McManus, S. (2003). Strategies for implementing professional development activities on college campuses: Findings from the OPE funded project sites (1999–2002). *Journal of Postsecondary Education and Disability, 17,* 59–76.

Getzel, E. E., & Finn, D. E. (2005). Training university faculty and staff. In E. E. Getzel & P. Wehman (Eds.), *Going to college: Expanding opportunities for people with disabilities* (pp. 199–214). Baltimore: Paul H. Brookes.

McGuire, J. M., Scott, S. S., & Shaw, S. F. (2003). Universal design for instruction: The paradigm, its principles, and products for enhancing instructional access. *Journal of Postsecondary Education and Disability, 17,* 11–21.

Scott, S. S., & Gregg, G. (2000). Meeting the evolving educational needs of faculty in providing access for college students with ld. *Journal of Learning Disabilities, 33,* 158–167.

Scott, S. S., & McGuire, J. M. (2005). Implementing universal design for instruction to promote inclusive college teaching. In E. E. Getzel & P. Wehman (Eds.), *Going to college: Expanding opportunities for people with disabilities* (pp. 119–138). Baltimore: Paul H. Brookes.

Scott, S. S., McGuire, J. M., & Foley, T. E. (2003). Universal design for instruction: A framework for anticipating and responding to disability and other diverse learning needs in the college classroom. *Equity and Excellence in Education, 36,* 40–49.

Wilson, K. E., & Getzel, E. E. (2001). Creating a supportive campus: The VCU professional development academy. *Journal for Vocational Special Needs Education, 23,* 12–18.

Professional development activities at VCU and Virginia Tech were developed under a grant from the U.S. Department of Education Office of Postsecondary Education (grant number P33A020046). However, the content of this chapter does not necessarily represent the policy of the Department of Education, and you should not assume endorsement by the federal government.

24

Promoters and Inhibitors of Universal Design in Higher Education

Sheryl E. Burgstahler

Earlier chapters have provided strategies for the implementation of universal design in higher education (UDHE). This chapter touches on factors that can promote or inhibit the widespread practice of UDHE; these include legislation, awareness, attitudes, diversity efforts, change processes, funding, and market forces. Roles that government, industry, educational entities, professional organizations, researchers, and consumers might play in the promotion of UDHE are also suggested. Topics discussed can increase the awareness of policymakers, researchers, and practitioners regarding issues that must be addressed in order to further the goals and processes of UDHE.

What would it take to make universal design in higher education (UDHE) as commonplace in higher education as recycling is in Seattle? Most people would know what UDHE is, accept it as the right thing to do, and make an effort to achieve it. Because of a shared belief, people would encourage one another toward the goal and, together, many small efforts would make a difference. The authors of this book make a compelling case that a more inclusive campus can result when UDHE is routinely applied to instruction, information technology, physical spaces, and services. Despite the promise of universal design (UD), however, this relatively new paradigm has not yet been widely embraced by U.S. colleges and universities.

PROMOTERS AND INHIBITORS

The following paragraphs touch on a few of the many factors that can serve to promote or inhibit the widespread application of UDHE: legislation, awareness, attitudes, diversity efforts, change, cost, and market forces.

Legislation

Campus responses to legislation can promote or inhibit the widespread adoption of UDHE. UDHE is inhibited when institutions focus on meeting minimum mandates for nondiscrimination, such as those that result in "ADA-compliant" physical spaces. On the other hand, UDHE is promoted when institutions look beyond minimal legal mandates and focus instead on broad institutional values and goals, such as those related to equity, diversity, inclusion, and campus climate.

Awareness

Today, lack of knowledge about UDHE inhibits its application. Relatively few faculty members and administrators are knowledgeable about the benefits, processes, and strategies of UD. With increased knowledge and resources, these practitioners could become promoters of UDHE. Awareness of practices at other institutions can also promote UDHE at an institution interested in keeping pace with the practices of its peers.

Attitudes

Discriminatory attitudes can create barriers to higher education. For example, *ableism* (Hehir, 2002, p. 3) is a devaluation of disability that

> results in societal attitudes that uncritically assert that it is better for a child to walk than roll, speak than sign, read print than read braille, spell independently than use a spell-check, and hang out with nondisabled kids, as opposed to other disabled kids.

Such attitudes perpetuate inequality and inhibit the acceptance of UDHE as a way to support social integration. The attitude of some faculty and staff that students with disabilities are an extra burden may also inhibit the adoption of UDHE, as is a "survival of the fittest" attitude about students in general.

A partial remedy to negative attitudes about underrepresented groups is the full participation of members of those groups in the campus environment, which can be achieved in part through the adoption of UD practices. As more students with diverse characteristics succeed in college and careers, negative attitudes may change for the better. Positioning UD as an approach that upholds the democratic principles of nondiscrimination and equal opportunity may promote its application.

Diversity Efforts

As Dr. Mark Emmert says in his foreword to this book, diversity efforts of many postsecondary institutions originally focused on gender and racial and ethnic issues. Institutions that have expanded their definition of diversity to encompass such characteristics as sexuality, religion, age, socioeconomic status, nationality, and disability are fertile ground for the promotion of the overarching concept of UD. Institutions with a narrower vision of diversity are less likely to embrace UDHE.

Change

An inhibitor to the acceptance of UDHE is adherence to "the way we have always done things." In contrast, forward-thinking campus administrators are promoters of

UDHE. The cause of UDHE can benefit from campus administrators who see the value of evolving the role of the disability services office to include a charge to consult with faculty and staff on UD and from faculty and staff willingness to embrace new roles in making campuses more inclusive. Promoters of UD can increase their impact by joining forces with others in advisory committees or working groups to further the practice of UD throughout the campus. Such UD promoters, for example, might work to have UD practices incorporated into campuswide initiatives to improve instruction. Routine consideration of teaching performance and service with respect to a diverse student body in faculty and staff evaluations can promote UD as well.

Cost

Time and cost are often reported as deterrents to the widespread application of UDHE. Until UD is routinely applied, extra time and resources may have to be expended to redesign inaccessible products and environments and to train and support staff in the practice of UD. However, setting incremental goals can minimize cost and thereby promote UDHE. For example, administrators of a distance learning program may employ UD practices each time a new course is developed or an existing course is updated. This sensible practice of addressing potential design barriers incrementally rather than all at one time serves to spread out costs over time.

Market Forces

The large and aging baby boomer population and the veterans of recent conflicts are increasing the demand for and availability of products and environments with built-in accessibility features. Campus administrators with purchasing authority are in a good position to promote UDHE by making it clear to vendors that accessibility is a consideration as they choose information technology and other products. By doing so they send a strong message to product developers, who are always seeking a competitive edge over companies that produce similar products. Conversely, purchasers who do not consider accessible and usable design when making institutional purchases inhibit widespread application of UDHE.

STAKEHOLDER ROLES FOR PROMOTING UNIVERSAL DESIGN IN HIGHER EDUCATION

Industry, institutions of higher education, professional organizations, researchers, consumers, and government can play important roles in promoting the widespread application of UDHE.

Industry

Industry can promote UD in a variety of ways: Hire a diverse workforce, involve consumers with a wide range of abilities and perspectives in product design and usability testing, make accessibility features readily apparent and promote them in advertising, and train sales representatives and other employees on accessibility and usability issues and universally designed product features as they are developed.

Institutions of Higher Education

Since implementation of UDHE may require a cultural shift, people and processes throughout the institution should be involved. Institutions can use print, video, and Web-based materials to increase awareness of UD practices, including disseminating UD guidelines customized to specific audiences (e.g., Webmasters, administrators, faculty), publishing articles on UD in campus periodicals, and delivering presentations on UDHE. All stakeholders should have access to training that is tailored to their specific application areas. Administrators can promote the adoption of UD practices by redefining the role of the disability services office to include proactively assisting faculty and staff in applying UD in their respective areas of responsibility. Campus units that offer professional development to faculty and staff can be encouraged to incorporate UD in their regular training options. Administrators can also adopt procurement policies that promote the purchase of universally designed products. Instructors can voice accessibility concerns to textbook publishers, use accessible technologies, apply UD to their instruction, and teach UD content in their courses.

Professional Organizations

Professional organizations can further UDHE by publishing UD articles in professional journals, offering presentations and exhibits on UD topics at conferences, and encouraging members to employ UD. Professional organizations can also promote consideration of the needs of students and staff with diverse characteristics in the evaluation of educational entities, such as in assessments of university quality.

Researchers

Efforts to get UD on the research agendas of disciplines such as technical communications, information sciences, education, and usability can promote its adoption in higher education. Researchers can examine the impact, efficacy, and cost of UDHE. There is also a need to further develop and validate guidelines and checklists to measure levels of application of UDHE to specific products and environments and to share best practices. Dissemination of research results can be tailored to specific audiences to encourage effective applications of UD. Industry and consumers can participate in the research agenda with the goal of creating more economically viable products and environments that employ UD.

Consumers

Consumers of higher education offerings can affect the adoption of UDHE through advocacy groups and individual input to various campus units. Individuals with disabilities tend to advocate only for specific accommodations when they are needed. A student UD advocate could take the next step of providing suggestions to the institution that would eliminate the need for that accommodation in the future. For example, a student who cannot access the content of a video on a Web site because it is not captioned might need to use a sign language interpreter to meet an immediate access need, but she could also suggest that captions be provided on videos in the future. Individuals with disabilities can further the adoption of UDHE by learning about access issues and solutions for their peers with different types of disabilities. This would help increase awareness and promote advocacy that goes beyond the specific needs of individuals with disabilities similar to their own. Similar efforts can make a more welcoming and usable campus for racial and ethnic minorities and other underrepresented groups.

Government

To promote UDHE, government agencies can fund research projects to apply UD to specific applications, disseminate information about UD, develop and enforce legislation and standards, and influence others by using accessible products and processes in their own agencies. Government could provide tax breaks to encourage companies to develop universally designed products and make accessible products more affordable. One current federal effort to promote UDHE is nine years of funding through the Office of Postsecondary Education of the U.S. Department of Education to promote successful postsecondary outcomes for students with disabilities, primarily through the professional development of faculty and administrators. To date, more than sixty projects have been funded in this program. One project, AccessCollege, supported the creation of the Center for Universal Design in Education, which develops and connects to resources that support applications of UD to instruction, services, technology, and physical spaces of institutions of higher education.

CONCLUSION

There is no magic formula for applying UDHE across campus. Clearly, much work needs to be done before the application of UD is as widespread in higher education as recycling is in the Northwest. However, the UDHE practices discussed in this book present models that others can adopt. For many, the only motivation needed for making UDHE efforts is the ultimate goal: to create an institution that is welcoming, accessible, and usable for all faculty, staff, students, and visitors.

REFERENCE

Hehir, T. (2002). Eliminating ableism in education. *Harvard Educational Review, 72*(1), 1–32.

This chapter is based on work supported by the U.S. Department of Education Office of Postsecondary Education (grant number P333A050064) and the National Science Foundation (Cooperative Agreement number HRD-0227995). Any opinions, findings, and conclusions or recommendations are those of the author and do not necessarily reflect the policy or views of the federal government, and you should not assume its endorsement.

Appendix:
Project Teams and Resources

Since 1992, the Disabilities, Opportunities, Internetworking, and Technology (DO-IT) Center at the University of Washington has worked to increase the representation of individuals with disabilities in higher education and employment. The three DO-IT projects described below were funded by the U.S. Department of Education Office of Postsecondary Education (OPE) to improve postsecondary academic outcomes for students with disabilities. Efforts from staff and team members in these projects led to the development of this book.

DO-IT PROF: PROFESSIONAL DEVELOPMENT FOR FACULTY AND ACADEMIC ADMINISTRATORS

In 1999, the U.S. Department of Education OPE funded the DO-IT Prof project (grant number P333A990042), in which professional development materials and training were provided to faculty and academic administrators nationwide to help them more fully include students with disabilities in their courses. Project efforts promoted universal design of instruction as a paradigm for maximizing learning for all students, including those with disabilities, and minimizing the need for academic accommodations. To extend impact and ensure that project products were applicable nationwide, project staff worked with a team of representatives from twenty-four postsecondary institutions, along with their partner schools, that had demographics different from their own. Project staff assigned to DO-IT Prof included

Sheryl Burgstahler, Principal Investigator and Director
Christina deMille, Project Coordinator
Tanis Doe, External Evaluator and Research Consultant
Deb Cronheim, Research Coordinator
Nancy Rickerson, Research Consultant
Tracy Jirikowic, Research Consultant
Linda Tofle, Publications Manager
Gale Devens, Publications Assistant
Dan Comden, Technology Accessibility Specialist
Marvin Crippen, Technology Specialist

Members of the DO-IT Prof project team and their partner institutions were as follows.

Carol Achziger
Arapahoe Community College, Littleton, Colorado
Partner: University of Northern Colorado, Greeley, Colorado

Victoria Amey-Flippin
Northeastern Illinois University, Chicago, Illinois
Partner: Oakton Community College, Des Plaines, Illinois

Alice Anderson
University of Wisconsin–Madison, Madison, Wisconsin
Partner: Madison Area Technical College, Madison, Wisconsin

Patricia Bunge
Guilford Technical Community College, Jamestown, North Carolina
Partner: North Carolina Agricultural and Technical State University,
    Greensboro, North Carolina

Deborah Casey-Powell
Florida Atlantic University, West Palm Beach, Florida
Partner: University of Florida, Gainesville, Florida

Rosemary Coffman
Lee College, Baytown, Texas
Partner: Rice University, Houston, Texas

Jill Douglass
Santa Fe Community College, Santa Fe, New Mexico

Mary Ann Ferkis
Purdue University, West Lafayette, Indiana
Partner: Ivy Tech Community College, Bloomington, Indiana

Pam Griffin
University of Minnesota–Duluth, Duluth, Minnesota
Partner: Fond du Lac Tribal and Community College, Cloquet, Minnesota

Beverly Boone Harris
Norfolk State University, Norfolk, Virginia
Partner: New River Community College, Dublin, Virginia

Nancy Hart
Lane Community College, Eugene, Oregon
Partner: Western Oregon University, Monmouth, Oregon

Elaine High and John Pedraza
Michigan State University, East Lansing, Michigan
Partner: North Central Michigan College, Petoskey, Michigan

Alison McCarthy Iovanna
Tunxis Community College, Farmington, Connecticut
Partner: Southern Connecticut State University, New Haven, Connecticut

Richard Jones
Arizona State University, Tempe, Arizona
Partner: South Mountain Community College, Phoenix, Arizona

Jana Long
Southwest Missouri State University, Springfield, Missouri
Partner: St. Louis Community College, St. Louis, Missouri

Ralph McFarland
Humboldt State University, Arcata, California
Partner: College of the Redwoods, Eureka, California

Richard Radtke
University of Hawaii–Manoa, Honolulu, Hawaii
Partner: Leeward Community College, Pearl City, Hawaii

Lisa Badia Rhine
University of Dayton, Dayton, Ohio
Partner: Sinclair Community College, Dayton, Ohio

Patricia Richter
Kutztown University, Kutztown, Pennsylvania
Partner: Thaddeus Stevens College of Technology, Lancaster, Pennsylvania

Vicki Roth
University of Rochester, Rochester, New York
Partner: Finger Lakes Community College, Canandaigua, New York

Al Souma
Seattle Central Community College, Seattle, Washington
Partner: Gonzaga University, Spokane, Washington

Chrystal Stanley
Drake University, Des Moines, Iowa
Partner: Des Moines Area Community College, Ankeny, Iowa

Marcia Wiedefeld
Loyola College in Maryland, Baltimore, Maryland
Partner: Community College of Baltimore County–Dundalk, Baltimore, Maryland

DO-IT ADMIN: PROFESSIONAL DEVELOPMENT FOR STUDENT SERVICE ADMINISTRATORS

In 2002, the OPE funded DO-IT Admin (grant number P333A020044), which expanded DO-IT Prof efforts to train student service administrators and staff as well as faculty. Project staff worked with a team of representatives from twenty-three postsecondary institutions, along with their partner schools, to maximize impact and to ensure that project products are applicable nationwide. DO-IT Admin project staff at the University of Washington included

Sheryl Burgstahler, Principal Investigator and Director
Lisa Stewart, Project Coordinator
Christina deMille, Research Coordinator
Tanis Doe, External Evaluator and Research Consultant
Linda Tofle, Publications Manager
Sue Wozniak, Publications Assistant
Terry Thompson, Technology Accessibility Specialist
Marvin Crippen, Technology Specialist

Members of the DO-IT Admin team and their partner institutions were as follows.

Alice Anderson
University of Wisconsin–Madison, Madison, Wisconsin
Partner: Madison Area Technical College, Madison, Wisconsin

Beatrice Awoniyi
Florida State University, Tallahassee, Florida

Meryl Berstein
Johnson and Wales University, Providence, Rhode Island
Partner: Community College of Rhode Island, Warwick, Rhode Island

Sharon Bittner
Des Moines Area Community College, Ankeny, Iowa

Deborah Casey-Powell
Green River Community College, Auburn, WA

Rosemary Coffman
Lee College, Baytown, Texas
Partner: Rice University, Houston, Texas

Jane Furr Davis
Hunter College, New York, New York
Partner: Columbia-Greene Community College, Hudson, New York

Jill Douglass
Santa Fe Community College, Santa Fe, New Mexico
Partner: College of Santa Fe, Santa Fe, New Mexico

Jim Gorske
University of South Carolina–Upstate, Spartanburg, South Carolina
Partner: Greenville Technical College, Greenville, South Carolina

Pam Griffin
University of Minnesota– Duluth, Duluth, Minnesota
Partner: Fond du Lac Tribal and Community College, Cloquet, Minnesota

Grace T. Hanson
Mt. San Antonio College, Walnut, California
Partner: California State University–Long Beach, Long Beach, California

Nancy Hart
Lane Community College, Eugene, Oregon
Partner: Southern Oregon University, Ashland, Oregon

Dyane Haynes
University of Washington, Seattle, Washington
Partner: Seattle University, Seattle, Washington

Elaine High and John Pedraza
Michigan State University, East Lansing, Michigan
Partner: North Central Michigan College, Petoskey, Michigan

Richard Jones
Arizona State University, Tempe, Arizona
Partner: South Mountain Community College, Phoenix, Arizona

R. Scott Laurent
University of Missouri–Kansas City, Kansas City, Missouri
Partner: Metropolitan Community College–Longview, Lee's Summit, Missouri

Rodney Pennamon
Georgia State University, Atlanta, Georgia
Partner: Gainesville State College, Oakwood, Georgia

Patricia Richter
Kutztown University, Kutztown, Pennsylvania
Partner: Lehigh Carbon Community College, Schnecksville, Pennsylvania

Sharon Robertson
University of Tennessee–Martin, Martin, Tennessee
Partner: Jackson State Community College, Jackson, Tennessee

Rosezelia Roy
Virginia State University, Petersburg, Virginia
Partner: J. Sargeant Reynolds Community College, Richmond, Virginia

Al Souma
Seattle Central Community College, Seattle, Washington
Partner: Seattle University, Seattle, Washington

Suzanne Tucker
Southern Connecticut State University, New Haven, Connecticut
Partner: Gateway Community College, New Haven, Connecticut

Linda Walter
Seton Hall University, South Orange, New Jersey
Partner: Raritan Valley Community College, Somerville, New Jersey

ACCESSCOLLEGE: SYSTEMIC CHANGE FOR POSTSECONDARY INSTITUTIONS

DO-IT Prof and DO-IT Admin team members identified the critical need for systematic change in policies, procedures, and practices in order for both universal design and reasonable accommodations for students with disabilities to be embraced at an institutional level. AccessCollege (OPE grant number P333A050064), began in 2005 and continues to offer and refine the successful professional development and resources for faculty and administrators of earlier projects. It complements those activities with capacity-building activities and the identification, validation, and application of Campus Accessibility Indicators to document institutional change toward more inclusive campuses and programs. Project staff at the University of Washington include

Sheryl Burgstahler, Principal Investigator and Director
Michael Richardson, Program Manager
Lisa Stewart, Project Coordinator
Elizabeth Moore, External Evaluator and Research Consultant
Rebecca C. Cory, Research Coordinator
Linda Tofle, Publications Manager
Rebekah Peterson, Publications Coordinator
Terry Thompson, Technology Accessibility Specialist
Marvin Crippen, Technology Specialist

Members of the *AccessCollege* team and their partner institutions are as follows.

Alice Anderson
University of Wisconsin–Madison, Madison, Wisconsin
Partner: Madison Area Technical College, Madison, Wisconsin

Beatrice Awoniyi
Florida State University, Tallahassee, Florida
Partners: Tallahassee Community College and Florida A&M University,
    Tallahassee, Florida

Meryl Berstein
Johnson and Wales University, Providence, Rhode Island
Partner: Community College of Rhode Island, Warwick, Rhode Island

Sharon Bittner
Des Moines Area Community College, Ankeny, Iowa
Partner: Iowa State University, Ames, Iowa

Barbara Brown
Kodiak College, Kodiak, Alaska
Partner: University of Alaska–Anchorage, Anchorage, Alaska

Deborah Casey
Green River Community College, Auburn, Washington
Partner: University of Washington, Seattle, Washington

Adele Darr
Arizona State University, Tempe, Arizona
Partner: South Mountain Community College, Phoenix, Arizona

Tim Dailey
Southwestern Oregon Community College, Coos Bay, Oregon
Partner: University of Oregon, Eugene, Oregon

Jim Gorske
University of Florida, Gainesville, Florida
Partner: Greenville Technical College, Greenville, South Carolina

Pam Griffin
University of Minnesota–Duluth, Duluth, Minnesota
Partner: Fond du Lac Tribal and Community College, Cloquet, Minnesota

Grace T. Hanson
Mt. San Antonio College, Walnut, California
Partner: California State University–Long Beach, Long Beach, California

Dyane Haynes
University of Washington, Seattle, Washington
Partner: Seattle University, Seattle, Washington

Elaine High and Virginia Walker
Michigan State University, East Lansing, Michigan
Partner: Kalamazoo Valley Community College, Kalamazoo, Michigan

Melissa Locher
Missouri Southern State University, Joplin, Missouri
Partner: Crowder College, Neosho, Missouri

Rodney Pennamon
Georgia State University, Atlanta, Georgia
Partner: Georgia Perimeter College, Clarkston, Georgia

Patricia Richter
Kutztown University, Kutztown, Pennsylvania
Partner: Lehigh Carbon Community College, Schnecksville, Pennsylvania

Sharon Robertson
University of Tennessee–Martin, Martin, Tennessee
Partner: Middle Tennessee State University, Murfreesboro, Tennessee

Rosezelia Roy
Virginia State University, Petersburg, Virginia
Partner: J. Sargeant Reynolds Community College, Richmond, Virginia

Audrey Annette Smelser
National Park Community College, Hot Springs, Arkansas
Partner: Henderson State University, Arkadelphia, Arkansas

Al Souma
Seattle Central Community College, Seattle, Washington
Partner: Seattle University, Seattle, Washington

Suzanne Tucker
Southern Connecticut State University, New Haven, Connecticut
Partner: Gateway Community College, New Haven, Connecticut

Linda Walter
Seton Hall University, South Orange, New Jersey
Partner: Raritan Valley Community College, Somerville, New Jersey

RESOURCES

The following comprehensive Web sites are designed to help faculty, administrators, and staff create welcoming, accessible, and usable environments, programs, and resources and to help students with disabilities prepare for and succeed in college. Select AccessCollege from http://www.washington.edu/doit/ to find links to these five Web sites.

- *The Faculty Room.* A space for faculty and academic administrators at postsecondary institutions to learn how to create classroom environments and academic activities that maximize the learning of all students, including those with disabilities.
- *The Student Services Conference Room.* A space for staff and administrators at postsecondary institutions to learn how to create facilities, services, and resources that are accessible to all students, including those with disabilities.
- *The Board Room.* A space for high-level administrators at postsecondary institutions to learn how to create and facilitate the development of programs and services that are accessible to all students, including those with disabilities.
- *The Student Lounge.* Resources to help students with disabilities prepare for and succeed in college.
- *The Center for Universal Design in Education.* A comprehensive Web site on principles, processes, guidelines, checklists, and promising practices for applying universal design to instruction, student services, information technology, and physical spaces.

DO-IT has created an extensive collection of short, focused printed publications, training videos, and comprehensive training materials and books that can be obtained from DO-IT or freely viewed online at http://www.washington.edu/doit/Brochures/.

The following free publications relate most directly to the topic of this book:

- Applications of Universal Design in Education
- Equal Access: Universal Design of Instruction
- Making Science Labs Accessible to Students with Disabilities
- Universal Design in Education: Principles and Applications
- Universal Design of Instruction: Definition, Principles, and Examples
- AccessCollege: Systemic Change for Postsecondary Institutions
- Self-Examination: How Accessible Is Your Campus?
- Effective Communication: Faculty and Students with Disabilities
- Invisible Disabilities and Postsecondary Education
- Working Together: Faculty and Students with Disabilities
- Working Together: Teaching Assistants and Students with Disabilities
- Equal Access: Universal Design of Advising
- Equal Access: Universal Design of Career Services
- Equal Access: Universal Design of Financial Aid
- Equal Access: Universal Design of Housing and Residential Life
- Equal Access: Universal Design of Libraries
- Equal Access: Universal Design of Recruitment and Undergraduate Admissions
- Equal Access: Universal Design of Registration
- Equal Access: Universal Design of Student Services
- Equal Access: Universal Design of Tutoring and Learning Centers
- Equal Access: Universal Design of Computer Labs
- Equal Access: Universal Design of Computing Departments
- Web Accessibility: Guidelines for Administrators
- World Wide Access: Accessible Web Design
- Equal Access: Universal Design of Distance Learning
- Real Connections: Making Distance Learning Accessible to Everyone

The following video presentations relate most directly to the topic of this book:

- Building the Team: Faculty, Staff, and Students Working Together
- Equal Access: Campus Libraries
- Equal Access: Student Services
- Equal Access: Universal Design of Computer Labs
- Equal Access: Universal Design of Instruction
- Invisible Disabilities and Postsecondary Education
- Real Connections: Making Distance Learning Accessible to Everyone
- Self-Examination: How Accessible Is Your Campus?
- Working Together: Faculty and Students with Disabilities
- World Wide Access: Accessible Web Design

The following comprehensive training materials are of particular interest to postsecondary faculty and administrators:

- Building the Team: Faculty, Staff, and Students Working Together—Presentation and Resource Materials
- Students with Disabilities and Campus Services: Building the Team—Presentation and Resource Materials
- Building Capacity for a Welcoming and Accessible Postsecondary Institution
- Making Math, Science, and Technology Instruction Accessible to Students with Disabilities—A Resource for Teachers and Teacher Educators

About the Authors

Linda Abarbanell is a doctoral candidate in human development and psychology at the Harvard Graduate School of Education. She studies the role of language, culture, and schooling in children's cognitive and conceptual development. Her research includes comparing English speakers in the United States with a Mayan-speaking population in Chiapas, Mexico.

Alice Anderson is the technology accessibility program coordinator in the Division of Information Technology at the University of Wisconsin–Madison. She plays a significant role in strategic planning, policy, and resource development in the area of technology accessibility and coordinates campus advisory committees that address accessibility for people with disabilities.

Susan B. Asselin, Ph.D., is a professor in the Special Education Teacher Preparation Program at Virginia Tech, where she works with aspiring and currently employed career and technical, general academic, and special educators. A former vocational educator with teaching experience and degrees in career and technical and special education, she prepares professionals for their evolving roles. Dr. Asselin received several grants funded by the Office of Special Education and Rehabilitative Services to prepare resource/transition educators, established the first regional transition services technical assistance center, and provided the groundwork for a statewide system of technical assistance with education and rehabilitation. Her publications and outreach efforts focus on personnel development and strategies for teaching diverse learners.

Kirsten Behling, Ph.D., has conducted research on and developed practices that create access to postsecondary education for individuals with disabilities. She has served as the coordinator for the Equity and Excellence in Higher Education project since 2001, working to educate college faculty members on the benefits of incorporating the principles of universal design into course development, instruction, assessment, and the environment. Dr. Behling has developed a Web site (www.eeonline.org) and videos, given presentations, and facilitated core teams on universal course design at several institutions of higher education.

Sheryl E. Burgstahler, Ph.D., directs the Accessible Technology division of UW Technology Services, including the Disabilities, Opportunities, Internetworking, and Technology (DO-IT) Center, at the University of Washington. DO-IT promotes the success of students with disabilities as well as the universal design of facilities, computer labs, Web pages, services, and on-site and online instruction. Dr. Burgstahler also founded and directs the Center on Universal Design in Education, which is funded by the U.S. Department of Education. She has published dozens of articles, book chapters, and books; taught at precollege, community college, and university levels; and delivered presentations at national and international conferences. Dr. Burgstahler and her projects have received numerous awards, including the Program Recognition Award from the Association of Higher Education and Disability, a mentoring award from the president of the

United States, the Trace Center Catalyst Award, and the Innovation Award from Career Opportunities for Students with Disabilities.

Deb Casey, Ph.D., is dean of student services at Green River Community College in Auburn, Washington. Dr. Casey has served in leadership positions in higher education, including assistant dean and 504 Compliance Officer at the University of Florida. She has published articles on diversity issues in colleges and universities and students with psychological disabilities in allied health sciences. She also wrote a chapter called "An Administrator Perspective: Universal Design in Allied Health Programs" in *Pedagogy and Student Services for Institutional Transformation: Implementing Universal Design in Higher Education*.

Rebecca C. Cory, Ph.D., is the research coordinator for DO-IT at the University of Washington. DO-IT research explores the educational attainment of students with disabilities and examines how to make college and university environments more accessible to people with disabilities. Dr. Cory has published and presented on issues of inclusive higher education at conferences and on campuses around the country. She has also taught undergraduate and graduate level courses in disability studies and research. She coedited the book *Building Pedagogical Curb Cuts: Incorporating Disability in the University Classroom and Curriculum*.

Samantha G. Daley is a doctoral student in human development and psychology at the Harvard Graduate School of Education. Her background includes working with high school and college students with learning disabilities. Her research focuses on the cognitive, social, and affective characteristics that predict success in this population.

Adele Darr, Ph.D., is the director of a disability resource center at the west campus of Arizona State University. Dr. Darr works with students with disabilities, faculty, and staff to promote universal design concepts within courses and colleges. She also reaches out to local high schools and community colleges to facilitate successful transitions to the university environment for students with disabilities. Dr. Darr spent more than twenty years as both a nurse and a teacher.

Imke Durre, Ph.D., is a climatologist for the National Oceanic and Atmospheric Administration. She holds a bachelor's degree in applied mathematics from Yale University and a doctoral degree from the University of Washington. Dr. Durre's work focuses on compiling international data from weather balloons and surface instruments into research-quality datasets.. She volunteers for the I Have A Dream Foundation and serves as a lead Mentor for blind and visually impaired students who are DO-IT participants.

Elizabeth Evans Getzel, M.A., is director of Postsecondary Education Initiatives at Virginia Commonwealth University's Rehabilitation Research and Training Center on Workplace Supports and Job Retention, a grant-funded center focusing on the education and employment issues of individuals with disabilities. She has extensive experience conducting research, evaluation, and training in the areas of college transition planning, postsecondary education, career planning and employment for individuals with disabilities, and faculty professional development that focuses on universal design principles. She has authored or coauthored journal articles and book chapters on transition, career development, postsecondary education, and employment and is coeditor of the book *Going to College: Expanding Opportunities for People with Disabilities*.

Scott Ferguson is 22 years old. Mr. Ferguson attended Shoreline Community College and is currently a senior majoring in political economics and history at the University of Washington.

Donald E. Finn, Ph.D., is assistant professor of Adult Education and Professional Development at Regent University in Virginia Beach, Virginia. He has developed and conducted workshops on inclusive instructional practices for classroom teachers and college/university professors that have been delivered across campuses in Virginia and at state and national education conferences. Dr. Finn has contributed chapters to books about effective instructional practices and has written articles for journals, newsletters, and other publications. Dr. Finn's research interests include the integration of various technologies into online and face-to-face instruction and effective curriculum design and delivery techniques for diverse students.

Elisabeth Goldstein, M.I.Arch, LEED® AP, is a planner/programmer at MITHUN, an architecture firm in Seattle. She has worked with postsecondary institutions on their master plans as well as new construction and renovation projects for student housing, academic buildings, and student service spaces. Her experiences as an accessibility designer and management consultant have made Ms. Goldstein keenly aware of the importance of understanding each client's unique needs and requirements to achieve the best design solutions.

Pam Griffin, M.A., is the coordinator of General Disability Services at the University of Minnesota–Duluth. She has more than fourteen years of experience providing academic accommodations to students with physical, psychological, systemic, and visual disabilities. Her work also includes providing resources and information to faculty and staff on accessibility and instructional strategies for students with disabilities. Additionally, she teaches Introduction to College Learning classes and applies universal design of instruction principles in her classes.

Wendy S. Harbour is a doctoral student in administration, planning, and social policy at the Harvard Graduate School of Education, where she recently completed a term as editor of the *Harvard Educational Review*. She is a teaching assistant in special education and disability-related courses at Harvard and is also a project director for PEPNet's Midwest Center for Postsecondary Outreach. Her publication experience includes coauthoring *Special Education for a New Century* and writing reports on the 2004 AHEAD survey of disability services providers.

Debra Hart, Ph.D., has more than twenty-five years of experience working with individuals with disabilities and directing national and local projects. She has codirected the Equity and Excellence in Higher Education project since 2001. Dr. Hart's work with the National Center on Postsecondary Educational Supports includes research, training, and technical assistance on creating access to college for students with intellectual disabilities. Dr. Hart has also worked on a collaborative project with staff from the Center for Applied Special Technology to provide training to high school faculty on universal design for learning. Topics of relevant published articles include creating access to postsecondary education for students with intellectual disabilities, how to integrate technology across the curriculum, and the coordination of services and supports in secondary transition to postsecondary education.

Jeanne L. Higbee, Ph.D., has a bachelor's degree in sociology, a master's degree in counseling and guidance, and a doctorate in educational administration. She currently serves as professor and interim director for the Center for Research on Developmental Education and Urban Literacy at the University of Minnesota. The author or editor of more than 100 books, monographs, and journal articles, she is an American College Personnel Association Diamond Honoree and Voice of Inclusion Medallion recipient. Dr. Higbee is the project director for PASS IT, which is funded by the U.S. Department of Education to enhance professional development in universal instructional design.

Cathy Jenner directs a U.S. Department of Education demonstration project, Ensuring Students with Disabilities Receive a Quality Higher Education, at Renton Technical College in Washington State. She has a bachelor's degree in psychology from the State University of New York–Plattsburgh. In the past she has served as the director of student services at the Resource Center for the Handicapped, a postsecondary technical institute serving individuals with disabilities. In 1994, Ms. Jenner became the founding manager of one of the nation's first One-Stop Employment and Training Centers, the Renton Career Development Center, which won several national awards for customer service. She also directed the start-up of a new King County program for dropout prevention, encompassing over twenty middle and high schools in King County.

Catherine Sam Johnston is a doctoral student at the Harvard Graduate School of Education. Her research focuses on adult online education, distributed learning, and emerging technologies.

Christopher J. Johnstone, Ph.D., is a research associate at the National Center on Educational Outcomes at the University of Minnesota and is director of International Initiatives and Relations for the College of Education and Human Development at the University of Minnesota. He has published several articles and book chapters on how universal design relates to large-scale assessment in K–12 education. He has investigated the implications of universal design of assessments in higher education, including contributing to an article on this topic in the *Journal of Postsecondary Education and Disability*. Dr. Johnstone's most recent research investigates disability issues in international settings, including a collaborative project on university accessibility in Kazakhstan.

Richard Jones, M.A., is a retired assistant director of Disability Resources at Arizona State University. He is interested in issues of accessible technology, especially for blind and visually impaired users. He served as a member of the DO-IT Prof and DO-IT Admin teams.

Leanne R. Ketterlin-Geller, Ph.D., is an assistant professor at the University of Oregon. Her interests include integrating the principles of universal design into the development of effective assessment procedures in mathematics and valid decision-making systems for students with diverse needs using the general education curriculum. Dr. Ketterlin-Geller's work is centered on using technology with embedded accommodations to provide a flexible assessment system that supports student needs. She has presented research and published articles and book chapters in the area of universal design for assessment, using data from large-scale and classroom-based assessments for decision-making and curriculum-assessment alignment.

Mike Litzkow is a professional software developer participating in a wide variety of research projects at the University of Wisconsin–Madison. He has worked on projects ranging from Grid computing systems, to parallel architecture simulators, to delivery of course lectures and instructional content over the World Wide Web. His current interests include developing technology for making multimedia, highly technical, interactive Web applications accessible to screen reader users.

Joan M. McGuire, Ph.D., is a professor emerita of Special Education in the Educational Psychology Department and codirector of the Center on Postsecondary Education and Disability at the University of Connecticut. Dr. McGuire's research interests include universal design for instruction (UDI); postsecondary disability program development, administration, and evaluation; and adults with learning disabilities. She served as the coeditor of the *Journal of Postsecondary Education* and has published widely in the fields of UDI and postsecondary education and support services for students with disabilities.

Karen A. Myers, Ph.D., is an associate professor in the Higher Education Graduate Program at Saint Louis University. Dr. Myers has been a college teacher and administrator for more than twenty-eight years and currently serves on the ACPA College Student Educators International Governing Board as the director of External Relations. In addition to classroom teaching, she facilitates online courses on disability, including her self-designed hybrid course entitled Disability in Higher Education and Society. She is a writer, researcher, consultant, and trainer in the area of disability and is the author of the book *The Way I See It: Bumping into Life with Low Vision*.

Eric Patterson, who is visually impaired, attends Portland State University. His major is marketing with a focus on information technology. He works in a campus computer lab, providing technical support to other students. Mr. Patterson views universal design as the process of designing classes, technology, services, and physical spaces so that they are accessible to everyone, including those with disabilities.

Lacey Reed is a student at Shoreline Community College and participates in therapeutic horseback riding in Washington state. Having multiple disabilities, she is one of the many beneficiaries of universal design. She has quadriplegia (both arms and legs) and athetoid (low muscle tone) cerebral palsy as a result of brain injury caused by lack of oxygen at birth. Her disabilities affect her whole body, including fine and gross motor movement and speech. Ms. Reed employs adapted computer equipment because she does not have dependable use of her hands, receives help with other activities from a personal care assistant, and operates a power wheelchair for mobility. Along with her physical disabilities, she also has specific learning and processing disabilities that require accommodations. Ms. Reed began participating as a DO-IT Scholar in high school and is now a DO-IT Ambassador, mentoring the younger Scholars as they transition to adult life.

Virginia Reilly, Ph.D., is the director of University Americans with Disabilities Act (ADA) Services at Virginia Tech. She served as president of the Association on Higher Education and Disability. Dr. Reilly has conducted research on standards of accessibility for higher education, is coauthor of the book *The ADA Coordinator's Guide to Campus Compliance*, and wrote a chapter in the book *Going to College*. She was awarded a research grant from the Virginia Board for People with Disabilities and has served as the project coordinator for the Southwest Virginia Assistive Technology System site. She is a member of the Virginia Higher Education Leadership Partners, which developed statewide guidelines for documentation of disabilities.

Michael Richardson is program manager for DO-IT at the University of Washington. He coordinates programs that serve to increase the participation of people with disabilities in challenging academic programs and careers. Before coming to DO-IT, Mr. Richardson worked with the state of Washington as a vocational rehabilitation counselor and regional coordinator of deaf and hard of hearing services. Mr. Richardson has personal experience with disability, having grown up with a progressive hearing loss, participating in Deaf culture, and using a cochlear implant.

Patricia J. Richter, M.A., is director of Disability Services at Kutztown University of Pennsylvania. She has served in this capacity for eight years, ensuring reasonable accommodations for students and employees at the university. Prior positions include assistant director of the ACT 101 Program at Kutztown University, a state program for access to higher education, and learning specialist in the Program for Learning Disabled College Students at Adelphi University, Garden City, New York. Ms. Richter holds a bachelor's degree from New York University and a master's degree in special education, specializing in psycho-educational disabilities, from New York University.

Olga Romero, Ph.D., has a doctorate in speech and hearing sciences from the Graduate Center of the City University of New York. She currently chairs the Special Education and Dual Language Education Department at the Bank Street College of Education, where she teaches courses in language development and disorders, learning disabilities, and bilingualism. She also coordinates projects for the Office of Students with Disabilities. Her interest in the academic success of graduate students with disabilities, combined with her expertise in the needs of English language learners, sparked her interest in universal design. Dr. Romero was director of a grant-funded demonstration project whose main goal was to ensure that college students with disabilities have full access to academic offerings through faculty development.

David H. Rose, Ed.D., is cofounder of the nonprofit research and development organization, Center for Applied Special Technology, and a lecturer in developmental neuropsychology and universal design for learning at the Harvard Graduate School of Education. Dr. Rose is the recipient of many awards, including the Computerworld/Smithsonian Award for Innovation in Education and is the author or editor of numerous articles, books, and educational software programs. He holds a doctorate from Harvard University.

Sally S. Scott, Ph.D., is director of Disability Services and associate professor of Special Education at Longwood University. She previously served as codirector of the Universal Design for Instruction Project at the University of Connecticut. Her expertise and research interests include postsecondary disability services, inclusive instructional design, adults with learning disabilities, and online teaching and learning.

Jessie Amelia Shulman is a Technology Leadership Program Associate at Washington Mutual. She graduated from the University of Washington with a bachelor's degree in informatics and a minor in dance. Before graduating, Ms. Shulman coauthored the article "A Web Accessibility Report Card for Top International University Web Sites." She began her involvement with DO-IT in 1998 as a DO-IT Scholar and has continued to serve as a Mentor.

Carson Smith is a senior at the University of Washington. A comparative literature major, he enjoys exploring connections across cultures: He studied in Prague and traveled across Eastern Europe and Turkey. In addition to his literary and cultural interests, Mr. Smith expanded his leadership skills by interning at NASA. He looks up to his great-uncle Pete Conrad, a person with dyslexia who did not let his disability prevent him from becoming the third man on the moon. Mr. Smith does not want his own dyslexia to define his opportunities in life. With the loan of adaptive technology from DO-IT, he hopes to make some giant leaps of his own by pursuing his passions in cultural studies and world literature.

Al Souma, M.A., is a rehabilitation counselor who coordinates disability support services at Seattle Central Community College. He speaks nationally on accommodating students with psychiatric disabilities in the classroom. His presentations to faculty and administrators offer suggestions on effectively serving students with mental health issues. Mr. Souma has presented dozens of workshops across the country, as well as seminars for national organizations such as the American College Personnel Association, the National Association of Student Personnel Administrators, and the Association of Higher Education and Disability (AHEAD). He has also presented work at the Sixth International Conference on Higher Education and Disability in Innsbruck, Austria. He received the 2002 Professional Recognition Award from AHEAD.

Andrea M. Spencer, Ph.D., is associate dean for Academic Affairs at Bank Street College of Education in New York City. In addition, she teaches online and traditional special education courses; supervises integrative master's projects; and collaborates with faculty in the development of programs, grant writing, and professional development opportunities for teachers in New York and abroad. Dr. Spencer's educational consultation has focused on problems of truant youth and advocacy for children with disabilities in public school systems. Before joining the Bank Street faculty, she supervised multiple special and alternative education programs for students with developmental disabilities, neurological impairments, and social-emotional and behavioral disorders in Connecticut, Maine, and Massachusetts.

Sarah Steele is a graduate of Seattle Pacific University (SPU). She is working part time in the music department at SPU, setting up a new master's program in sacred music. Ms. Steele is 22 years old and lives in Redmond, Washington with her parents and two younger siblings. She uses an electric wheelchair to get around. She has fibrodysplasia ossificans progressiva, a rare disease that causes muscle to turn to bone.

Terry Thompson is a senior computer specialist with UW Technology Services and DO-IT at the University of Washington. He works to promote technology accessibility for students with disabilities in education and careers. Mr. Thompson has more than fifteen years of experience in the accessibility field and has presented internationally at numerous conferences, seminars, and workshops. He has consulted widely with local and state government, private industry, and K–12 and postsecondary education entities on technology access issues.

Martha L. Thurlow, Ph.D., is director of the National Center on Educational Outcomes and senior research associate at the University of Minnesota. During the past decade, Dr. Thurlow's work has emphasized the need to obtain valid, reliable, and comparable assessment measures while ensuring that the assessments are truly measuring the knowledge and skills of students with special needs rather than their disabilities or limited language when these are not the focus of the assessment. Her research studies have covered a range of topics that include participation decision-making, accommodations, universal design, computer-based testing, graduation exams, and alternate assessments.

Susan Yager, Ph.D., is an associate professor of English at Iowa State University and the associate director of Iowa State's Center for Excellence in Learning and Teaching. Her chief research interests are medieval British literature and the scholarship of teaching and learning, especially as it pertains to literary studies.

Index

Note: Information contained in figures and tables are indicated by an italic *f* and *t* respectively.

Abarbanell, Linda, 45–59, 295
ableism, 280
access skills, 75–77, 78
AccessCollege, 39, 171–172, 178, 193, 283, 290–292
accessibility, of assessment, 74–75
accessible design, 9–10, 191
accommodation
  inviting discussion, 85–86
  marginalization by, 249
  planning for, 94–95
  reducing need for, 68
  and UD, 10–12, 62
Accommodations—Or Just Good Teaching? (Hodge and Preston-Sabin), 69
ADHD (attention deficit hyperactivity disorder), 62
adjustable-height furnishings, 203–205
administrative empowerment, 251
admissions process, 155
affective learning, 28–29, 47
American College Personnel Association, 160
Americans with Disabilities Act of 1990 (ADA), 9, 10, 73, 168, 189, 191, 219, 250
Anderson, Alice, 177–186, 225–233, 295
Architectural Barriers Act of 1968, 9
Arizona State University, 105–108
Asselin, Susan, 267–277, 295
assessment, of UD implementation, 69
assessment, student
  access skills, 75–77, 78
  approaches to, 77–79
  constructive feedback, 65–66
  elements of, 74
  of engagement and motivation, 47–48

multiple expressions of knowledge, 67–68, 78, 121
  postsecondary challenges for, 75–77
  and psychiatric disabilities, 101–102, 102*t*
  successful methods of, 93–94
  training for developing tools, 79–80
  UCD methods, 119–121, 120*t*
  UD principles and, 141
  web-based products, 56–58
assistive technology, 92, 184, 213–214, 236, 239–240
Assistive Technology Act of 1998, 6–7
Association of Higher Education and Disability (AHEAD), 39
attention differences, 5
attitudes, 280
autism spectrum disorders, 5, 56, 79, 180, 182–183
awareness, of student diversity and UD, 127–129, 145–146, 148–149, 148*f*, 274, 280

behaviorist theory, 30*t*
Behling, Kirsten, 295
blind students, 68–69
Bowe, Frank, 26
brain injuries, 5, 6, 51, 97, 188
buildings. *See* physical spaces/facilities
Burgstahler, Sheryl, 23–43, 167–175, 187–197, 213–224, 247–253, 279–283, 295–296

Campus Accessibility Indicators, 251–252
Casey, Deb, 97–104, 296
Center for Applied Special Technology (CAST), 28, 110, 220
Center for Excellence in Language and Teaching (CELT), 128–133
Center for Learning and Teaching Excellence (CLTE), 105–108
Center for Universal Design, 7–9, 26, 189, 191

Center for Universal Design in Education,
9, 292
classroom
    discussions, 52–53
    environment and design, 62–64, 84–86,
        121–122, 132–133
closed-circuit television, 239
cognitive demands, of lectures, 51–52
collaborative work, 58, 87
College of the Redwoods, 238–239
communication
    differences, 5–6
    skills, 63, 86–87, 171, 173*t*
communication technology
    distance learning and UDI, 35–36, 37*t*
computer labs, 235–244
constructivism, 30*t*
content-area knowledge, 76
Cory, Rebecca, 177–186, 247–253, 296
costs, and UD, 257, 263, 281
course design, application of UD to
    assessment methodology, 56–58
    assessment methods, 119–121, 120*t*
    core team for design, 112–114
    course web site, 55
    curriculum, 114–116, 115*t*
    and discussion groups, 52–53
    engagement and affect, 58–59
    environmental considerations, 121–122
    instructional methods, 48–55, 116–119,
        117*t*–118*t*
    and lecture format, 48–52
    multimedia, 55
    sustaining implementation, 122–124
    and textbooks, 53–55
course materials, 48–56, 162
curriculum planning, UCD methodologies,
    114–116, 115*t*

Daley, Samantha, 45–59, 296
Darr, Adele, 105–108, 296
deaf, and hearing differences, 49, 92
Descriptive Video Services, 69
design, traditional, 3
differentiated instruction, 30*t*
disabilities. *See also* psychiatric disabilities
    and ADA legislation, 10–11
    communicating with individuals with, 173*t*
    continuum model, 7
    course completion rates, 255
    disability resource/services offices, 130
    disclosure of, 63

faculty awareness of, 127–129, 145–146,
        148–149, 148*f*
    "invisible" disabilities, 4, 62, 97–98, 146
    physical environments and, 179–182
    prevalence, 160
    UD in professional preparation programs,
        135–142
discussion boards, 162
discussion groups, and UD, 52–53
Disguised: A True Story (Moore & Conn), 190
distance learning, 35–36, 37*t*
distributed intelligence, 58
diversity, of student population, 4–6, 109,
        113, 135, 146, 248–249
DO-IT Admin project, 288–290
DO-IT (Disabilities, Opportunities, Internet-
        working, and Technology), 9, 26
    about, 285
    Campus Accessibility Indicators, 251–252
    *Equal Access: Universal Design of Computer
        Labs,* 237
    Equal Access: Universal Design of Instruction,
        33, 178, 182
    guidelines and examples, 32–35, 34*t,* 170,
        178
    staff, 285–290
    strategies for application of UDI, 110–111
    web resources of, 172–174, 293
DO-IT Prof project, 285–287
Durre, Imke, 83–96, 296
dyslexia, 53

Electronic and Information Technology
        Accessibility Standards, 241
Elements of Universally Designed Assessments
        (Thompson, Johnstone, & Thurlow),
        74
engagement and motivation, 47–48, 58–59
English as a second language, 49
Equal Access: Universal Design of Instruction
        (Burgstahler), 33, 178, 182
Equity and Excellence in Higher Education
        project
    about, 110–112
    assessment methods, 119–121, 120*t*
    curriculum, 114–116, 115*t*
    environmental considerations, 121–122
    instructional methods, 116–119, 117*t*–118*t*
    sustaining implementation, 122–124
    UCD core team, 112–114, 122
Estrella Mountain Community College,
        208–209*f*

eTeach, 225–232
evaluation. *See* assessment, of UD implementation
expectations, communicating, 64–65
extended time, 67, 94, 236

facilities. *See* physical spaces/facilities
faculty
    awareness of student diversity and needs, 127–129, 145–146, 148–149, 148*f*, 274, 280
    case study methods for training, 135–142
    development centers and UD, 129–131
    implementing UD, 150–156, 153*t*–154*t*
    institutional support, 131–133
    promoting interest in UD among, 149–150, 274–275
    retirement projections, 135–136
    training, 38–39, 106, 123–124, 135–142, 145–156, 268–269
    UD's benefits and challenges, 68–69
faculty training. *See* training, faculty, in UD
feedback, providing student, 93
Ferguson, Scott, 177–186, 296
Finn, Donald, 267–277, 296–297

Getzel, Elizabeth Evans, 267–277, 296
goals, instructional, 47, 64
Goldstein, Elisabeth, 297
good practice, and UD, 31–32, 31*t*
Griffin, Pam, 177–186, 297
group discussions, 52–53

Harbour, Wendy, 45–59, 297
Harrison, Marc, 6, 188
Hart, Debra, 297
hearing differences, 5, 49
Higbee, Jeanne, 61–72, 297
higher education, UD and. *See* Universal Design in Higher Education
Higher Education Disability Support–Universal Design Principles (HEDS-UP), 145–156
HTML, 242

Implementation Plan for Web Accessibility, 221–222
inclusion
    responsibility of, 11–12
industry, and UD, 281
information technology. *See also* technological spaces, Universal Design in

computer lab design, 235–244
distance learning and UDI, 35–36, 37*t*
documentation, 216
guidelines for UD, 215–216
input/controls, 215
institutional commitment to accessibility, 221–222
manipulations, 215–216
as natural supports, 66–67, 91–93
output/displays, 215
safety, 216
software design, 220, 241–242
in student services, 172*t*, 183–184
UD for telecommunications, 219–221
UD for Web design, 217–219
Institute for Community Inclusion, 110
institutional change
    characteristics of, 247–252
    collaborative implementation model, 267–277
    effective support of, 131–133
    overcoming inertia, 280–281
    project management of, 255–265
instructional practices
    assessing learning outcomes, 141
    case studies for improving, 139–141
    delivering instruction, 140
    good practice, and UD, 31–32, 31*t*
    instructional cycle, 138–139
    multiple methods for access, 88–91
    planning instruction, 139–140
    and psychiatric disabilities, 100, 101*t*
    in Universal Course Design (UCD), 116–119, 117*t*–118*t*
interaction, promoting, 68, 86–87
"invisible" disabilities, 4, 62, 97–98. *See also* psychiatric disabilities
Iowa State University, 127–133
Iowa State University–Ames, 203
iPod, 118

JAWS screen reader, 229
Jenner, Cathy, 255–265, 297–298
Johnston, Catherine Sam, 45–59, 298
Johnstone, Christopher, 73–81, 298
Jones, Richard, 105–108, 298

Ketterlin-Geller, Leanne, 73–81, 298

learning-centered instruction, 30*t*
learning
    differences, 5

learning *(continued)*
  disabilities, 5, 10, 28, 29, 51, 67, 79, 145,
    146–156, 173, 261
  networks, 28–29
  styles, 29–31, 67, 91, 114–115, 159
lectures, UD and
  methods, 48–52, 116–119
  multimedia web-based, 225–232
  promoting interaction, 68
legislation, 280
lighting and sound, 205–206, 211
Litzkow, Mike, 225–233, 298

Mace, Ronald, 6, 168, 188–189
marginalization, 249
Massachusetts Institute of Technology,
    206–208, 207*f*
McGuire, Joan, 135–143, 298
mental health disabilities. *See* psychiatric
    disabilities
mentors, 51, 101, 112–114, 122–124
models, 57, 158–159
Moore, Patricia, 190
motivation, 85
multimedia, 55, 225–232
multiple means of
  expression, 29
  engagement, 29
  representation, 29
Myers, Karen, 157–164, 298–299

National Center on Accessible Media, 220
National Instructional Materials Accessibility
    Standard (NIMAS), 38, 55
North Carolina State University, 7–9, 26,
    189, 191, 240–241
notes, and note-taking
  in lecture class, 50–51

Oklahoma State University, 239–240

Patterson, Eric, 177–186, 299
pedagogy. *See* instructional practices
Pedagogy and Student Services for Insti-
    tutional Transformation (PASS IT)
    program, 163
personal-response units, 132
physical accessibility. *See* physical spaces/
    facilities
physical differences, 5
physical spaces/facilities
  adjustable-height furnishings, 203–205

building entrances, 200–202, 200*f*, 201*f*,
    210
classrooms, 62–64, 84–86, 121–122,
    132–133, 202–204*f*, 210
furnishings and equipment, 203–209, 211
history of Universal Design of, 188–191
lighting and sound, 205–206, 211
process for applying UD, 193–196, 194*f*,
    210
student needs, 87–88
in student services, 179–182
UD guidelines for, 191–193, 192*t*
podcasts, 116, 118, 162
population demographics, 190, 248–249
postsecondary assessment
  about, 73–75
  approaches for, 77–79
  challenges, 75–77
  training for developing tools, 79–80
procurement and purchasing, 179
professional development. *See* training,
    faculty, in UD
professional organizations, and UD, 282
project management, 256–264
psychiatric disabilities
  about, 98–99
  assessment strategies, 101–102, 102*t*
  class assignments, 102, 103*t*
  teaching strategies, 100, 101*t*
  and UD, 99–100
psychological disabilities, 62
public awareness, 189–190

recognition learning, 28–29
Reed, Lacey, 177–186, 299
Rehabilitation Research and Training Center
    (VCU), 267–277
Reilly, Virginia, 267–277, 299
Renton Technical College, 255–265
researchers, and UD, 282
Richardson, Michael, 83–96, 299
Richter, Patricia, 177–186, 299
Riley, Richard, 37
Romero, Olga, 145–156, 299–300
Rose, David, 45–59, 300

scaffolding, 57
Scott, Sally, 135–143, 300
screen readers, 228–231
Section 504, 9, 73, 168, 189, 242, 250
Section 508, 241, 243
self-advocacy skills, 63, 85–86, 180

Shulman, Jessie Amelia, 83–96, 300
sign language/ASL, 49, 51, 68, 92
signage, 200
Smith, Carson, 83–96, 300
sociocultural approach, 30t
software. *See* information technology
Souma, Al, 97–104, 300
Spencer, Andrea, 145–156, 300–301
spoken language attributes, 48–49
Standards for Educational and Psychological Testing (NCME), 75
Steele, Sara, 83–96, 301
stereotyping, 84
strategic learning, 28–29
student-centered learning, 106–107
student services
    computer labs, 236–237
    events, 184–185
    guidelines for applying UD, 170–172t
    information resources and technology, 183–184
    physical environments and products, 179–182
    planning, policies, and evaluation, 178–179
    process for applying UD, 168–169f
    staff, 182–183
    and UD, 167–168
    UD resources, 172–174
students
    as higher education consumers, 282–283
    learning styles, 29–31, 67, 91
    participation in UD course development, 123
    perceived needs as learners, 147–148, 148f
    student characteristics, 4f
study guides, 66–67
syllabus/syllabi, 63, 114–116, 115t, 151

target skills, assessment, 76–77
teacher training. *See* training, faculty, in UD
teachers. *See* faculty
Teaching Every Student in the Digital Age: Universal Design for Learning (Rose & Meyer), 54
teaching philosophies, and UD, 29–32, 30t, 31t
technological spaces, Universal Design in, 213–222
telecommunications, 219–221
tests. *See* assessment, student
text-to-speech software, 7, 11, 27t
textbooks, and UD, 53–55

Thompson, Terry, 235–244, 301
Thurlow, Martha, 73–81, 301
time considerations, 94
training, faculty, in UD, 38–39, 106, 123–124
    case study methodology, 135–142
    HEDS-UP, 145–156
    program implementation, 268–269
    UD in professional preparation programs, 135–142

Universal Course Design (UCD)
    about, 110–112
    assessment methods, 119–121, 120t
    core team, 112–114, 122
    curriculum, 114–116, 115t
    environmental considerations, 121–122
    instructional methods, 116–119, 117t–118t
    sustaining implementation, 122–124
Universal Design for Learning (UDL)
    about, 28–29, 45–46
    assessment methodology, 56–58
    course web site, 55
    and discussion groups, 52–53
    engagement and affect, 58–59
    and lecture format, 48–52
    multimedia, 55
    and textbooks, 53–55
Universal Design in Education (Bowe), 26
Universal Design in Higher Education. *See also* institutional change
    about, 3–4
    applying, 14–15, 15t, 16f
    Campus Accessibility Indicators, 251–252
    collaborative implementation, 267–277
    and diversity, 4–6
    examples, 16f
    principles
        CAST, 110
        DO-IT, 32–35, 34t
        North Carolina State University, 7–9
    project management, 256–264
    promotors and inhibitors of, 279–281
    reasons to adopt model, 248–250
    research focus, 80
    resources, 292–294
    shareholders, and roles, 17, 248, 281–283
Universal Design of Instruction (UDI)
    about, 23–24, 61
    acceptance and promotion, 36–39
    distance learning, 35–36, 37t
    principles of, 25–29, 27t, 137t–138t, 153t–154t

Universal Design of Instruction *(continued)*
  process for, 24–25
  and psychiatric disabilities, 99–103
  strategies for applying, 32–35, 34*t*
Universal Design, products and
    environments
  accessible design, 9–10
  accommodations, 10–12, 62
  definition of, 12–13
  history and meaning, 6–7
  process, 12–14, 13*f*
  usable design, 10
university faculty. *See* faculty
University of Connecticut, 27–28
University of Massachusetts–Boston, 110
University of Oregon–Eugene, 200–202
University of Washington, 39
University of Wisconsin–Madison,
    225–233
usable design, 10, 191

validity, of assessment, 74–75
video, 49, 152
Virginia Commonwealth University, 267–271,
    275–277
Virginia Tech, 271–275
visual aids, 51–52, 91
visual differences, 5, 68–69, 229–231

Web Accessibility Initiative (WAI), 217–218,
    221–222, 228–229
web authoring tools, 225–233
web sites
  access to, 183, 242–243
  accessible multimedia lectures on, 225–233
  in assessment, 57
  UD for Web design, 217–219
World Wide Web Consortium (W3C),
    217–219

Yager, Susan, 127–133, 301